CORINNE FENNESSY

READING LIFE

Longman

Boston Columbus Indianapolis New York San Francisco Upper Saddle River
Amsterdam Cape Town Dubai London Madrid Milan Munich Paris Montréal Toronto
Delhi Mexico City São Paulo Sydney Hong Kong Seoul Singapore Taipei Tokyo

Editor in Chief: Eric Stano
Acquisitions Editor: Kate Edwards
Editorial Assistant: Lindsey Allen
Development Editor: Paul Sarkis
Senior Supplements Editor: Donna Campion
Senior Media Producer: Stefanie Liebman
Marketing Manager: Tom DeMarco
Production Editor: Ellen MacElree
Project Coordination and Composition:
   Integra Software Services, Inc.
Cover Design Manager: Wendy Ann
   Fredericks
Cover Photos: *Clockwise from top left:*
   Stephan Sollfors/Alamy; Fuse/Getty Images;
   PM Images (Phil Leo/Michael Denora)/
   Photodisc/Getty Images; Ariel Skelley/Blend
   Images/Getty Images; Fuse/Getty Images;
   and Monty Rakusen/Cultura/Getty Images
Photo Researcher: Rona Tuccillo
Senior Manufacturing Buyer: Dennis J. Para
Printer and Binder: Courier/Kendallville
Cover Printer: Coral Graphic Services, Inc.

Design Development and
Art Direction: Stuart Jackman
Page Layout: The Book Makers
Cover Design: Stuart Jackman

For permission to use copyrighted material, grateful acknowledgment is made to the copyright holders on pages 547–548, which are hereby made part of this copyright page.

ISBN-10-205-63294-7 (student ed.)
ISBN-13: 978-0-205-63294-7 (student ed.)

ISBN-10 0-205-75545-3 (instructor's ed.)
ISBN-13: 978-0-205-75545-5 (instructor's ed.)

2 3 4 5 6 7 8 9 10—CRK—14 13 12 11

Longman
is an imprint of

www.pearsonhighered.com

DETAILED CONTENTS

CHAPTER 1 PLAN TO SUCCEED

CHAPTER 2 THE FOUR-STEP READING PROCESS

CHAPTER 3 **VOCABULARY SKILLS**

CHAPTER 4 TOPICS AND STATED MAIN IDEAS

CHAPTER 5 SUPPORTING DETAILS

CHAPTER 6 PATTERNS OF ORGANIZATION—PART 1

CHAPTER 7 PATTERNS OF ORGANIZATION—PART 2

CHAPTER 8 **DRAWING CONCLUSIONS**

CHAPTER 9 IMPLIED MAIN IDEAS AND CENTRAL POINT

CHAPTER 10 CRITICAL READING AND THINKING

PREFACE

More than twelve years ago, when I started teaching college preparatory reading, the textbooks available at that time required students to struggle through the reading selections and extensive multiple-choice practice exercises. My students did not understand how either their textbook or their college preparatory reading course related to their lives or future goals. I saw the need for a textbook that would relate what they learned in the classroom to real-life applications, including academic reading and real documents they will encounter outside of school.

Research has shown that students who are engaged in the learning process are more successful than passive learners. When students are motivated, they are more likely to participate in the learning process. To accomplish this, they need materials and activities that are related to their academic and personal needs. They also need interesting articles that will inspire them to succeed and opportunities to discuss and engage in critical thinking. *Reading for Life* engages students in reading through an activities-based learning approach to help them master key reading skills and strategies.

Learning Principles Incorporated into *Reading for Life*

Reading for Life is shaped by several pedagogical principles backed by research. First, students are most successful when they are active learners. Students learn best by participating, not by just listening or reading extensively about how to do something. Furthermore, this text teaches reading as a thinking process by taking students through the steps of reading actively. As you go through each chapter, you will find a multitude of instructive features that support the active learning approach. Furthermore, in order to support instructors, the Annotated Instructor's Edition includes complete lesson plans that enable instructors to easily incorporate active learning, collaborative learning, and closure activities.

Second, student motivation increases when the material students are reading is related to their lives and their goals. Each chapter in this text is focused on a different career domain. Moreover, I have carefully chosen highly motivating selections about real people who have overcome challenges and have succeeded. These selections lead students through the process of reading actively to help them master key reading skills and strategies. The selections also provide critical thinking questions for discussion or writing.

Third, research has shown that collaborative learning is one of the most effective ways that students learn. In response to this, many of the activities and assignments in *Reading for Life* are done in pairs or teams. This book provides ample opportunities for students to talk through their thinking processes and to learn from each other. This also benefits students who have an auditory learning style, who learn best by listening and speaking. In addition, it reinforces active learning by engaging more students in the learning process.

Chapter Features in *Reading for Life*

The multitude of features within every chapter of *Reading for Life* supports the book's goal to engage students in preparatory college reading through active learning and real-life connections.

HOW *Reading for Life* MAKES READING REAL

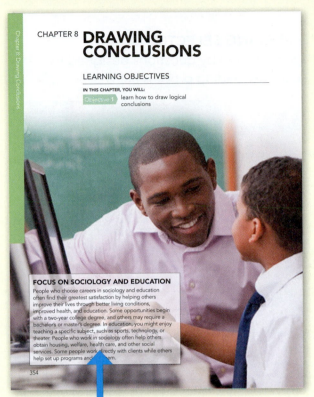

CHAPTER 8 **DRAWING CONCLUSIONS**

LEARNING OBJECTIVES

IN THIS CHAPTER, YOU WILL:

Objective 1 — learn how to draw logical conclusions

FOCUS ON SOCIOLOGY AND EDUCATION

People who choose careers in sociology and education often find their greatest satisfaction by helping others improve their lives through better living conditions, improved health, and education. Some opportunities begin with a two-year college degree, and others may require a bachelor's or master's degree. In education, you might enjoy teaching a specific subject, such as sports, technology, or theater. People who work in sociology often help others obtain housing, welfare, health care, and other social services. Some people work directly with clients while others help set up programs and run them.

354

Each chapter is organized around a **CAREER THEME** to inspire students about different career options.

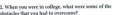

Arethea Moise, Registered Nurse

ON THE JOB INTERVIEW

1. How did you become interested in being a nurse?
I was born to become a nurse. As a child, I played nurse with my dolls and helped care for my younger brother and sister. I had midwives and nurses in my family back in Jamaica.

2. When you were in college, what were some of the obstacles that you had to overcome?
I was a single mom, and I was able to live at home with my parents while I went to college. I had to get up at 5 a.m. to go to clinicals. I had to take care of my son after classes and study hard to keep up my grades.

3. Did you ever think about quitting and giving up on getting a degree?
There were many times I wanted to quit. The hardest times were when my son cried when I had to leave him to go to classes. I also became so exhausted that at one point I had to drop a class and retake it because I was overworked and became ill. But I came back stronger and took the class again successfully.

4. Where do you work now, and what do you like about your job?
I am working as a nurse at Dr. Philips Hospital in Orlando, Florida. I love my job there because, as a preceptor, I monitor the new nurses who are just starting out. I am also finishing up my master's degree and teaching part-time. What I like most about my job is being able to help people through difficult times. It is so rewarding, and I love what I do.

5. What do you dislike about your job?
The long shifts are hard. Sometimes I have to work 12 to 14 hours in one shift. And sometimes it's hard working with nurses who are not team players. Everyone is on teams, and we help each other out. My unit works great together, but once in a while there is someone who is not cooperative, and she or he will make things more difficult than they need to be.

6. If you could give college students one piece of advice, what would it be?
First, stay focused on your goal. Discouraging things will happen in your life, and you have to be determined to succeed. Having a degree has changed my whole life. I was able to buy a home and have the security of knowing I will always have a good job. Second, talk to an academic counselor at your school to make sure you are taking the right courses. Without the right courses, you won't get accepted into the nursing program.

7. What are your plans for the future?
I am completing my master's degree, and I teach part-time now at the community college. I may decide to do it full-time some day. I love the enthusiasm of the students who are so excited about becoming nurses. I am married now and my husband is in medical school. But I know I will be able to find a good job wherever I go because of the demand for nurses. I love this career, and I can't imagine doing anything else.

55

ON THE JOB INTERVIEW boxed features show real people who are presently working in careers related to that chapter's theme and who share personal experience and advice.

CREDIT CARD AGREEMENT

REAL-LIFE READING

If you apply for a credit card with a bank or other financial institution, you should read the terms of the credit card agreement carefully. The following is an excerpt (part) of a credit card agreement. Use the four-step reading process as you read, and then answer the questions that follow to check your comprehension. Preview the selection first, and then read it and answer the questions that follow with your team.

TERMS AND CONDITIONS

FEES: We may charge your account for the following fees. The application and payment of a fee will not release you from responsibility of the action which caused the fees.

LATE PAYMENT. We may charge a $25.00 late fee to your account if you do not pay at least the minimum payment by the stated due date. In addition to the late fee, we will cancel any temporary low rate offers if your payment is late more than one billing cycle during the promotion. We will charge an additional late fee of 10% of your balance for each billing cycle that your account is past due.

OVER THE LIMIT. If you go over your credit limit or cash advance limit by $50.00 or more, we will add an additional $30 Over the Limit fee to your account for each billing cycle that you remain over your credit limit.

RETURNED PAYMENT. If you make a payment on your account with a check from some other financial institution and that check is not honored by the financial institution on which it is drawn, you will be charged a fee of $35.00

RETURNED CHECK. If you write a check from your account and that check is not honored because your account is in default or over the limit, we will charge you a fee of $35.00

CASH ADVANCE FEE. An additional finance charge will be added to your account each time you obtain a cash advance. This additional finance charge will be 8% of the amount of the cash advance with a maximum of $30.00. Internet transactions are exempt from the cash advance fee

ENTIRE BALANCE DUE: If you fail to make a required payment when due or default on any other term in this agreement, we can declare the entire balance of your account due and payable at once without notice. We can also demand complete immediate payment if you make any false or misleading statement on your application or if you die or file for bankruptcy.

COLLECTION COSTS: To the extent permitted by applicable law, you agree to pay all costs and disbursements, including reasonable attorney fees, incurred by us in legal proceedings to collect or enforce your indebtedness.

166

REAL-LIFE READING selections show students the value of reading skills to situations in everyday life.

HOW *Reading for Life* ENGAGES STUDENTS THROUGH ACTIVITIES

WHAT DO YOU ALREADY KNOW? questions begin each reading selection so that students can connect their prior knowledge with the reading topic.

The **READING SELECTIONS** are accompanied by questions designed to keep the reading process active.

Reading 2 — What Do You Already Know?

1. Have you ever known anyone with a disability? Describe how this person coped with the disability and any technology he or she used for assistance.

2. Do you know anyone who has served or is serving in the military? What did (does) this person do? Was this person ever involved in a war? Share what you know.

Directions: As you read this article, practice the four-step reading process. Preview the article, and then write on the following lines one or two questions that you would hope to have answered.

As you read, answer the questions in the margins to check your comprehension.

"Bionic Soldiers"
BY CORINNE FENNESSY
Copyright © by Corinne Fennessy. Reprinted by permission of the author.

With advanced technology, amputees who have lost limbs in battle are now able to regain mobility through the use of advanced, highly technical artificial limbs. This article illustrates how amputees are benefiting from this amazing technology.

1 George Perez, a Puerto Rican paratrooper from the 82nd Airborne Division, remembers traveling on a road outside of Fallujah, Iraq. When a bomb blasted their Humvee, he flew through the air and hit the ground. Then he tried to get up and saw that his left foot was folded backward onto his knee and his combat boot stood in the road a short distance away—still laced.

2 George Perez is determined to regain the strength and abilities he had before losing his leg to the roadside bomb in Iraq. "I'm not ready to get out of the Army yet," he says. "I'm not going to let this little injury stop me from what I want to do." Perez is one of at least four amputees from the 82nd Airborne Division who decided to re-enlist. With a new carbon-fiber prosthetic leg, Perez intends to show that he can still run,

328

Reading 2

jump out of a plane, and pass all of the other challenging paratrooper tests so he can go back to active duty next year.

3 Surgeons tried to save part of his leg, but an infection necessitated the amputation of his leg just below the knee joint. After he recuperated and received his prosthetic leg, Perez asked a visiting general if he could stay in the army. "They told me, 'It's all up to you, and how much you want it,'" he says. "If I could do everything like a regular soldier, I could stay in."

4 Perez has worked hard to become accustomed to his prosthetic leg. He began exercising by doing push-ups in bed. Soon he was walking, and then running. Perez gets his inspiration from other paratroopers in the 82nd Division who have lost limbs in combat and have re-enlisted.

5 Due to advances in prosthetic technology, many soldiers are able to live their lives normally after losing one, two, or more limbs. Some have chosen to return to active duty wearing a prosthetic leg or arm.

6 The process of creating a prosthetic limb begins at the Walter Reed Hospital's **Orthotics** and Prosthetics laboratory. First, a custom-fit socket is made for the prosthetic. Each one is made to fit the individual amputee. The prosthetist creates a mold for a socket in about 20 minutes. Next, a sheet of plastic is heated until it is pliable, and then it is formed over the foam mold. It is trimmed and sanded, and then the amputee is given a fitting. They continue to make adjustments until it fits snugly and comfortably over the residual limb.

7 Next, the amputees move into occupational and physical therapy.

orthotics
(or-THOT-ix): the branch of medicine dealing with prosthetic aids.

How did George Perez lose his leg?

What are three types of prosthetic arms each amputee must learn to use?

U-REVIEW sections appear immediately after students practice key reading skills to enable closure.

3. Identify the relationship within the following sentence: As a result, individuals with Type C behavior pattern experience the same low risk for stress-related heart disease as do those with Type B behavior pattern.
   a. definition   c. cause and effect
   b. listing   d. compare and/or contrast

4. Identify the relationship between sentences 8 and 9.
   a. definition   c. cause and effect
   b. listing   d. compare and contrast

5. How are the major details organized?
   a. They define the different types of behavior patterns while at the same time comparing and contrasting the different types.
   b. They show the causes of different behavior patterns.
   c. They show the effects of different behavior patterns.
   d. They give examples of different behavior patterns.

U-Review

On the following lines, write whether the statements are true or false. If the statement is false, correct it to make it true on the lines provided.

1. When looking for a paragraph's overall pattern, you should look at the minor supporting details.

2. The main idea will often give a clue to the paragraph's pattern of organization.

3. Sometimes the transitions in the sentences do not match the overall relationship being shown in a paragraph.

4. You should ask yourself, "How are the major supporting details organized?"

5. Every sentence in the paragraph will have the same pattern of organization as the whole paragraph.

257

VIEWPOINT: Copyright Infringement on the Internet

A copyright is a legal right of ownership to created materials such as music, books, films, or other materials. In October of 2007, Jammie Thomas was found guilty of posting 24 songs on the Internet service *Kazaa* without getting permission from the copyright holders. Thomas was fined $222,000 in damages to the Recording Industry Association of America (RIAA).

Read the following letters to the editor about copyrighted music, and then answer the questions that follow.

Dear Editor:

Suing someone for over $200,000 just because she copied a few songs from a CD onto the Internet is absurd! The Internet is supposed to be a place of sharing information and ideas. How can ideas be shared if people are sued every time they download something? It should be like an online library where everything can be shared for free. Most of the music being shared is done by musicians and singers who are well paid and should be willing to share. Besides, people who upload or download parts of TV shows don't always realize that they are breaking a law. Suing someone for $200,000 is too harsh. What's next, censorship?

Signed,

Free to Be Me

Dear Editor:

No one should upload copyrighted music, books, or films onto the Internet without getting the permission of the creators. Many people depend on the sales of their products to make a living. If their products are available free on the Internet, who will go out and buy them? Musicians, authors, artists, and filmmakers deserve to get paid for what they do. Stealing products off the Internet is no different than going into a store and stealing CDs, DVDs, or books off the shelves. Many people have invested their hard work, time, and money to produce these works. Giving them away for free is a form of theft. The only way to stop this kind of theft is to continue to issue harsh penalties to those who break copyright laws.

Signed,

Advocate for Artists

336

The **VIEWPOINT** feature includes "letters to the editor" that offer opposing arguments related to a real-life issue. This section is designed to help students develop their critical thinking skills.

A variety of **GAMES AND ACTIVITIES** is included to further engage students in active and collaborative learning.

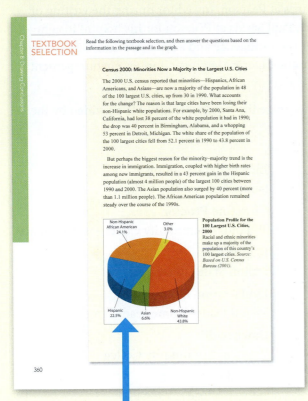

Every chapter includes **TEXTBOOK SELECTIONS** to help students learn to read academic material, including how to read **TEXTBOOK GRAPHIC AIDS.**

Abundant **PRACTICES** and **SKILL-BUILDING EXERCISES** are included so students can apply the key reading and study skills.

ADDITIONAL CHAPTER FEATURES IN *Reading for Life*

■ Metacognitive strategies are taught and self-assessment surveys appear at the end of each chapter to help students learn how to become more efficient learners.

■ End-of-chapter review sections review key concepts using a variety of study skills such as note cards, diagrams, charts, and concept maps.

READING LAB ASSIGNMENTS direct students to MyReadingLab. com for additional practice of skills, reading comprehension, and research opportunities.

ACKNOWLEDGMENTS

I would like to acknowledge Kate Edwards at Pearson, my editor during the writing of this book, for her guidance and support; Paul Sarkis at Pearson for his helpful insight; the staff at Integra Software Services for their diligence and advice; Dorling Kindersley (DK) in London for their design; my mother, Doris Metzinger, for her encouragement; and my husband, Craig, for his patience and support.

Similarly, I would like to gratefully recognize the invaluable insights provided by the following colleagues and reviewers:

Taddese Addo
Community College of Denver

Dale Boyle
Community College of Rhode Island

Kathleen Carlson
Brevard Community College

Judy Covington
Trident Technical College

Nikka Harris
Rochester Community College

Cathy Hunsicker
Dalton State College

Kimberly Jones
College of Southern Idaho

Susie Khirallah-Johnston
Tyler Junior College

Mary Nielsen
Dalton State College

Elizabeth O'Scanlon
Santa Barbara City College

Christine Proctor
St. Louis Community College at Meramac

Regina Ray
Dalton State College

Linda Saumell
Miami Dade–Homestead Campus

Dawn Sedik
Valencia Community College

Alan Shuttleworth
Sierra College

Dr. Phebe Simmons
Blinn College

TC Stuwe
Salt Lake Community College

READING for LIFE

CHAPTER 1 PLAN TO SUCCEED

LEARNING OBJECTIVES

IN THIS CHAPTER, YOU WILL:

Objective 1 understand why teamwork is an effective way to learn.

Objective 2 set short-term, midterm, and long-term goals.

Objective 3 identify how to manage your time more effectively.

Objective 4 understand how to organize a notebook.

Objective 1 — TEAMWORK: GETTING TO KNOW YOUR CLASSMATES

One of the most important qualities that employers look for in potential employees is that of a "team player." Employers know that good ideas, products, and services become even better when more people are involved in the creative process.

Some people do not warm up to the idea of working in teams. They prefer to work alone, and this is understandable. But in the real world, you also have to be able to work with other people. Getting along with others, sharing ideas, supporting each other, and helping each other are key skills in teamwork.

Get into groups of two or three, and take turns interviewing each other. Try to find out something unique about the other person. Think about what you would like to know about someone who is sitting across the aisle or across the room. Questions should include his or her first and last name (spelled correctly), why he or she is in college, careers the student finds interesting, hobbies, what the student does in his or her spare time, part-time jobs, and so on. Jot down the information you gathered in the space provided below. Next, introduce the student you interviewed to the class. When you introduce this person, be sure to speak loudly and clearly enough so that everyone can hear you.

Today I met

....

....

....

Objective 2 — SETTING GOALS

To succeed at anything in life, you must have plans and goals. Setting goals and mapping out a plan to reach those goals will greatly help you achieve them.

Goals should be set high, but they should also be realistic. Do not settle for second best when planning your future. Don't stop at becoming the manager or the supervisor. Aim for the top position—the president of the company—if that's what you want. Have faith in your ability to do the things you want to do, and then go out and do them.

If you fail along the way, and you *will* sometimes, just learn from your mistakes. Do not be discouraged by setbacks or failure, for failure is how we learn to succeed. Successful people do not let failure defeat them. Every great invention and every new process that has been developed has come by trial and error. As the famous animal psychologist Cesar Millan says, "Mistakes don't bother me because that's how I learn."

Write Down Your Goals

Write your own goals on the spaces provided below. They can be about anything, not just school. Aim high, but be realistic. Try to be as specific as you can when writing goals, and describe how you will accomplish them. (Use notebook paper if you require more space.)

EXAMPLE:

"By the end of this semester, I will get As in all of my classes. (How?) I will stick to my study schedule, do all of my homework, study for tests, and attend all of my classes on time."

In the next month, I will:

....

....

By the end of this semester, I will:

....

....

By the end of next semester, I will:

....

....

In a year, I will:

....

....

In two years, I will:

....

....

In five years, I will:

....

....

....

Keep this list in your book or in your notebook. If you change your goals, make changes to your list. At the end of the month, check to see if you accomplished your "one month" goals. Continue to check this list at least once a month to see if you are on track for your longer-term goals. If you find that you are wandering off track, set some new goals that will help you to get back on track; write them in the space below.

EXAMPLE:

Old goal:

"By the end of the semester, I will get As in all of my classes."

New goal:

"My new goal is to get an A in reading class and a B+ in math class."

(How will you accomplish this?)

*"I will get extra tutoring in math, see my instructor for help,
go to the math center or lab, spend more time
(an extra three hours each week) practicing math skills,
and study more for tests and quizzes."*

After you have filled in your goals, share them with a small group. Listen for specific strategies on how each person intends to accomplish his or her goals. Remember to encourage one another and tell each other, "You can do it! Just don't give up!"

At the end of this semester, keep this list of goals in a safe place at home. Every once in a while, take it out and read it. Ask yourself if you have accomplished any of your goals. Then look into the mirror and tell yourself what you will do to make them happen.

The old adage "Quitters never win and winners never quit!" holds true especially in college. Start over if you must, but don't become discouraged and drop out. No matter what job you will have in life, you will always benefit from having a college education. Just keep on going to college, and you *will* earn that degree.

TIME MANAGEMENT: BUILDING A STUDY SCHEDULE

"A goal without a plan is just a wish." –Antoine de Saint-Exupéry

To succeed at anything, you must start with a good plan. Putting ideas down on paper or on the computer helps to make them real, giving them shape and form. It is also a good way of thinking through problems. Seeing something visually helps you see things you didn't think of when you just went over it in your mind. Your first plan for success in college should be to make a study schedule. Simply telling yourself, "I'll do my homework when I have time between classes and my job" is not going to work once the semester gets going and your life becomes busier than you ever believed it could possibly be.

Take a few minutes now to plot out time each day for review, to study for tests, and to do homework. A good general rule is to plan one hour of study time each week for each hour of class time. So for each course that meets three hours a week, you need to set aside a minimum of three hours of study time. The more difficult the course is for you, the more time you will need to spend on studying.

Even if you don't have a written homework assignment to complete for the next class, you still have homework: studying and reviewing. In future chapters, you will learn why it's important to study even when you don't have an assignment or a test coming up.

So decide now when you will study. Choose a time when you know you will be awake and not sleepy or tired, and not interrupted by distractions. Make it known to all of your family and friends that you need to study and would appreciate it if they would not interrupt you, call you, text you, or chat online with you at those times. Turn off your phone during study time. You need to concentrate when you study, or you will find yourself forgetting what you learned. That's a waste of time you will not be able to afford.

HERE'S WHAT YOU SHOULD PUT ON THE STUDY SCHEDULE:

- When you are in class and traveling to or from school
- When you are at a job or other regular commitments
- When you can study, do homework, and review
- When you'll eat three meals a day and sleep at least seven hours a night
- When you can relax with friends and family
- When you worship or volunteer

"Something's Gotta Give"

There are only 24 hours in a day, and like the old song says, "Something's Gotta Give," meaning you can't do it all. If you find that you don't have the time to study that you need, you must cut down on something else, such as watching TV, playing video games, talking on the phone, or even working too many hours. Give up some of life's frills, or take fewer trips to the mall. You might find that your new schedule actually helps you to concentrate on the important things in life instead of on the things that eat up your time and money but offer no long-term benefits.

Once you have completed your schedule, stick to it! Hang it on your wall. Make an extra copy for your notebook or your car. The important thing is not to let any distractions invade your study time. If a true emergency comes up, then reschedule your study time, but don't neglect it.

Success is all about making the right choices and following through. If you get off track on your schedule, make every effort to get back on track as soon as possible. Make adjustments when needed, but don't cheat yourself out of your study time. When the grades arrive, you don't want to feel disappointed because you didn't give it your best effort.

Daily Planners

Take advantage of any free planning calendars that your college or local businesses might offer. You can also use an appointment calendar on your cell phone or computer. Get into the habit of writing something down every day, even if it's a simple reminder, such as "Buy a notebook." Write down homework assignments, long-term assignments, project due dates, reminders about tests or papers the week before they are due, and anything else that you want to remember. Also record information about your study partners in each class, such as their e-mail addresses or phone numbers. Developing habits takes time. Practice good habits daily, and they will become a part of your normal routine.

STUDY PLAN

Sunday	Monday	Tuesday	Wednesday	Thursday	Friday	Saturday
7:00 a.m.	7:00 a.m.	7:00 a.m.	7:00 a.m.	7:00 a.m.	7:00 a.m.	7:00 a.m.
8:00	8:00	8:00	8:00	8:00	8:00	8:00
9:00	9:00	9:00	9:00	9:00	9:00	9:00
10:00	10:00	10:00	10:00	10:00	10:00	10:00
11:00	11:00	11:00	11:00	11:00	11:00	11:00
12:00 p.m.	12:00 p.m.	12:00 p.m.	12:00 p.m.	12:00 p.m.	12:00 p.m.	12:00 p.m.
1:00	1:00	1:00	1:00	1:00	1:00	1:00
2:00	2:00	2:00	2:00	2:00	2:00	2:00
3:00	3:00	3:00	3:00	3:00	3:00	3:00
4:00	4:00	4:00	4:00	4:00	4:00	4:00
5:00	5:00	5:00	5:00	5:00	5:00	5:00
6:00	6:00	6:00	6:00	6:00	6:00	6:00
7:00	7:00	7:00	7:00	7:00	7:00	7:00
8:00	8:00	8:00	8:00	8:00	8:00	8:00
9:00	9:00	9:00	9:00	9:00	9:00	9:00
10:00	10:00	10:00	10:00	10:00	10:00	10:00
11:00	11:00	11:00	11:00	11:00	11:00	11:00
12:00 a.m.	12:00 a.m.	12:00 a.m.	12:00 a.m.	12:00 a.m.	12:00 a.m.	12:00 a.m.

College Readiness Checklist

Are you ready for college? Put a check mark next to the following tasks that you have already completed, and circle the ones that you still need to do.

☐ **1.** Purchase all required texts and materials for each course.

☐ **2.** Keep a copy of your schedule in your notebook.

☐ **3.** Read the syllabus for each course so you will know what your professors expect of you.

☐ **4.** Make a study schedule of when you will study and do homework each day.

☐ **5.** Know where to go to get extra help if needed.

☐ **6.** Keep an assignment notebook or appointment program in your cell phone to record dates for short-term assignments, long-term assignments, and tests.

☐ **7.** Have a place set up for doing homework, complete with supplies and away from distractions.

☐ **8.** Inform your friends and supervisor at work that you are in college and will have to arrange your work schedule and free time around your study time.

☐ **9.** Get your student I.D. card.

☐ **10.** Make arrangements for travel to and from classes, for babysitters, or for other responsibilities outside of school.

☐ **11.** Pay for classes by the date payment is due (or you'll be dropped from the classes).

Add any other tasks not included on this list that you still have to do:

....

....

....

....

....

....

....

....

MyReadingLab

MyReadingLab is a Web site published by Pearson Education. The lab assignments in this text will coordinate with the skills that are taught in this course.

Once you are registered to use MyReadingLab, your name and all of your scores will be recorded and saved. But only you and your instructor will be able to see your results. You will have a secure password to access your scores.

One of the benefits of an online reading lab is that you can work on it at any time and from anywhere you have Internet access.

What Is in MyReadingLab?

On this Web site, there are passages to read and questions to answer for skills practice, much like the exercises in this book. These exercises will give you additional independent practice and immediate feedback on your answers. The site will also give you explanations for incorrect answers. The questions are mostly multiple choice, with a few questions where you must type in an answer.

Besides the skills practices, there are also vocabulary exercises, study skills resources, and Lexile readings. A Lexile is a type of score that tells you your overall comprehension, based on how many multiple-choice questions you answered correctly. The Lexile readings are on a variety of topics, and you can select the ones you want to read.

As you improve in your reading comprehension, you will be given stories at higher reading levels. At each level, you choose which stories interest you. The more questions you answer correctly, the higher your Lexile score will go. By the end of the course, you will see an improvement in your Lexile score if you read carefully and answer the questions to the best of your ability.

MyReadingLab is designed to be user friendly and interesting. Remember that the purpose of the lab is to help you to improve your reading comprehension. If you take shortcuts and don't put in your best effort, you will not see much improvement. Make a commitment to do the work seriously. Plan enough time in your study schedule to complete the lab assignments without rushing through them. Do them to the best of your ability, and you will see improvement over the duration of the course.

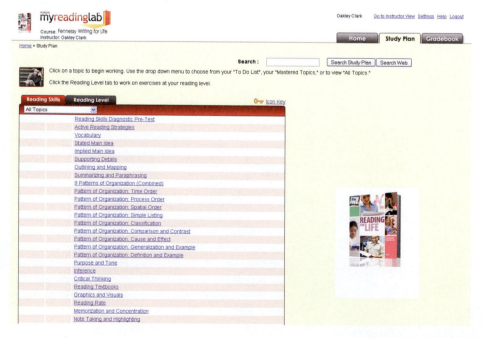

Objective 4

ORGANIZING YOUR NOTEBOOK

Keeping your papers organized is one of the most important keys to success in college. In a very short time, you will have more papers than you'll know what to do with. Throwing them into your book bag or shoving them anywhere into your notebook will only lead to frustration and wasted time when you need them later. Get into the habit of taking the time to put things away in their proper places. Once you see how much it improves your learning experience, you'll want to apply it to all of your other courses as well.

Staying organized requires self-discipline. Most students will say, "I don't have time to use a notebook!" Yet they are the ones who waste the most time trying to find papers. Putting papers in a notebook will actually *save* you time. You won't be frustrated or feel that things are out of control, and you may even see higher grades.

Here's what to do:

1. Buy a big three-ring binder with pockets inside, a pack of notebook paper, and dividers. Also buy a small hole-puncher that will fit into your book bag. Don't waste money on binders or notebooks that are too thin to hold all of your class papers. Buy a set of dividers for each course you are taking. It's okay to use the same notebook for two or three classes, but if you are taking more than that, you may wish to use two notebooks of different colors. For example, Mindy has reading and math on Mondays and Wednesdays, so she has one notebook for those subjects. She also takes speech and humanities on Tuesdays and Thursdays, so she uses a different-colored notebook for those classes. Using two different-colored notebooks will help you avoid the mistake of bringing the wrong notebook to class.

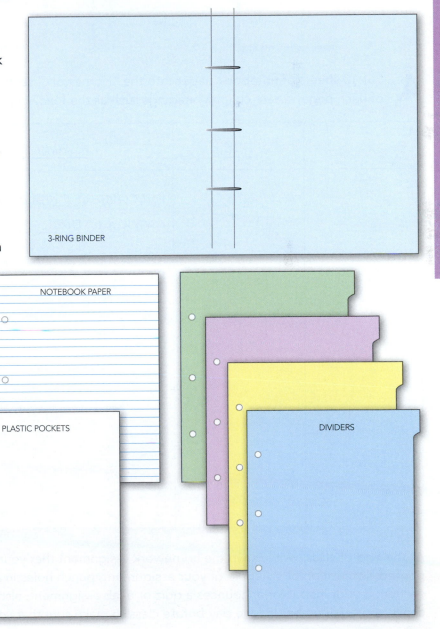

3-RING BINDER

NOTEBOOK PAPER

PLASTIC POCKETS

DIVIDERS

2. Make labels for your reading course dividers. Your instructor will suggest the best way to label your dividers, but for a start, you can label them:

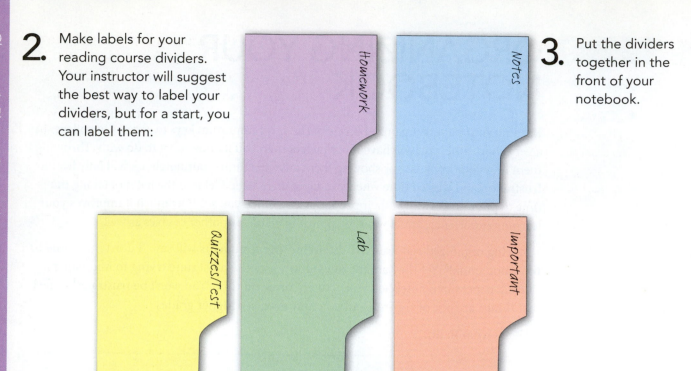

Homework

Notes

Quizzes/Test

Lab

Important

3. Put the dividers together in the front of your notebook.

4. Put 10 sheets of notebook paper into the "Homework" section. At the top of each page, create column headings such as the following:

	DATE	ASSIGNMENT	DUE
	06.01.2010	read chapter 4 and answer review questions	06.07.2010

At the end of class, write down the homework assignment that your instructor announces. If there is a printed description or schedule of your assignment, punch holes in it and put it into the "Homework" section. If your instructor announces a quiz or a lab assignment, also write it in this section. Don't forget to check your assignment list the day *before* class to make sure that you will be prepared!

5. Punch holes in the instructor's syllabus and put this after the tab labeled "Important." The syllabus contains all of the most important information about the course. The "Important" tab is where you will keep all the course-related handouts that you are given by your instructor, such as the syllabus, the course schedule, information about labs, and other important papers that you will need.

6. Put about 25 sheets of notebook paper into the "Notes" section. This is where you will write down things like vocabulary definitions, class notes, and anything else you need to learn in this course. Don't mix other courses' notes in this section, such as math notes. This section is strictly for reading notes only.

7. When you complete a homework assignment, put it into the notebook at the *front* of the "Homework" section so it will be ready to hand in at the beginning of class. Remember to include your name, the date, and the title of the assignment at the top, and page numbers if necessary. Don't use class time to get your papers ready to hand in. Instructors generally do not appreciate watching students tear out sheets of paper, write their names on them, ask for a stapler, or do other similar tasks that should be done outside of class.

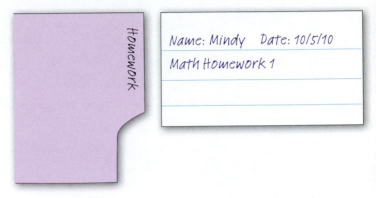

8. When papers are returned to you, take a minute to put them back into the "Homework" section of your notebook. Don't stuff them just anywhere! Each time you add a new paper, add it to the back so that the papers will be in chronological order. That way when you need to go back to find an assignment to verify a grade or to study, it will be easier to find.

9. Save all of your papers and tests until you have your final grade at the end of the semester. Rarely, but occasionally, you may want to ask an instructor how he or she arrived at your final grade. Your papers are important evidence of your work.

10. Use stick-on notes, colored stick-on tabs, or highlighters to mark important pages in your notebook. For example, if you have made a chart of transitions that you will want to refer back to, add a colorful tab that will help you find it more easily.

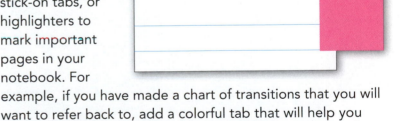

Keeping a notebook can actually give you a sense of satisfaction and accomplishment. Take a minute at the end of every class and study session to put things into your notebook in the right place. The next time you look for that homework assignment, you'll know exactly where it is.

Follow the same procedure for your other courses. If you use spiral notebooks for taking notes, buy the ones with three holes so they will fit into your large notebook in the "Notes" section. You can still take them out when you want to write in them, but put them back into the notebook for safe keeping.

U-Review

Take a few minutes to think about the answers to the following questions. Then pair up with someone and take turns asking each other the questions. Allow your partner time to answer. When finished, if he or she leaves out any information, you should give it. Continue taking turns until all of the questions are answered.

1. Why is setting goals important?

....

....

....

2. Why should you set up a study schedule?

....

....

....

3. Why is it important to keep an organized notebook?

....

....

....

4. What is the syllabus, and what should you do with it?

....

....

....

5. What should you do after you have completed your homework?

....

....

....

STUDY SKILL CHAPTER REVIEW

Creating tables or charts is a good way to summarize and chunk information. They are useful tools for studying in any subject.

   Complete the missing information in the following chart about what we learned in Chapter 1.

TOPIC	WHY USE IT	HOW TO USE IT
SETTING GOALS		Write down realistic short-term, midterm, and long-term goals, with a plan on how I will achieve them.
STUDY SCHEDULE	Planning my time is good time management. It will help me set aside time for homework and studying, which will help me get better grades.	
DAILY PLANNER		Write in my assignments, tests, quizzes, and papers, with the dates when they are due. Include reminders the week before long-term assignments are due.
ORGANIZING A NOTEBOOK		Set up a notebook with dividers for each subject. Keep all course materials organized in the notebook.

READING LAB ASSIGNMENTS

1. Go online to MyReadingLab, and log in as a student.

2. Look in the section of the home page titled "Other Resources." Under "Getting Started," click on the "Study Skills Website." Then click on "College Success Strategies," and complete the survey.

3. Under the section "Other Resources," click on the "Study Skills Website." Under "Life Skills," click on "Time Management," and take the survey to determine how you manage your time.

LEARNING REFLECTION

Think about the skills and concepts discussed in this chapter. What have you learned in this chapter that will help your reading comprehension and enable you to do well in college?

SELF-EVALUATION CHECKLIST

Rate yourself on the following items using the following scale:

1 = strongly disagree
2 = disagree
3 = neither agree nor disagree
4 = agree
5 = strongly agree

1. I completed all of the assigned work on time. ....

2. I understand all of the concepts in this chapter. ....

3. I contributed to teamwork and class discussions. ....

4. I completed all of the assigned lab work on time. ....

5. I came to class on time. ....

6. I attended class every day. ....

7. I studied for any quizzes or tests we had for this chapter. ....

8. I asked questions when I didn't understand something. ....

9. I checked my comprehension during reading. ....

10. I know what is expected of me in the coming week. ....

CHAPTER 2

THE FOUR-STEP READING PROCESS

LEARNING OBJECTIVES

IN THIS CHAPTER, YOU WILL:

Objective **1**   identify how to improve reading comprehension using the four-step reading process.

FOCUS ON HEALTH SCIENCES

This chapter focuses on careers in the medical field and the academic preparation needed to specialize in this area. Most pre-med students need to take courses in math and science, including biology, microbiology, and chemistry. As you explore the readings and textbook selections in this chapter, think about how your own interests and skills might fit into a career in the medical field. If you are interested in technology, you may like to work as a radiologist, a cardiovascular technician, or a sonographer. People with a love for the arts or music can use art and music therapy to help children, disabled adults, and patients with psychological disorders. Or perhaps you'd like to go into physical and occupational therapy, where you can help rehabilitate others after a serious illness or injury. The health sciences is a career field where the need for skilled professionals will always exceed the supply.

Objective 1

THE FOUR-STEP READING PROCESS

Has this ever happened to you? After reading an article or a chapter in a book, you closed the book and said, "I have no idea what I just read!" This type of "forgetting" what we just read is a common occurrence and usually happens because we weren't thinking about what we were reading. Our eyes were engaged, but our brains were not. This happens because we are not reading actively. We start on page one and continue until we finish the book or the chapter, and then close the book and think about something else. The result is that we cannot remember what we have read a day, an hour, or even minutes later.

In college, you will be given reading assignments on a regular basis for nearly all of your courses. You will be expected to understand the concepts that you read about and be ready to explain them in class or on a quiz. Some of the reading assignments will be more challenging than any you were given in high school. You might find yourself saying, "There's no way I can read all that and remember it!" But you *can* recall information for all of your college reading assignments if you develop the good habits described here. Reading actively will also help you to be successful in your career because you will remember and understand any materials that you will be expected to read.

STEP 1
Preview Before You Read

STEP 2
Read Actively

STEP 3
Highlight and Annotate

STEP 4
Review

STEP 1
Preview Before You Read

Previewing is important because it gets your brain thinking about the topic that you will be reading about. It gives your brain time to recall information you already know about the topic. It also helps you to understand the new information more easily. Your brain creates pathways for recalling information. Each time you recall information about a topic and learn new information, it will strengthen your understanding and improve your recall.

Previewing also allows you to decide how you will approach the material. Some things should be "skimmed" over, and other things should be read more slowly for better comprehension and recall. While previewing, you can decide what's important to remember and what is not.

Much of your reading in college will be in textbooks. Always read with a pencil in your hand and a highlighter. This habit will help you to read faster and more efficiently. Begin by looking over the reading selection:

- Read the title and bold headings.
- Look at pictures, graphs, diagrams, charts, or any other visual aids.
- Read the chapter introduction.
- Read the chapter summary.
- Read questions at the end of the chapter.
- Read words in bold print, such as key terms.
- Read the first sentence of each section.

As you preview, think of some questions you hope will be answered in the reading. For example, here are some headings from the textbook *Introduction to Biology*: "Chemistry and Cells," "Genetics," and "Animal Physiology." Each of these should be turned into a question. For instance, for "Genetics" you might ask, "What is genetics?" As you read that section, you will look for the answer to that question. This gives you a purpose for reading. You will be searching for the answer to the question, and you will be more focused on what you are reading and less likely to forget what you just read.

Practice Writing Preview Questions

Turn the following headings into questions. Begin with words such as *who, what, when, where, why,* or *how.*

"Blood Types"

....

.... ?

"The Effects of Smoking"

....

.... ?

"Sports Injuries"

....

.... ?

Practice Previewing

Read the underlined text in the following passage. These are the parts you should read while previewing the material.

Sample preview questions:

- What is this passage about?
- What is dizziness, and what are some common causes of it?
- How should a person with dizziness be treated?

DIZZINESS

Read the title and introduction. ──────▶ Dizziness is a feeling of being unbalanced or spinning, and it is a common symptom that can be caused by any number of conditions. Most commonly, it occurs when someone has not eaten or has an inner ear infection. Other causes of common dizziness are stress and viral infections.

Treatment

Read the heading and first sentence of the paragraph. ──────▶ Most causes of dizziness are not serious, and the symptom can be treated by having the patient sit or lie down. Give the patient something to drink, and find out when he or she last ate. Often a few slow deep breaths will help restore oxygen to the brain. If the dizziness does not go away, or happens frequently, a physician should be consulted. If dizziness is accompanied by chest pain, difficulty in breathing, sudden weakness, numbness or tingling, or severe bleeding, call emergency services immediately. This could be the sign of a stroke or heart attack.

Read the last paragraph or summary. ──────▶ As in any medical emergency, it is best to keep the patient calm, comfortable, and relaxed until the problem goes away or until medical assistance arrives. When the patient feels the dizziness has passed, advise him or her to stand up slowly and to get plenty of rest and fluids over the next 24 hours.

STEP 2
Read Actively

Reading actively means that you are reading to find answers to your preview questions. As you read, look for important points that the author is making about the topic. Usually there is a main idea and several major details to explain or prove the main idea. Ask yourself, "What is this selection about?" and then, "What's the most important point about this topic?" Read to find the answers, and you will be able to stay focused on what you are reading. If you find yourself getting distracted, stop and repeat the preview questions you are trying to answer.

Read one section at a time, such as the paragraphs under one heading. If you find the answers to your preview questions, underline them so you can find them later. Read the whole paragraph before you underline, or you might find yourself underlining the whole thing. By underlining the most important ideas only, you are chunking information and making it easier to remember. Your memory can fill in the details once you focus on the big idea. Try to limit your highlighting and underlining of a section to about 25 percent or less. You will underline more in some paragraphs than others, depending on how many major points are made.

STEP 3
Highlight and Annotate

Make sure you have underlined the author's main point, if it is stated. Then, make notes in the margins of your text; this is called "annotating." Doing this will help you to remember what you read. It will also help you to review and summarize the information into a "word byte"—a single word or phrase that describes what the section is about. Furthermore, it will help you find information quickly later when you need to go back to look up answers to questions or take notes.

When you need to review, you will save time by reading just the notes in the margins and highlighted information. If you do not have room in your margins for short notes, or if you are planning to sell your book at the end of the semester, buy some small sticky notes, such as Post-it® notes, and write on them instead.

Example

The main idea—notice how the topic is underlined in the title and its definition is underlined in the first sentence. All definitions to key terms are important, so always underline them.

Make note of sentences that begin with transition words like "first," "second," or "third." These are often important points.

Use abbreviations, like "Def" for "definition" and "Ex" for "example."

Numbering major details will help you remember them. In this case, the two types of businesses are numbered: for-profit and nonprofit.

Getting Down to Business

Types of Business

A business is any activity that provides goods or services to consumers for the purpose of making a profit. When Phil Knight *Def: Business* and Bill Bowerman, his running coach at the University of Oregon, created Blue Ribbon Sports (the predecessor of Nike), they started a business. The product was athletic shoes, and the company's founders hoped to sell shoes to runners for more than it cost to make and market them. If they were successful (which they were), they'd make a profit.

Before we go on, let's make a couple of important distinctions concerning the terms in our definitions. First, whereas Nike produces and sells goods (athletic shoes, apparel, and equipment), many businesses provide services. Your bank is a service company, as is your Internet provider. Airlines, law firms, movie theaters, and hospitals are also service companies. Many companies provide both goods and services. For example, your local car dealership sells goods (cars) and also provides a service (automobile repairs).

For-profit businesses

1st: For-profit
Goods vs. Services
Ex: Nike: Goods
Ex: Bank: Service
Goods AND services companies
Ex: Car dealership

2nd: Nonprofit org.
Ex: Post office, Red Cross

Second, some organizations are not set up to make profits. Many are established to provide social or educational services. Such not-for-profit (or nonprofit) organizations include the U.S. post office, museums, almost all colleges and universities, the Sierra Club, and the American Red Cross. Most of these organizations, however, function in much the same way as a business. They establish goals and work to meet them in an effective and efficient manner. Thus, most of the business principles introduced in this course also apply to nonprofits.

Nonprofits: function like for-profit businesses

(From *Exploring Business* by Karen Collins. Copyright © 2008 by Karen Collins. Reprinted by permission of the author.)

You can also use sticky notes over the edge of a page to mark the page or describe it for easy reference later. Often students are hesitant to write in their textbooks, but annotating is such a powerful learning tool that you can't afford to skip it. It is well worth the investment in your textbook if you earn good grades by highlighting and annotating.

Chunking Information

Your brain is wired to store information in different stages. It first stores it in your immediate memory, which only lasts about 30 seconds. If you want to remember this information for a class or a quiz, you'll need to move it to your working memory. And, like a moving truck that can only move one truckload at a time, your brain will only be able to handle a limited amount of material at once. That's why you need to learn material in chunks. Stopping at the end of a section and reviewing what you just read helps your brain to remember and understand it better. Begin by asking yourself questions about what you just read, like:

"What did I just read about?"
"What was the most important idea the author tried to explain?"
"What other important points explain the main point?"

Try answering these three questions about the textbook selection "Getting Down to Business" in the example on the preceding page. You can look at the notes in the margins to help you.

If you want to learn this material, you will need to move it into your long-term memory. To do this, you must make sure that the material *makes sense* and *has meaning* for you.* The more you can meet these two requirements, the better you will remember what you just read. One way to do this is to try to think of your own examples and how the concepts apply to them. This helps you to connect what you learn to what you already know.

*Adapted from David A. Sousa, *How the Brain Learns*. Thousand Oaks: Corwin Press, 2006, p. 48.

Look at the definition for a business in the textbook selection "Getting Down to Business" on page 22. Can you think of other examples (besides the ones mentioned in the text) that fit this description? In the following spaces, jot down a couple of examples of businesses that you know. According to the definition, they must be in business to make a profit.

Businesses:

....

Next, the author discussed businesses that produce goods and those that provide services. Write your own examples of these types of businesses:

Goods:

....

Services:

....

Then, the author discussed businesses that provide both goods and services. Give your own examples of this:

Goods and Services:

....

Finally, the author discussed nonprofit businesses. Write two of your own examples:

Nonprofit:

....

Next, check your recall of the textbook selection by answering these questions. Try to answer the questions without looking back. Check when you are done to see if you answered the questions correctly.

1. What is the definition of a business?

2. What are two different types of businesses, and what is one example of each type?

The important thing to remember about active reading is that you are *active*, not just passing your eyes over the page. You are looking for answers to questions, making decisions about what is important and should be underlined, summarizing and making notes in the margins, and then making sense and meaning of what you just read. You go back over it again and *think* about what you read and how it relates to what you already know. You reread parts of it to highlight or annotate. And by providing the extra examples of your own, your brain makes connections between what you already know and what you are learning. The more that you practice this process, the more quickly and efficiently you'll be able to do it.

STEP 4

Review

You should review new material every day. That's why it's important to set aside time to study even when you don't have a quiz or specific assignment that is due. During your study time, read through your class notes and test yourself. One easy way is to read the notes you made in the margins or in your notebook. As you are reading, try to explain what they mean. Imagine that YOU are the instructor trying to teach it to the class. If you have forgotten the information, this means it is not in your long-term memory yet. You need to review it again by going back and reading the sentences you underlined or highlighted. Try making up questions and writing the answers down. You can use note cards to write the questions on one side and the answers on the back. Practice answering them with a friend, or read them aloud. Try making a computer aid or graphic aid, such as a table, chart, concept map, or diagram to help you study.

If you spend 15 or 20 minutes reviewing material every night for each class you are taking, you will have a much stronger understanding and recall for what you are learning in class. You can earn those top grades and qualify for scholarship money, too.

This is why sticking to a study schedule is so important in college. Don't shortchange yourself by skimming through the text or not reading it at all. By doing that, you will be wasting your time and the money you spent on tuition. One thing is true: Students who take shortcuts in their learning fail faster than everybody else. Is that what you want? Or do you want to pass your courses with good grades? Investing time is as important as investing money in your education.

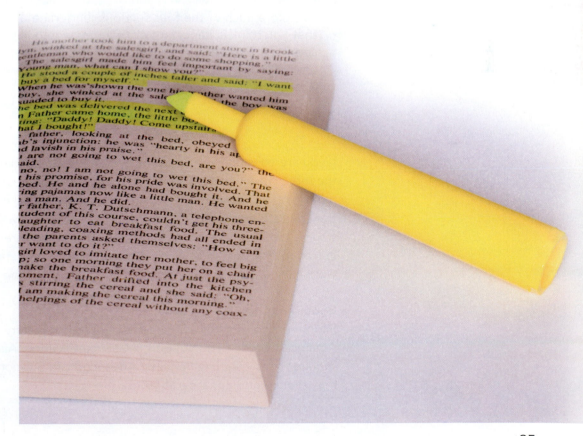

Practice

1.

1. Preview the article "Flight Nursing" with your team. Share any information you know about the topic with your learning partners before you start.

2. Underline the parts of the article that you read during your preview.

3. Write two questions you expect to have answered in this article. When writing preview questions, let your curiosity guide you. What information would YOU like to learn about this subject? Also notice clues in the photos and bold print to help you think of questions.

Write your preview questions here:

1. ....

....

....

2. ....

....

....

....

4. Share what you wrote with your team.

5. Read silently to find the answers to your questions. Don't be concerned if your questions are not answered. Simply looking for the answers that will help you to stay focused as you read. After you complete each of the four sections, underline or highlight anything that you think is important or that you would like to bring to someone else's attention later. If you find answers to your questions, underline them. Remember not to underline more than about a quarter of what you have read.

"FLIGHT NURSING"

If you are considering a career as a flight nurse, you have chosen one of the most challenging and rewarding jobs in the field of nursing. As a flight nurse, you will be involved with both emergency and non-emergency air transportation of injured or critically ill patients. You will provide care to trauma victims and monitor their vital signs as they are flown to hospitals. It is a job that demands excellent physical condition and a willingness to work in harsh conditions, often with long hours around the clock.

Requirements
Flight nursing requires a bachelor's degree in registered nursing with Advanced Cardiac Life Support (ACLS) certification. Also, it usually requires certification in Pediatric Advanced Life Support (PALS). Some jobs may require additional certification.

Employment

Flight nurses are employed by trauma centers in hospitals, the military, and public and private transport companies. Employers look for nurses with three to five years of nursing experience and someone who is willing to perform physically demanding work. When not on flight duty, these nurses have to also be willing to perform routine tasks. Flight nurses can make anywhere from $50,000 to $85,000 a year, depending on where they work.

Resources

For more information on what it is like to be a flight nurse, go to DiscoverNursing.com and read articles about real flight nurses. You can also request more information from the National Flight Nurses Association (NFNA) in Denver.

AFTER READING

6. When you have finished reading, summarize what the passage was about in one or two sentences. How would you describe this selection to someone who hasn't read it? Be brief and very general in your description.

My summary of "Flight Nursing":

....

....

....

....

....

Practice

2. For short articles, preview by reading the title, the headings, and the first sentence of each paragraph. Preview the following selection, and then answer the questions that follow. Underline everything that you previewed.

1. What is the topic? ....

....

2. What is one question you hope to have answered in this selection?

....

....

THE BUSINESS OF HEALTH CARE

[1]Medical fields urgently need people who are able to manage the business of health care. [2]Health administration is a growing field needing trained supervisors, managers, and directors. [3]They are responsible for managing large or small health care facilities such as hospitals, clinics, doctors' offices, veterinarian's offices, and health insurance companies. [4]These professionals help to improve the quality of patient care while keeping costs under control. [5]Health administrators need good computer skills, as well as good communication skills. [6]People with strong business skills are needed to help patients receive the best possible care available to them.

Requirements

[7]To become a health administrator, you will need to have a bachelor's degree in business or health administration. [8]Besides general education courses, you will need to take courses in business, law, and health care. [9]To find out more, search the Internet or see a college career counselor.

Now, go back and read the article. Finally, review by answering the following questions.

1. What do health administrators do?

....

2. What kinds of skills do health administrators need?

....

3. What is the main requirement for health administration?

....

Practice

3. Practice the four-step reading process with the following article by previewing, reading actively, highlighting and annotating, and reviewing. First, preview by reading the title and first sentence of each paragraph, and highlight what you previewed. Based on your preview, answer the first two questions.

1. What is the topic (subject) of this article?

....

2. What are two questions that you expect this article will answer?

....

....

ultrasound: Sound waves are sent into the subject and then bounce back to create an image.

MEDICAL SONOGRAPHERS

[1]A medical sonographer uses **ultrasound** technology to help physicians diagnose illnesses and see inside the patient's body. [2]Sonography uses sound waves to create an image of what is inside the body. [3]Pregnant mothers can see their unborn babies. [4]Doctors can watch a patient's heart valves pumping blood through the body. [5]Other areas of the body are also examined with sonography. [6]Sonographers are trained to use the ultrasound equipment to record images that are transmitted. [7]Sonographers are also trained how to get the best images of the area they are recording. [8]They examine the images to make sure that they are clear and decide which ones to send to the physician.

Special Areas in Sonography
[9]Diagnostic medical sonographers may specialize in one area of medicine such as obstetrics or female reproductive systems. [10]Or they may choose to specialize in abdominal sonography to examine the liver, kidneys, and other organs of the abdomen. [11]In neurosonography, sonographers specialize in imaging the brain. [12]Cardiac sonographers are trained to record images of the heart and cardiovascular system.

Skills Needed
[13]Sonographers need good communication skills because they must be able to explain what they are doing to patients and answer questions that physicians may have. [14]They must also be comfortable using high-tech equipment because they will be trained to use it and maintain it. [15]They will also need to update their training when technology is improved. [16]Sonographers can find employment with a two-year or a four-year degree. [17]This is a field where job openings are expected to remain high.

Practice

Now read actively, looking for answers to your questions. Mark the answers if you find them, reading one section at a time.

Next, highlight and annotate by underlining the answers to your questions, plus any important points that interested you. Make brief notes in the margins to describe what each paragraph is about.

Finally, review by answering the following questions.

1. How does sonography work?

....

2. In what different areas of the body do sonographers specialize?

....

3. What kind of skills and training are needed to become a sonographer?

....

....

TEXTBOOK SELECTION

Preview the following textbook selection as a team. Each member of the team should choose one or two of the questions below. If there are more questions than people on your team, the whole team can work on the leftover questions. When you find the answer, underline it in the textbook. When your team has finished all five questions, take turns sharing your answers.

QUESTIONS

1. What is the topic (subject) of the information in this selection?

....

2. What are some specific subjects that will be discussed?

....

3. What do the pictures, charts, and diagrams show?

....

4. Based on what you previewed, write one question about the selection you can use to ask another team.

....

5. What do you already know about some of these topics?

....

....

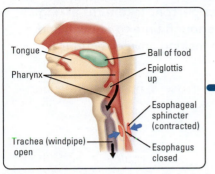
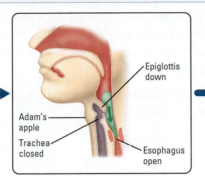
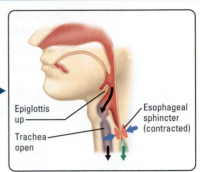

(a) Not swallowing. When you're not swallowing food or drink, air travels freely through the trachea (black arrows). The esophagus is closed because the esophageal sphincter, a ring of muscles, is contracted (blue arrows).

(b) Swallowing started. Once the food reaches the back of the mouth, a swallowing reflex is triggered. The top of the trachea rises against the epiglottis, closing the air passage, while the esophagus opens because the sphincter relaxes. Food travels down the esophagus (green arrow).

(c) Swallowing finished. Once swallowing is completed, the esophageal sphincter contracts, and air once again flows freely through the trachea.

Figure 22.8 The pharynx and swallowing. Like crossing guards at a dangerous intersection, the epiglottis and the esophageal sphincter direct the flow of traffic through the pharynx. You can see this action in the bobbing of your Adam's apple every time you swallow.

The Pharynx

The chamber called the **pharynx,** located in your throat, is an intersection of the food and breathing pathways. It connects the mouth to the esophagus, but the pharynx also opens to the trachea, or windpipe, which leads to the lungs. When you're not swallowing, the trachea entrance is open, and you can breathe. When you swallow, a reflex moves the opening of the trachea upward and tips a door-like flap called the epiglottis to close the trachea entrance **(Figure 22.8)**. The closing of the trachea ensures that the food will go down the esophagus. Occasionally, food begins to "go down the wrong pipe," triggering a strong coughing reflex that helps keep your airway clear of food.

The Esophagus

The **esophagus** is a muscular tube that connects the pharynx to the stomach. Imagine trying to move a tennis ball through a sock open at both ends. The ball will not just fall through, but you could move the ball along by pinching repeatedly just behind the ball until it pops out the other end. Your esophagus moves a ball of food by a similar mechanism. The action is called **peristalsis,** rhythmic waves of muscular contractions that squeeze the food ball along the esophagus **(Figure 22.9)**. This muscular action ensures that you can swallow even when standing on your head. Peristalsis continues throughout the length of the alimentary canal, propelling food all the way along.

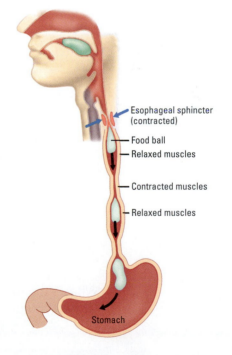

Figure 22.9 The esophagus and peristalsis. The wavelike muscular action called peristalsis squeezes balls of food through the esophagus to the stomach. Muscles of the esophageal wall contract just behind the food ball and relax just ahead of it.

CHAPTER 22   Nutrition and Digestion   491

(From *Essential Biology with Psychology*, 2e by Campbell, Reece, and Simon. Reprinted with permission of Pearson Education, Inc. Upper Saddle River, NJ.)

U-Review

THINK, PAIR, AND SHARE

First, answer the following questions about the chapter by yourself. If you need to, go back and look up the correct answers. After you have completed your answers, pair up with another person. Take turns asking each other the questions. Give your partner enough time to answer, and wait until he or she is done answering before making any corrections or additions to the answer.

1. What is the first step in the four-step reading process, how is it done, and why should you do it?

....

....

....

....

2. What is the second step in the reading process, how is it done, and why should you do it?

....

....

....

3. What is the third step in the reading process, how is it done, and why should you do it?

....

....

....

4. What is the fourth step in the reading process, how is it done, and why should you do it?

....

....

....

Reading 1   Vocabulary Preview

The following vocabulary words are from the article "Bayflite Down." With a partner or in a team, choose the correct meanings of the underlined words in the following sentences. Use context clues (LEADS), word part clues, and parts of speech to help you figure out the meanings.

1. The baby was born with a <u>congenital</u> (kon-JEN-i-tl) heart defect, which needed surgery.

    a. having had since birth

    b. heart

    c. friendly

    d. necessary

2. When someone is unconscious, the first thing you should check is the person's <u>respiration</u> (res-pur-A-shun). If he or she is not breathing, it could be due to a blocked airway.

    a. sweat

    b. hope

    c. breathing

    d. heartbeat

3. Karen works as a <u>respiratory therapist</u> (RES-pur-a-tor-ee THER-a-pist) to help people with breathing problems.

    a. someone who helps people with emotional problems

    b. someone who helps people with breathing problems

    c. someone who helps people with heart problems

    d. a machine to assist breathing

4. The baby was lying inside an <u>Isolette</u> (eye-so-LET) when the nurse came to give her medicine.

    a. crib

    b. box

    c. machine

    d. a type of incubator for babies

5. The tall <u>mangroves</u> (MAN-grovz) that grow in swampy areas provide shelter and food for wildlife.

    a. a type of tropical tree or shrub that grows in swamps

    b. a swamp

    c. a place where animals and fish live

    d. shelters

Reading 1

6. You should note the locations of <u>egress</u> (EE-gress) on a plane in case of an emergency evacuation.

   a. parachutes

   b. wings

   c. exit

   d. food preparation

7. Even though I called him to the dinner table three times, Robbie was <u>oblivious</u> (ob-LIV-ee-us) to my calls because he was so interested in the TV show.

   a. angry

   b. unaware of

   c. listening for

   d. ignoring

8. She wants to be a <u>neonatal</u> (nee-o-NATE-al) nurse because she loves taking care of babies.

   a. nursing home

   b. physical therapy

   c. full-time

   d. having to do with young babies

9. We drove on the <u>causeway</u> (KOZ-way) over the bay to get to the city.

   a. a type of bridge

   b. ferry

   c. tunnel

   d. street

10. The spinning <u>rotors</u> (RO-terz) of the helicopter caused my hat to blow off.

    a. motors

    b. fans

    c. blades

    d. engines

Reading 1 What Do You Already Know?

1. Have you ever experienced a medical emergency yourself or with someone you know? Describe what happened.

2. What do you know about medical transportation using helicopters?

Directions: As you read this article, practice the four-step reading process. Preview the article, and then write on the following lines one or two questions that you would hope to have answered.

....

....

....

....

As you read, answer the questions in the margins to check your comprehension.

Adapted from

"Bayflite Down"

BY DIANE MUHL-LUDES

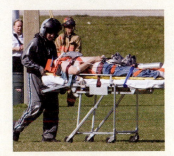

From *Guideposts Magazine*, June 2003. Copyright © 2003 by Guideposts. Reprinted with permission.

She was a flight nurse transporting a seriously ill baby to another hospital, until something went terribly wrong.

1   Our pilot opened the back doors of the Bayflite 3 medical transport helicopter and pushed aboard a stretcher. I walked beside it, keeping a close eye on the 10-day-old girl with weak lungs and a <u>congenital</u> heart problem who was in an <u>Isolette</u>. Beneath her was the equipment monitoring her condition. Heartbeat. <u>Respiration</u>. I checked the oxygen monitor. The baby's levels were down

2   My partner, Kevin, and I went into action. Kevin is a <u>respiratory therapist</u>, and I'm a critical-care transport nurse.

3   I strapped myself into the seat at the foot of the stretcher for the one-hour flight from Naples to St. Petersburg. The helicopter's <u>rotors</u> roared into action. Glancing out the window I noticed the baby's parents huddled on the edge of the landing pad. Something about the way the husband had his arm around his wife touched me. I thought, 'I wish I could speak to my husband Scott again.'

What is Diane preparing to do?

35

Reading 1

4   Scott was an RN too. Our busy schedules pulled us in 10 different directions at once. All too often the only time we had to talk was on the phone during a shift. That morning we'd gotten into an argument about what our son was doing at school. It wasn't a huge matter, but the discussion got heated, and I hung up without saying good-bye. Immediately I was sorry. I called him back as soon as I had a chance, but all I got was the answering machine. I left a message: "Scott, please say a little prayer for me. I'm flying tonight."

5   I plugged my earphones into the helicopter intercom system. Kevin sank down in the seat to my left. "All secure?" the pilot's voice crackled over the headset as the chopper lifted off. "Doing fine," I said. The baby was fidgeting inside the Isolette, but her numbers on the monitors had **stabilized**. It was crucial she breathe on her own.

stabilized: kept at a steady level

6   Kevin pointed to the oxygen levels. I got up to reposition the baby. We could not hear each other over the roar of the rotors. Sign language was the only way to talk. I nodded. He nodded.

What was Diane feeling at this time, and why did she feel that way?

7   The vibrations of the helicopter were settling the baby down. I wish they'd settle me down too, I thought. My last conversation with my husband had left me with a bad feeling.

8   Outside the sky was darkening. I had a sense we were flying over water or a mangrove swamp. I hated flying over water. If the copter crashed, it would flip over and sink because of the weight of the rotors. Going in mangroves is just as bad because of the thick trees **mangling** the rotors and making operations impossible.

mangling: twisting

9   Maybe it was a good idea I had asked Scott to pray for me, I thought. I was so uneasy around water that I'd never even worked up the nerve to go on the Skyway Bridge by myself. It was probably right beneath us now, spanning Tampa Bay. Soon we'd land. Soon I'd be home. Scott and I could talk through everything.

10   BOOM! An explosion rocked the helicopter.

11   "What's that?" I yelled.

12   "Hang on!" the pilot shouted over the intercom.

horrific: horrible

13   A **horrific** grinding noise started somewhere to my left. My gaze locked on Kevin's. He looked back in wide-eyed terror. My heart raced. Flames jumped just outside the window.

14   *We're on fire!* I thought in a panic. *We're going to crash!*

15   "Mayday, Mayday! Bayflite 3 is going down!" the pilot called into the radio. We were spinning like a top now, falling from the sky.

16   The water! We'll sink in the water or in a mangrove swamp!

17   "Brace yourself!" the pilot yelled over the intercom. I reached out and grabbed Kevin with my left hand, then grabbed hold of the stretcher with my right.

18   "Help us!" I screamed out loud. Thoughts whirled through my mind. Why hadn't I said good-bye to Scott that morning? Why were my last words spoken in anger?

19   "Mayday, Mayday! We're going down!" I heard over the **intercom**. I didn't want to think about what was below.

20   There was a tremendous jolt. The rear of the helicopter slammed down violently. Another jolt, more violent than anything I'd ever felt. The nose hit something hard. My hips collided with the seat and the shoulder harness cut across me. The helicopter skidded wildly.

21   "Egress! Egress!" I heard over the intercom.

22   Kevin pushed hard against the door on his side and leaped out, oblivious to the flames. I half fell, half jumped out. My feet landed on something solid. Pavement? My eyes caught spots of bright lights shining toward me in the darkness. Cars! We'd landed on the causeway, just a strip of highway in the bay. Traffic was headed straight for us! I jumped up and down frantically flagging traffic in the highway.

23   A car slammed on the brakes a few yards away. Another screeched to a halt. Flames shot over the top of the helicopter 20 feet into the air. The pilot grabbed a small fire extinguisher. A truck driver dashed out with another extinguisher.

24   "We've got to get the baby out of there!" I shouted. If I carried her in my arms, how would I keep her stable without the equipment and monitors?

25   "We have to open the doors in the back and bring out the whole Isolette and stretcher!" I yelled to the others. "Fast!"

26   All I could think about were those flames hitting the chopper's gas tanks and the explosion that would follow. We raced to the back. While the pilot hit the flames with his extinguisher, Kevin undid the clasps on the back doors.

intercom: the on-board communication system

What do you think will happen next?

Reading 1

Where did the helicopter land?

27   POP! POP! POP! The clasps fell apart. He tried again, yanking open the doors. Kevin and I grabbed the stretcher and pulled it out to the highway. Kevin and I took off running, rolling the stretcher away from the helicopter. We checked the baby's condition. Breathing fine. Heartbeat normal. She was safe. I ran to a stopped car. "Please call 911!" I shouted. I raced to another car and asked for a cell phone. I called the neonatal floor and told them we'd gone down. "We're on the 1-275 Causeway," I said. "The baby's doing fine, but we need another chopper."

28   I gave the nurse my home phone number. "Please call my husband, Scott, and tell him I'm all right." I wanted to add, "Tell him I love him and I'm sorry."

29   I rushed back to the Isolette and wrote down the baby's vital signs, trying not to think about getting on the helicopter they were sending to pick us up. I heard the sound of its rotors before I saw it appear through the smoke from the fire. Kevin and I loaded in the Isolette, and we took off.

30   We buzzed across the bay, into the night sky. We landed at Bayfront Medical Center and rushed the baby through the tunnel under the hospital to the neonatal intensive care unit.

31   Doctors and nurses swooped down and took her away. Finally, my job was over. I sank down in a chair at the nurse's station, my head in my hands. Just then Scott came rushing in. He didn't say a word. He just wrapped me up in his arms. That was all I needed. "It's all right," he said. "It's all right now."

32   "Did you get my message?" I asked. "Yes," he said. "I was praying for you."

33   I thought of all of the things that could have gone wrong that day. We could have crashed in the bay. We could have landed in the swamp. We could have been hit by a car on the causeway—or hit a car. The baby could have been hurt in the crash.

34   But she was safe. We were all safe, and now I had Scott beside me. I took Scott's hand in mine. Even when we disagree, Scott and I know what's really important.

1,004 words divided by .... minutes = ... words per minute

Reading 1 Thinking About What You Read

It is a good habit to summarize everything you read to strengthen your comprehension.

Directions: Complete the following summary of "Bayflite Down" by filling in the blanks.

Transport nurse, ..., saved ....after the medical transport ....she was riding in crashed on the .... The baby was being taken to .... because of a .... Another .... arrived and took them safely to ....

Comprehension Questions

The following questions will help you to recall the main idea and the details of "Bayflite Down." Review any parts of the article that you need to in order to find the correct answers.

LITERAL COMPREHENSION

1. What is the topic (subject) of this article? (Who or what is this article about?)
   a. flight nursing
   b. an emergency helicopter landing
   c. neonatals
   d. Diane's career as a flight nurse

MAIN IDEA

2. What is the main idea of the article? (What is the most general statement that tells the most important point of the article?)
   a. A sick baby was transported to another hospital by helicopter.
   b. While transporting a sick baby to another hospital, the helicopter made an emergency landing on the Tampa Bay causeway.
   c. A helicopter caused a crash.
   d. Flight nursing can be dangerous.

SUPPORTING DETAILS

3. What problem was Diane facing as she began her flight?
   a. She didn't know how to help the sick baby.
   b. She was afraid of flying.
   c. She had an argument with her husband that morning.
   d. She had to land the helicopter on a bridge.

Reading 1

4. **Why was Diane afraid of flying over water or swamps?**

   a. She thought they may have alligators in them.

   b. She knew that if the helicopter crashed, it would sink.

   c. She didn't have much confidence in the pilot's ability to navigate over water.

   d. She couldn't swim.

5. **What did Diane notice after they landed?**

   a. Traffic was heading toward them.

   b. There was an ambulance waiting to take them to the hospital.

   c. The baby was not breathing.

   d. The pilot was unconscious.

6. **What thoughts ran through Diane's mind as the helicopter was going down?**

   a. She wished she hadn't spoken in anger to her husband that morning.

   b. She realized she couldn't swim.

   c. She wanted to call the hospital and tell them what had happened.

   d. She thought about her son's problems in school.

DRAWING CONCLUSIONS

7. **What happened after they landed on the causeway?**

   a. An ambulance came and took the baby to the hospital.

   b. Another helicopter came and took the crew and the baby to the hospital.

   c. A driver on the causeway offered to take them to the nearest hospital.

   d. The first department's emergency rescue team took the baby to the hospital.

VOCABULARY IN CONTEXT

Using context clues and word part clues, determine the best meaning for the underlined word in each of these sentences. If necessary, use a dictionary.

8. **It was <u>crucial</u> she breathe on her own (paragraph 5).**

   a. desperate   **c.** extremely important

   b. not important   **d.** considerable

9. **"<u>Mayday</u>, Mayday! Bayflite 3 is going down!" the pilot called into the radio (paragraph 15).**

   a. the day of the month   **c.** a command to jump

   b. emergency   **d.** a person's name

10. **It was probably right beneath us now, <u>spanning</u> Tampa Bay (paragraph 9).**

   a. turning   **c.** circling

   b. swimming   **d.** crossing

Reading 1 Vocabulary Practice

Use the vocabulary words from the following Word Bank to complete the sentences. Write the words into the blanks provided.

WORD BANK

congenital	respiration	respiratory therapist	Isolette
mangroves	egress	oblivious	neonatal
causeway	rotors		

1. The pediatric nurse placed the newborn infant into a(n) ....

2. Damian was not allowed to play on his high school football team because the doctor found that he had a(n) .... heart defect.

3. We paddled our canoes around the .... looking for rare birds and wildlife in the swamp.

4. The emergency medical technician checked the patient's pulse and ....

5. José is .... to Maria's flirting with him. He hasn't a clue how she feels about him.

6. The .... of the helicopter collided with the signal tower and crashed.

7. Janeka wanted to be a(n) .... so she could treat people with breathing problems.

8. Working in the .... unit of the hospital, Cassandra got used to the sound of crying babies.

9. A crash on the .... caused a huge traffic jam for nearly two hours.

10. In case of an emergency, it is a good idea to note the best route of .... from your office building.

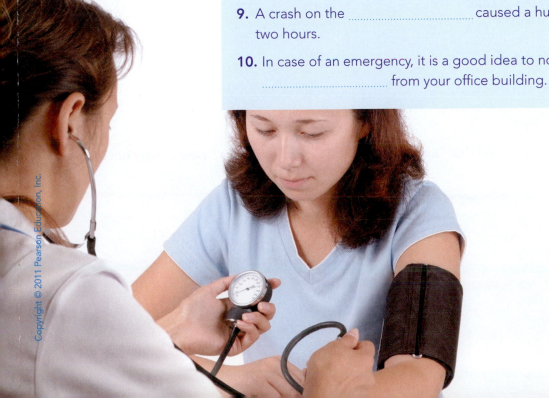

41

Reading 1 Questions for Writing and Discussion

Review any parts of the article you need to answer the following questions.

1. What personal characteristics would a good flight nurse need to have?

....

....

....

2. What lesson do you think Diane learned about what is important in life?

....

....

....

3. What actions in the article showed that Diane is well suited for her profession?

....

....

....

4. What feelings did Diane display during the article that showed her "human side"?

....

....

....

5. Do you feel that Diane should be regarded as a hero? Why or why not?

....

....

....

Reading 1 Vocabulary Practice—Crossword

Read the clues at the bottom. Fill in the crossword with the words in the Word Bank.

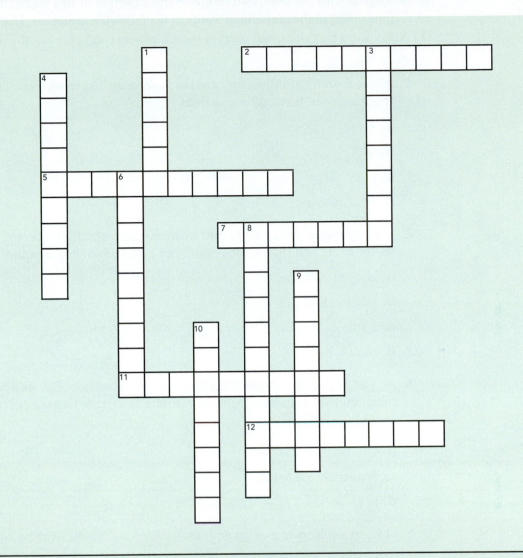

WORD BANK

CAUSEWAY	CONGENITAL	CRUCIAL	EGRESS
INTERCOM	ISOLETTE	MANGROVES	NEONATAL
OBLIVIOUS	REPOSITION	RESPIRATION	SATURATED

ACROSS
2. having this since birth
5. to put in position again
7. extremely important
11. filled with
12. communication system

DOWN
1. exit
3. newborn (adj.)
4. tropical trees or shrubs
6. not aware
8. breathing
9. a type of baby incubator
10. a bridge

Reading 2 Vocabulary Preview

The following vocabulary words are from the article "An Illegal Immigrant Turned Brain Surgeon with His Own Two Hands." With a partner or in a team, choose the correct meanings of the underlined words in the following sentences. Use context clues (LEADS), word part clues, and parts of speech to help you figure out the meanings.

1. It was a grim (GRIM) existence: He lived in an old truck camper—without the truck—in the middle of a field.

   a. great

   b. old

   c. impossible

   d. depressing

2. In psychology class we learned how to watch children interact (in-ter-ACT) and then wrote down our observations in a report.

   a. cooperate together

   b. surf the Internet

   c. fight

   d. put on a play

3. At age 14, Quiñones qualified for an accelerated (ak-SELL-er-a-ted) program that prepared students for jobs as elementary school teachers.

   a. faster than regular

   b. shorter than regular

   c. financially assisted

   d. popular

4. "I wasn't willing to put up with that injustice," (in-JUS-tis) he says.

   a. fairness

   b. something that is harmful

   c. something that is unfair

   d. political

5. In the spring of 1993, his mentor (MEN-tor), Hugo Mora, looked over his transcripts and told him he stood a good chance of getting into Harvard Medical School.

   a. supervisor

   b. friend

   c. someone who competes with another

   d. someone who gives advice to another

6. Dr. Q now specializes in a high-tech form of brain surgery called motor mapping, in which an electrical <u>stimulator</u> (STIM-u-la-tor) is used to locate sensitive areas.

    a. a medical instrument

    b. something that is like another thing

    c. a type of drill

    d. technician

7. "Not only is he a talented and <u>conscientious</u> (kon-shee-EN-shus) surgeon, but he's very sensitive to the needs of patients," says Dr. Henry Brem, director of neurosurgery at Johns Hopkins.

    a. popular

    b. responsible about one's duties

    c. joyful

    d. awake

8. Quiñones studied medicine at Harvard Medical School to become a <u>neurosurgeon</u> (NER-o-sir-jin) because he was interested in the human brain.

    a. a new surgeon

    b. a doctor who specializes in nerves

    c. a brain surgeon

    d. a surgeon who works on children

9. Every day, Carlita worked <u>painstakingly</u> (pains-TAKing-lee) on her wedding gown, sewing every single stitch and bead by hand.

    a. carelessly

    b. without effort

    c. causing pain

    d. with great care and attention

10. The camp where we stayed was in such a <u>remote</u> (re-MOTE) location that we had to hike two hours to reach it from the nearest road.

    a. easy to find

    b. far from civilization

    c. unbelievable

    d. unreachable

Reading 2   What Do You Already Know?

1. Do you know anyone who has moved from another country? Why did he or she move, and what was this person's experience like?
2. Have you ever traveled to a country where you didn't know the language? Describe your experiences.

> **Directions:** As you read this article, practice the four-step reading process. Preview the article, and then write on the following lines one or two questions that you would hope to have answered.
>
> ....
>
> ....
>
> ....
>
> ....

As you read, answer the questions in the margins to check your comprehension.

"An Illegal Immigrant Turned Brain Surgeon with His Own Two Hands"

(Adapted from "With His Own Two Hands" by Max Alexander from *Reader's Digest*, February 2008. Copyright © 2008 by The Reader's Digest Association, Inc. Reprinted by permission of *Reader's Digest*.)

He was an illegal immigrant making a living picking tomatoes. Now Alfredo Quiñones-Hinojosa excels in a different field—as a top brain surgeon.

1   The hot sun seared his skin as Alfredo Quiñones-Hinojosa bent in the field to pick tomatoes. It was work few Americans would do for just $155 a week, and most of his co-workers on this 10,000-acre farm in central California were, like Quiñones, illegal Mexican immigrants. It was a grim existence: He lived in an old truck camper—without the truck—in the middle of a field.

2   But Quiñones was different from the other workers. He carried an English dictionary in his pocket and studied it every day. He was studying to become an American.

3   It had been a year since Quiñones jumped the fence in Calexico. His cousin was supposed to be waiting for him on the American side. Instead he was met by the U.S. Border Patrol. Half an hour later, Quiñones was back in Mexico.

4   Figuring the border police would never expect the same guy to cross in the same spot on the same night, he went over the fence again. This time, his cousin was there. Quiñones hopped in his car, and the two roared off into the night toward El Centro. It was January 2, 1987, Quiñones's 19th birthday.

5   The oldest of Sostenes Quiñones and Flavia Hinojosa's five children, Alfredo began work at age five, pumping gas at his father's Pemex station. That's where the family also lived, on a dusty road 37 miles south of the border town of Mexicali. It was hard work, but Quiñones didn't mind. He also got to drive the cars now and then, perched on a stack of pillows.

6   In 1976 the Mexican government devalued the peso, throwing the country into an economic depression. "We lost everything, just like that," Quiñones says with a snap of his fingers. "I remember going to the back of the house to find my father crying."

7   His father turned to his brothers, who were working in the United States as migrant farm workers. They supplied the family with sacks of potatoes and beans. Quiñones helped bring in extra money by working at a taco stand.

What was Quiñones's childhood like growing up in Mexico?

8   Still, he kept up with school. "My father kept telling me, 'You want to be like me? Just never go to school.' And I was not going to follow the same path." At age 14, Quiñones qualified for an accelerated program that prepared students for jobs as elementary school teachers. Each morning, he rose at 4:30 a.m. to take a bus to the school. There was no bus home in the afternoon, so he hitchhiked—or walked—in the blistering heat.

9   He graduated near the top of his class. But because his family had no political connections, he says, he was assigned a teaching job at a remote school far down the Baja peninsula. "I wasn't willing to put up with that injustice," he says.

10   Shortly after that, he decided to leave Mexico in search of better options. He had been to America twice before, doing summer labor. So on his arrival, Quiñones headed with his cousin for the San Joaquin Valley to work in the fields. "I picked tomatoes, cauliflower, broccoli, corn, and grapes."

11   After a year, he had saved $8,000—almost all of his pay. "I ate what I was picking," he says. "I wore the same pair of jeans the whole year."

12   When Quiñones looked up from the dirt, the best job he could see was driving the big tractors. The drivers were skilled, and they supervised crews. Quiñones was soon behind the wheel of plows and ditch diggers.

Reading 2

What accomplishments did Quiñones achieve? How did he achieve them?

How did Quiñones make his way through college?

He learned how to service the engines and qualified for a temporary work permit. "I had that hunger in my gut," he says.

13   He moved to Stockton, California, and took a job in a rail yard so he could attend night school at San Joaquin Delta College, learning English. His first job, shoveling sulfur, was the worst of his life—smelly and filthy. Once again, he scrambled to acquire new skills, this time as a welder repairing valves on tank cars. Within a year, he'd become a foreman. With his English improving, Quiñones switched to the night shift and began full-time studies in science and math. To make ends meet, he also tutored other students.

14   After graduating with an associate's degree in 1991, Quiñones was accepted to the University of California, Berkeley. He moved to a low-rent district in Oakland, getting by on a combination of scholarships, loans, a small grant, and, as always, work. He became a teacher's assistant in three departments and also took a job at a men's clothing store.

15   Quiñones excelled at Berkeley, getting straight As in advanced classes, writing his honors thesis on the role of drug receptors in the brain and teaching calculus on the side. In the spring of 1993, his mentor, Hugo Mora, looked over his transcripts and told him he stood a good chance of getting into Harvard Medical School. Quiñones had been to a doctor only once in his life.

16   Harvard Medical School accepted him, and Quiñones moved east in the fall of 1994. A year later, Quiñones became a U.S. citizen. Quiñones gave the commencement address when he graduated from Harvard and continued his training, in neurosurgery, at the University of California, San Francisco. It was an exciting but challenging prospect. Could an illegal Mexican fieldworker become a brain surgeon? It didn't seem possible.

17   The University of California turned out to be a low point in Quiñones's American journey. "Neurosurgery has been reserved for people who come from a long line of medicine," he says carefully. "It's rare that you have someone like me go into this highly demanding field, where lots of patients die." He admits there were times, when he worked 130 hours a week for $30,000 a year, when he considered quitting. "I felt what my father felt, not being able to put food on the table for my family," he says. "But I had a dream."

18   Known as "Dr. Q" by his patients, he now specializes in a high-tech form of brain surgery called motor mapping, in which an electrical stimulator is used to locate sensitive areas. He prepares to remove a brain tumor. "Let's have complete silence, please," he says,

Reading 2

How did Quiñones achieve his success as a neurosurgeon?

and the operating room falls quiet. He touches the stimulator to the brainsurface, and the woman's arm twitches—a spot to avoid. Eventually he determines a safe path to the tumor, which he <u>painstakingly</u> removes, piece by piece, with electrical forceps.

19   "Dr. Q" is a relatively young doctor, and his colleagues are already impressed. "Not only is he a talented and <u>conscientious</u> surgeon, but he's very sensitive to the needs of patients," says Dr. Henry Brem, director of neurosurgery at Johns Hopkins. "And he's a joyous person—full of enthusiasm and the mission to do good for the world."

20   It's now after seven, and Dr. Q has been working for 12 hours. Other surgeons are going home for the weekend, but he is headed for his research laboratory in downtown Baltimore. The doctor's busy schedule means little time relaxing with his wife and three children— Gabriella, eight, David, six, and Olivia, two.

21   "I think my background allows me to <u>interact</u> with my patients in a more humanistic way," Dr. Q says. "When they're scared, I'm one of them. I'm just lucky that patients allow me to touch their brains, their lives. When I go in, I see these incredible blood vessels. And it always brings me back to the time I used to pick those huge, beautiful tomatoes with my own hands. Now I am here, looking at the same color—that bright red that just fills the brain with nutrition and wonder. I'm right there in the field, and I'm just doing it."

1,320 words divided by .... minutes = ... words per minute

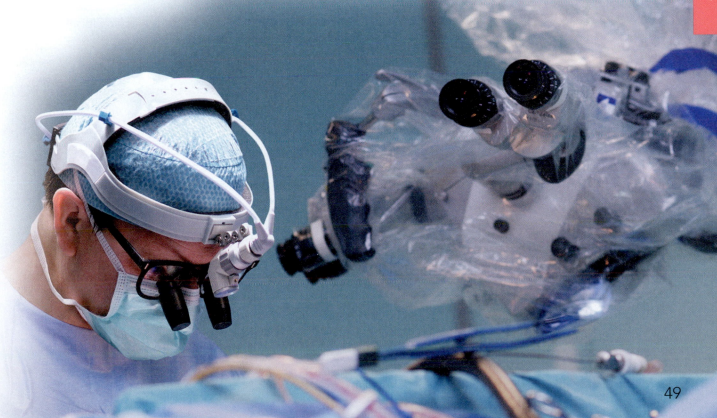

Reading 2 Thinking About What You Read

It is a good habit to summarize everything you read to strengthen your comprehension.

Directions: Complete the following summary of "An Illegal Immigrant Turned Brain Surgeon with His Own Two Hands" by filling in the blanks.

(Who?) ...., an illegal immigrant from .... , worked in .... , where he (did what?) .... He put himself through .... to become a doctor. He is now a successful .... in a hospital.

Comprehension Questions

The following questions will help you to recall the main idea and the details of "An Illegal Immigrant Turned Brain Surgeon with His Own Two Hands." Review any parts of the article you need to in order to find the correct answers.

LITERAL COMPREHENSION

1. What is the topic (subject) of this article? (Who or what is this article about?)
   a. illegal immigrants
   b. neurosurgery
   c. Alfredo Quiñones-Hinojosa
   d. Mexican doctors

MAIN IDEA

2. What is the main idea of this article? (What is the most general idea that tells the most important point of the article?)
   a. Alfredo Quiñones-Hinojosa entered the United States as an illegal immigrant and went to medical school at Harvard University.
   b. Alfredo Quiñones-Hinojosa faced hardship in the United States.
   c. The hot sun seared his skin as Alfredo Quiñones-Hinojosa bent in the field to pick tomatoes.
   d. Alfredo Quiñones-Hinojosa, an illegal immigrant, put himself through college and medical school to become a neurosurgeon.

SUPPORTING DETAILS

3. Why did Alfredo Quiñones-Hinojosa leave Mexico?
   a. He wanted to get a better job in teaching.
   b. He wanted to pick crops in America.
   c. His parents, brothers, and sisters had already moved there.
   d. He wanted to get a better paying job.

4. How did Alfredo Quiñones-Hinojosa get his associate's degree?

   a. He received a scholarship to pay for his tuition.

   b. He saved his money and attended school while working as a welder and tutoring other students.

   c. He asked his cousins to help him pay for his tuition.

   d. He took online classes.

DRAWING CONCLUSIONS

5. One of the main reasons Dr. Quiñones is so successful is that:

   a. He was determined to get an education and was willing to work hard for it.

   b. He had a family to help him get through college and medical school.

   c. He knew he could get a scholarship from Mexico.

   d. He was satisfied with what he had.

6. All of the following sentences about Dr. Quiñones are true except:

   a. He is Mexican.

   b. Dr. Quiñones is married with three children.

   c. Besides being a neurosurgeon, Dr. Quiñones also works at a research lab in Baltimore, Maryland.

   d. He is an only child.

7. When Dr. Q's father had told him, "You want to be like me? Just never go to school," he meant that:

   a. Alfredo should not go to school.

   b. Alfredo should be like him.

   c. If Alfredo didn't get an education, he would end up poor like his father.

   d. If he wanted to be like his father, he should go to school.

VOCABULARY IN CONTEXT

Using context clues and word part clues, determine the best meaning for the underlined word in each of these sentences. If necessary, use a dictionary.

8. The government <u>devalued</u> the peso, and his father lost almost all of his money (paragraph 6).

   a. increased in value   c. produced

   b. decreased in value   d. spent

9. "His first job, shoveling <u>sulfur</u>, was the worst of his life—smelly and filthy." (paragraph 13)

   a. sand   c. quickly

   b. a strong chemical powder   d. painfully

10. He worked hard to get promoted; within a year, he'd become a <u>foreman</u> (paragraph 13).

   a. a manager   c. a type of welder

   b. a member of a crew   d. a tutor

Reading 2 Vocabulary Practice

Use the vocabulary words from the following Word Bank to complete the sentences. Write the words into the blanks provided.

> **WORD BANK**
>
> | | | | | |
> |---|---|---|---|---|
> | grim | accelerated | injustice | mentor | stimulator |
> | interact | conscientious | neurosurgeon | painstakingly | remote |

1. The surgeon used an electronic .... to map out the various areas of the brain.

2. Shakara took an honors course in biology, which was a(n) .... version of the regular course.

3. Roberto is a(n) .... student. He always studies for tests and hands in his work on time.

4. The economic state of the country was .... because there were few jobs and many people were out of work.

5. Because she specialized in studying the human brain, Natasha became a ....

6. To make sure that she had not misspelled any words on her essay, Nina went through every line very ....

7. The veterinary students had to observe the chimpanzees .... with each other.

8. In high school, Ming's physics teacher became her .... by helping her decide on a major and encouraging her to apply for college.

9. Paying women less than men for the same job is a(n) .... that still exists in many places.

10. Sofia chose a college in a(n) .... location, 50 miles away from the nearest city, so she would not have any distractions from her studies.

Reading 2 Questions for Writing and Discussion

Review any parts of the article you need to answer the following questions.

1. Dr. Q said in the article, "But I had a dream" (paragraph 17). What do you think his dream was?

....

....

....

2. Why was Dr. Q able to accomplish all that he did?

....

....

....

3. How was Quiñones different from other farm workers who worked with him in the field?

....

....

....

4. Do you think Quiñones made a good decision to come to the United States, even if he had to do it illegally? Why or why not?

....

....

....

5. In what ways are Diane Muhl-Ludes (the transport nurse in the first reading selection) and Alfredo Quiñones-Hinojosa alike?

....

....

....

....

Reading 2 Vocabulary Practice—Word Maze

In the word maze below, find the following vocabulary words and search for their closest meanings in the surrounding boxes. The meaning of a vocabulary word must touch the box where the word can be found. Circle or shade in the boxes that contain the words and their meanings to find the path through the maze. The first word is done for you.

WORD BANK

grim	mentor	accelerated	conscientious
injustice	painstakingly	remote	interact
stimulator	neurosurgeon		

START

(grim)	old	impossible	thoughtful
small	(depressing)	injustice	fight
smile	aware of	mentor	boss
unpleasant	manager	friend	advisor
torrid	vehicles	accelerated	causeway
harmful	quickly	went faster	speeding
political	injustice	prejudice	location
unfairness	judicial	criminal	believable
painfully	painstakingly	carelessly	studying
carefully	without effort	causing pain	interesting
remote	controller	obvious	attention
unlikely	faraway	online action	play a part
very hot	between acts	interact	associate
saturated	actions	play	cooperate
a disease	faraway	conscientious	aware of
mortar	like another	imitate	responsible
unlike	electro plug	stimulator	interesting
emergency	medical device	nerve doctor	specialist
nursing	new surgeon	neurosurgeon	type of fish
internet website	nerve surgeon	nervous doctor	brain surgeon

FINISH

Arethea Moise,
Registered Nurse

1. How did you become interested in being a nurse?

I was born to become a nurse. As a child, I played nurse with my dolls and helped care for my younger brother and sister. I had midwives and nurses in my family back in Jamaica.

2. When you were in college, what were some of the obstacles that you had to overcome?

I was a single mom, and I was able to live at home with my parents while I went to college. I had to get up at 5 a.m. to go to clinicals. I had to take care of my son after classes and study hard to keep up my grades.

3. Did you ever think about quitting and giving up on getting a degree?

There were many times I wanted to quit. The hardest times were when my son cried when I had to leave him to go to classes. I also became so exhausted that at one point I had to drop a class and retake it because I was overworked and became ill. But I came back stronger and took the class again successfully.

4. Where do you work now, and what do you like about your job?

I am working as a nurse at Dr. Philips Hospital in Orlando, Florida. I love my job there because, as a preceptor, I monitor the new nurses who are just starting out. I am also finishing up my master's degree and teaching part-time. What I like most about my job is being able to help people through difficult times. It is so rewarding, and I love what I do.

5. What do you dislike about your job?

The long shifts are hard. Sometimes I have to work 12 to 14 hours in one shift. And sometimes it's hard working with nurses who are not team players. Everyone is on teams, and we help each other out. My unit works great together, but once in a while there is someone who is not cooperative, and she or he will make things more difficult than they need to be.

6. If you could give college students one piece of advice, what would it be?

First, stay focused on your goal. Discouraging things will happen in your life, and you have to be determined to succeed. Having a degree has changed my whole life. I was able to buy a home and have the security of knowing I will always have a good job. Second, talk to an academic counselor at your school to make sure you are taking the right courses. Without the right courses, you won't get accepted into the nursing program.

7. What are your plans for the future?

I am completing my master's degree, and I teach part-time now at the community college. I may decide to do it full-time some day. I love the enthusiasm of the students who are so excited about becoming nurses. I am married now and my husband is in medical school. But I know I will be able to find a good job wherever I go because of the demand for nurses. I love this career, and I can't imagine doing anything else.

VIEWPOINT: Assisted Suicide

Medically Assisted Suicide: Should It Be Legal in Every State?

Read the following letters to a newspaper editor on assisted suicide, and then answer the questions that follow.

Dear Editor:

YES! Assisted Suicide Should Be Legalized!

Assisted suicide means that a patient who is suffering or terminally ill can get lethal drugs from a doctor to end his or her own life. Everyone should have the right to choose when he or she wants to die, not the government. Patients should be allowed to choose when and how they will die instead of suffering needlessly. Forcing someone to stay on life support for 10 or 20 years makes no sense. It causes more suffering for the patients and their families. Let the dying have the right to die with dignity!

Signed,

Miss Liberty

Dear Editor:

NO! Assisted Suicide Should NOT Be Legalized!

No one has the right to decide when he or she wants to die. Helping someone to end one's own life is a form of murder. Making it legal will encourage more people to do it, even when there might be a small hope for a recovery. Dying patients might feel pressured by their families to end their lives instead of spending money on hospital or nursing home care. People who benefit financially from this may pressure doctors to perform assisted suicides. Patients who are temporarily depressed or in pain may decide to end their lives needlessly. And there is always hope that some new medical procedure, drug, or a miracle will rescue the dying.

Signed,

Defender of the Weak

Critical Thinking

1. A *point of view* is the author's opinion about a topic. To find the author's point of view, ask yourself, "How does this author feel about this issue?" What is the author's point of view about assisted suicide in the first letter?

   ....

   ....

2. What is the author's point of view about assisted suicide in the second letter?

   ....

   ....

3. Which letter do you agree with, and why?

   ....

   ....

   ....

4. What could be the consequences of legalizing assisted suicides, according to the second letter?

   ....

   ....

   ....

   ....

5. Under what conditions, if any, do you think a doctor should be allowed to assist someone who wishes to commit suicide?

   ....

   ....

WRITE YOUR THOUGHTS

Write a letter to the editor stating your own feelings about assisted suicide. What do you think should be done? Use a separate sheet of paper.

Living Will

In life you will have to read and understand many important documents. Read the following Living Will document, and then answer the questions that follow. Use the four-step reading process as you read, and then answer the questions that follow to check your comprehension.

LIVING WILL

I,................., intend that this document states my wishes regarding my medical care if I am unable to communicate them otherwise. I declare that I am of sound mind and body and that I have not been influenced by anyone in regard to these statements. This declaration must be honored as my legal right to accept or refuse medical treatment.

For this declaration to be valid, my doctor and another doctor must review my condition. They must both agree that I am not able to regain consciousness, and that I am incapable of living without a life support system. If I am unable to participate in decisions regarding my medical care, the declarations in this living will must be followed.

I wish that my medical treatment will be as follows: ....

....

My family, my medical caregivers, and my medical facility shall not be held for any criminal liability as a result of following the wishes expressed in this document.

If I change my mind regarding these wishes, I may communicate it in any way at any time to my family or health care providers.

Signed copies of this declaration are to be regarded as legal as the original.

After careful consideration, I declare that I understand and I accept the consequences of my expressed wishes in this document.

Signed,

....
(Declarant's signature)   (Declarant's name printed)

....
(date)

STATEMENT OF WITNESSES

We the witnesses of this document declare that the declarant is of sound mind and body and has made this declaration without undue influence or fraud.

....
Signature of witness 1   Printed name of witness 1

Address ....

....
Signature of witness 2   Printed name of witness 2

Address ....

....

Note: This is an example of a living will and is not a legal document.

Questions

1. What does this document do?

   a. It gives the doctor the right to decide what kind of medical treatment to give the person named in the document.

   b. It gives the family the right to decide what kind of medical treatment to give the person named in the document.

   c. It states that the person will give up all of his or her rights to decide upon what medical treatment to get.

   d. It describes the declarant's (the patient's) wishes regarding his or her medical treatment if he or she cannot communicate them later.

2. What does the word "declarant" mean?

   a. The person who witnesses the document.

   b. The person who is completing the document and is named in the document.

   c. The person who will give the medical care.

   d. Someone who is a family member of the patient.

3. According to the document, which of these statements is not true?

   a. Two doctors must agree that the person is unable to continue life without life support.

   b. If the patient should die as a result of respecting this living will, the family and the doctors will be held responsible.

   c. The person named in the document declares to have normal mental abilities.

   d. The person filling out this form can change his or her mind about what is on this document.

4. True or false: All signed copies of this document are as legal as the original.

   a. True

   b. False

5. True or false: The document must be signed before two witnesses.

   a. True

   b. False

BUILDING VOCABULARY

Throughout this course, you will be introduced to word parts that make up many words in the English language. Study the following word parts, and then answer the questions that follow.

Prefixes	**Roots**	**Suffixes**
sub- *under*	-mit-, -mis- *to send*	-tion, -sion- *action, state of*
pre- *before*	-script-, -scribe- *to write*	

1. What English words can you create from the lists of word parts above?

....

....

2. Using a dictionary, look up the meanings of any of the words you wrote that you can't define. Use one of the words you wrote in a sentence that reveals its meaning with a context clue:

....

....

....

CHAPTER REVIEW PRACTICE #1

Use the four-step reading process to read the passage and answer the questions.

STEP 1: Preview

1. What is the topic of this passage?

....

2. What is one question you expect to have answered in this article?

....

....

STEP 2: Read actively to find answers to your questions.

STEP 3: Highlight (or underline) and annotate key points and answers to your questions.

Dietitians and Nutritionists

If you love food and cooking, you may want to consider a career in the medical field. Dietitians and nutritionists are people who plan meals, manage food service systems, conduct research, and help patients learn how to follow special diets. There are several different types of careers in nutrition.

Clinical dietitians work in hospitals, nursing care homes, or other large institutions to plan meals and special nutrition programs for patients. They work with doctors and nurses to decide on the best diets for patients with special dietary needs. They may also work directly with patients to help them understand how their diets will help them to improve their health.

Community dietitians talk to people about nutrition in clinics, health agencies, and other health care organizations. They may also work in the food industry to analyze foods and provide nutritional information. Their job is to help professionals understand the benefits of good nutrition.

Management dietitians work in large institutions and act as managers and supervisors. They work in large health care facilities, companies, schools, and prisons. They manage the food services and plan meals as well as prepare records and reports.

Consultant dietitians work in businesses, such as supermarkets, sports teams, or companies. They do menu planning, budgeting, and nutritional counseling. They advise their clients on the best diets to follow, how foods should be stored and prepared, and what the costs of foods will be.

Whatever type of job dietitians and nutritionists have, they all need good people skills, good communication skills, and a love of food and good nutrition.

STEP 4: Review Questions

1. What are the four different types of dietitians' jobs described here?

....

....

....

2. What skills do all of these jobs require?

....

....

....

3. Which is the correct meaning of the word "analyze" as it is used in paragraph 3?

a. to define

b. to separate into parts

c. to examine in detail

d. to figure out how to do something

61

CHAPTER REVIEW PRACTICE #2

Use the four-step reading process to read the passage and answer the questions.

STEP 1: Preview

1. What is the topic of this passage? ....

2. What is one question you expect to have answered in this article?

....

STEP 2: Read actively to find answers to your questions.

STEP 3: Highlight (or underline) and annotate key points and answers to your questions

Sports Medicine

[1]Sports medicine is a field where job opportunities are expected to grow much faster than the supply. [2]As long as there are athletes, there will always be a need to prevent and treat injuries.

[3]Athletic trainers are often on the sidelines of many sports events, ready to jump in to attend to an injured player or competitor and to provide immediate care. [4]Besides treatment, athletic trainers help prevent injuries by teaching players how to use injury-preventing equipment, as well as how to avoid becoming injured on the playing field.

[5]Athletic trainers work with doctors and other health care providers in colleges, high schools, hospitals, clinics, and professional sports teams. [6]They may spend much time outdoors on the sidelines of playing fields, or indoors in hospitals and clinics, depending on the job.

[7]Others who are with professional sports teams may do a great deal of traveling and work long hours. [8]They are responsible for the safety and health of their players, which can be stressful when the team's success depends on an injured player. [9]Despite the challenges of being a professional team's trainer, many athletic trainers are in stiff competition for these positions. [10]Other trainers work in private training organizations for athletes who wish to prepare themselves for national and international competitions, such as marathons or the Olympics.

[11]Athletic trainers will continue to be in careers that offer a variety of opportunities for working in a sports environment. [12]For more information on how to become an athletic trainer, use the Internet or see a career counselor at your college.

STEP 4: Review Questions

1. What are some of the different places where athletic trainers may work?

....

....

....

....

2. What are athletic trainers in professional sports teams required to do?

....

....

....

....

3. Why is the job of professional sports team athletic trainers more demanding than other athletic trainers' jobs?

....

....

....

....

CHAPTER REVIEW PRACTICE #3

Use the four-step reading process to read the passage and answer the questions.

STEP 1: Preview the selection and answer the questions.

1. What is the topic of this selection? ....

2. What is one question you expect to have answered in this selection?

....

STEP 2: Read actively to find answers to your questions.

STEP 3: Highlight (or underline) and annotate key points and answers to your questions.

What Is Cancer?

replicates: copies

[1]Cancer is a disease that begins when a single cell **replicates** itself when it should not. [2]Cell division is the process a cell undergoes in order to make copies of itself. [3]This process is normally regulated so that a cell divides only when more cells are required and when conditions are favorable. [4]A cancerous cell is a rebellious cell that divides without being given the go-ahead.

[5]Cells that divide continually cause a pileup of cells that form a lump or tumor. [6]A tumor is a mass of cells that has no apparent function in thebody. [7]Tumors that stay in one place and do not affect surrounding structures are said to be **benign** (be-NINE). [8]Some benign tumors remain harmless; others become cancerous. [9]Tumors that invade surrounding tissues are malignant, or cancerous. [10]The cells of a malignant tumor can break away and start new cancers at distant locations through a process called **metastasis**.

(From *Biology: Science for Life*, 2e by Colleen Belk and Virginia Borden Maier. Copyright © 2007 by Colleen Belk and Virginia Borden Maier. Reprinted by permission of Pearson Education, Inc., Upper Saddle River, NJ.)

STEP 4: Review Questions

1. What is cancer?

....

....

2. How is a tumor formed?

....

....

3. What is the difference between a malignant tumor and a benign one?

....

....

....

TEXTBOOK PRACTICE

Preview the following paragraphs, then read actively and answer the questions.

STEP 1: Preview the textbook selection and answer the questions.

1. What is the topic of this selection?

....

....

2. What is one question you expect to have answered in this selection?

....

....

STEP 2: Read actively to find answers to your questions.

STEP 3: Highlight (or underline) and annotate key points and answers to your questions.

Genes and Chromosomes
(jeans & KROME-a-soams)

[1]Each normal sperm and egg contains information about "how to build an organism." [2]A large portion of that information is in the form of genes— segments of DNA that contain specific pieces of information about the **traits** of a living being.

> traits: characteristics

Genes Are Instructions for Making Proteins

[3]Genes carry instructions about how to make proteins. [4]These proteins may be either structural (like the protein that makes up hair) or functional (like the protein lactase, which breaks down sugar). [5]Proteins give cells—and, by extension, organs and individuals—nearly all of their characteristics.

Genes in Combination

[6]Imagine genes as being roughly like the words in an instruction manual. [7]Words can have one meaning when they are alone (for instance, saw) and another meaning when used in combination with other words (see-saw). [8]Words can even change meaning in different contexts ("saw the wood" versus "sharpen the saw"). [9]Some words are repeated frequently in any set of directions, but other words are not. [10]It is the presence of certain words and their combination with other words that determines which instruction is given.

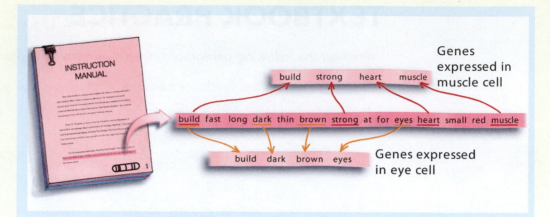

Figure 6.2 Genes as words in an instruction manual. Different words from the manual are used in different parts of the body, and even when the same words are used, they are often used in special combinations. In this way, the manual can provide instructions for making and operating the variety of body parts we possess.

(From *Biology: Science for Life*, 2e by Colleen Belk and Virginia Borden Maier. Copyright © 2007 by Colleen Belk and Virginia Borden Maier. Reprinted by permission of Pearson Education, Inc., Upper Saddle River, NJ.)

STEP 4: Review Questions

1. What does DNA contain?

....

....

....

....

2. What are two types of proteins found in genes?

....

....

....

....

3. How are genes like words in an instruction manual?

....

....

....

....

LEARNING R

Think about the skills and c
learned in this chapter that
you to do well in college? V
your learning?

....

....

SELF-EVALUA

Rate yourself on the followir
1 = strongly disagree
2 = disagree
3 = neither agree nor disagr
4 = agree
5 = strongly agree

1. I completed all of the ass

2. I understand all of the co

3. I contributed to teamwor

4. I completed all of the ass

5. I came to class on time.

6. I attended class every da

7. I studied for any quizzes

8. I asked questions when I

9. I checked my comprehen

10. I know where to go if I ne

PEARSON
myreadingla

For support in meeting this chapt
and select Active Reading Strateg
Materials section, and then comp
Activities section. Check your res

incompatible: not able to be combined with

TEXTBOOK GRAPHIC AIDS

Read the following chart, and then answer the questions that follow.

BLOOD TRANSFUSION COMPATIBILITY AND INCOMPATIBILITY		
Recipient	Compatible donors	**Incompatible** donors
Type 0	Type 0	Type A Type B Type AB
Type A	Type 0 Type A	Type B Type AB
Type B	Type 0 Type B	Type A Type AB
Type AB	Type 0 Type A Type B Type AB	None

(From *Biology: Science for Life*, 2e by Colleen Belk and Virginia Borden Maier. Copyright © 2007 by Colleen Belk and Virginia Borden Maier. Reprinted by permission of Pearson Education, Inc., Upper Saddle River, NJ.)

1. **What does the chart show?**

   a. blood types

   b. blood types that are common

   c. blood transfusion compatibility and incompatibility

   d. rare blood types

2. **What blood types are described as recipients (who receive the blood transfusion)?**

   a. types A and B

   b. types A, B, and AB

   c. types A, O, and B

   d. types A, B, AB, and O

3. **What kind of blood is compatible for type O recipients?**

   a. type O only

   b. types A and B

   c. types A, B, and AB

   d. none

4. **For recipients with type A blood, which are incompatible donors?**

   a. types B and AB

   b. types O and A

   c. types A and AB

   d. types O and B

5. **For recipients with type AB blood, which donors are compatible?**

   a. types A and B only

   b. all types

   c. types A, B, and O

   d. none

STUDY SKILL C

At the conclusion of each chapter
you review the important concep
your own study aids for other cou
future. For this chapter we use a
here. Flow charts show actions in
following chart with the missing o

THE FOUR-STEP READING PRO

STEP **1**

by finding the topic
and making up
questions.

STEP **2**

Read actively by

READING LAB

REVIEW PRACTICE

1. Go online to MyReadingLab a
   Reading Strategies."

2. Go online to MyReadingLab a

CAREER EXPLORATION

1. Research a career in a medical
   in doing. Do online or library re
   about your findings. Include inf
   (degrees, certificates, or license
   appeals to you, and an educatio
   more about the various kinds c
   the U.S. Department of Labor

2. Interview someone working in
   interviews in this textbook in th
   10 questions that you would lik
   up an appointed time that wou
   you.

   Write down the person's answe

STUDY SKILL: SUMMARIZING

At the end of each article in Chapters 1 and 2 you are asked to write a brief summary of what you have just read. A **summary** is a brief description that states the main idea and major points of an article in your own words. The length of a summary depends on the length of the material you are summarizing, your purpose for summarizing, and the requirements of the assignment.

READING AND SUMMARIZING

As you read the following paragraph, notice how the main points have been underlined and are included in the summary.

Water

Water makes up approximately 60-70% of your body, and it is important for everything from temperature regulation, digestion, absorption, and blood formation to waste elimination. Water is especially important for physically active people. A person engaged in heavy exercise in a hot, humid environment can lose 1 to 3 liters of water per hour through sweating. Losing as little as 5% of body water causes fatigue, weakness, and the inability to concentrate; losing more than 15% can be fatal. You should consume 8-10 cups of water per day through foods and beverages. People who experience excess sweating, diarrhea, or vomiting or who donate blood may have higher water requirements.

(From *Total Fitness and Wellness*, 5e by Scott K. Powers and Stephen L. Dodd. Copyright © 2009 by Scott K. Powers and Stephen L. Dodd. Reprinted by permission of Pearson Education, Inc., Upper Saddle River, NJ.)

THE SUMMARY

Read the following summary of "Water":

Water makes up 60% to 70% of the body and is important for its major functions, including temperature regulation, digestion, absorption, blood formation, and waste elimination. Losing water causes fatigue, weakness, and the inability to concentrate, and losing too much can be fatal. Most people require 8 to 10 cups of water per day.

MAKING A SUMMARY

Read the following paragraph. Underline the information that you think should be included in a summary.

Epidemics

Epidemics are diseases that spread rapidly through a population. Once a person comes in contact with the disease-causing germ, he or she may become infected. Infectious diseases are spread in many different ways. First, exposure to body fluids such as saliva, blood, or semen can spread disease. Examples of diseases that are spread this way are sexually transmitted diseases, the common cold, or flu. Another way diseases spread is through an intermediate host, such as an insect. Lyme disease and rabies are spread through intermediate hosts. Third, inhaling a virus from the air after someone coughs or sneezes can spread diseases such as colds or the flu. Finally, ingesting (eating foods containing the germs) also spreads diseases like food poisoning and Mad Cow disease.

YOUR SUMMARY

Now use the information you underlined to help you write a summary in your own words. Try to be as brief as possible but not leave out important information.

CHAPTER 3 VOCABULARY SKILLS

LEARNING OBJECTIVES

IN THIS CHAPTER, YOU WILL:

Objective **1** use context clues and word part clues to identify the meanings of unfamiliar words.

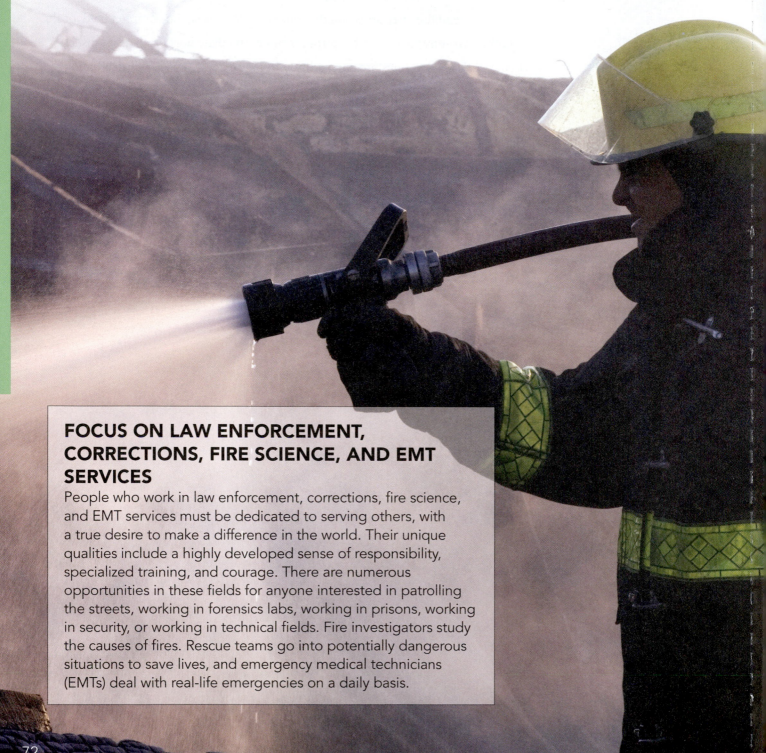

FOCUS ON LAW ENFORCEMENT, CORRECTIONS, FIRE SCIENCE, AND EMT SERVICES

People who work in law enforcement, corrections, fire science, and EMT services must be dedicated to serving others, with a true desire to make a difference in the world. Their unique qualities include a highly developed sense of responsibility, specialized training, and courage. There are numerous opportunities in these fields for anyone interested in patrolling the streets, working in forensics labs, working in prisons, working in security, or working in technical fields. Fire investigators study the causes of fires. Rescue teams go into potentially dangerous situations to save lives, and emergency medical technicians (EMTs) deal with real-life emergencies on a daily basis.

DEVELOPING VOCABULARY SKILLS TO IMPROVE COMPREHENSION

What do you do when you're reading and you come to a word you don't know? Skip over it? Sound it out? Look it up in a dictionary? Ask someone else?

If you could figure out the meanings of new words without having to ask someone else or look them up in a dictionary, you would save time, and you would learn many more new words. There simply isn't enough time to look up the thousands of new words you will be exposed to in college. Skipping over them isn't wise, either, because you will never learn new words that way. Many of the new words you encounter will be terms that you must know in order to understand the key concepts of the material you are studying. Knowing the meanings of more words will unlock the author's message. What tools do you already use for figuring out the meanings of unfamiliar words?

Objective 1

USING CONTEXT CLUES TO DETERMINE WORD MEANINGS

"Using context clues" means looking at the information in the sentence or paragraph to help you figure out the meaning of the unknown word.

When you come across a word you don't recognize, look at the words around it that you do know to find some clue as to the meaning of the word. There are several different types of clues you should look for:

1. Look for **synonyms** (words that mean the same thing) in the sentence.

    The cliff was <u>stratified</u>; each layer held several types of colorful rock.

What word in this sentence gives you a clue for the meaning of *stratified*?

2. Look for **definitions** set off by transitions, commas, parentheses, brackets, or dashes.

   • Transitions: Words and phrases such as "means," "refers to," "defined," "is," and "are" can be helpful because they indicate a definition is to follow. Notice the transitions in bold in the following sentences. They signal that a definition is to follow.

      <u>Doo-wop</u> **is** a style of jazz singing.

      <u>Lampreys</u> **are** a snake-like fish.

   • Commas: Definitions for a term are often included in a phrase set off by commas.

      The <u>pulmonary circuit,</u> *a pathway for the oxygen-depleted blood to return to the heart,* is pumped by the right side of the heart.

- Parentheses: Often a term will be defined in parentheses.

  At the dinner party, we ate raclette *(a Swedish dish of potatoes and cheese)* and drank wine.

- Brackets: Terms may also be defined in brackets.

  The process of photosynthesis *[how plants convert sunlight to energy]* can be demonstrated with a simple experiment.

- Dashes: Sometimes dashes are used to set off the definition of a word.

  The student improved his retention—*his ability to remember what he learned*—by previewing before he read the chapter.

- Explanations: Sometimes words are explained in descriptive ways rather than in exact definitions.

  A platypus *has a bill like a duck, has webbed feet like a duck, has fur and a tail like a beaver, lays eggs like a bird, and has poisonous spurs on its ankles.*

3. Look for **examples** of what the term is describing and for transitions, like the following, that indicate an example will follow: "such as," "known as," "for example," "to illustrate," "like," "including."

   Some herbivores, **like** the elephant, giraffe, and tapir, will feed on low-hanging trees or plants.

What are herbivores?

4. Look for **antonyms** (the opposite of what the unfamiliar word means). These words show contrast and are often signaled by transitions such as:

on the other hand	however	instead
but	unlike	on the contrary
yet	although	as opposed to
conversely	despite	in contrast

   Unlike the smooth rocks found in many streams and river beds, the rocks along the northeastern seacoast can be very craggy.

Which word states the opposite of *craggy*? What does *craggy* mean?

5. General sense, or "**logic**": To get a general sense of the sentence, place a finger over the unfamiliar word. Read the sentence saying "blank" for the word under your finger. Then try to put a word in the sentence that makes sense, using the clues in the sentence and paragraph to help you. Use logic and reasoning skills to figure out the meaning of the unknown word.

   She spoke and acted with such animosity toward the man who hit her car that I was surprised he didn't get angry.

What does *animosity* mean? What clues help you figure out the meaning of *animosity*?

Sometimes you may have to read several sentences or a complete paragraph to figure out the unknown word, as in the following paragraph:

> The morning sun sparkled on the ruffled surface of the lake. A steady breeze drifted from the south. The air was crisp and clear, and the sky a brilliant blue. Only wisps of feathery clouds chased the wind. It was <u>propitious</u> weather for sailing.

What does *propitious* mean? What clues in the paragraph help you to determine the meaning of the word *propitious*?

Think like a detective and figure out the meanings of unfamiliar words by looking for "LEADS": Logic of the passage, Examples, Antonyms, Definitions, and Synonyms.

STUDYING VOCABULARY

There are several ways you can learn the meanings of many new words and terms. Flash cards are still a popular study method, where you write a vocabulary word on one side of a note card and the definition on the other, and then use them to quiz yourself. Another way to study vocabulary words is to record them on your cell phone. You can text them to yourself or record a voice message to yourself. Keep replaying the messages or reading the texts until you have memorized the meanings. You can also make yourself a study sheet with the definitions and examples of how the terms are used and read it often. Another method you could use is to download free puzzle software and create a crossword or other type of puzzle using the terms and their definitions. You could even trade puzzles with a study partner to test each other. Be creative, and use your strongest learning style to study. Make it fun, and you will learn the terms easily.

Practice

1. Use context clues (LEADS) to determine the meanings of the underlined words in the following sentences.

1. The college would not give Damien his transfer credits until it could <u>verify</u> (VER-i-fy) his grades from the last school he attended.
   - **a.** test
   - **b.** prove
   - **c.** deny
   - **d.** lessen

2. The data from the graph showed that there were more <u>felonies</u> (FEL-un-eez) committed in theft than in fraud.
   - **a.** major crimes
   - **b.** prisons
   - **c.** fraud
   - **d.** situations

3. The realtor tried to reach an agreement with the homebuyer and the seller, but they reached an <u>impasse</u> (IM-pass) on the price.
   - **a.** impossible
   - **b.** bargain
   - **c.** a deadlock
   - **d.** delay

4. Rakeisha is such an <u>extrovert</u> (EX-tro-vert) that she would never be too shy to ask for seconds at the dinner table.
   - **a.** shy person
   - **b.** overweight person
   - **c.** funny person
   - **d.** outgoing person

5. The newlyweds were very <u>elated</u> (ee-LAY-ted) at their wedding reception, but the bride's mother was depressed.
   - **a.** sad
   - **b.** direct
   - **c.** happy
   - **d.** angry

Practice

2. Use context clues (LEADS) to determine the meanings of the underlined words in the following sentences.

1. Mr. Martinez gives us a five-minute quiz at the beginning of each class. We have learned to write very <u>succinctly</u> (sus-SINKT-lee) to finish on time.

   a. easily

   b. long

   c. briefly and to the point

   d. essay

2. The <u>cataract</u> (CAT-er-act) falls almost 200 feet, splashing into a deep lake, where tour boats pass this beautiful display of nature.

   a. eye disease

   b. waterfall

   c. bird

   d. enormous

3. Our cat is so <u>inquisitive</u> (in-QUIZ-i-tiv) that she will often get herself trapped in unlikely places.

   a. talented

   b. carefully

   c. sweet-tempered

   d. curious

4. As a teacher, Mr. Collins is quite a <u>sage</u> (SAYJ); he often sounds like an encyclopedia.

   a. a wise person

   b. a fool

   c. boring

   d. journey

5. The suspect <u>succumbed</u> (sa-KUM-d) to the stress of intense questioning and admitted to stealing the money from the victim.

   a. misunderstood

   b. took

   c. gave in to

   d. arrangement

Practice

3. Use context clues (LEADS) to determine the meanings of the underlined words in the following sentences. Consider the parts of speech when deciding the best definition.

1. The customer was <u>outraged</u> (OUT-raj'd) that his dinner arrived cold.
    a. not impressed
    b. angry
    c. overcharged
    d. happy

2. The meeting <u>convened</u> (kon-VEEN'd) at 7:00 p.m. with the Pledge of Allegiance to the flag.
    a. began
    b. continued
    c. ended
    d. was postponed

3. She has <u>aspirations</u> (as-pir-AY-shuns) to become a doctor and help children in poor neighborhoods.
    a. dreams or ambitions
    b. efforts
    c. strongly
    d. hopeful

4. After his favorite team was defeated in the championships, Jamal was very <u>morose</u> (muh-ROSE).
    a. pleased
    b. relaxed
    c. rested
    d. depressed

5. The blue whale is a <u>leviathan</u> (lev-EYE-ah-then). In fact, it is the largest creature on earth.
    a. mammal
    b. something that is narrow
    c. something that is huge
    d. heavy

TEXTBOOK SELECTION Read the following textbook selection. Try to determine the meanings of the underlined words using context clues.

External Examination of the Crime Scene

¹A firearm has the <u>potential</u> of providing some excellent fingerprints and must be examined carefully. ²It should be handled by the checkered portion of the *pistol grip* and similar areas on long arms. ³You cannot get prints from these areas. ⁴*Do not put anything into the muzzle of the firearm.* ⁵There is entirely too much evidence you can ruin by doing this. ⁶As just mentioned, in contact or near-contact wounds, blood and tissue is sometimes <u>ingested</u> into the muzzle. ⁷Also of concern is that the <u>striations</u> found on the bullet are imparted for the most part in the end 1 inch or less.

⁸TIP: After recovery of prints on the firearm, you can use your fingerprint brush to dust the **serial number** and other markings on the firearm and then place these <u>lifts</u> in your notes or notebook. ⁹By following this procedure it can never be <u>insinuated</u> that you might have recorded the number incorrectly, because you have the actual impression.

QUESTIONS

1. What is the meaning of the word <u>potential</u> (po-TEN-shal) as it is used in sentence 1?

   a. possibility **c.** advantage

   b. characteristic **d.** idea

2. What is the meaning of the word <u>ingested</u> (in-JES-ted) as it is used in sentence 6?

   a. eaten **c.** disturbed

   b. taken inside of **d.** digested

3. What is the meaning of the word <u>striations</u> (stry-AY-shuns) as it is used in sentence 7?

   a. gunpowder **c.** dangers

   b. points **d.** markings

4. What is the meaning of the word <u>lifts</u> as it is used in sentence 8?

   a. picking up

   b. fingerprints or other impressions that have been picked up

   c. something added into shoes

   d. machines that lift loads

5. What is the meaning of the word <u>insinuated</u> (in-SIN-you-ay-t'd) as it is used in sentence 9?

   a. inserted **c.** suggested

   b. imprinted **d.** helpful

U-Review

Get together in teams. Pass around a copy of the table below. Every team member must fill in one of the empty boxes until the table is complete.

TYPE OF CONTEXT CLUE	EXPLANATION OF WHAT IT IS	EXAMPLE SENTENCE
1.	The general logic of the sentence or paragraph helps to determine the meaning of a word.	After winning the game, Ricky gloated, calling the other team "losers."
2. Examples		Context clues, such as synonyms and antonyms, can help you determine the meaning of a word.
3.		Instead of making a profit for the year, our business ended up with a deficit.
4. Definition		A pseudonym is a false name that authors often use when publishing books.
5.	A word that means the same as the unknown word can be found in the sentence.	The newspaper was sued for libel because it had written several lies about the mayor.

WORD PARTS: PREFIXES, ROOTS, AND SUFFIXES

How do you like to make sandwiches? Do you put a lot of meat on two slices of bread? Do you add lettuce and tomatoes? Each time you change the ingredients, you make a different kind of sandwich.

Like sandwiches, words are made up of different parts. When you change the parts, you can make new words. There are three different word parts that make up many words in English: prefixes, roots, and suffixes. Many of these came from the ancient Latin and Greek languages. Once you get to know the meanings of some of these word parts, you will be able to figure out the meanings of many new words without a dictionary. The context clues in the sentences will also confirm your understanding of the word. You may already know many of these word parts.

1. **Prefixes** come at the beginning of a root word. They often change the meaning of a word. What's the difference between *correct* and *incorrect*?

   What does the prefix *in-* do to the meaning of the word *correct*?

2. The **root**, or **base**, of the word contains its meaning. It can come at the beginning, middle, or end of a word:

   football, barefoot, footstep, footpath

3. The **suffix** comes at the end of a word and often changes the function of the word or the meaning:

   loving, lovable, lovely, lover, lovesick

Tips to Keep in Mind

1. Some words have no prefixes or suffixes, like the word *pass*. But we can add a prefix to make *impasse*. Note how the spelling changed and an *e* was added to the end of the word.

2. Sometimes the spelling of a word may change as prefixes and suffixes are added, but the root of the word still has the same meaning.
   For example:

   > Because of the rockslide, the road was *impassable*.

   Adding the suffix *-able* (meaning "a condition of being able") to the word *impasse* (a noun) makes a new word:

   im + pass + able = impassable (an adjective)

   (not) + pass + (able to) = (not able to pass through)

3. Some word parts can have more than one meaning. For example:

   In the word *incapable*, the prefix *in-* means "not."

   In the word *inborn*, the prefix *in-* means "into."

81

Tables of Prefixes, Roots, and Suffixes

PREFIXES

PREFIX	MEANING	EXAMPLES
ab-	away from	abnormal, abstain
ad-	to, toward	advance, adjacent
anti-	against	antiwar, antisocial
auto-	self	autobiography, automobile, autograph
bi-	two	bicycle, bimonthly, binoculars
circum-	around	circle, circumference
com-	with, together	common, community
con-	with, together	connect, confide, construct
de-	down, away	descend, deject (cast down)
dia-, di-	through, across	diameter, diagonal
dis-	apart, away from	disinterested, discomfort, disengage
e-	out of, from	elect (choose out of), eject (throw out)
ex-	out of, from	exhaust, expel
hyper-	over	hypertension, hyperactivity
hypo-	under	hypodermic
il-	not	illegal, illegible (not readable)
im-	not	imperfect, impolite, impossible
in-	not	incorrect, invisible, ingenious
ir-	not	irregular, irrational, irresponsible
un-	not	unfinished, undamaged
im-	into	impress, import
in-	into	incorporate, inscribe, inside, inborn
inter-	between	interview, interstate
intra-	within	intrastate
mal-, male-	bad, wrong	malfunction, malnutrition
micro-	small	microscope, microbiology
mono-	one, single	monologue, monotheism, monorail

PREFIXES (continued)

PREFIX	MEANING	EXAMPLES
peri-	around	perimeter, periscope
poly-	many, several	polygon, polygamy
post-	after	postgraduate, postpone
pre-	before	precede, predict (to tell before)
pro-	for, forward	promote, project, progress (to step forward)
re-	again, back	repeat, recede, regress (step back)
sub-	under	submarine, subject, subhuman, subterranean
sur-, super-	over, above	superhuman, superego, surpass
syn-, sym-, syl-, sys-	with, together	symphony, synonym, system, syllable
tele-	distant, far off	telephone, telepathy, television, telegram
trans-	across	transatlantic, transport (carry across)

Tables of Prefixes, Roots, and Suffixes (continued)

COMMON ROOTS

ROOTS	MEANING	EXAMPLES
act	act on	actor, action
ann, enni	year	anniversary, annual
aqua, aque	water	aquatic, aquarium
aud	sound	auditorium, audible
bio	life	biography, biology, antibiotic
cis	to cut	scissors, incisive
cess	to stop	cease, recess
cred	believe	incredible, credibility, credit
de	away	depart, deliver, descend
demo	people	democracy, epidemic
derm	skin	dermatitis, dermatology
duct	to bring or take	reduction, deduct, conduct
equ	equal	equal, equity, equality
gam	marriage	monogamy, polygamy
geo	earth	geology, geography
graph	writing, printing	biography, telegraph, geography
ject	throw	inject, reject, subject, project
magn	large	magnify, magnate, magnificent
man	hand	manufacture, manual, manuscript
metri, meter	measure	geometric, thermometer, metric
min	small	minority, minute
mit, miss	send	permit, submission, mission
mor, mort	death	mortal, immortality
neuro	nerve	neurosurgeon, neuron, neurobiology
path	feeling, suffering	sympathy, telepathy, pathology
phobia	exaggerated fear	claustrophobia, arachnophobia
phon, phone	sound	symphony, telephone
port	carry	portable, transport, report

COMMON ROOTS (continued)

ROOTS	MEANING	EXAMPLES
psych	soul, spirit, mind	psychology, psychic
scope	to look	telescope, horoscope, midroscope
sec, sect	cut	dissect, section
struct	to build	construct, instruct
terr	earth	territory, terrestrial
therm	heat	thermal, thermos, thermometer
vit	life	vital, revitalize, vitamin
zoo	animal	zoo, zoology

SUFFIXES

SUFFIX	DEFINITION	EXAMPLE
-able	the condition of being able to	flammable, likable, touchable
-ion	a state, a condition, or a quality of	discussion, mission
-ive	a state or quality	festive, instructive
-ment	a state, a condition, or a quality of	engagement, commencement
-y	quality of	sunny, sugary, funny
-ate	an action	operate, calculate, communicate
-cide	kill	patricide, infanticide, herbicide, suicide
-ectomy	cutting	appendectomy, tonsillectomy
-er, -or	one who	actor, teacher, lawyer, doctor
-ist	one who	pianist, vocalist, psychiatrist
-ic, -tic, -ical, -ac	having to do with	surgical, dramatic, biblical
-ism	the belief in	terrorism, communism, Judaism
-ly	in the manner of	quietly, quickly, happily
-less	without	hopeless, careless, sunless
-logy	study of	biology, geology
-ward	in the direction of	toward, forward, backward

Practice

1. Using the tables of prefixes, roots, and suffixes, write the meanings of these prefixes and roots. Then, use these word parts to complete the missing word parts in the paragraph that follows. The first one is done for you.

PREFIXES

mono- *one*

poly-

bi-

ROOTS

gam- *marriage*

cent-

tri-

Polygamy and Monogamy

Before the 11th century, Jewish men practiced *poly-* gamy, which allowed them to have many wives at once. After the 11th century, most Jewish men practiced _____ gamy, which only permitted marriage to one wife. Even today, some countries, such as Sudan in Africa, still practice poly _____, and have numerous wives. In most Western countries, it is illegal to have two wives or husbands; therefore, _____ gamy is considered a crime in the United States. In England between the 17th and 19th _____ uries, the term _____ gamy referred to someone who had three wives or husbands at the same time.

2. Use the tables of prefixes, roots, and suffixes to complete the following story.

The Florida bank robber had a(n) _____ genious plan. He walked to _____ the front of the bank carrying a(n) _____ folio and looked around. He cautious _____ approached the tell _____ 's window and _____ mitted a withdrawal slip. On it he had written, "I want a cashier's check for $100,000. This is a stick up, and I have a gun!" The teller looked _____ prised, and said, "Yes, sir. I understand. I will be happy to make this _____ action for you. First, I'll need to see your driver's license, and then I'll write the check." The robb _____ reached into his wallet and gave it to her. She copied down his name, address, and license number, then wrote out the check and handed it to him. He _____ parted the building and raced off in his car. Minutes later, the police _____ tained and arrested him from the information he gave to the teller!

U-Review

For each of the following sentences, write "T" if the statement is true or "F" if the statement is false. As you go over the answers with your team, discuss why the false statements were false.

1. .... The part of the word that carries the meaning is the root.
2. .... All words have a prefix, a root, and a suffix.
3. .... Some prefixes may have more than one meaning.
4. .... The spelling of a word part sometimes changes.
5. .... A word never has more than one prefix or suffix.

Reading 1 Vocabulary Preview

The following vocabulary words are from the article "Dangerous Duty." With a partner or in a team, choose the correct meanings of the underlined words in the following sentences. Use context clues (LEADS), word part clues, and parts of speech to help you figure out the meanings.

1. The felon (FELL-un) finally collapsed when Deputy Martin managed to shoot him in the leg.
   a. a major crime
   b. a person who commits a major crime
   c. an injured person
   d. someone having a prison record

2. The three gunmen were alone in the house, with easy access to the adjoining (add-JOIN-ing) garage.
   a. newly built
   b. unfinished
   c. attached to the house
   d. distant from

3. "Bullets were ricocheting (rik-o-SHAY-ing) everywhere off the concrete floor," she recalls.
   a. shooting
   b. falling
   c. bouncing
   d. falling

4. "When you go through something like that," she says, reflecting on her ordeal (or-DEEL), "mindset is really important. I was not going to die in that garage."
   a. effort
   b. an idea
   c. orders
   d. a difficult experience

Reading 1

5. "When you go through something like that," she says, reflecting on her ordeal, "mindset (MIND-set) is really important. I was not going to die in that garage."

   a. a state of mind or thought

   b. stubbornness

   c. refusal

   d. agreement

6. The suspects had planned to steal the contraband (KON-tra-band) from Isola's husband, Clinton, who had hidden marijuana and cash in the house.

   a. money

   b. something illegal

   c. something helpful

   d. large

7. The president of the United States awarded the officer a medal of valor (VAL-or) for her bravery in protecting the children.

   a. bravery

   b. distinction

   c. award

   d. reward

8. The officer recuperated (ree-KOOP-er-ate-ed) from her gunshot wounds and is now a detective in the sheriff's department.

   a. was relieved

   b. was injured

   c. was healed

   d. was promoted

9. She bought a bridal gown for her forthcoming (forth-COM-ing) wedding in September.

   a. honest

   b. fourth in a row

   c. late

   d. coming soon

10. "In retrospect (RET-ro-spekt), I wish I had majored in nursing instead of business."

    a. looking down

    b. looking back

    c. looking ahead

    d. looking inside

Reading 1 What Do You Already Know?

1. Have you ever experienced or heard of a situation in which a member of the police department, fire department, or EMT services rescued you or someone you know? Describe the situation.

2. If you saw some children in danger, would you be willing to take a risk to save them? Why or why not?

> **Directions:** As you read this article, practice the four-step reading process. Preview the article, and then write on the following lines one or two questions that you would hope to have answered.
>
> ....
>
> ....
>
> ....
>
> ....
>
> ....

As you read, answer the questions in the margins to check your comprehension.

"Dangerous Duty"

BY CORINNE FENNESSY

Copyright © by Corinne Fennessy. Reprinted by permission of the author.

1   The early May morning was pleasantly warm. Isola Marino* secured the seat belt straps on her two-year-old twins, seated in the back of her mini-van. She called for her eight-year-old son, Dustin,* from the garage adjoining her house.

2   "Hurry or you'll be late for school," she warned.

3   As soon as everyone was buckled in, she began to back out of her driveway from her small suburban home in Pine Hills, Florida. Suddenly, she saw three men carrying guns surrounding her van and she jammed on the brake. One of the men yelled as he yanked open the door and grabbed Isola by the arm. He dragged her out of the car as her son screamed, "Mommy!"

4   The third man got into the van and drove it back into the garage. After locking the children inside, he went into the house. The other two men demanded that Isola tell them where all her cash was hidden, and she begged them not to harm her children.

5   Dustin was terrified by these strange men who had dragged his mother away and locked him and his sisters in the car. But the eight-year-old noticed that his mother's purse was still sitting on the front seat. He found her cell phone and dialed 911.

6   A patient operator on the 911 line got the information she needed from Dustin and told him to keep calm and stay in the van until the police arrived.

Reading 1

7   Two Orange County Sheriff's deputies arrived on the scene, followed by Deputy Jennifer Fulford and a trainee. When the police arrived, the men inside the house sent Isola to answer their knock and tell them that everything was fine. Isola knew this would be her only chance to save her children, even if she were killed for alerting the police.

8   "Is everything all right, ma'am?" asked the deputy.

9   "No!" she cried, "Please, save my children!" She pointed to the garage just before she was yanked back and the door was slammed shut.

10   The deputy heard shouting from inside and ran back to the other deputies. Deputy Jennifer Fulford looked back at the van parked in the open garage.

Why did the deputies go into the garage?

11   "I'm going to try to get those kids," Deputy Fulford declared, as she drew her weapon and hurried to the garage. Deputy Martin followed her.

12   Just then, three shots were fired from inside the house into the garage. Both deputies dropped down behind the van. The door to the house opened and one of the gunman named Jenkins fired at Deputy Fulford. She returned fire with her Glock .45, striking Jenkins, but he kept on firing as he went down.

13   Deputy Fulford was worried that someone would hit the kids inside the van. If there were only some way to get them out—but it was too dangerous. Dustin was flattened face down on the front seat in terror as the twins screamed from the back.

14   Another gunman suddenly emerged from the house and fired across the hood, hitting Deputy Fulford four times. Bullets ricocheting off the concrete floor struck her again and again. Glass exploded. Fulford went down and Jenkins, who was still alive, shot her in the shoulder of her shooting arm.

15   The gun dropped from her hand onto the floor, but she grabbed it with her left hand and saw the second gunman coming. She fired off two rounds, hitting him twice in the head. But even that didn't stop him. He stumbled into the driveway and shot at Deputy Martin, hitting him in the shoulder. He grabbed his shoulder in pain and squeezed off one more round, hitting the felon in the leg and bringing the man down with a thud.

What happened to Deputy Fulford and Deputy Martin?

16   The shooting stopped, and Deputy Fulford lay bleeding on the floor of the garage. She felt light-headed and lost consciousness momentarily.

17   She was thinking about her beautiful bridal gown, the one that she would wear to her forthcoming wedding with firefighter Tom Salvano. She wondered if she'd ever get the chance to wear that elegant dress, or walk down the aisle on her father's arm at her wedding.

18   "Hey, Fulford! Are you OK?" her partner, Kevin Curry, called to her.

19   "No! Please help me get out of here!" she cried. She knew she had been hit several times and she was losing blood fast. She knew she could die. But she had a mindset that she wasn't going to die in this garage. Not today.

20   The other deputies got the children safely out of the van and gave Deputy Fulford assistance while Isola was rescued from inside the house.

21   Deputy Fulford and Deputy Martin were rushed to the nearest hospital. Fulford underwent surgery for 7 gunshot wounds and recuperated within four months. Two of

Reading 1

What happened to Isola and her children?

the felons died from their injuries; the third one was convicted and sentenced. At the house, police had found over 340 pounds of the husband's marijuana and $54,000 in cash. Isola was charged with trafficking <u>contraband</u> and sent to jail for committing a <u>felony</u>. Her children went to live with relatives.

22   Jennifer Fulford is now Detective Jennifer Salvano. She and Tom were married and she was promoted to detective. She now investigates cases of child abuse. For her bravery, she received the Presidential Public Safety Officer Medal of <u>Valor</u> and the American Deputy Sheriff's Association named her Deputy of the Year for the United States. She was also named Deputy Sheriff of the Year in Florida.

23   After the <u>ordeal</u> she was asked if she is a hero, and she replied,

24   "No, just doing my job!"

*The names of these persons were changed for their privacy.

Shipley, Stephen "United States Law Enforcement Officer of the Year," *Central Florida Lifestyle Magazine,* July 2008.

Gutierrez, Redro R., Curtis, Henry P., and Mckay, Rich "7 Bullets Couldn't Stop Orange Deputy–She and Another Injured Patrol Officer Outgunned Three Home Invaders Who Had Ambushed Them," *The Orlando Sentinel,* Thursday, May 6, 2004.

Smith, Larry "I Wasn't Going to Die There" (Deputy Jennifer Fulford), *Parade.com,* Sept. 18, 2005.

921 words divided by .... minutes = ... words per minute

Thinking About What You Read

It is a good habit to summarize everything you read to strengthen your comprehension.

Directions: Begin by filling in the details for "Dangerous Duty." on the lines below, using the information from the article.

In May ...., Deputy Sheriff .... rescued

....from three men

with guns. She and her partner were .... but managed to

....

Reading 1 Comprehension Questions

The following questions will help you to recall the main idea and the details of "Dangerous Duty." Review any parts of the article that you need to in order to find the correct answers.

LITERAL COMPREHENSION

1. **What is the topic (subject) of this article? (Who or what is it about?)**

   a. a rescue

   b. Deputy Jennifer Fulford's rescue of three children

   c. three children trapped in a car during a gunfight

   d. a woman who was taken hostage

MAIN IDEA

2. **What is the main idea of the story? (What is the most general statement that tells the most important point?)**

   a. Deputy Fulford risked her own life to protect the lives of three children.

   b. Three men took a woman hostage.

   c. The police stopped three men from harming a family.

   d. An eight-year-old boy called 911 to save his family.

SUPPORTING DETAILS

3. **When one of the men, Jenkins, started firing at her, Deputy Fulford:**

   a. ran back to her patrol car and called for backup.

   b. returned fire and shot him.

   c. got into the van.

   d. got hit in the right shoulder and lost her weapon.

4. **After she was shot, Deputy Fulford:**

   a. was thinking about her retirement.

   b. was thinking about a promotion.

   c. tried to climb into the van to get the kids.

   d. was thinking about her forthcoming wedding.

DRAWING CONCLUSIONS

5. **The three suspects had attacked the family because:**

   a. they knew that Isola's husband had cash and marijuana in the house.

   b. they wanted to take the family hostage and demand money.

   c. they were running from the police.

   d. they were terrorists.

Reading 1

6. Deputy Fulford made the decision to go into the garage because:

   a. she planned to go into the house through the garage.

   b. she wanted to protect the children in the van.

   c. she was told to go in by Deputy Martin.

   d. she tried to stay out of the line of fire.

7. How did the children end up alone in the van inside the garage?

   a. The gunmen took them out to the garage.

   b. The mother put the children in the van for safety when she saw the gunmen.

   c. After the mother was taken, one gunman drove it into the garage.

   d. The children ran into the garage and locked themselves inside the van.

8. With which statement would the author probably agree?

   a. The criminals were planning to kill the entire family.

   b. The criminals didn't know there was money and marijuana in the house.

   c. The eight-year-old boy was a hero for calling 911.

   d. The mother of the children didn't know there was 341 pounds of marijuana in the house.

VOCABULARY IN CONTEXT

Using context clues and word part clues, determine the best meaning for the underlined words in the following sentences. If necessary, use a dictionary.

9. "The three gunmen were alone in the house, with easy access to the adjoining garage" (paragraph 1).

   a. two-car

   b. attached

   c. spacious

   d. separate

10. "Bullets were ricocheting everywhere off the concrete floor," she recalls (paragraph 3).

    a. sliding

    b. coming from

    c. bouncing off

    d. sinking in

Reading 1 Vocabulary Practice

Use the vocabulary words from the Word Bank to complete the following sentences. Write the words into the blanks provided.

WORD BANK

felon	adjoining	ricochet	ordeal	valor
contraband	mindset	forthcoming	recuperated	retrospect

1. Rita and her best friend had .... rooms at the dormitory.

2. As a convicted ...., Mr. Smith was serving a lengthy jail sentence.

3. Firefighters who rescue people in dangerous situations must have .... and strength.

4. After surviving the hurricane that destroyed her home, Mrs. Lopez didn't want to talk about her ....

5. To succeed in college, you must have the .... that you can and will succeed.

6. In ...., I wish now that I had met with my academic advisor so that I would have taken the right courses for my major.

7. The man injured in Tuesday's fire has .... and has been sent home from the hospital.

8. Thinking about her .... graduation from college, Shanika decided to throw a big party.

9. Hidden inside the truck's seats, the officers discovered the .... that was being smuggled across the border.

10. A speeding bullet can .... off a hard surface and strike someone nearby.

Reading 1 Questions for Writing and Discussion

Review any parts of the article you need to answer the following questions.

1. Think about the actions that Deputy Fulford took to protect the lives of the children in the car. Describe how she showed courage and a sense of responsibility to protect and serve.

   ....

   ....

   ....

2. Describe how teamwork was important to Deputy Fulford's success in protecting the children inside the car.

   ....

   ....

   ....

3. In your opinion, do you think that the mother, Isola, should have been sentenced? Why or why not?

   ....

   ....

   ....

4. What qualities are needed in a good police officer, firefighter, or rescue worker?

   ....

   ....

   ....

5. What do the actions of the eight-year-old boy who called 911 tell you about this child?

   ....

   ....

   ....

Reading 1 Vocabulary Practice

Together with your team, use the clues in the first column to unscramble the jumbled words in the second column. Then, use the letters in the circles to unscramble a phrase.

WORD BANK

RICOCHET   VALOR   ORDEAL   ADJOINING   FORTHCOMING

MINDSET   RETROSPECT   FELONY   CONTRABAND   RECUPERATED

CLUES (Note: Clues are not definitions, just "clues")	SCRAMBLED WORDS	WORD
1. Reconsidering	TCERROPSET	R Ⓞ T R O S P Ⓔ C T
2. Connected	NINIGOADJ	_ _ _ _Ⓞ_ _ _ _
3. Attitude	SEIMNTD	_ _ _ _ _Ⓞ_ _
4. Suffering	LARDOE	_ _ _ⓄⓄ_
5. Heroes	ROLVA	_ _ _ _Ⓞ
6. Illegal	RACADBOTNN	Ⓞ_ _ _Ⓞ_ _Ⓞ_ _
7. Future	HOMONRCGIFT	Ⓕ_ _Ⓞ_ _ _Ⓞ_ _ _
8. Healthy	RAUPETCEDER	_ _Ⓞ_Ⓞ_ _Ⓞ_ _
9. Bullets	TECHIRCO	_ _ _ _Ⓞ_ _Ⓞ
10. Kidnap	ENLOFY	_Ⓞ_ _ _

Write the letters from inside the circles on the following lines. Use them to unscramble the phrase. (The picture is a clue.)

_ _

P _ _ _ _ _ _ _   _ _ K _ _

P _ _ _ _ _ _

Reading 2 Vocabulary Preview

The following vocabulary words are from the article "Father's Day Rescue." With a partner or in a team, choose the correct meanings of the underlined words in the following sentences. Use context clues (LEADS), word part clues, and parts of speech to help you figure out the meanings.

1. Firefighters are protected from heat and flames by fire-retardant (ree-TAR-dent) clothes and boots.

   a. slow

   b. waterproof

   c. fire resistant

   d. accelerated

2. The crowd that stood watching the house on fire appeared agitated (AJ-i-tay-ted) and almost panicky.

   a. fearful and anxious

   b. bored

   c. angry

   d. interested

3. Bystanders (BY-stand-ers) filled the street, watching the firefighters battling the blaze.

   a. people who stand around and watch something

   b. people who are involved in something

   c. people who help others

   d. stands for people to sit on

4. The little girl's pathetic (pa-THET-ik) attempt to find her mother in the crowd drew sympathy from those around her.

   a. hopeful

   b. upset

   c. angry

   d. causing pity

5. The blazing house was an inferno (in-FER-no) that shot smoke more than a hundred feet in the air.

   a. a furnace

   b. a chimney

   c. a raging fire

   d. a container for burning something

Reading 2

6. I waved my arms **frantically** (FRAN-tik-lee) to try to stop the oncoming traffic from hitting the child who had fallen off of her bike.

   a. in a funny way

   b. in a panicked manner

   c. hopefully

   d. like a bird

7. When an elderly man fell down in the supermarket, the **EMTs** arrived first on the scene.

   a. firefighters

   b. emergency medical technicians

   c. doctors

   d. emergency trucks

8. Smoke **billowed** (BILL-owed) from the open front door.

   a. puffed out in clouds

   b. seeped through

   c. blew fast

   d. disappeared

9. One of the presents my daughters gave me was a T-shirt **emblazoned** (em-BLAY-zund) with the words "World's Coolest Dad."

   a. on fire

   b. something burned

   c. written in bold letters

   d. engraved

10. The fire was so **torrid** (TOR-id) that it melted the television and computer.

    a. big

    b. close

    c. extremely hot

    d. exciting

Reading 2   What Do You Already Know?

1. Share what you know about how firefighters work together to put out fires.

2. Do you know anyone who has had a fire emergency and had to call the fire department? Describe what happened.

> Directions: As you read this story, practice the four-step reading process. Preview the article, and then write on the following lines one or two questions that you would hope to have answered.
>
> ....
>
> ....
>
> ....
>
> ....

As you read, answer the questions in the margins to check your comprehension.

Adapted from

"Father's Day Rescue"

BY DON HAWLEY

From *Guideposts Magazine*, June 2005. Copyright © 2005 by Guideposts. Reprinted by permission.

It's the crisis every firefighter worries about most—a child trapped in a burning house. This true account tells how one fireman in Pocahontas, Illinois, almost didn't survive to tell this story.

1   We ate a big breakfast at a local restaurant, like we did every Father's Day. One of the presents my daughters gave me was a T-shirt emblazoned with the words "World's Coolest Dad." That was good enough for me. After church I put the shirt on. Then we left for a car show the next town over. That was our Father's Day tradition.

2   Just as we headed out the front door, my volunteer fire-department pager went off. "Nuts," I thought. "Maybe it's just a brush fire and they won't need me."

3   But the dispatcher's voice crackled: "Attention, Pocahontas-Old Ripley firefighters! House fire on Simpson Street. Repeat. House fire on Simpson Street."

4   "Gotta go," I said.

5   I left my family on the front porch, ran to my car, jumped behind the wheel and took off.

6   Again came the dispatcher's voice: "There is a child inside. Repeat. A child is trapped inside the house."

Reading 2

7   I drove to the firehouse, all the while hoping it would just be a false alarm. That happens a lot. We'd get to a house fire and find everyone standing outside in the yard, safe.

8   I got to the firehouse in minutes. Another firefighter, Tom Smith, and the chief were waiting.

9   "Tommy, Don, take truck two-five-three. Roll!" he ordered. "The rest of the guys will be right behind you."

10   Tommy and I threw on our fire-retardant clothes and boots.

11   "What do you think?" Tommy asked, "False alarm, maybe?" But it was more of a hope than an opinion.

12   Tommy and I rolled in Truck 253, siren ripping through the otherwise peaceful Sunday afternoon. As the first on the scene, our job was to make sure everyone was out of the house, locate the nearest hydrant, and then wait for backup. And there was another backup. Prayer. I always pray before going in to a fire..

13   The truck screeched around the corner onto Simpson. A small crowd had gathered in front of number 907. They appeared agitated, almost panicky. Smoke billowed from the one-story house's open front door. Tommy grabbed the radio.

14   "Truck two-five-three on scene. Advise all units: We have smoke; this is a working fire!

15   We lurched to a stop. The bystanders swarmed us.

16   "The baby's inside!" one yelled. "Do something, quick!"

17   First Tommy and I had to put on our air packs. We wouldn't stand a chance without oxygen. Someone—a neighbor, I figured—stood in the doorway of the house holding a garden hose, a pathetic jet of water spurting in vain. A large man burst through the door, sputtering and coughing, red eyes streaming with tears.

18   "Please hurry!" he called. "My boy's still in there. I couldn't get to him!"

19   Tommy and I glanced at each other. I knew what he was thinking. No time to wait for backup. Together we raced toward the house. We heard a voice behind us.

20   Battalion Chief Steve Brown was on scene. Backup would be here soon. Steve yanked the garden hose from the neighbor and headed inside.

21   "Let's move," he said. Tommy and I plunged through the doorway. Curtains of fire ate away at the walls and ceiling. The place was an inferno. And all we had was a garden hose. That wouldn't cut it. I prayed that those other firefighters would get here on the double and we would find the child.

22   Tommy and I worked as a pair. We got down on all fours. Every few seconds I reached out to touch Tommy or I felt him touch me. Maintain contact, I reminded myself. That's one of the first rules. Trying to find Tommy if I lost him would mean a delay, possibly death; for me, for Tommy, and for the child in the house.

23   The smoke quickly grew thicker until it was pitch-black. One thing you don't realize about a fire until you're in one is how loud the sound is. Flames roared in our ears. Pieces of ceiling smashed down on our backs. Ashes were everywhere. The blistering heat sucked sweat from our skin.

Why didn't Tommy and Don wait for backup?

Reading 2

24   "Anyone here?" I shouted. No answer.

25   Tommy and I searched every inch of the first two rooms. No child. My hand knocked into a wall. We followed it down a hallway. I strained to see something through the smoke. I couldn't discern what it was, so I reached for it. A table leg, then a chair; it must be the dining room. Tommy and I felt all around under the table. Again, nothing.

26   "Next room!" I shouted.

27   I knew the layout of these houses. The only room left was the kitchen. We crawled from one end of it to the other. The torrid flames roared louder. How long would it be before the roof collapsed?

28   "This is it!" I yelled to Tommy. "We have to get out!"

29   All at once a vision was put into my head—that father begging us to save his child. We couldn't give up. Not today, I thought. There still might be a chance. I tapped Tommy on the arm and motioned him to follow. "Let's try here!" I shouted. I reached out. Thick black smoke flowed through my empty fingers. Then my hand landed on something. Another chair leg? No, too thin. I squeezed gently. It was soft. It felt like . . . an arm.

30   "Tommy, I've got him! I've got him!" I screamed.

31   I snatched the boy up in one arm and frantically waved ahead of me with the other, half crawling, half crouching. Stay low. Move fast. My breathing was a roar inside my fire hood. Sweat blinded me, but it didn't much matter. I couldn't see anyway.

32   Tommy kept close behind, tapping me again and again. I was out the front door before I could make out a glimpse of daylight. I stood up and ran with the boy to a safe distance. I put him down on the lawn. His face was gray, his body limp, and his chest still. He couldn't have been more than two years old. I tore off my mask and started mouth-to-mouth.

33   "Breathe!"

34   Finally he sputtered and took a breath. Then another. Slowly color rose in his face. Our EMTs started him on oxygen and loaded him into our ambulance. It looked like he would be fine. Once the fire was under control, Tommy and I stripped off our gear and sat in the shade of a maple, drinking ice water a neighbor had given us.

35   I looked down at myself. I still had on my "Coolest Dad" T-shirt. Filthiest dad was more like it. Those black stains would never come out.

36   "Look at this," I said, pointing to my shirt, "You can hardly see what it says anymore."

37   The neighbor who'd given us water just smiled. "That's okay," he said. "Today you guys gave another dad the greatest gift anyone ever could."

Why did Don feel that they had to get out of the house?

How did they find the missing child?

1,160 words divided by _____ minutes = _____ words per minute

Reading 2 Thinking About What You Read

It's a good habit to summarize everything you read to strengthen your comprehension.

Directions: Complete the summary of "Father's Day Rescue" by filling in the following blanks.

Firefighter, (who?) ...., risked his own life to ....

who was .... He and his partner, (who?) ....

...................................., found the two-year-old boy (where?)...................................

and took him out to the ...., who gave the boy ....

The boy was saved on (when?).................................... .

Comprehension Questions

The following questions will help you to recall the main idea and the details of "Father's Day Rescue." Review any parts of the article that you need to find the correct answers.

LITERAL COMPREHENSION

1. **What is the topic (subject) of this article? (Who or what is this article about?)**

   a. firefighting

   b. a firefighter's rescue of a child

   c. finding a child in a house fire is difficult

   d. an Illinois firefighter

MAIN IDEA

2. **What is the main idea of the article? (What is the most general statement that tells the most important point of the article?)**

   a. Firefighters have a very dangerous job.

   b. Don Hawley, a firefighter, risked his life to save a child trapped in a burning house.

   c. We ate a big breakfast at a local restaurant, like we did every Father's Day.

   d. A firefighter spent his Father's Day battling a house fire.

SUPPORTING DETAILS

3. **When Truck 253 arrived at the scene of the fire:**

   a. there were two other fire trucks and a crew of firefighters already on the scene.

   b. they were the first firefighters to arrive.

   c. they found an ambulance and EMTs treating the victims of smoke inhalation.

   d. it started to thunder with lightning.

4. The first things that Tommy and Don were expected to do at the scene of the fire were to:

   a. hook up the hoses and begin spraying the roof.

   b. check to see if anyone needed an ambulance or immediate medical attention.

   c. decide how many fire trucks were needed at the scene and call in a report.

   d. make sure everyone was out of the house, locate the nearest hydrant, and then wait for backup.

DRAWING CONCLUSIONS

5. The firefighter decided to risk staying in the house longer because:

   a. he envisioned the father begging him to save his child.

   b. he had made a promise to the parents to find their child.

   c. he heard the child crying.

   d. a backup crew had arrived to help in the search.

6. With which statement would the author most likely agree?

   a. The child had started the fire.

   b. Both firefighters, Don and Tommy, showed great courage.

   c. Tommy and Don had been inside the burning house once before.

   d. People are careless with matches.

7. Which one of the following is an accurate conclusion you can make based on the information in the article?

   a. In a burning house, it is best to stay close to the floor on your hands and knees.

   b. Firefighters should be paid more money for what they do.

   c. The fire was probably started on purpose.

   d. Old houses are fire hazards.

VOCABULARY IN CONTEXT

Use context clues, word part clues, and parts of speech to determine the meanings of the underlined words in each of these sentences. If necessary, use a dictionary.

8. I couldn't <u>discern</u> (dis-SERN) what it was, so I reached for it (paragraph 25).

   a. agree   b. follow

   c. determine   d. allow

9. Someone—a neighbor, I figured—stood in the doorway of the house holding a garden hose, a pathetic jet of water spurting in <u>vain</u> (VAYN) (paragraph 17).

   a. without hope of success   b. upright

   c. cold   d. in streams

10. I was out the front door before I could make out a <u>glimpse</u> (GLIMPS) of daylight (paragraph 32).

    a. window   b. a quick look

    c. scene   d. a time period

Reading 2 Vocabulary Practice

Fill in the missing information in each row of the following table using the vocabulary words from "Father's Day Rescue."

WORDS	DEFINITIONS	SENTENCES
1.	nervous or anxious	The customers became .... while waiting in line after the clerk asked for a price check.
2. billowed	....	Smoke .... out of the old house after it began to burn.
3. bystanders	....	The .... crowded around the wrecked car to see who would be taken out.
4. emblazoned	....	The team's name was .... across the side of the bus in large bold letters.
5.	in a panicked manner	We waved our arms .... trying to flag down a police car after the accident happened.
6. torrid	....	The .... forest fire drove the animals away from the flames.
7.	a raging blazing fire	The forest was a(n) .... , fueled by the dry timber and high winds.
8.	causing pity	The victims who had lost their homes to the fire were a(n) .... sight.
9. retardant	....	Building houses with flame- .... materials will help control house fires.
10. EMTs	....	The .... began to give oxygen to each of the firefighters who suffered from smoke inhalation.

Reading 2   Questions for Writing and Discussion

Review any parts of the article you need to answer the following questions.

1. How did Don Hawley and Tom Smith show that they are courageous and committed to saving the lives of other people?

....

....

....

2. What made Don Hawley decide to stay in the burning house longer than he should have? Do you think you would have made the same decision that he did? Why or why not?

....

....

....

3. Describe how teamwork was important to Don's survival and success in finding the little boy.

....

....

....

4. What do you think would have happened if Don Hawley had decided to quit looking for the boy when the situation became dangerous?

....

....

....

5. Do you think that firefighters and law enforcement personnel should be paid more for what they do? Why or why not?

....

....

....

Reading 2 Vocabulary Practice

First, complete the following sentences using the vocabulary words in the Word Bank. Then, find and circle the words on the puzzle grid. The words may be horizontal, vertical, diagonal, or backwards. If you need a hint, look in the row number shown after each sentence.

WORD BANK

agitated	billowed	bystanders	EMT
inferno	emblazoned	pathetic	frantically
torrid	retardant		

1. The men in the lifeboat waved their arms .... when they saw a ship approaching (row 5).

2. When they arrived at the burning house, it looked like a blazing .... (row 1).

3. The .... tried to revive the woman who was suffering from smoke inhalation (row 2).

4. Pajamas made of fire- .... fabrics protect children from burns (row 6).

5. The sight of the charred house, still smoking and in ruins, was .... (row 9).

6. The fire truck had "Fire Company No. 12" .... across the side (row 2).

7. A small crowd of .... stood watching the firefighters shooting water on the burning roof (row 13).

8. The heat from the .... fire was so hot that we all moved away (row 5).

9. The little boy became .... when he realized that his puppy was missing (row 11).

10. Smoke .... out of the broken windows as the building burned out of control (row 15).

Reading 2 Vocabulary Practice—Puzzle Grid

	A	B	C	D	E	F	G	H	I	J	K	L	M
1	E	M	P	O	N	I	U	R	X	L	P	A	X
2	Z	T	U	A	F	N	I	T	M	E	H	U	P
3	Q	A	R	T	Y	F	U	D	I	M	O	A	R
4	I	N	S	O	F	E	D	I	R	B	W	A	Z
5	F	A	T	H	E	R	S	R	H	L	E	P	F
6	G	O	O	M	T	N	A	D	R	A	T	E	R
7	P	O	R	U	Y	O	T	O	R	Z	W	Q	A
8	L	K	R	H	G	F	C	T	A	O	D	S	N
9	S	P	I	P	U	T	N	I	K	N	E	N	T
10	P	I	D	G	A	U	P	O	T	E	W	Y	I
11	W	A	A	G	I	T	A	T	E	D	O	A	C
12	B	O	S	T	F	H	H	U	N	C	L	K	A
13	B	Y	S	T	A	N	D	E	R	S	L	B	L
14	L	U	B	L	A	B	U	Y	T	A	I	T	L
15	R	G	U	M	A	B	N	A	F	I	B	I	Y
16	Y	O	E	C	H	T	A	J	V	J	C	S	K

VIEWPOINT: Video Surveillance

Read the following letters to the editor about video surveillance and whether they violate our right to privacy, and then answer the questions that follow.

Dear Editor:

The use of video camera surveillance in recent years has increased sharply due to advances in digital technology. Although the law permits video surveillance in public, more laws should be passed to limit its use. Having cameras everywhere infringes on the right to privacy. Just having so many cameras in place could lead to an abuse of their use. People who may not wish to be photographed for personal reasons have no say about it. And it's not just private companies that use them. Many government agencies—including police—are keeping a watchful eye on us. If we're not criminals, why do we have to be treated like them?

Signed,

Aggravated

Dear Editor:

I fully support the use of video surveillance cameras by the police, the FBI, the CIA, or anyone else who has a right to use them. Without video surveillance, many criminals would never be found and would go unpunished. Knowing that video surveillance cameras are in place also helps prevent crime. I would rather shop at a store where I know we are being watched because I feel safer. When a criminal is caught because his or her face is seen on a video, this benefits everyone. Without video surveillance, we would have a lot more crime than we presently have. So I say, "Put up all the cameras you want! I have nothing to hide!"

Signed,

Smiling for the Camera

Critical Thinking

1. A *point of view* is the author's opinion about a topic. To find the author's point of view, ask yourself, "How does this author feel about this issue?" What is the author's point of view about video surveillance in the first letter?

   ....

2. What is the author's point of view about video surveillance in the second letter?

   ....

   ....

3. With which letter do you agree, and why?

   ....

   ....

   ....

4. What could be the consequences of having no limits on video surveillance?

   ....

   ....

   ....

5. What could be the consequences of having too many limits on video surveillance?

   ....

   ....

   ....

WRITE YOUR THOUGHTS

Write a letter to the editor stating your own feelings about video surveillance cameras. What do you think should be done? Use a separate sheet of paper.

DRUG TESTING CONSENT FORM

Read the following Drug Testing Consent Form, which is a form some job applicants are required to fill out. Use the four-step reading process as you read, and then answer the questions that follow to check your comprehension.

consent: to give permission

initial: first one

metabolites: chemical substances

JOB APPLICANT FINALIST
DRUG TESTING **CONSENT** FORM

I, ..., as a job applicant finalist for a full-time position at the Acme Painting Company, do hereby agree to submit to the physical examination of my person in conjunction with my employment with the company.

I further agree to an **initial** test and a confirmation test as required in accordance with the provisions of the company, a copy of which I have received prior to the execution of this drug testing consent form, and more particularly described as follows:

Initial Test. The following cutoff levels shall be used when first screening specimens to determine whether they are positive or negative for these drugs or **metabolites**. All levels equal to or exceeding the following shall be reported as positive:

Amphetamines 1,000 ng/ml	Barbiturates 300 ng/ml
Cannabinoids 100 ng/ml	Methadone 300 ng/ml
Cocaine 300 ng/ml	
Opiates 300 ng/ml	

Confirmation Test. The following confirmation cutoff levels shall be used when analyzing specimens to determine whether they are positive or negative for these drugs or metabolites. All levels equal to or exceeding the following shall be reported as positive:

Amphetamines 500 ng/ml	Barbiturates 150 ng/ml
Cannabinoids 15 ng/ml	Methadone 150 ng/ml
Cocaine 150 ng/ml	
Opiates 300 ng/ml	

I understand that consent to the tests described above in accordance with the above described policy of the company is a condition of my initial employment with the company, and I further understand that a confirmed test result that is positive may result in denial of my employment.

I further release and hold harmless the company from and against any claims, losses, liability, judgments, costs or expenses of any nature which I may have with regard to or which may arise out of any drug testing I undergo in compliance with the company's policy.

I hereby authorize any physician or drug testing laboratory to release to the company all information concerning the results of my initial or confirmation tests together with all relevant reports, data and medical records pertaining to any such test. I further authorize the company to discuss all tests results with the personnel of the testing facility and with the consulting physician.

Witness Signature   Applicant's Signature   Date

Questions

1. **What is the topic of this form?**

   a. a consent form for drug testing only

   b. a consent form for a physical examination only

   c. a consent to have a physical examination and a drug test

   d. none of the above

2. **What happens if your first test result is above the limits shown for any of the chemicals being tested?**

   a. You will be required to take another test (a confirmation test).

   b. You will be reported to the police.

   c. You will be denied employment.

   d. You will be sent for drug counseling.

3. **What does the form state about who is responsible for any costs or expenses?**

   a. The company will pay for all costs and expenses.

   b. The drug testing center will pay for the expenses.

   c. The applicant must pay for the test.

   d. If there are any costs, the company is not responsible for paying them.

4. **True or false: The results of the test are sent to you and no one else.**

   a. true

   b. false

5. **True or False: Your results may be discussed with a consulting physician and the personnel of the testing facility.**

   a. true

   b. false

111

Lieutenant David Scott

PEPPERELL (MASSACHUSETTS) POLICE
DEPARTMENT

How did you become interested in becoming a police officer?

My father was in the police force, and I spent a lot of time around police officers when I was growing up.

What training or education have you had?

When I was younger, I joined the auxiliary police force to get experience. I received training and got to ride in the squad car with a professional police officer to get some experience in the job. After I graduated from college, I went into the police academy and completed my training there.

What do you like about your job?

I most like being able to help people at some of their worst times in life. In my job you get involved in other people's lives, including family problems, drugs, or other criminal activity. In a community like Pepperell, Massachusetts, you get to know a lot of people and become involved with them on a more personal level than in big cities. I liked doing the D.A.R.E. program with kids. It enabled me to get to know more kids, who later became teenagers. That kind of contact can make a difference for some kids. It's also gratifying when people you have helped through a tough time come back and say thank you.

What do you dislike about your job?

Sometimes the hours conflict with family plans now. When I first started, I volunteered for nights and overtime because there were more opportunities to get involved during those times.

What about the danger police officers face?

Yes, the danger is always there, but if you stay alert and keep up with training, you can stay relatively safe. It's a part of the job that we all accept.

When you were in college, did you have to overcome any obstacles to succeed?

Not in college, but when I tried to get into the police force after graduation, there weren't a lot of openings. So I paid for my own training at the police academy in order to get an advantage over other applicants.

What's the advantage of having a college degree as a police officer?

I think it makes you a better officer—more well rounded—and it gives you more opportunities in law enforcement.

What are your plans for the future?

I am working on a master's degree in criminal justice, so I plan to have that completed soon.

What advice do you have for college freshmen who may be considering a career in law enforcement?

Get involved in some of the different aspects of police work. There are programs like the Explorer Program, the Junior Police Academy, or Citizens Academy. This will help you find out more about the job. In school, take classes in criminal justice, and do an internship if your college offers it. It's a great career for the right people.

BUILDING VOCABULARY

Throughout this course, you will be introduced to word parts that make up many words in the English language. Study the following word parts, and then answer the questions that follow.

Prefixes	Roots	Suffixes
trans- *across*	-port- *to carry*	-able *a condition of being able to*
e-, ex- *out*	-act- *to act on*	-er, -or *one who*
re- *again*		

What English words can you create from these word parts?

....

....

....

....

....

Using a dictionary, look up the meanings of any of the words you wrote that you can't define. Use one of the words you wrote in a sentence that reveals its meaning with a context clue:

....

....

....

TEXTBOOK GRAPHIC AIDS

Study the following graph, and then answer the questions that follow.

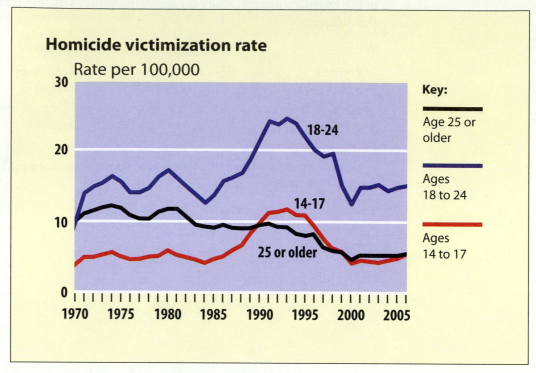

Homicide victimization rate

(Based on U.S. Bureau of Justice Statistics, http://bjs.ojp.usdoj.gov/content/glance/homage.cfm.)

1. What does this graph show?

   ....

2. Which age group had the highest homicide victim rate per 100,000 for all years represented in the chart?

   ....

3. Which age group had the lowest homicide victim rate per 100,000 in the year 1985?

   ....

4. During what years did the homicide victim rate peak at its highest number?

   ....

5. About how many homicide victims per 100,000 were there in 2005 for the 18–24 group?

   ....

CHAPTER REVIEW PRACTICE #1

Use word part clues to choose the correct meanings of the underlined words in the following sentences. If necessary, refer back to the tables of prefixes, roots, and suffixes from earlier in this chapter to help you determine the meanings of the words.

1. Ryan wanted to become a <u>dermatologist</u> (der-ma-TOL-uh-jist).

   a. belonging to a political party

   b. one who studies people

   c. one who studies the skin

   d. dentist

2. He took a <u>circuitous</u> (sir-KYOU-it-us) route to the fair.

   a. direct

   b. long way around

   c. short

   d. fast

3. The woman showed <u>antipathy</u> (an-TIP-path-ee) toward her neighbor.

   a. kindness

   b. dislike

   c. not interested

   d. interest

4. Steve <u>reverted</u> (re-VERT-ed) to his bad behavior as soon as he came home from rehab.

   a. went back to again

   b. went forward

   c. came to

   d. went against

5. The captain was awarded a <u>posthumous</u> (POSS-tyoo-mus) award.

   a. before his death

   b. after his death

   c. famous

   d. costly

CHAPTER REVIEW PRACTICE #2

Read the following passage, and then choose the best meaning for each underlined word as it is used in the sentence. Use context clues (LEADS), word part clues, and parts of speech to help you determine the best meaning.

SAR dogs are "search and rescue" dogs, trained to assist police and rescue workers in an emergency, and respond immediately to commands given by hand signals. If a dog passes the obedience test, it must then go through intensive training. Dogs must complete the agility course by jumping from various heights, out of windows, and by walking on balance beams. Next, the dogs are trained to follow a scent. Their sense of smell is hundreds of times more acute than a human's. When tracking scented items, the dogs must disregard all distractions that are placed in their way. The training is done in a large rural area outside of town where the dogs are trained to locate the items in a specific amount of time, and sit down at their handler's side.

1. If a dog passes the obedience test, it must then go through intensive training.
   a. something done on purpose
   b. something intended to be done
   c. very difficult
   d. easily done

2. Dogs must complete the agility course by jumping from various heights, out of windows, and by walking on balance beams.
   a. ability
   b. the ability to move quickly and accurately
   c. intelligence
   d. obedience

3. Their sense of smell is hundreds of times more acute than a human's.
   a. accurate
   b. serious
   c. deadly
   d. attractive

4. When tracking a scent, the dogs must disregard all distractions that are placed in their way.
   a. dislike
   b. having no feelings for
   c. disobey
   d. ignore

5. The training is done in a large rural area outside of town…
   a. open
   b. city
   c. countryside
   d. housing tracts

CHAPTER REVIEW PRACTICE #3

Read the following passage, and then choose the best meaning for each underlined word as it is used in the sentence. Use context clues (LEADS), word part clues, and parts of speech to help you determine the best meaning.

Correctional officers in state and federal prisons watch over roughly 1.5 million offenders who are underlined incarcerated at any given time. Correctional officers maintain security to prevent disturbances, assaults, and escapes. To make sure that inmates are orderly and obey rules, correctional officers watch the activities of inmates. They also settle disputes between inmates and enforce discipline. Correctional officers sometimes inspect the facilities. They check cells and other areas of the institution for unsanitary conditions, fire hazards, and any evidence of infractions of rules. In addition, they routinely inspect locks, window bars, grilles, doors, and gates for signs of tampering.

1. Correctional officers in state and federal prisons watch over roughly 1.5 million offenders who are incarcerated (in-CAR-sir-ate-ed) at any given time.

   a. not honest

   b. put into

   c. imprisoned

   d. called to

2. They also settle disputes (dis-PYOOTS) between inmates and enforce discipline.

   a. arguments   c. matches

   b. lawsuits   d. displays

3. They check cells and other areas of the institution for unsanitary (un-SAN-i-tar-y) conditions, fire hazards, and any evidence of infractions of rules.

   a. unusual   c. not busy

   b. not clean   d. perfect

4. They check cells and other areas of the institution for unsanitary conditions, fire hazards, and any evidence of infractions (in-FRAK-shuns) of rules.

   a. sections

   b. parts of something

   c. correcting

   d. violations

5. In addition, they routinely inspect locks, window bars, grilles, doors, and gates for signs of tampering (TAM-per-ing).

   a. opening

   b. harmful changes

   c. illegally using

   d. leaving

TEXTBOOK PRACTICE

Read the following passage, and then choose the best meaning for each underlined word as it is used in the sentence. Use context clues (LEADS), word part clues, and parts of speech to help you determine the best meaning. To check your answers, substitute your answer for the underlined word to see if the sentence makes sense and does not change the meaning.

Adapted from "The Hunt for Eric Rudolph"

With shattering glass, splitting brick, and shredding human flesh, the explosion engulfed the New Woman All Women Health Care clinic in Birmingham, Alabama, on January 20, 1996. In an instant, an off-duty city police officer lay dead and a nurse severely injured. With a crude-but-lethal mix of dynamite and nails, the mysterious antiabortion clinic terrorist had struck again. But this time, witnesses spotted a truck near the clinic and had the presence of mind to get the license number. Police quickly identified the vehicle owner—a 32-year-old former U.S. Army demolitions man who lived in a remote area at the western end of North Carolina. The chase would wind across some of the country's most rugged and foreboding terrain as well as back in time. Rudolph's bombs had a signature in the nails they used. That signature and other clues allowed authorities to tie Rudolph to several bombings in the Atlanta area, including the knapsack bomb detonated in the midst of the 1996 Olympics in Atlanta's Centennial Park.

1. With shattering glass, splitting brick, and shredding human flesh, the explosion engulfed (en-GULF'd) the New Woman All Women Health Care clinic in Birmingham, Alabama, on January 20, 1996.

   a. split

   b. completely overcame

   c. heard

   d. within

2. With a crude-but-lethal mix of dynamite and nails, the mysterious antiabortion (ant-eye-a-BOR-shun) clinic terrorist had struck again.

   a. insane

   b. for abortion

   c. against abortion

   d. doing abortions

3. The chase would wind across some of the country's most rugged and foreboding (for-BODE-ing) terrain as well as back in time.

   a. threatening

   b. interesting

   c. beautiful

   d. peaceful

4. Rudolph's bombs had a <u>signature</u> (SIG-na-chur) in the nails they used.

   a. where someone signs his or her name

   b. permission

   c. brand name

   d. a clue as to who committed the crime

5. That signature and other clues allowed authorities to tie Rudolph to several bombings in the Atlanta area, including the knapsack bomb <u>detonated</u> (DET-oh-nate-ed) in the midst of the 1996 Olympics in Atlanta's Centennial Park.

   a. dangerously

   b. container

   c. practiced

   d. exploded

STUDY SKILL CHAPTER REVIEW

A good way to review material for a test is to make note cards. Complete the following note cards for Chapter 3.

Context Clues

Context clues: look at the information in the sentence or paragraph to ....

....

Types of Context Clues

1. Logic of the passage: ....

....

Ex: The <u>precipice</u> was dangerously steep and unsafe to climb.

2. Examples: ....

Ex: <u>Marsupials</u> include kangaroos and opossums.

---

3. .... The sentence gives a word that means the opposite of the unfamiliar word. Ex: My health insurance was <u>comprehensive</u>, but Marco's **didn't cover everything**.

4. .... The sentence gives the meaning of the word or term, using

....

Ex: Smoking is my one vice (bad habit).

5. .... The sentence gives a word that means the same as the unfamiliar word.

Ex: Although she gave her <u>testimony</u> in court, most of her statements were untrue.

Word Parts

.... Part added to the beginning of a word that often changes the meaning of the word.

Ex: true, <u>un</u>true

Roots: Part that has the ....

Ex: bare<u>foot</u>, <u>foot</u>ball, <u>foot</u>ing

Suffixes: ....

Ex: act, ac<u>tion</u>, ac<u>tivate</u>, ac<u>tivity</u>

READING LAB ASSIGNMENTS

SKILL REVIEW

1. Go online to MyReadingLab and do the practices and tests for "Vocabulary."

COMPREHENSION IMPROVEMENT

2. Go online to MyReadingLab and read two Lexile Reading Level stories and answer the questions. Practice using the four-step reading process as you read them.

CAREER EXPLORATION

3. Go to www.livecareer.com, and take the Career Inventory test to find out what careers are best for you.

4. Go online to MyReadingLab and click on "Research Navigator." From the drop-down menu, select "Criminal Justice." Think of a topic you would like to know more about, such as "auto theft" or "Internet crime," and then search for that topic. Print out the article. Underline unfamiliar words, and then use context clues and word part clues to write your own definitions for the words. Check your definitions with a dictionary.

5. Go online to www.bls.gov/home.htm and search for a career that you would like to learn more about. Print out the information you find. Present the ideas in the article to your team or your class.

LEARNING REFLECTION

Think about the skills and concepts presented in this chapter. What have you learned that will help your reading comprehension and enable you to do well in college? Which learning strategy helped you the most in your learning?

STAYING ON TRACK

Write your thoughts about the following questions on the lines provided.

1. Go back to Chapter 1, and read your short-term goals. Are you still on track to meet your short-term goals? If not, how do you plan to get back on track to meet those goals?

2. Are you sticking to the study schedule you created in Chapter 1? Are you finding that you have enough time to study and do homework? If not, what changes will you do to make the time?

SELF-EVALUATION CHECKLIST

Rate yourself on the following items, using the following scale:

1 = strongly disagree

2 = disagree

3 = neither agree nor disagree

4 = agree

5 = strongly agree

1. I completed all of the assigned work on time.   ....

2. I understand all the concepts in this chapter.   ....

3. I contributed to teamwork and class discussions.   ....

4. I completed all of the assigned lab work on time.   ....

5. I came to class on time.   ....

6. I attended class every day.   ....

7. I studied for any quizzes or tests we had for this chapter.   ....

8. I asked questions when I didn't understand something.   ....

9. I checked my comprehension during reading.   ....

10. I know what is expected of me in the coming week.   ....

For support in meeting this chapter's objectives, go to the Study Plan in MyReadingLab and select Vocabulary. Read and view the resources in the Review Materials section, and then complete the Recall, Apply, and Write exercises in the Activities section. Check your results by clicking on Gradebook.

STUDY SKILL: DEVELOPING SELF-CONFIDENCE IN READING

Many students in reading courses begin the semester by stating, "I stink at reading. I've never been any good at it." Beginning any course with a defeatist attitude will make failure easy. It's one way of giving yourself permission to fail. You've already decided that you can't succeed, so you expect failure and won't be disappointed when it happens. For some students, this attitude exists not only in their reading classes but also in their English classes, their math classes, and any other class that looks as if it may be too difficult. If you are one of these students, you need to overcome this self-defeatist attitude and give yourself the opportunity to succeed.

Everyone has at least one challenging class in college. Many students will drop the class and try to find something easier, but some of those challenging classes are required courses that you must pass to get your degree. But you can change your attitude by taking a different approach.

The term *self-efficacy* means your belief in your own ability to succeed. It may seem magical, but students who have confidence in their ability to learn can be more successful in college than those who have the same ability but do not have confidence.

How do you get that confidence that you need to succeed?

Try following these steps:

STEP 1	**RECALL PAST SUCCESSES**
	Think about something that you have done in your life that you were successful in doing, such as a sport or hobby that you mastered or a talent that you have. Thinking about your past success reminds you that you do have the ability to succeed. Spend five minutes thinking about things you have done well in the past, and make a list of them.

STEP 2	**AVOID NEGATIVE THINKING**
	Thinking negatively about yourself only makes it more likely that you will fail. You need to change this habit and replace it with a different way of thinking. The next time you begin making negative remarks to yourself, stop and accept the fact that you made an error. Even the smartest students make mistakes. But smart people aren't defeated by mistakes, they learn from them. Instead of negative thinking, think about what you can do to fix the problem, and add the phrase, "I will do better next time." Changing your self-talk can change your attitude, but it will take plenty of practice. Over a period of time, you will begin to see a change.

STEP 3	**FIND SOLUTIONS TO YOUR PROBLEMS**
	Think about the areas in your life that give you the most trouble. Is it forgetting to do homework? Not having enough time for studying? Lacking motivation? Problems are a distraction and a source for negative thinking. You should think about solutions to your problems instead of dwelling on them or ignoring them. If you can't come up with a solution, ask friends, classmates, or family members for their ideas.

STEP 4	**TRY TO FIND A ROLE MODEL SUCH AS A CLASSMATE OR A FRIEND**
	What do successful people specifically do that makes them successful? What strategies do they use? Talk to someone you think is sucessful and ask questions to gain ideas.

STEP 5

DON'T FALL INTO THE HABIT OF COMPARING YOURSELF TO OTHERS

Am I smarter than him? Is she prettier than me? Those kinds of questions do nothing to improve your self-confidence. The truth is, there will always be someone else who is smarter, better looking, richer, or more popular than you, and there will always be someone else who is not as smart, as good looking, or as rich as you. Focus on yourself, and only compare yourself to yourself. Are you doing better at something today than you were a year ago? Look for opportunities to praise yourself for your own growth and success.

STEP 6

TAKE BABY STEPS

The old saying "Rome wasn't built in a day" means that things take time. Often people are impatient to achieve their personal goals, and they expect immediate results or they give up. Set small achievable goals to solve your problems, and keep track of your own success. For example, instead of saying, "I'm going to lose 20 pounds this month," make the goal smaller and more attainable by saying, "I'm going to lose two pounds this week."

STEP 7

AFTER YOU HAVE DECIDED UPON A SOLUTION TO A PROBLEM, STICK TO YOUR PLAN AND DON'T GIVE UP IF YOU DON'T SEE IMMEDIATE RESULTS

Develop patience. Self-discipline and self-control are key factors to success. Just setting goals and doing nothing about them will not help you succeed. Keep in mind that some problems may take longer to solve than you had planned. But stay on track and keep trying. Eventually, you will succeed.

STEP 8

CELEBRATE YOUR SUCCESSES—EVEN THE SMALL ONES

It's easy to beat yourself up over your mistakes and ignore your successes. When you do succeed (like getting a good grade or losing a pound), give yourself some praise. Share your success with someone else whom you know will be happy for you. Stay away from people who speak negatively about you. Hearing negative things about yourself on a regular basis can be emotionally draining, and you'll begin to believe what they are saying.

STEP 9

BE A RISK TAKER

You've heard the old cliché about the turtle who can't move ahead unless he sticks his neck out. The same is true with humans. You must take some risks in life in order to move ahead. But with risk taking comes the responsibility to learn from your mistakes if you fail. Many of the famous people you will read about in this book had failures before they succeeded. But they learned from their mistakes and believed that they would eventually succeed.

STEP 10

FAILURE IS NOT AN OPTION

Promise yourself that you will not allow yourself to fail in reading, in school, in life, in your relationships—whatever it is. Learning from your mistakes will help you find success in whatever you want to achieve.

EVALUATING SOLUTIONS TO PROBLEMS

Once you have a list of solutions for a problem, you should evaluate them. Think about the advantages and disadvantages of each solution and make a table like the one below.

Problem: I need a job

Solutions	Advantages	Disadvantages
1. Hand out copies of my résumé.	People will know I'm looking for a job and see my qualifications and experience. Easy to hand out to employers, friends, neighbors, or anybody!	Costs involved for making copies and time needed to hand them out.

125

CHAPTER 4 TOPICS AND STATED MAIN IDEAS

LEARNING OBJECTIVES

IN THIS CHAPTER, YOU WILL:

Objective **1** identify the topic of a reading selection.

Objective **2** select the stated main idea.

FOCUS ON BUSINESS AND PERSONAL FINANCE

Throughout the readings in this chapter, you will learn about building wealth and managing money. You will also learn about careers in business and finance and read about real people who have started their own successful businesses. Perhaps you can turn your passion into a profitable business, making money doing what you love. This chapter will help you understand the skills that are needed to be successful in business and with your personal finances.

TOPICS, STATED MAIN IDEAS, AND TOPIC SENTENCES

Topic: the subject of a reading selection.

Knowing who or what a selection is about is the first step in understanding what you are reading. Knowing the general **topic** can help you better understand the points that are being made.

It's important to identify the topic of the selection you are reading because knowing the topic will put you on the right track to finding the main idea. The topic is usually mentioned or referred to in the sentence containing the main idea.

Objective **1**

How to Find the Topic

Begin by asking, "Who or what is this selection about?" Next, look for the subject that is most frequently mentioned in the reading, usually a word or phrase that is repeated often in the subjects of the sentences. A topic is a subject, like surfing, Egypt, classic cars, or 19th-century poets. Topics are not complete sentences. Paragraphs may have the topic as a title but not always. For example, a paragraph on the best seafood restaurants in town may have a catchy title that does not state the topic plainly, like "Fishing for Great Dining."

Directions: As you read the following paragraph, ask yourself, "Who or what is this about?" Underline any words or phrases that give you a clue.

There are several key elements that make a great leader in business. First, you must have good leadership skills. Good leaders are good listeners and have excellent communication skills. They know how to read people and inspire them. Also, they must be dedicated to learning their business. The best business leaders constantly look for new ways of doing things to gain new customers while continuing to maintain their present ones. Third, good leaders in business have goals. They know what they want to accomplish and how they are going to do it within a specific time frame. Having these key elements can make anyone a good business leader.

1. Which of the following topics is the best "fit" for this passage?
   a. business
   b. leaders
   c. good business leaders
   d. leadership

127

Getting the Specific Topic

Finding the right topic to fit the passage is like finding a pair of shoes that fit. Some topics are too broad; some are too narrow. One that is just right will fit the passage perfectly. Read the following passage, and as you read, try to find the topic of this passage. Ask yourself, "Who or what is this passage about?"

Underline any words or phrases that give you a clue to the topic.

An IRA, or individual retirement account, is a savings and investment program for your personal finances so that you will have income after you retire. There are several different types of IRAs. One type is known as the traditional IRA. This IRA will allow you to contribute up to $3,000 of your annual salary to a retirement fund before the salary is taxed. For example, if you made a salary of $50,000 a year, you would be able to save $3,000 into a traditional IRA and only be taxed on the remaining $47,000. This lowers your income tax and allows you to invest the money until you reach the age of 59½, the age when you may begin to withdraw the money.

1. Which of the following topics is the best "fit" for this passage?
   a. IRAs
   b. retirement accounts
   c. investing money
   d. saving money

Answers (b), (c), and (d) are too broad because they include other ways to save not described here. Answer (a), IRAs, is the perfect fit for this passage because most of the sentences in the paragraph describe the traditional IRA.

Specific versus General Topics

As you have seen in the example above, some topics are broader than others. When a passage has a wide variety of details and can be broken down into subtopics, it will have a broad topic. But if a passage discusses only one thing, it will have a narrower (more specific) topic.

Look at the following groups of words, and circle the broadest topic in each row:

1.	2.	3.
notebook	New York	sports equipment
pens	Texas	basketball
school supplies	California	tennis racket
highlighter	United States	basketball hoop

Now look at the following groups of topics. Number them in order from the most general (1) to the most specific (4). The first set is done for you.

EXAMPLE:

1. books (This is the broadest term; all of the subtopics below could fall into this category.)

2. novels (Novels are a type of book, and they contain both items listed below.)

3. paragraphs (Paragraphs are in novels and include sentences.)

4. sentences (Sentences make up a paragraph.)

1.
- [ ] team sports
- [ ] pitchers
- [ ] baseball
- [ ] sports

2.
- [ ] Ford Motor Co.
- [ ] U.S. auto manufacturers
- [ ] manufacturers
- [ ] American manufacturers

3.
- [ ] bushes with flowers
- [ ] bushes
- [ ] red roses
- [ ] roses

4.
- [ ] actors
- [ ] entertainers
- [ ] film actors
- [ ] Brad Pitt

5.
- [ ] iPhone
- [ ] cell phone companies
- [ ] technology companies
- [ ] Apple

Practice

1. Read the following paragraphs, and underline any clues that help you determine the topics. Then, write the topic that best fits each paragraph on the line below.

If you apply for a credit card or a loan and you're turned down, it may be because of your credit history. In some cases, if you have never borrowed money before, you may not have a credit history. In other cases, you may have borrowed money but have been late on your payments, or you may have a poor credit history due to fraud—specifically, identity theft. One way to find out about your credit history is to get a credit report. Your bank can direct you where to get one, or you can look online for credit reports. It is recommended that consumers check their credit history once every two or three years.

The topic of this passage is:

....

2. Read the following paragraphs, and underline any clues that help you determine the topics. Then, write the topic that best fits each paragraph on the line below.

Stocks, also known as *equity shares*, are units of ownership in a company. If a company wants to raise money to develop new products or services, it may sell shares of the company. The price of a stock is determined by its demand. The demand to buy the stock may go up when investors feel the stock may make them a good profit. Typically, investors buy stocks at a lower price and hold onto them until the price of the stock goes up. Then they sell the stocks and keep the profit. The stock market is constantly changing due to many factors. However, like all products, the price of stocks will increase when the demand to buy increases, and it will decrease when the demand to buy decreases.

The topic of this passage is:

....

3. Read the following paragraphs, and underline any clues that help you determine the topics. Then, write the topic that best fits each paragraph on the line below.

When a company needs money to make the business grow, it may go to a bank and ask for a loan, but this means the company will have to begin making monthly payments in addition to paying an interest charge. Another way to raise the money is to sell bonds. A bond is just a loan from investors. Bonds have the principal (the amount borrowed) and interest (the lending fee) due at a much later date, called the "maturity date."

Practice

Companies can sell bonds to raise money without having to pay them back immediately in monthly payments. Unlike stockholders, bondholders do not own any share of the company. Also, bonds have a maturity date when they must be paid back with interest, whereas stocks can be held indefinitely.

The topic of this passage is:

....

....

TEXTBOOK SELECTION

Read the following paragraph, and underline any clues that help you determine the topic. Then, write the topic that best fits the paragraph on the line below.

If you are a first-time borrower and have no credit history, it may be difficult to get a bank loan. You may want to think about joining a credit union. A credit union is like a bank, but it is owned by its members. The board of directors and loan committee are elected by the members of the credit union. In the United States, credit unions typically charge lower interest rates on loans and pay higher interest dividends on savings accounts than most banks. Credit unions offer many of the same services as banks. Some credit unions are small and run by a few members, while others are huge with several billion dollars in resources and more than a hundred thousand members.

The topic of this passage is:

....

....

....

U-Review

For each of the following sentences, write "T" if the statement is true or "F" if the statement is false. As you go over the answers with your team, discuss why the false statements were false.

1. .... Topics tell us who or what the reading passage is about.
2. .... Topics are complete sentences.
3. .... Topics are often found in the sentence that states the main idea.
4. .... Topics are usually not found in titles or bold print.
5. .... Knowing the topic will help you find the main idea.

Stated Main Ideas

Finding the main idea of a reading passage is the most important part of reading comprehension. Knowing the key message that the author is trying to get across will unlock many other supporting roles.

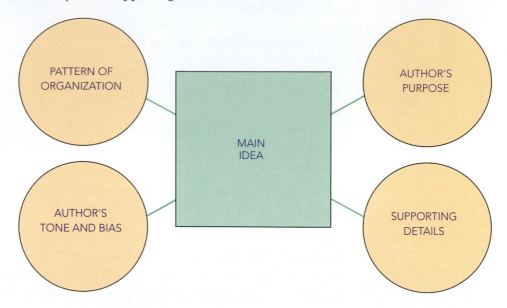

Characteristics of a Main Idea

> The **main idea** is the most important point that the author is making about the topic.

A **main idea** is always a complete sentence that states an important point about the topic. That's why you can often find the topic in the main idea sentence. Main ideas are never questions; they're always statements.

Mark which of the following statements would be considered stated main ideas.

1. .... There are several benefits to having a college degree.
2. .... Ways to save money for college.
3. .... How to get financial assistance in college
4. .... Finding money to pay for college can be a challenge.
5. .... What are the best ways to save for college?

Main Idea Styles

Authors use different styles to convey main ideas.

1. Some main ideas will introduce the major points that the paragraph will discuss.

There are *several types* of marketing methods that would be appropriate for this product. (The several types would be the major details.)

Three main factors are important to consider when deciding upon the correct way to solve a crime. (The three factors would be the major details.)

2. Some main ideas are a summary of the paragraph.

> Mozart was one of the most influential composers of all time. (The major details would explain why he was the most influential composer.)

> Thomas Edison worked tirelessly to create new inventions and processes. (The major details would explain how he worked to create new inventions and processes.)

3. In definition pattern paragraphs, the definition of the term is the main idea. It is usually followed by an explanation and may include examples in the supporting details

> **Immediate memory** is the temporary memory where information is processed briefly (in seconds) and subconsciously, and then is either blocked or passed on to working memory.

> **Self-concept** is the perception of who we are and how we fit into the world.*

4. Other main ideas may be a conclusion of a study, experiment, or discussion.

> The results of the study show that, over the period of a lifetime, students who do not get a college degree will earn less than half the income of those who do.

> In conclusion, it is often difficult to prove arson as the cause of a fire.

When a main idea is stated in a sentence, it is known as the **topic sentence**. Remember that a main idea is an idea. It can be stated or implied. But when it is stated, it is found in the topic sentence. Also remember that a topic sentence is always a complete sentence, never a phrase, and it is never a question. The most common mistake made when searching for a topic sentence is to choose one of the supporting details. To make sure you have the right topic sentence, you must always check by asking yourself, "Do most of the sentences in the paragraph tell me more about this idea?"

> A **topic sentence** is the sentence that states the main idea, the author's most important point.

Sometimes students draw a conclusion about what they have read, thinking that it is a main idea. Conclusions are also based on the details, but a conclusion is often not the same thing as the main idea. For example, which of these statements is the main idea, and which one is a conclusion?

> a. *Pinocchio* is about a puppet who became a real boy whose nose grew longer every time he told a lie.

> b. You should never tell lies because you will only bring misfortune upon yourself.

The main idea tells what the story was about, whereas the conclusion is an inference you make based on the details in the story. Sentence (a) is the main idea, and (b) is a conclusion of the story.

Knowing the main idea is the key to good comprehension and will help you in many other aspects of your learning: in writing good paragraphs and essays, in highlighting, and in note taking.

*From *How the Brain Learns* by David Sousa. Copyright © 2005 by Sage Publications, Inc. Reprinted by permission of Sage Publications, Inc.

Stated Main Idea: Checking Your Answer

Once you have found the topic sentence, you should check to see if the other sentences tell you more about it. If they don't, then look again for a sentence that might better state the author's most important point. Always choose a statement that is general enough to relate to the details discussed in the paragraph. In the following paragraph, the topic and the topic sentence are underlined. Most of the other sentences help to prove the topic sentence.

Have you ever been to a restaurant and stood there next to an empty desk waiting to be seated? Or once you were seated, did you have to wait more than five minutes for a waiter to approach your table? Even after the meal, did you become frustrated trying to get the waiter's attention so you could get your check? If you've experienced any of these things, then you know how important it is to have good customer service. Customers who have a poor experience at a restaurant or any other business are not likely to come back and may even tell their friends about it. Customer service is one of the most important factors in a business.

Practice Finding the Topic and Topic Sentence

Read the following paragraph. Find the topic by underlining the subject that is most often mentioned. Then, decide which sentence states the main point that the author is trying to make about the topic. This will be the topic sentence. When you think you have found it, ask yourself, "Do most of the other sentences tell me more about this idea?" If the answer is yes, you have the correct topic sentence.

When trying to save money, you need to know about your options. Most people save their money in a savings account at a bank. They are paid interest from the bank for allowing the bank to hold and use their money. If you save money in a money market account, your interest rate will be determined by how well the stock market is doing. Although you won't lose any of your original investment, you won't be making much interest when interest rates are low. Another way to save money is to buy a certificate of deposit, or CD. You cannot cash in the certificate until it reaches a certain age, but CDs are a good investment if you don't need the money right away.

1. What is the topic of this passage?
   a. savings accounts
   b. money market accounts
   c. banking
   d. ways to save money

2. What is the topic sentence?
   a. Most people save their money in a savings account at a bank.
   b. When trying to save money, you need to know about your options.
   c. If you save money in a money market account, your interest rate will be determined by how well the stock market is doing.
   d. Saving money today will keep you from financial trouble in the future.

Where to Find the Topic Sentence

Topic sentences can be found anywhere in a paragraph, but there are some places where they are more likely to appear.

Topic Sentence at the Beginning

Topic sentences are often the first sentence of the paragraph, as in the following paragraph. Notice that the topic is in bold print, and it is mentioned in the topic sentence.

One way of investing money is to purchase **real estate**. Most people want to buy **real estate** not only as an investment but for a place to live. Others may want to lease out the property to renters so they can make money. But investing in **real estate** is like any other investment—there are no guarantees of making money. In fact, buying the wrong property or buying when real estate prices are going down can result in losing money. When there are not enough buyers or renters to match the flood of properties on the market, real estate won't sell. Many people can get behind in their taxes and mortgage payments and lose their property to the banks who lent them the money to buy it.

Topic Sentence at the End

Sometimes the topic sentence comes at the end of a paragraph, as in the following passage.

A **loan** is an amount of money borrowed from a lender. Most **loans** are paid back in regular monthly payments, plus an interest charge. The interest charged on a **loan** can be high or low, depending upon the terms of the **loan** contract. If the interest rate is high, the cost of the **loan** will be high. A borrower must also look at the terms of the **loan** contract. Questions like, "Can I pay off the loan at any time?" and "What happens if I am late on my payment?" should be answered in the contract. Some lenders have high fees or increase the interest rate of your loan for being late on payments. There are many factors to consider when taking out a **loan**.

Topic Sentence in the Middle

In some cases, the topic sentences appears in the middle of the paragraph, as is shown here.

When a company or bank loans money to a borrower, it will often ask for something as "**collateral**." This is usually some type of property such as a car or real estate that can be held until the loan is paid off. The lender will hold the title (ownership papers) of the car, or place a "lien" (a claim) on the real estate. **Collateral** is used to secure a loan to make sure that the lender receives some sort of repayment if a loan is not paid back. This means that the lender must be paid back first when the **collateral** is sold. If the borrower does not pay back the loan, or is late on payments for a certain number of months, the lender can keep the **collateral**.

Topic Sentences in the First and Last Sentences

Often an author will want to emphasize an important point. To do this, the author may present the topic sentence first and then restate the same idea again at the end. Usually, a repeated topic sentence is stated in different words but has the same key idea. Notice how the topic sentences in this paragraph are similar but not identical:

135

<mark>Beware of borrowing money from **loan sharks**, because you may end up in serious trouble</mark>. People who loan money with extremely harsh terms are known as "**loan sharks**." Their customers are usually people who are desperate, poor, and not well informed about borrowing money safely. **Loan sharks** sometimes commit criminal acts if the payments are late. Some **loan sharks** threaten or even assault borrowers for missing payments. They charge very high interest rates, which make it impossible for the loans to ever be paid back. Or they may have hidden terms in their contracts that allow them to charge extra fees or take away personal property as collateral. <mark>Borrowing from **loan sharks** is a dangerous way to get money, no matter how badly it's needed.</mark>

TIPS ON TOPIC SENTENCES

Here are some things to keep in mind about topic sentences:

- They are always complete sentences, never a phrase or a question.
- They state the author's most important point about the topic.
- They are explained or proved by most of the other sentences in the paragraph.
- They are broad statements that are general enough to include all the details in the paragraph.
- They are not the same as inferences or conclusions.
- Topic sentences usually mention the topic or make a reference to the topic.

Practice

1. Read the following groups of sentences. One item is the topic, one is the topic sentence, and the others are sentences that explain or prove the topic sentence. These are known as supporting details. Label each item T = topic, TS = topic sentence, or SD = supporting detail.

Example:

*TS*____ Using the Internet is one way to conduct business online.

*SD*____ Pop-up ads can appear on Web sites to advertise new products or services.

*T*____ Internet Business

*SD*____ A "shopping cart" is a feature that allows people to buy products online.

Group 1

_____ A business plan is a written plan that shows how a business will be conducted.

_____ It includes details about how much it will cost to start and run the business.

_____ Business plans predict about how much money the business will make in the next few years.

_____ Business plans

Practice

Group 2

.... Examples of small businesses are hair salons, restaurants, newsstands, or locksmiths.

.... Small businesses

.... There are many different kinds of small businesses.

.... The term "small business" means businesses with less than 100 employees.

Group 3

.... Franchises

.... Some popular franchises include fast-food restaurant chains, convenience stores, and gas stations.

.... Franchises are branches of a large corporation that owns a chain of small businesses with the same brand name and same products or services.

.... Franchise owners enjoy the benefits of a large corporation but must pay a percentage of their profits to the corporation.

Group 4

.... There are several reasons why more than half of all new businesses go bankrupt within the first five years.

.... Many new businesses do not have enough money to keep them going during the years when they are trying to get established.

.... Some new businesses fail because the managers do not have enough experience in management.

.... New businesses failures

Group 5

.... Start-up capital

.... One source of start-up capital is to sell shares of stock in the company.

.... Sometimes private investors will give money to a new business in return for a percentage of the business.

.... New businesses need money to get started, known as "start-up capital."

2. **In each of the following paragraphs, underline the topic and locate the topic sentence.**

APR means the annual percentage rate that you will pay as interest on your loan. The APR is determined by the lender and the general economy. Some lenders charge much higher APRs than others. If you have a credit card, your APR for charging purchases may be less than the APR for transferring balances to other credit cards or for cash advances. Sometimes the APR changes depending on how much money you owe or your credit score. Often credit card companies will

Practice

advertise a low introductory <u>APR</u> for anywhere from 3 to 6 months, and then it will increase. When taking out a loan, you need to know not only your <u>APR</u> but also the terms under which it may change, so read the loan or credit card application carefully.

1. What is the topic of this paragraph?

   a. loans

   b. APRs

   c. credit cards

   d. applying for a loan

2. What is the topic sentence of this paragraph?

   a. APR means the annual percentage rate that you will pay as interest on your loan.

   b. The APR is determined by the lender and by the general economy.

   c. Sometimes the APR changes depending on how much money you owe or your credit score.

   d. When taking out a loan, you not only have to know your APR, but the terms under which it may change, so read the loan or credit card application carefully.

Oprah Winfrey was born in Mississippi to a poor, single mother. They moved to the inner city of Milwaukee, where life was hard. She earned a scholarship to Tennessee State University, where she majored in communications. After a series of successful jobs as a news anchor, she moved to Chicago to host a morning talk show. Her popularity gave her so much success that she soon had her own show and moved into film acting. Oprah Winfrey is a role model for women everywhere because she overcame poverty and hardship to achieve great success. Oprah always found new ways to stay challenged. She started her own magazines and her own television and film production company, which were a huge success. For three years in a row, she was the world's leading African American billionaire, worth more than $2.5 billion. But Oprah's success is more than financial. She has raised millions of dollars for charities and donated millions of her own money. She has won many awards for her humanitarian efforts, making her one of the most influential and generous women in the world.

1. What is the topic?

   a. Oprah's TV show success

   b. the world's richest woman

   c. Oprah Winfrey

   d. rich women

Practice

2. What is the topic sentence?

   a. Oprah Winfrey was born in Mississippi to a poor, single mother.

   b. Oprah Winfrey is a role model for women everywhere because she overcame poverty and hardship to achieve great success.

   c. For three years in a row, she was the world's leading African American billionaire, worth more than $2.5 billion.

   d. She has won many awards for her humanitarian efforts, making her one of the most influential and generous women in the world.

If you purchase an item with your credit card, you may withhold payment if the product is damaged or of poor quality. First, you must try to resolve the problem with the company that sold you the goods. Under the Fair Credit Billing Act (a federal law), you can have payment withheld if the sale took place within 100 miles of your home address and it is worth $50 or more. If you can't get a refund, write to your credit card company or call its customer service number. Otherwise, you will lose your rights to stop payment. Your credit card company will investigate the claim, and if it is approved, you will not have to pay for the item.

1. What is the topic of this paragraph?

   a. withholding a credit card payment   **c.** credit cards

   b. returning damaged goods   **d.** the Fair Credit Billing Act

2. Which of the following is the topic sentence for this paragraph?

   a. First, you must try to resolve the problem with the company that sold you the goods.

   b. If you can't get a refund, write to your credit card company or call its customer service number.

   c. Your credit card company will investigate the claim, and if it is approved, you will not have to pay for the item.

   d. If you purchase an item with your credit card, you may withhold payment if the product is damaged or of poor quality.

When Larry Page was a student at the University of Michigan, he loved turning his creative ideas into useful technology. After he graduated with his bachelor's and master's degrees in computer science, he enrolled in the PhD program at Stanford University. There he met another student who was also interested in the Internet, Sergey Brim. Together, they created a computer program to find data more easily and tried it on the Stanford University Web site. It worked so well that they decided to create their own company and named it Google. Today, both young men are listed in *Forbes* magazine's richest people in the world. Each of them has a net worth close to $20 billion. Larry Page and Sergey Brim created one of the most successful Internet companies in history—Google.

1. What is the topic? (Who or what are most of the details about?)

   a. Larry Page   **c.** Google

   b. Sergey Brim   **d.** Larry Page and Sergey Brim

Practice

2. **What is the topic sentence?**

   a. When Larry Page was a student at the University of Michigan, he loved turning his creative ideas into useful technology.

   b. Together, they created a computer program to find data more easily and tried it on the Stanford University Web site.

   c. It worked so well that they decided to create their own company and named it Google.

   d. Larry Page and Sergey Brim created one of the most successful Internet companies in history—Google.

TEXTBOOK SELECTION

Read the following textbook selections, underline the topics, and then answer the questions that follow.

The field of marketing is extensive—and so are the opportunities for someone graduating with a marketing degree. While one person may seek out the excitement of an advertising agency that serves multiple clients, another might prefer to focus on brand management at a single organization. For someone else interested in marketing, working as a buyer for a retail chain is appealing. A few people might want to get into marketing research. Others might have an aptitude for supply chain management or *logistics management*, the aspect of supply chain management that focuses on the flow of products between suppliers and customers. A lot of people are attracted to sales positions because of the potential financial rewards.

(From *Exploring Business* by Karen Collins. Copyright © 2008 by Karen Collins. Reprinted by permission of the author.)

QUESTIONS

1. **What is the topic?**

   a. logistics management   **c.** sales

   b. management   **d.** marketing

2. **Which of the following is the topic sentence for this paragraph?**

   a. The field of marketing is extensive—and so are the opportunities for someone graduating with a marketing degree.

   b. A few people might want to get into marketing research.

   c. For someone else interested in marketing, working as a buyer for a retail chain is appealing.

   d. Others might have an aptitude for supply chain management or logistics management, the aspect of supply chain management that focuses on the flow of products between suppliers and customers.

Have you ever wanted to go surfing but couldn't find a body of water with decent waves? You no longer have a problem: the newly invented PowerSki JetBoard makes its own waves. This innovative product combines the ease of waterskiing with the excitement of surfing. A high-tech surfboard with a 40-horsepower, 40-pound watercraft engine, the PowerSki JetBoard has the power of a small motorcycle. Where do product ideas like the PowerSki

JetBoard come from? How do people create products that meet customer needs? How are ideas developed and turned into actual products? How do you forecast demand for a product? How do you protect your product ideas? In this chapter, you'll learn the answers to many questions about products.

To see the PowerSki JetBoard in action, visit the company's Web site at www.powerski.com. Watch the streaming videos that demonstrate what the JetBoard can do. (Rider in photo is Chad Montgomery, son of Robert E. Montgomery, Inventor of the PowerSki JetBoard and Flat Engine Technology.)

(From *Exploring Business* by Karen Collins. Copyright © 2008 by Karen Collins. Reprinted by permission of the author.)

QUESTIONS

1. What is the topic?
   a. PowerSki JetBoard
   b. surfing
   c. products
   d. selling products

2. Which of the following is the topic sentence for this paragraph?
   a. Have you ever wanted to go surfing but couldn't find a body of water with decent waves?
   b. This innovative product combines the ease of waterskiing with the excitement of surfing.
   c. You no longer have a problem: the newly invented PowerSki JetBoard makes its own waves.
   d. In this chapter, you'll learn the answers to many questions about products.

U-Review

List six ways you can identify a topic sentence of a paragraph. Then, check your answers with your team to see if there are any you forgot. (Hint: If you need help getting started, go back and reread "Tips on Topic Sentences.")

1. ....

2. ....

3. ....

4. ....

   ....

5. ....

6.

....

Bonus Question: What question should you ask to check if you have the correct topic sentence?

....

Reading 1 Vocabulary Preview

The following vocabulary words are from the article "Escaping the Debt Trap." With a partner or in a team, choose the correct meanings of the underlined words in the following sentences. Use context clues (LEADS), word part clues, and parts of speech to help you figure out the meanings.

1. If you look at money from the wrong <u>perspective</u> (per-SPEK-tiv), it can cause a lot of unhappiness. (Hint: The root is "spect," meaning "to see or view.")

   a. proportion

   b. viewpoint

   c. amount

   d. idea

2. Rather than trying to break down words into their parts, some people prefer to read them with a <u>holistic</u> (hole-IS-tik) approach.

   a. in sections

   b. the whole thing

   c. solid

   d. unusual

3. Patients with <u>terminal</u> (TER-min-ul) diseases are not expected to live. (Hint: The root, "term," is from the Latin root "terminus," meaning "to end.")

   a. serious

   b. unexpected

   c. fatal

   d. watchful

4. It was so <u>sweltering</u> (SWELL-ter-ing) on the day of the parade that many of the marchers fainted from the heat.

   a. extremely hot

   b. mild

   c. chilly

   d. important

Reading 1

5. He invited me to open a charge account at his store, but I <u>declined</u> (dee-KLINE 'D) his offer.

   a. accepted

   b. listened to

   c. didn't accept

   d. questioned

6. The <u>forlorn</u> (for-LORN) look on Jim's face told me that his team had lost the basketball game.

   a. sad

   b. angry

   c. happy

   d. long

7. Even though Jamika finds math difficult, her <u>perseverance</u> (per-sa-VEER-ence) has enabled her to pass Algebra with a B.

   a. presence

   b. hardness

   c. determination

   d. frustration

8. If you trust me with your apartment while you are gone, I promise to be a good <u>steward</u> (STOO-ard) and make sure everything is kept safe until you return.

   a. caretaker

   b. babysitter

   c. waiter

   d. cook

9. The lessons I learned about hard work were <u>imprinted</u> (im-PRINT-ed) upon me by my mother, who was always busy working.

   a. written on

   b. impressed upon

   c. given to

   d. taken from

10. After her car accident, Jaya got into a <u>funk</u>, and nothing seemed to cheer her up.

    a. junk car

    b. dance

    c. situation

    d. depressed mood

Reading 1 What Do You Already Know?

1. Do you owe money on credit cards or student loans?

2. What kinds of things do you buy with credit cards?

> **Directions:** As you read this article, practice the four-step reading process. Preview the article, and then write on the following lines one or two questions that you would hope to have answered.
>
> ....
>
> ....
>
> ....
>
> ....

As you read, answer the questions in the margins to check your comprehension.

"Escaping the Debt Trap"

BY CORINNE FENNESSY

Many students rely heavily on credit cards to get through college. Some graduates owe thousands of dollars on credit cards in addition to their college loans, digging themselves into a financial hole so deep that they see no escape. Here's how one couple found a way out of the debt trap.

1   Dana was afraid to open her mailbox. She dreaded seeing the envelopes with red warnings stamped "Final Notice" and "Overdue" stabbing at her. Dana took a few deep breaths before opening the bills. Upon opening each one she sunk deeper into depression until she was feeling forlorn and crying.

2   She sank into a funk and pushed the bills aside, thinking, "How can I ever pay all these bills?" She and her boyfriend Kyle barely made enough at their part-time jobs to cover their living and college expenses. She hated the unpaid bills, the calls from collection companies, and the threats from the car leasing company. She felt as if she had a terminal disease with no cure.

3   One bill from a credit card company showed that Kyle had purchased a new phone for himself. She became so enraged that when he came home, she started yelling at him about the bill. He accused her of spending money at her salon every month.

4   Like many couples, Dana and her boyfriend, Kyle, were always fighting about money. They fought over how much the other one spent and what was purchased. Each blamed the other for the desperate financial situation they faced. Dana reasoned that their debt problem was ruining their relationship. Before they had become so deeply in debt, they had been a happy couple. But now, their financial problems were the source of every argument. Dana knew she couldn't go on like this. She loved Kyle, but hated what was happening to their relationship. One day, Dana's girlfriend suggested that she and Kyle go for some counseling—financial counseling.

Why were Dana and Kyle arguing?

Reading 1

5   What they learned from the financial counselor surprised them. The counselor offered a new perspective about money. Instead of focusing on the negative aspect of their debt, he suggested that they should take a holistic approach and learn to manage their money more efficiently. It would mean making sacrifices for a while until they could get back on their feet. They discovered that even though they owed more than their combined income, there was a way for them to climb out of debt and start to save money. Both Dana and Kyle had to learn to become better stewards of their financial resources. The counselor asked if they would be willing to give it a try. Neither of them declined the challenge.

6   First, they had to write down the amounts they owed and all of their expenses, along with the annual percentage rate (APR) on their credit cards. One of their credit cards had an APR of 24% and the other only 15%. Their counselor told them to pay off the high interest credit card by transferring the balance onto their lower interest card, and then closing the high interest credit card account.

7   Next, they looked at how much of their budget was used to pay rent. It was over 36% of their total budget—way too high. Dana and Kyle agreed to look for a cheaper place to live that wouldn't cost more than 25% of their budget but wouldn't leave them sweltering in the summer without air conditioning. It took some shopping, but they finally found a smaller place they liked that was almost half of the rent they were currently paying.

8   Dana had a car loan payment and Kyle had a car lease payment due each month. They decided to keep one car and sell the other. If both of them needed transportation at the same time, they would ask friends or relatives for a ride or take the bus, the subway, or ride a bike. This would save money on car payments, insurance, gas, and repairs.

9   "The first rule of finance is to pay yourself first," the counselor told them. Saving money had always seemed impossible to Dana and Kyle, so the counselor suggested that they let their bank do their saving for them. Each month, their bank would transfer a small amount out of their checking and put it into a savings account. This would help them establish an emergency fund and to save for a down payment on a house. Eventually they would have enough in the fund to cover the cost of a car repair or a dentist's bill so they wouldn't have to keep using their credit card and getting deeper into debt.

10   Their financial counselor suggested that they try going on a "no spending spree" for two weeks. Neither of them would spend any money, except to pay bills, pay rent, or buy food. They were put on a strict budget for food expenses, which meant no eating out or buying prepared foods. They would have to eat dinner at home and make their own lunches and drinks to take to school. To help them spend less at the supermarket, the counselor told them about several websites where they could download coupons, and he suggested buying store brands or buying bulk foods at the local farmers' markets

11   Both Kyle and Dana had expensive cell phone contracts. To reduce their phone charges, they started using the Internet for free long distance calls. They also shopped around and found phone plans with low prepaid monthly fees for unlimited text messages and email, and enough talk minutes each month, saving them over $100 each month.

12   Both of them also agreed to give up spending money on themselves. Dana conceded to do her own hair and nails instead of going to a salon and Kyle agreed

What advice did the financial counselor give Dana and Kyle?

What was the "no spending spree" that Dana and Kyle agreed to do?

145

Reading 1

to give up his daily coffee at Starbucks and drink homemade brew from a thermal mug. They couldn't buy any new clothes, so they dug through their closets to find clothes they hadn't worn in a while or traded some clothes with friends and siblings.

13   Their financial counselor also suggested that they try to find additional income. Dana and Kyle went through all of their possessions to find items they no longer used and they held a yard sale at a friend's house. They also asked friends and family if they had any clothes or items they would like to donate. Not only did the yard sale bring them $257, they had a lot of fun interacting with people who came to buy, and they were able to donate the goods that weren't sold to a local charity. After putting that money into their savings account, they both looked for additional part-time work. Dana began babysitting for neighbors and Kyle started washing and waxing cars for his friends. The extra money helped pay for groceries, gas, and school supplies.

14   Learning to live within their means was not easy. It took a lot of <u>perseverance</u> to stick to a budget. They soon realized that they had been spending money to get immediate gratification instead of waiting until they could really afford the things they wanted. "Buying something new made us feel good for a while," Dana said, "until the bill came in."

15   "It was really hard at first," Kyle admitted, "I wasn't used to saying 'no' to myself for things I really felt I deserved to have. Now I know that much of the stuff I wanted I can actually live without and feel okay about it."

16   For three months, Kyle and Dana didn't go out to movies, restaurants, or clubs. They went to the library to borrow movies to watch at home while sharing a bowl of popcorn. They enjoyed the local parks and joined a campus club to volunteer at a soup kitchen. Instead of going out on weekends, they invited friends over and asked everyone to bring something to eat or drink. They soon found they had more fun and more friends than ever before.

17   After three months of staying on their "no spending spree" and paying down their debt, Kyle and Dana found they actually had some money left over at the end of the month. This was split up into four parts: one part for savings, one part for making additional payments on their credit card, another part for donating to charity, and the fourth part for spending on themselves. Now they can go out once a month to an inexpensive restaurant and not feel guilty.

18   "Getting a special treat at the end of the month means more now because we've had to work hard to earn it," says Dana. "As soon as we pay off our credit card, we're going to start putting those monthly payments into our savings account. We have learned how to manage our money by spending less and saving more. Now that we're saving money, I don't worry about it anymore. We just try to limit our spending to the things we need and not the things we want. I've also learned that there are some things more important than money. I was so focused on our debt that I didn't see what a great guy Kyle is, or how important it is to have friends who care about you. And no matter how poor you think you are you can always spare something for somebody who has less than you. I know that someday we will be able to afford the things we want once we are both working full-time. The lessons we learned have been <u>imprinted</u> on us forever. We'll never be into more debt than we can handle ever again."

Chatzky, Jean "Saving Money During Hard Financial Times." *Reader's Digest Magazine* at www.rd.com.
Hochman, David "My Family's No-Buy Experiment." *Reader's Digest Magazine* at www.rd.com.
"Mission Possibilities" from *Thrivent Magazine,* Fall 2010 Vo. 108 No. 657 at www.thrivent.com.

How did Dana and Kyle change their money management style?

1,562 words divided by .... minutes = ... words per minute.

Reading 1 Thinking About What You Read

It is a good habit to summarize everything you read to strengthen your comprehension.

Directions: Briefly answer the following five questions, and then use this information to write a summary of the article "Escaping the Debt Trap."

1. Describe the subject (who and what)?

....

....

2. Action (what happened?)

....

....

3. How?

....

....

4. When?

....

....

5. Why?

....

....

Use your summary notes to write a two- or three-sentence summary of the article on the lines below. In your own words, describe what the article was about and why the author wrote it.

....

....

....

....

Reading 1 Comprehension Questions

The following questions will help you to recall the main idea and the details of "Escaping the Debt Trap." Review any parts of the article that you need to find the correct answers.

LITERAL COMPREHENSION

1. What is the topic (subject) of this article?

   a. money

   b. saving money

   c. getting out of debt

   d. Kyle and Dana's relationship

MAIN IDEAS

2. What is the main idea of the article? (What is the most general statement that tells the most important point of the article?)

   a. After meeting with a financial counselor, Kyle and Dana learned how to manage their finances and get out of debt.

   b. Dana and Kyle went to see a financial counselor.

   c. Getting out of debt requires perseverance.

   d. You should never go into debt because it can ruin your life.

3. What is the main idea of paragraph 9?

   a. The first rule of finance is to pay yourself first.

   b. Saving money had always seemed impossible to Dana and Kyle, so the counselor suggested that they let their bank do their saving for them.

   c. Each month, their bank would transfer a small amount out of their checking and put it into a savings account.

   d. Eventually they would have enough in the fund to cover the cost of a car repair or a dentist's bill so they wouldn't have to keep using their credit card and getting deeper into debt.

4. What is the main idea of paragraph 13?

   a. Their financial counselor also suggested that they try to find additional income.

   b. Dana and Kyle went through all of their possessions to find items they no longer used and they held a yard sale at a friend's house.

   c. Not only did the yard sale bring them $257, they had a lot of fun interacting with people who came to buy, and they were able to donate the goods that weren't sold to a local charity.

   d. After putting that money into their savings account, they both looked for additional part-time work.

SUPPORTING DETAILS

5. According to the article, Kyle and Dana saved money all the following ways except

   a. transferring their credit card balance to a lower interest card

   b. reducing the cost of their phone plans

c. moving into a cheaper place to live

d. buying all their clothes at a thrift store

6. **What did Dana and Kyle discover after living for three months on a "no spending spree"?**

a. They realized they didn't need to buy things.

b. They were glad to get their credit cards back.

c. They had some money left over to spend.

d. They were no longer in debt.

DRAWING CONCLUSIONS

7. **What did the financial counselor mean when he said, "The first rule of finance is to pay yourself first"?**

a. You should save some money first and use the rest for expenses and debt reduction.

b. You should pay your debts first.

c. You should keep your paycheck and spend it on yourself.

d. You should save your paycheck for yourself.

8. **From reading the article, you can conclude that (choose all that apply):**

a. Dana and Kyle no longer spend money on restaurants and movies.

b. To become debt-free, both partners must be willing to change their attitudes about spending and agree on how to manage their money.

c. People often spend money as a way to satisfy an emotional need.

d. People should not use credit cards.

VOCABULARY IN CONTEXT

Using context clues and word part clues, determine the best meaning for the underlined words in each of these sentences. If necessary, use a dictionary.

9. They realized that they had been spending money to get immediate <u>gratification</u> instead of waiting until they could really afford the things they wanted.

a. satisfaction

b. response

c. recognition

d. investment

10. Instead of focusing on the negative <u>aspect</u> of their debt, he suggested that they should take a holistic approach and learn to manage their money more efficiently.

a. respect

b. side

c. discouraging

d. reward

Reading 1 Vocabulary Practice

Use the vocabulary words from the Word Bank to complete the following sentences. Write the words into the blanks provided.

> **WORD BANK**
>
> holistic   terminal   sweltering   declined   forlorn
> perseverance   funk   perspective   steward   imprinted

1. If you apply for a loan and you are .... , you can apply for one at another bank or credit union.

2. If you have the right .... about money, you will have a healthy financial outlook.

3. Instead of trying to write every little detail about the book in your report, just write a more .... summary of the entire novel.

4. The day my team won the championship will be .... in my memory forever.

5. Mrs. Jones was diagnosed with a .... disease, but her treatment was so successful that she is now expected to live a long life.

6. On a(n) .... day like today, the best thing to do is to stay in a cool, air-conditioned room, or go swimming.

7. No one thought Ming would be able to finish college and become an artist, but her hard work and .... paid off, and now she works as an illustrator.

8. A small boy who looked very .... asked me if I had seen his lost puppy.

9. Dave got into a serious .... after his girlfriend left him for another guy.

10. Because Tina is too young to manage her inheritance, her uncle is her financial .... until she reaches the age of 18.

Reading 1 — Questions for Writing and Discussion

Review any parts of the article you need to answer the following questions.

1. What are some things Dana and Kyle learned from their experience?

2. How was Dana's attitude about money different at the end of the story from the beginning, and why do you think she changed?

3. What new perspectives about money did the financial counselor bring to Dana and Kyle?

4. Dana says she learned that some things are more important than money. What do you think some of those things are?

5. Kyle and Dana used to buy things because it was enjoyable. What other ways did they discover how to enjoy themselves that didn't cost money?

Reading 1 Vocabulary Practice—Speed Quiz

DIRECTIONS: *The object of the game is to be the team with the most matched sets of cards.*

1.

Using an index card of 1/4 sheet of paper, copy **one** of the numbered items from the lists below. Your instructor will inform you about which item(s) to copy onto the card(s). (Some students may have to make more than one card to get all 30 cards made.) Label the word cards with a "W" and the definition cards with a "D" as illustrated below.

2.

There are three matching cards for each set: the vocabulary word card, the definition card, and the sentence card. When your instructor tells you to begin, in your teams, match as many sets of 3 cards as you can, matching the word with its definition and the sentence it completes. With the remaining cards that do not match any of your sets, trade cards with other teams.

3.

Lay out the cards into rows as illustrated on the right.

4.

When time is called, the team with the most correctly matched sets of cards wins.

| W sweltering | D very hot | It was such a _____ day, our ice cream cones quickly melted |

W Cards (Words)	**D Cards (Definitions)**	**Sentence Cards**
1. holistic	11. turned down	21. It is such a(n) _____ day that I think I would rather swim than go running.
2. terminal	12. determination	22. The _____-looking dog poked his nose through the fence and whined for attention.
3. sweltering	13. referring to the whole thing	23. If you have enough _____, you can succeed at just about anything.
4. declined	14. viewpoint	24. A hospice is a care center for patients with _____ illnesses.
5. forlorn	15. caretaker	25. In _____ medicine, they treat the whole body instead of just one part.
6. perseverance	16. sad, pitiful	26. Serving in the military during a war gave Juan a new _____ on life.
7. perspective	17. final, ending, or fatal	27. I offered to buy James a new basketball, but he _____ my offer.
8. steward	18. impressed upon	28. I promised my brother that I would be a good _____ of his new car if he let me borrow it for a few days.
9. imprinted	19. depressed mood	29. Keisha fell into a(n) _____ after she lost her dream job.
10. funk	20. very hot	30. The memory of 9-11 will be _____ on me as long as I live.

Reading 2 Vocabulary Preview

The following vocabulary words are from the article "Taryn Rose: Taking a Risk on Shoes." With a partner or in a team, choose the best meaning of the underlined words in the following sentences. Use context clues (LEADS), word part clues, and parts of speech to help you figure out the meanings.

1. When Maria's mother needed a hip replacement, it was performed by an orthopedic (or-tho-PEA-dik) surgeon.

   a. the special medical area of the brain

   b. the special medical area of the skeleton

   c. the special medical area of dental surgery

   d. highly skilled

2. That dress is so fashionable that you look absolutely chic (sheek) in it!

   a. heavy

   b. skinny

   c. stylish

   d. terrible

3. During the first six months after we opened our new restaurant, it was such grueling (GROOL-ing) work that I came home exhausted every night.

   a. very difficult

   b. short

   c. cruel

   d. simple

4. My boyfriend is in medical school, and he must apply for a fellowship (FELL-o-ship) because he can't afford to pay the tuition fees.

   a. a group of people at a social event

   b. partners

   c. a grant for financial aid

   d. guardian

5. At the sound of the ship's horn, the passengers began to embark (em-BARK) onto the ship.

   a. get off

   b. get on board

   c. pay their way

   d. resist

Reading 2

6. Before deciding to go into business, it is important to get feedback from <u>focus groups</u> (FO-cus groups) to find out if people think your idea is valuable.

   a. photographers

   b. a group of people at a reunion

   c. a group starting a business

   d. a group who answers questions about a new product or service

7. To reach <u>potential</u> (po-TEN-shel) buyers, Jasmine sent out flyers advertising her new makeup kits.

   a. possible

   b. late

   c. sellers

   d. wealthy

8. In American Government class, we learned that the <u>demographics</u> (dem-o-GRAF-iks) of the country show that the majority of citizens are mostly older baby boomers—people over the age of 55.

   a. candidates

   b. government

   c. population data

   d. photos for magazines

9. In the United States, the smallest <u>segment</u> (SEG-ment) of the work force consists of Asians and Pacific Islanders.

   a. population

   b. section or part

   c. to break up

   d. people

10. Although I try to watch my diet, I sometimes <u>indulge</u> (in-DULJ) in a hot fudge sundae.

    a. to forgive

    b. to refuse

    c. to give in to

    d. eat

Reading 2 What Do You Already Know?

1. What are your favorite styles or types of clothes or shoes? What brands of clothing or shoes do you like?
2. Have you ever taken a risk to do something in which you believed you would succeed? Describe the situation.

> **Directions:** As you read this article, practice the four-step reading process. Preview the article, and then write on the following lines one or two questions that you would hope to have answered.
>
> ....
>
> ....
>
> ....
>
> ....

As you read, answer the questions in the margins to check your comprehension.

"Taryn Rose: Taking a Risk on Shoes"

BY MARIA BARTIROMO

Adapted from "Dreamers: The Risk Taker," by Maria Bartiromo. *Reader's Digest* (www.rd.com, July 2008).

After graduating from college, Taryn Rose went on to do her residency as an orthopedic surgeon. She wanted to change her career path but was afraid of failure. It would mean taking risks and starting all over again. But she followed her heart's desire, and it led her to a new and exciting future.

MADE FOR WALKING

1 After working 36-hour shifts as a resident in <u>orthopedic</u> surgery, Taryn Rose knew a lot about sore feet. But unlike most of her colleagues, she turned her pain into profit: Today she is CEO of Taryn Rose International, a $28 million company that makes <u>chic</u> and comfortable shoes.

2 A Vietnamese refugee who came to the United States when she was eight, Rose assumed she'd follow in the footsteps of her physician father. For a while, she did, getting her medical degree from the University of Southern California and choosing a <u>grueling</u> training in orthopedic surgery.

155

Reading 2

Why did Taryn Rose want to give up her career as a doctor?

3   But when the time came to apply for post-residential <u>fellowships</u>, Rose found her heart was no longer in medicine. "I felt like a part of me, the part that loves to learn new things, that likes adventure, would be dying."

4   Rose had always loved shoes, especially high heels. When her fellow residents headed home after long hours on their feet, "I would make my way to Neiman Marcus for some retail therapy," she says. What if, she wondered, she gave up her career to learn how to make stylish shoes that could stand up to a day's work?

5   Rose realized the only thing stopping her was her "fear of failure. I could hear my friends and family saying, 'Why did you leave a secure job?' If I failed, would I be okay facing them? And I thought, 'So what? I can go back to do a fellowship.' I started to accept that it would be okay to say, 'I failed, but I tried.' Once I was comfortable with that idea, the fear dissolved. I realized I feared regret more than failure. And after you <u>embark</u> on the path you choose, there is nothing acceptable but success."

6   But first, Rose had to learn the shoe business. "The great thing about a medical education is that it teaches you how to learn," she says, "because every case and every patient is different." Rose had become friends with a salesclerk who knew people in the shoe industry in Italy. She made the introduction and headed off to Milan, Italy, to learn how to make shoes.

7   She didn't have the money to conduct <u>focus groups</u> on her <u>potential</u> market. "My research was done sitting on the couch at Neiman Marcus, asking women what they wanted from shoes. Then I studied the <u>demographics</u>. Baby boomers are the largest <u>segment</u> of the population; they have the most money and their feet are going to hurt as they age."

No Regrets

How did her college education help her in learning how to start a business?

8   With the data to back her up, Rose got a $200,000 loan from the Small Business Administration in 1998. She wore out a lot of her own shoe leather showing samples to independent shoe stores and buyers at upscale department stores.

9   "Someone told me it costs $10 million to start a new brand," Rose says. She didn't have $10 million, but she had a good story, and it got picked up by a lot of magazines. Taryn Rose International was on its way. "I did everything at the beginning: the designing, the marketing, the accounts receivable," Rose recalls. "There were moments when I was so frustrated, I remember crying. The client is saying, 'Where are my shoes?' The vendor is saying, 'Where is my payment?' But when you're faced with saving a patient, you don't think about giving up."

Reading 2

10   Her natural sense of optimism also helped. "If someone tells me we're $200,000 short of our goal, I'll say, 'Let's sit down and see how we can bring up those numbers.'"

11   Handmade in Italy of the finest leathers, the shoes are designed for comfort, for women and men. They range from $200 to $400 a pair. Rose makes sure they're also available through discount catalogs and websites as well as her warehouse sale. "My family started out in this country with nothing, so I don't have a problem selling to a discount catalog. Today's discount catalog customer may one day be a luxury customer."

How did Taryn Rose deal with problems in the business?

12   Now that she can indulge her love of shoes, Rose owns about 200 pairs and, she adds, "a warehouse of 20,000 more that I can borrow from at any time!"

13   Rose has no regrets about leaving medicine. "What I'm doing is not all that different from what I was doing as a physician. The goal is the same, to relieve pain. A former professor told me, 'You're helping hundreds of thousands of people with your shoes. As a surgeon, you would have helped only the few who made it to your office. You're having a much greater effect.'"

14   Looking back, Rose admits she caught a couple of lucky breaks. "To me, luck is about being prepared for those opportunities that come knocking. You have to have an open mind, the right skills, and all your senses working to see what opportunities present themselves. Luck can open the door, but you still have to walk through it." Preferably, in a pair of good-looking, great-feeling shoes.

What advice does Taryn offer to someone starting a business?

15   It's barely eight years since Rose, now 40, started her business. The shoes can be found in more than 220 stores worldwide. There are four boutiques in the United States and one in Paris, France. The business has been so successful that she has expanded her product line by adding handbags. Taryn Rose International footwear boutiques are found in Beverly Hills; New York; Las Vegas; San Jose; and Seoul, Korea. Her products are also sold in hundreds of department stores, including Neiman Marcus, Bloomingdale's, SAKS Fifth Avenue, Nordstrom, Lord & Taylor, and Harrods of London as well as online at tarynrose. com. Taryn Rose International has become a successful name brand in women's fashion around the world.

1,004 words divided by _____ minutes = _____ words per minute

Reading 2 Thinking About What You Read

It is a good habit to summarize everything you read to strengthen your comprehension.

> Directions: On the following lines, write a two- or three-sentence summary of the article. "Taryn Rose: Taking a Risk on Shoes." In your own words, describe what the article was about and why the author wrote it.
>
> ....
>
> ....
>
> ....
>
> ....

Comprehension Questions

The following questions will help you to recall the main idea and the details of "Taryn Rose: Taking a Risk on Shoes." Review any parts of the article that you need to find the correct answers.

LITERAL
COMPREHENSION

1. **What is the topic of this article?**

   a. the shoe business   **c.** an orthopedic surgeon

   b. Taryn Rose Shoes   **d.** Taryn Rose

MAIN IDEAS

2. **What is the main idea of the article?**

   a. To be successful, you need to take risks.

   b. Taryn Rose left her career as a doctor to start a successful shoe company.

   c. After working 36-hour shifts as a resident in orthopedic surgery, Taryn Rose knew a lot about sore feet.

   d. Luck can open the door, but you still have to walk through it.

3. **What is the topic sentence of paragraph 13?**

   a. Rose has no regrets about leaving medicine.

   b. The goal is the same, to relieve pain.

   c. You're helping hundreds of thousands of people with your shoes.

   d. You're having a much greater effect.

4. **What is the topic sentence of paragraph 15?**

   a. It's barely eight years since Rose, now 40, started her business.

   b. There are four boutiques in the United States and one in Paris, France.

   c. The business has been so successful that she has expanded her product line by adding handbags.

   d. Taryn Rose International has become a successful name brand in women's fashion around the world.

SUPPORTING DETAILS

5. According to the article, when Taryn Rose wanted to give up medicine to start her own company, what was stopping her at first?

   a. Her parents forbid her to quit her career as a doctor.

   b. She didn't have the money needed to start a business.

   c. She was afraid of failing.

   d. She didn't know how to start a business.

6. According to the article, Taryn Rose has also started to sell:

   a. luggage

   b. hats

   c. briefcases

   d. handbags

7. According to Taryn Rose, what does having "luck" mean?

   a. when things just all seem to go in your favor

   b. when someone offers you a lot of money to start your business

   c. when you have prepared yourself for opportunities with an open mind and the right skills

   d. when customers really want what you have to offer

DRAWING CONCLUSIONS

8. What does Taryn Rose mean when she says, "Luck can open the door, but you still have to walk through it"?

   a. You can't be lucky all the time.

   b. You may get lucky and get an opportunity, but you still have to do the work to be successful.

   c. You can't expect luck to help you.

   d. If a door opens for you, you will be successful.

VOCABULARY IN CONTEXT

Using context clues and word part clues, determine the best meaning for the underlined word in each of these sentences. If necessary, use a dictionary.

9. Her natural sense of <u>optimism</u> also helped. "If someone tells me we're $200,000 short of our goal, I'll say, 'Let's sit down and see how we can bring up those numbers'" (paragraph 10).

   a. positive thinking

   b. direction

   c. negative thinking

   d. confusion

10. "Luck can open the door, but you still have to walk through it. <u>Preferably</u>, in a pair of good-looking, great-feeling shoes" (paragraph 14).

   a. if at all possible

   b. probably

   c. for certain

   d. never

Reading 2 Vocabulary Practice

Use the vocabulary words from the Word Bank to complete the following sentences. Write the words into the blanks provided.

WORD BANK

| orthopedic | chic | grueling | fellowship | segment |
| embark | focus groups | potential | demographics | indulge |

1. When the breakfast food company created its newest cereal product, it hired several .... to gather feedback about the product.

2. Taking six classes proved to be too .... for Nadia, so she dropped one class.

3. A(n) .... surgeon told me I needed to have surgery on my foot after it was broken during football practice.

4. All of the .... candidates for student government president first had to gather signatures before they could be put on the ballot.

5. Samantha's new hairstyle looks so .... that I'm sure her boyfriend will like it.

6. Our travel guide told us that we were about to .... on the biggest and newest cruise ship ever built.

7. According to the .... of this state, there should be more baby boomers employed than people in younger age groups.

8. Even though Gary is on a strict diet, he still likes to .... in eating a bowl of popcorn on the weekends while watching a game on TV.

9. Drug abuse has invaded every .... of our society—the poor, the middle class, and the wealthy.

10. If Carlo is granted a(n) .... by the university, he will enter the graduate program and study finance.

Reading 2 **Questions for Writing and Discussion**

Review any parts of the article you need to answer the following questions.

1. When did Taryn know that being an orthopedic doctor was not the right career for her?

2. When Taryn Rose decided she wanted to make shoes for a living, she had to overcome her fears. What were these fears and how did she overcome them?

3. Even though she started her shoe business from scratch, Taryn Rose became very successful. How do you think she became so successful? What lessons can you learn from her?

4. Do you think her time spent learning to become a doctor was a waste of time for Taryn Rose, or do you think it was useful to her in her career as a business woman?

5. What kind of business would you be interested in operating? Describe it.

Reading 2 Vocabulary Practice—Team Password

Directions: The object of this game is to correctly guess the word in three tries.

List A | List B

List A	List B
For 3 pts: vertebrae For 2 pts: ankles and knees For 1 pt: having to do with bones	For 3 pts: evening gown For 2 pts: high-heel shoes For 1 pt: very stylish
For 3 pts: final exams For 2 pts: digging a deep hole For 1 pt: very difficult work	For 3 pts: college _____ For 2 pts: professor's assistant For 1 pt: a grant for financial aid
For 3 pts: aircraft For 2 pts: train station For 1 pt: to get on board	For 3 pts: marketing For 2 pts: product survey For 1 pt: it gives feedback about a new product or service
For 3 pts: a good business idea has it For 2 pts: not actual For 1 pt: possible	For 3 pts: minorities For 2 pts: senior citizens For 1 pt: population data
For 3 pts: citrus fruit has it For 2 pts: in geometry, a line_____ For 1 pt: section or part	For 3 pts: shopping spree For 2 pts: eating chocolate cheesecake For 1 pt: to give in to

1.

Divide the team into two opposing teams, or play one team against another.

2.

Each team will take one list of clues, list A or list B. These can either be torn out of the book or copied onto paper. You may only have one list when you begin the game.

3.

Decide which team will go first. A member of that team will read the first clue to the other team. The other team has 15 seconds to guess the word. There are three clues on each card: the first two are hints; the third clue is the definition. If team members guess the word correctly with only the first clue, they get three points. If they need the second clue to guess the word, they get two points. If they guess it on the third clue, they get one point. If they cannot guess the word after all clues have been given, no points are awarded, and the play goes to the opposing team, who will read its first clue.

4.

The correct answers are found in the instructor's edition. After all the clues have been read, the team with the highest score wins.

5.

When a team correctly identifies a word, the team sets aside that card and draws a new card from the pile, which it will use on its next turn.

6.

Continue playing until all the cards are played or time is called. The team with the most points wins.

WORD LIST
If you decide to use this word list, leave it face up on the table as you are playing:

indulge   segment   grueling   demographics
potential   embark   fellowship   focus group
orthopedic   chic

Adam Metzinger,
Trust Administrator

What is your career, and how did you become interested in it?

I work as a trust administrator for a large financial institution in the Global Trust Department. We handle some of the financial deals for governments or large corporations. For example, if a government or corporation wanted to fund a large project like building a bridge or a power plant, the financial deal would be handled by our department.

What is your training and education?

I earned my bachelor's degree in sociology and criminal justice, and then my master's in business administration.

Did you ever consider quitting when you were in college?

Not really. Some courses were harder than others. While I was doing an internship for my bachelor's degree, I worked as a salesman for a brokerage firm on Wall Street. I found that I wasn't really interested in being a salesman, so I learned something important from that, plus I gained the experience in business that I needed to get this job.

What do you like about your job?

I enjoy lots of things, especially the variety of work that I do. I move around some very large sums of money, which are used for many different purposes all around the world. Each project is unique, and I get to do business on an international scale.

What do you dislike about your job?

I have no dislikes, but working with huge sums of money carries a lot of responsibility, so I have to read everything very carefully, looking at every detail in the contracts.

If you could give college students one piece of advice, what would it be?

My best advice is, even if you do nothing else, go to class. Your professor will get to know you, and you can learn a lot just by being there.

VIEWPOINT: Illegal Immigration

Read the following letters to the editor about the guest-worker program and then answer the questions that follow.

Dear Editor:

I think the guest-worker program to allow immigrants into our country to work should not be instituted. Under this program, foreign workers would be given a temporary pass that would allow them to come here and work. Many other people who want to come into the country have been waiting years and paying thousands of dollars in applications and fees to come here legally. Is it fair to allow temporary workers to get in sooner and cheaper? Who is going to keep track of them and make sure they leave when their time is up? I think the guest-worker program is a bad idea. It will only encourage more temporary immigrants to come here.

Signed,

Citizen Taxpayer

Dear Editor:

The guest-worker program is a great idea. It would allow immigrants to enter the country legally to earn a wage. Their willingness to work for the minimum wage helps to lower the cost of goods and services by keeping prices low. This will keep business and manufacturing here instead of sending work overseas. That's good for the country's economy. The guest-worker program would reduce the number of people trying to enter the country illegally. It would lessen the need for border patrol agents and costly resources that are needed to keep illegal aliens out of the country. Also, we would know who is applying to enter the country, and we could screen out any unwanted individuals. The guest-worker program is a good program for everyone—citizens and immigrants.

Signed,

Liberty for All

Critical Thinking

1. A *point of view* is the author's opinion about a topic. To find the author's point of view, ask yourself, "How does this author feel about this issue?" What is the author's point of view about the guest-worker program in the first letter?

   ....

   ....

2. What is the author's point of view about the guest-worker program in the second letter?

   ....

   ....

   ....

3. Which letter do you agree with, and why?

   ....

   ....

   ....

4. What could be the consequences of allowing immigrants to come into the country to live and work temporarily?

   ....

   ....

5. What could be the consequences of not allowing illegal immigrants to come into the country to live and work temporarily?

   ....

WRITE YOUR THOUGHTS

Write a letter to the editor stating your own feelings about the guest-worker program. What do you think should be done with illegal immigrants? Use a separate sheet of paper.

CREDIT CARD AGREEMENT

If you apply for a credit card with a bank or other financial institution, you should read the terms of the credit card agreement carefully. The following is an excerpt (part) of a credit card agreement. Use the four-step reading process as you read, and then answer the questions that follow to check your comprehension. Preview the selection first, and then read it and answer the questions that follow with your team.

TERMS AND CONDITIONS

FEES: We may charge your account for the following fees. The application and payment of a fee will not release you from responsibility of the action which caused the fees.

LATE PAYMENT. We may charge a $25.00 late fee to your account if you do not pay at least the minimum payment by the stated due date. In addition to the late fee, we will cancel any temporary low rate offers if your payment is late more than one billing cycle during the promotion. We will charge an additional late fee of 10% of your balance for each billing cycle that your account is past due.

OVER THE LIMIT. If you go over your credit limit or cash advance limit by $50.00 or more, we will add an additional $30 Over the Limit fee to your account for each billing cycle that you remain over your credit limit.

RETURNED PAYMENT. If you make a payment on your account with a check from some other financial institution and that check is not honored by the financial institution on which it is drawn, you will be charged a fee of $35.00

RETURNED CHECK. If you write a check from your account and that check is not honored because your account is in default or over the limit, we will charge you a fee of $35.00

CASH ADVANCE FEE. An additional finance charge will be added to your account each time you obtain a cash advance. This additional finance charge will be 8% of the amount of the cash advance with a maximum of $30.00. Internet transactions are exempt from the cash advance fee

ENTIRE BALANCE DUE: If you fail to make a required payment when due or default on any other term in this agreement, we can declare the entire balance of your account due and payable at once without notice. We can also demand complete immediate payment if you make any false or misleading statement on your application or if you die or file for bankruptcy.

COLLECTION COSTS: To the extent permitted by applicable law, you agree to pay all costs and disbursements, including reasonable attorney fees, incurred by us in legal proceedings to collect or enforce your indebtedness.

Questions

1. Which of the following will not happen if you do not make a minimum payment by the date due?

   a. You will be charged a $35 late fee.

   b. The company will cancel any temporary low-rate offers if the payment is late more than one billing cycle during the promotion.

   c. The company will allow you to make an additional payment the following month with no penalty.

   d. The company will charge an additional late fee of 10% of the balance for each billing cycle that the account is past due.

2. Identify the following statement as true or false. If it is false, correct it to make it true: For each billing cycle that you charge an amount $50 or more over your credit limit, the company will charge you a $50 fee.

   a. True   b. False

   ....

   ....

3. For which of the following will you be charged a $35 fee? (Choose all that apply.)

   a. a check written from another bank that is not honored by this credit card company

   b. not paying the minimum amount by the due date

   c. if a check is returned because your account is in default or over the limit

   d. each time you make a cash advance

4. Identify the following statement as true or false. If you give false or misleading information on your credit card application, or if you declare bankruptcy, you will be required to pay the entire account balance immediately.

   a. True   b. False

5. Identify the following statement as true or false. If your account is not paid when due and you face legal action because of this, you will be responsible to pay all fees that are charged by the attorneys or the collection agencies.

   a. True   b. False

BUILDING VOCABULARY

Throughout this course, you will be introduced to word parts that make up many words in the English language. Study the following word parts, and then answer the questions that follow.

Prefixes
in- *into*
de- *away; reverse*

Roots
duct- *to bring, to take*
cis- *to cut*

Suffixes
-tion, -sion *action, state of*
-ive- *a state or quality*

What English words can you create from these word parts?

....

....

....

....

....

Using a dictionary, look up the meanings of any of the words you wrote that you can't define. Use one of the words you wrote in a sentence that reveals its meaning with a context clue:

....

....

....

TEXTBOOK GRAPHIC AIDS

In business, operations managers often use program evaluation and review technique (PERT) charts for complex schedules. These charts diagram the activities required to produce a good, specify the time required to perform each activity in the process, and organize activities in the most efficient sequence. The following is a PERT diagram showing the process for producing one "hiker" bear at Vermont Teddy Bear. Study the diagram, and then answer the questions that follow.

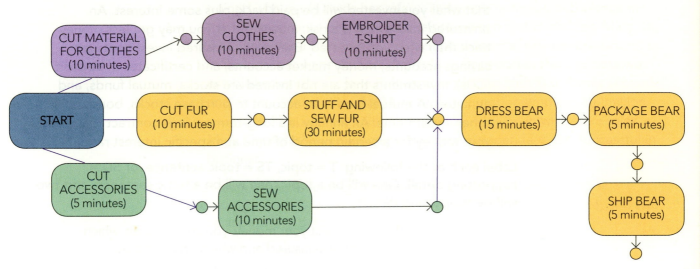

(From *Exploring Business* by Karen Collins. Copyright © 2008 by Karen Collins. Reprinted by permission of the author.)

1. **What is the topic of this chart?**
   a. children's toys
   b. manufacturing stuffed animals
   c. PERT chart for making a Vermont Teddy Bear
   d. sewing

2. **What does PERT stand for?**
   a. package, export, receive, and transport
   b. program evaluation and review technique
   c. preview examples and revise technology
   d. program explanation and review technique

3. **Which stage of the process takes the most time?**
   a. cutting material for clothes
   b. cutting accessories
   c. dressing the bear
   d. stuffing and sewing the fur

4. **Which three steps can occur all at the same time?**
   a. cut material for clothes, cut fur, cut accessories
   b. sew clothes, embroider shirt, stuff and sew fur
   c. cut accessories, sew accessories, dress bear
   d. dress bear, package bear, ship bear

5. **For the purple portion of the assembly line, what is the total time needed to complete the operations?**
   a. 10 minutes
   b. 45 minutes
   c. 30 minutes
   d. one hour

CHAPTER REVIEW PRACTICE #3

Read the following paragraph. Circle the topic, and underline the topic sentence. Then, complete the exercises that follow.

After your insured property has been damaged or stolen, you may make a claim with your insurance company. The insurance company conducts an investigation, and, if your claim is approved, you will be paid for a repair or complete replacement. Insurance companies hire specialists to conduct these investigations. An insurance investigator is a person who examines all the evidence on a claim and reports his or her findings to the insurance company. Insurance investigators do much of the same work as law enforcement investigators and may also be called to testify in court during a lawsuit. The salaries of insurance investigators vary depending on the company they work for and the area in which they specialize. Most insurance investigators have some college or technical school education.

Label each of the following T: = topic, TS = topic sentence, or SD = supporting detail. One will be a topic, one will be a topic sentence, and two will be supporting details.

1. .... An insurance investigator is a person who examines all the evidence on a claim and reports his or her findings to the insurance company.

2. .... Insurance investigators

3. .... Insurance investigators do much of the same work as law enforcement investigators and may also be called to testify in court during a lawsuit.

4. .... Most insurance investigators have some college or technical school education.

5. Identify the meaning of the underlined word in the following sentence: The salaries of insurance investigators <u>vary</u> depending on the company they work for and the area in which they are most informed.

   a. are high

   b. are different

   c. are unimportant

   d. individual

TEXTBOOK PRACTICE

Preview the following paragraphs, then read actively and answer the questions.

Why Do Businesses Fail?

Why do more than half of all new small businesses go out of business within the first five years? And why do one-third of all new businesses go out of business within the first two years? There are many reasons why most new businesses do not make it, and often it is a combination of things that cause them to fail. First, if the business idea was not a good one to begin with, it has a poor chance of success. By doing a little research to find out what people think about your idea first, you can avoid wasting time and money on an idea that won't succeed. The second most common reason is that going into business always takes more start-up capital than people think it will. They underestimate how much they will need to keep going during the first few years. Third, many new business owners have no experience in running a business. The best way to learn is to first take an interim job as a manager in the same business and gain some knowledge of how to avoid mistakes. And fourth, sometimes growing too fast can cause a company to fail. When the sales orders keep coming, and there is not enough stock to fill them or employees to do the job, customers become unhappy.

(From *Exploring Business* by Karen Collins. Copyright © 2008 by Karen Collins. Reprinted by permission of the author.)

Label each of the following: T = topic, TS = topic sentence, or SD = supporting detail. One will be a topic, one will be a topic sentence, and two will be supporting details.

1. .... The second most common reason is that going into business always takes more start-up capital than people think it will.

2. .... Reasons why new businesses do not make it

3. .... There are many reasons why most new businesses do not make it, and often it is a combination of things that cause them to fail.

4. .... First, if the business idea was not a good one to begin with, it has a poor chance of success.

5. Identify the meaning of the underlined word in the following sentence: The best way to learn is to first take an <u>interim</u> job as a manager in the same business and gain some knowledge of how to avoid mistakes.

   a. intern's

   b. first

   c. high-paying

   d. temporary

STUDY SKILL CHAPTER REVIEW

You can make an effective study guide using a sheet of notebook paper.

1.
Starting with the bottom, fold up your notebook paper four times, about every five lines, until you have just the top portion of your paper showing.

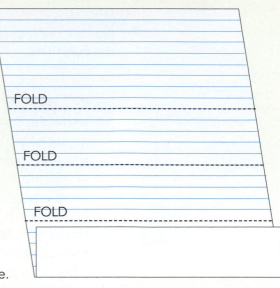

FOLD

FOLD

FOLD

2.
Write a review question on the top line.

QUESTION #1: What is a topic?

Question 1

Answer 1

Question 2

3.
Unfold the paper once, and write the answer to the question on the lines below the fold. Beneath that, write question #2.

4.
Each time you unfold the paper, write the answer to the question before it and the next question. For example, on the next unfolding, you'd write the answer to question #2 and then write question #3 below it. Continue using both sides of the paper.

5.
After you have created your study guide, read the questions one at a time, giving the answer, and then check your answer by unfolding the paper. Keep the study guide handy, in your purse or pocket, so you can review it often

Create a study guide for Chapter 4 by copying the following questions on your folded notebook paper and looking up the answers in this chapter.

QUESTION #1: What is a topic?

#1 Answer:

Question #2: What is a main idea?

#2 Answer:

Question #3: What is a topic sentence?

#3 Answer:

Question #4: How do you check to determine if you have found the topic sentence?

#4 Answer:

Question #5: Where are topic sentences found in a paragraph?

#5 Answer:

Make up some of your own questions and answers for the back of the paper.

READING LAB ASSIGNMENTS

STATED MAIN IDEA

1. Go online to MyReadingLab and click on the Study Plan tab. Do the practices and tests for Stated Main Idea.

COMPREHENSION IMPROVEMENT

2. Go online to MyReadingLab and click on the Reading Level tab. Choose a story to read, and then answer the questions that follow.

SKILL APPLICATION

3. Look at the list of learning objectives at the beginning of the chapter. What applications could these have in your career or in real life? List some ways that you will be able to use the skills taught in this chapter. For example, you can find the topic and main idea in a business report for your job. In what other ways can this skill be used?

CAREER EXPLORATION

4. To find out more about a specific business career, go online to www.bls.gov/oco and search for an occupation. This site will tell you what the job is like, what the outlook is for employment, and current salary and educational requirements. Print the article, and then preview, read, highlight, and annotate it.

LEARNING REFLECTION

Think about the skills and concepts presented in this chapter. What have you learned in this chapter that will help your reading comprehension and enable you to do well in college? Which learning strategy helped you the most in your learning?

....

....

....

....

....

....

....

SELF-EVALUATION CHECKLIST

Rate yourself on the following items, using the following scale:

1 = strongly disagree
2 = disagree
3 = neither agree nor disagree
4 = agree
5 = strongly agree

1. I completed all of the assigned work on time. ....

2. I understand all the concepts in this chapter. ....

3. I contributed to teamwork and class discussions. ....

4. I completed all of the assigned lab work on time. ....

5. I came to class on time. ....

6. I attended class every day. ....

7. I studied for any quizzes or tests we had for this chapter. ....

8. I asked questions when I didn't understand something. ....

9. I checked my comprehension during reading. ....

10. I know what is expected of me in the coming week. ....

For support in meeting this chapter's objectives, go to the Study Plan in MyReadingLab and select Stated Main Ideas. Read and view the resources in the Review Materials section, and then complete the Recall, Apply, and Write exercises in the Activities section. Check your results by clicking on Gradebook.

STUDY SKILL: TEST TAKING

As you read the following section on test taking, practice the four-step reading process:

STEP 1 Preview → **STEP 2** Read actively → **STEP 3** Highlight and annotate → **STEP 4** Review

Many students suffer from test anxiety and become so stressed that they cannot recall the information they need to answer questions correctly. There are many stress-relieving techniques that can help, such as taking deep breaths, or visualizing your success on the test. Positive self-talk is an important part of reducing stress. Reminding yourself that you know the material and can answer the questions correctly is much better than thinking that you are doomed to fail even before you start. Using alcohol or other "helpers" will only worsen your brain's ability to think clearly.

IMPORTANT TIPS FOR TEST TAKING

Prepare *Being prepared means STUDYING*

Maybe in the past you have studied and did not see results. The reason could be the *way* that you studied. Here are some tips to help you prepare:

- **Prepare for the test by taking good notes.** Keep your notebook up to date, and use any prepared notes from the instructor.

- **Use a variety of methods to study.** If you know your learning style, you can use particular study methods that match your style. Try using flash cards, voice recordings, outlines, question-and-answer cards, diagrams, maps, and other aids to find what works best for you.

- **Study every day, even if it's only for 20 minutes.** Short study times of 15 to 20 minutes each day for a week are much more effective than 2 hour sessions.

- **Divide the material into sections.** Study one section each day, and review the previous sections afterward because your brain remembers the first thing you learn the best.

- **Know when the test will be given.** You can't do your best when the test comes as a surprise.

- **Know what will be on the test and the format.** (essay, objective, true-false, etc.)

- **Form a study group to ask each other questions.** Split up the chapter so each person is responsible for teaching and reviewing one part with the group.

- **For application courses such as math, reading, or English make sure you know the rules, formulas, and procedures.** *Use what you have been taught to do.*

STUDY TIPS

- **If you find yourself getting sleepy while studying,** take a five-minute break to get a drink of water and walk around. Do some exercises to get your blood circulating and add more oxygen into your blood.

- **Take advantage of any free tutoring** services available at your school. Many colleges have free tutoring services, and you only need to ask for an appointment. Ask your instructor or go online to your school's Web site to find tutoring.

EFFECTIVE LEARNING

There are two things you need to do before you can learn effectively. First, you must correctly understand the material; it must *make sense to you*. Second, the learning must have meaning for you.* Think of ways that you can use the information or how you can apply it to situations in your own life.

THE DAY BEFORE THE TEST

Get your materials ready the day before the test. If you need a #2 pencil, a pen, a good eraser, an electronic scanning answer sheet, or a composition booklet, don't wait until the test starts to find out that you don't have them.

THE DAY OF THE TEST

Testing day begins the night before. ALWAYS get a good night's rest and eat a nutritious breakfast. Water, protein, and glucose (a type of sugar found in fruit) are all important brain fuel. Drinks with excessive amounts of caffeine can cause your thinking to become unfocused. Leave early for the test. Do a brief review of the material while waiting to start, but don't start studying new information. Concentrate on what you feel you know already.

AT THE TEST

Read through the questions before you begin, paying close attention to the instructions. Underline the verbs that tell you what you must do, such as "explain," "define," "give an example," "tell how," "give reasons," etc. Also note how many parts there are to each question. If there are two parts, you must answer both parts to get full credit. Find out whether you must answer in pencil or in ink and if you can write on both sides of the paper.

EXAMPLE

"Explain four causes of the Civil War, and give five effects of the War."

Note the word "explain." That does not mean you can just list the causes; it means you must provide specific details about them

Notice how many items you must answer. Some directions tell you to answer all of the questions, while others allow you to choose a certain number.

Note how many points each section is worth so you can concentrate on the questions worth the most points. Be aware of how much time you have to complete the test, and don't spend excessive time on one question.

- **Never change an answer unless you are *sure* that the answer you have is wrong.** Usually your first choice is correct. Before you hand in your paper, go over it again to make sure you answered every single question that you were supposed to answer.
- **Leave no blanks.** If you're having a hard time finding the correct answer, eliminate the two least correct answer choices and then make an educated guess based on factual information or logical reasoning. Leaving a question blank will guarantee a wrong answer, but if you guess by choosing between two answers, you have a 50% chance of getting it right.
- **Be sure you leave no stray marks or smudges on electronic-scoring answer sheets.**

*Adapted from David A. Sousa, *How the Brain Learns*. Thousand Oaks: Corwin Press, 2006, p. 48.

CHAPTER 5 SUPPORTING DETAILS

LEARNING OBJECTIVES

IN THIS CHAPTER, YOU WILL:

Objective 1 — recognize the difference between major and minor details.

Objective 2 — describe how concept mapping is used to better understand major and minor details.

FOCUS ON HOSPITALITY AND TOURISM

There is an incredible amount of opportunity in the fields of hospitality and tourism because they include so many different occupations. People who love food, entertaining, or travel often find a job they love in one of these areas. One benefit is that you can choose your working environment, such as in a restaurant or a hotel in a national park. If you like to travel, you might become a tour guide in any number of places where you'd like to live. Cruise ships and casinos also offer numerous opportunities for employment, as do theme parks, airlines, and railway companies.

Objective 1 — MAJOR AND MINOR DETAILS AND TRANSITIONS

If a friend called you and said, "I just had the most amazing thing happen to me!" you would probably want to know more details. What kinds of details would you expect? You might hear, "I was called into one of my professor's offices and he told me I have been nominated to receive a full scholarship to a four-year college," or "I was walking down the street and I found two $100 bills lying on the ground." **Supporting details** should explain, prove, or illustrate your main idea. Try creating a few supporting details for these topic sentences with your team:

> **Supporting details** provide information that tells us more about the author's main idea.

1. There are several important things to consider when choosing a college.
2. Here are four good reasons to get a college degree.
3. There are several factors to consider when choosing a major in college.

When Details Do Not Support

In college, you will have to write several papers. Good writing is concise. That means that it does not have a lot of *irrelevant* details that do not support the author's main idea. In your team, look at the list of details under each of the following topic sentences, and cross out the ones that do not support the main idea.

EXAMPLE:

Topic sentence: Learning a foreign language has many advantages.

a. Knowing another language can make you more valuable as an employee.

b. ~~Learning another language can be difficult.~~

c. Being able to speak another language enables you to learn more about other people's cultures.

d. Speaking a foreign language will make it easier to communicate when you travel.

To find out whether a sentence supports the main idea, ask yourself, "Does this sentence tell me more about the main idea?" If it doesn't, then it is not a supporting detail and should be crossed out.

Practice

Cross out or circle the detail that does NOT support the topic sentence.

1. Topic sentence: The hospitality industry is an exciting and challenging field in which to work.

    a. Some hotels feature luxurious working environments.

    b. Managers often work 10 hours a day.

    c. Many travelers enjoy vacation cruises.

    d. Large hotel and airline companies offer employees free travel and discounts.

2. Topic sentence: The most famous railway transportation system in Europe is the TVG train system in France.

    a. The TVG serves more than 150 cities in France and Europe.

    b. The United States does not have a national unified rail system.

    c. The trains in the TVG travel at about 186 mph.

    d. The ride on the TVG is amazingly smooth.

3. Topic sentence: The rental car business is a large part of the travel industry in the United States.

    a. Some agencies charge more than others for daily rentals.

    b. More than 5,000 car rental companies operate in the United States.

    c. About 75 percent of the car rental business is situated around airports.

    d. The top four rental agencies maintain about 625,000 rental cars.

4. Topic sentence: Air travel has become an important factor in the tourism industry.

    a. Many airlines offer vacation packages that include hotel and rental cars.

    b. During any time of the day, about 4,500 airplanes are flying over the United States.

    c. Jet aircraft have made it possible to visit places that were not accessible before.

    d. Low airfares help to boost hotel occupancy and increase tourism.

5. Topic sentence: Cruise ships have become a popular vacation choice.

    a. Many ships feature nonstop entertainment for their passengers.

    b. Some ships offer casinos and live entertainment.

    c. The Diamond Princess is longer than two football fields and carries up to 2,670 passengers.

    d. The market for cruise ship vacations has increased dramatically in recent years.

Major and Minor Details

Major details give us more information about the main idea.

There are two types of details in all writing: **major details** and minor details.

Major Supporting Details

perishability
(pair-ish-a-BIL-i-tee): In this context, it means not producing an income.

In the following example, the topic is highlighted, the topic sentence is underlined, and the major details are numbered and italicized.

> *¹ The hospitality industry is one that is open for business 365 days a year*. For this reason, it depends heavily on shift work. *² The industry is also dependent upon good customer service that will encourage guests to come back again and again. ³ Another characteristic of the hospitality industry is the **perishability** of its products, for instance, hotel rooms*. Rooms that are vacant for the night are a financial loss to the hotel owner. These are some of the characteristics of the hospitality industry that make it a challenging industry in which to work.

Here is another way to see the information in this paragraph:

Topic: The hospitality industry

Topic sentence: These are some of the characteristics of the hospitality industry that make it a challenging industry in which to work.

Major supporting details:

- The hospitality industry is one that is open for business 365 days a year.
- The industry is also dependent upon good customer service that will encourage guests to come back again and again.
- Another characteristic of the hospitality industry is the perishability of its products, for instance, hotel rooms.

As mentioned earlier, you can make sure that a sentence is a major supporting detail by asking yourself, "Does this sentence tell me more about the main idea or topic sentence?" If it does, then it is a major detail. Another way to find the major details of a paragraph is to turn the main idea into a question. The answers to the question will be the major details.

For example:

Main idea:
There are many benefits to getting regular exercise. (What are the benefits of getting regular exercise?)

Main Idea:
The events that led to the American Revolution can be traced back to more than a decade before it began. (What are the events that led to the American Revolution?)

Minor Supporting Details

Authors also use **minor details** to tell us more information about the major details.

Notice in the earlier example how the first major detail is followed by a minor detail, which explains the first major detail:

Minor details tell us more information about the major details. They usually follow the major detail they explain.

> **Major detail:**
> The hospitality industry is one that is open for business 365 days a year.
>
> **Minor detail:**
> For this reason, it depends heavily on shift work.
>
> **Major detail:**
> Another characteristic of the hospitality industry is the perishability of its products, for instance, hotel rooms.
>
> **Minor detail:**
> Rooms that are vacant for the night are a financial loss to the hotel owner.

How Supporting Details Work

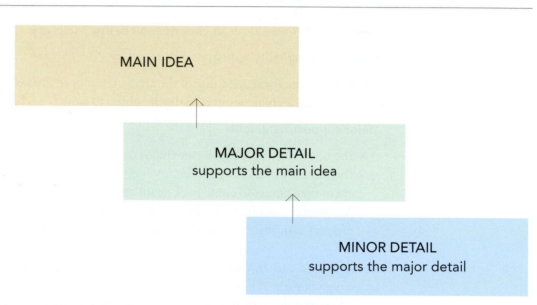

MAIN IDEA

MAJOR DETAIL
supports the main idea

MINOR DETAIL
supports the major detail

All good writing follows a certain structure. In college you will have to write many papers. Your professors will expect you to organize your thoughts in a logical manner, like in the diagram above.

Transitions

Transitions, or "signal words," are words or phrases that help show relationships between ideas and can introduce supporting details. There are hundreds of transitions in the English language, and each one of them serves a different function. You will learn more about transitions in future chapters. For this chapter, focus on the transitions that introduce supporting details. Most of these are called "listing transitions" (because they list details). Here are some of the most common listing transitions:

first	one	too	for one thing	and
second	another	in addition	moreover	besides
third	also	additionally	furthermore	final(ly)

In the following example, the topic sentence is underlined and the transitions are highlighted and italicized.

<u>Bianca wants to own her own travel agency for several reasons.</u> *First,* she would like to be independent and not have to worry about relying on an employer for her income. If things slow down in the travel industry, she could be laid off. *Second,* she would like to have the opportunity to make as much money as she wants and not be limited to an hourly wage. Instead of making just a weekly salary, she wants to get commissions from every booking she makes. *Third,* she wants flexible hours that let her decide when she wants to work. With a child at home and another one on the way, she would like to work at her home computer and on the phone.

Notice how the minor details tell us more about each major detail:

Major supporting detail #1:

She would like to be independent and not have to worry about relying on an employer for her income.

Minor supporting detail:

If things slow down in the travel industry, she could be laid off.

Major supporting detail #2:

She would like to have the opportunity to make as much money as she wants and not be limited to an hourly wage.

Minor supporting detail:

Instead of making just a weekly salary, she wants to get commissions from every booking she makes.

Major supporting detail #3:

She wants flexible hours that let her decide when she wants to work.

Minor supporting detail:

With a child at home and another one on the way, she would like to work at her home computer and on the phone.

THESIS STATEMENTS

A **thesis** is the main idea of a selection of two or more paragraphs on the same topic.

When an author writes several paragraphs on the same topic, the main idea of the entire selection is called a **thesis**.

In longer selections, the topic sentence of each paragraph actually plays a new role within the larger context of the essay. It becomes a major supporting detail for the thesis statement. Keep in mind, however, that when discussing a single paragraph, the stated main idea is still called the topic sentence. The following selection is an example of how topic sentences of paragraphs can act as major details for a thesis statement. The thesis statement is highlighted; each major detail that supports the thesis is underlined.

Classifications of Hotels

There are many different classifications of hotels. The AAA Auto Club of America classifies hotels by a five-diamond classification system.

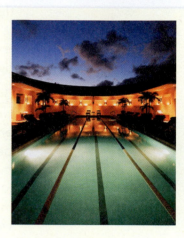

A one-diamond hotel is one that offers minimal services and no luxuries. It has a simple roadside appeal with limited landscaping. The lobby is small, with limited seating for guests. The art on the walls may look low budget. Guest rooms are small and barely meet industry standards.

A two-diamond hotel offers more services than a one-diamond hotel. It has average roadside appeal and some basic landscaping. There are some seats in the lobby, which typically features a medium-sized front desk, carpeted floors, and perhaps some plants for décor. The guestrooms meet the industry standards.

A three-diamond hotel has upgraded services to guests. It has very good roadside appeal with attractive landscaping. The lobby is spacious with carpeting and seating arranged in groups. Plants and art decorate the lobby, and there are luggage carts for guests to use.

A four-diamond hotel offers high-level guest services and hospitality. It has excellent roadside appeal and professionally groomed landscaping. The lobby is spacious and decorated in wood or marble. There may be background music, and the furniture and carpets are of high quality. Rooms are spacious and exceed industry standards.

A five-diamond hotel offers every possible service any guest could want, and it is all done perfectly. It has outstanding roadside appeal with gorgeous landscaping and an elegant entrance. The lobby is spacious and impressive in its quality of furniture and art. Fresh floral arrangements grace the tables. The guest rooms are large and luxurious.

Notice how the topic sentence of each paragraph acts as a major detail to support the main idea stated in the thesis. Understanding this relationship will help you to comprehend your textbooks more clearly.

Practice

1. Read each of the following sentences and label them as follows (each set will contain one of each):

T   = topic
TS = topic sentence
MA = major supporting detail
MI = minor supporting detail

EXAMPLE:

........*TS*........ **a.** Technology helps the restaurant business in many ways.

........*T*........ **b.** Technology in the restaurant business

........*MA*........ **c.** Palm-sized computers are used by servers to send an order to the kitchen.

........*MI*........ **d.** The chef can see these orders on a large computer in the kitchen.

Set 1

.... **a.** Executive chefs

.... **b.** If they order too much food, it will spoil, but if they order too little, the restaurant cannot meet its clients' needs.

.... **c.** Executive chefs must estimate how much food to order.

.... **d.** Among their many tasks, executive chefs are responsible for ordering food.

Set 2

.... **a.** The training and education of food service managers is important to health and safety.

.... **b.** Food that is not stored correctly will rot quickly.

.... **c.** Food service managers must know the correct procedures for storing food and keeping it fresh.

.... **d.** Food service manager training

Set 3

.... **a.** Except for schools, most of these places are open seven days a week and require shift work and sometimes long hours.

.... **b.** Places where food service managers work

.... **c.** Food service mangers may work in restaurants, cafeterias, schools, factories, casinos, and cruise ships.

.... **d.** There are a variety of places where food service managers can work.

Practice

Set 4

.... **a.** Franchising allows a hotel business to use the name brand and financing of a large corporation.

.... **b.** The hotel owner must agree to the terms of the contract with the franchising company.

.... **c.** Franchising

.... **d.** For example, the hotel must agree to use the franchise company's name and meet its standards.

Set 5

.... **a.** Resort hotels

.... **b.** Some resort hotels have package deals for skiers.

.... **c.** A resort hotel offers more than rooms; it offers activities such as golf, swimming, tennis, and skiing.

.... **d.** Guests can get a ski ticket and a hotel room for less than the cost of each one separately.

2. Read the following paragraph. Underline and label the topic sentence with "TS," and underline the major details. Then, answer the questions that follow.

People who enjoy playing games like lotteries, card games, and other games of chance can find employment in the casino industry. Most gaming-service employees work in casinos, and their work can vary from management to surveillance and investigation. *One* career opportunity is as a gaming supervisor. This is someone who oversees the games and the personnel in a specific area. Gaming supervisors make sure that players and workers are following the rules and will explain them clearly if needed. *Another* career opportunity is as a gaming manager. Gaming managers prepare work schedules and are responsible for hiring and training new personnel. *Finally*, gaming dealers are also employed to operate games such as blackjack, roulette, and craps. To become qualified for one of these positions, you will need a degree in hospitality or special training to become licensed by your state's casino control board or commission.

1. What is the topic?
   a. gaming supervisors
   b. casinos
   c. gambling
   d. gaming careers

Practice

2. **What is the topic sentence?**

   a. People who enjoy playing games like lotteries, card games, and other games of chance can find employment in the casino industry.

   b. Most gaming-service employees work in casinos, and their work can vary from management to surveillance and investigation.

   c. One career opportunity is as a gaming supervisor.

   d. To become qualified for one of these positions, you will need a degree in hospitality or special training to become licensed by your state's casino control board or commission.

3. **Which of the following is not a major supporting detail?**

   a. One career opportunity is as a gaming supervisor.

   b. Another career opportunity is as a gaming manager.

   c. Gaming supervisors make sure that players and workers are following the rules and will explain them clearly if needed.

   d. Finally, gaming dealers are also employed to operate games such as blackjack, roulette, and craps.

4. **Identify the minor detail that supports the following major detail: "Another career opportunity is as a gaming manager."**

   a. To become qualified for one of these positions, you will need a degree in hospitality or special training to become licensed by your state's casino control board or commission.

   b. Gaming managers prepare work schedules and are responsible for hiring and training new personnel.

   c. Most gaming-service employees work in casinos, and their work can vary from management to surveillance and investigation.

   d. This is someone who oversees the games and the personnel in a specific area.

5. **Which of the following transitions were used to introduce the major details?**

   a. most, one, finally

   b. one, another, to

   c. this, to, they

   d. one, another, finally

Practice 3.

Read the following paragraph. Underline and label the topic sentence with "TS," and underline the major details. Then, answer the questions that follow.

When you go to a restaurant, do you think about all the different operations that are taking place at the same time? Hosts or hostesses decide where patrons should be seated. Waiters and waitresses take orders, chefs prepare the food, bussers clean the tables, and managers make everything run smoothly. Being a food service manager is a job with many responsibilities. One of the responsibilities is to hire and train good employees. Food service managers must also schedule these employees for various shifts. In addition, they must make sure that groceries are ordered for the kitchen and the quality of the food is good. Food service managers supervise the employees to make sure the restaurant is kept clean and that guests are not kept waiting too long. Also, food service managers must deal with a lot of paperwork to pay employees, bills, and taxes, and to keep track of expenses.

1. What is the topic of this selection?

   a. food service managers   c. employees in a restaurant

   b. hosts and hostesses   d. restaurants

2. What is the topic sentence?

   a. When you go to a restaurant, do you think about all the different operations that are taking place at the same time?

   b. Hosts or hostesses decide where patrons should be seated.

   c. Being a food service manager is a job with many responsibilities.

   d. Also, food service managers must deal with a lot of paperwork to pay employees, bills, and taxes, and to keep track of expenses.

3. Which of the following is a major detail that supports the topic sentence?

   a. Hosts or hostesses decide where patrons should be seated.

   b. Waiters and waitresses take orders, chefs prepare the food, bussers clean the tables, and managers make everything run smoothly.

   c. When you go to a restaurant, do you think about all the different operations that are taking place at the same time?

   d. One of the responsibilities is to hire and train good employees.

4. Which of the following transitions were used to introduce the major details?

   a. there are, being, one

   b. one, in addition, also

   c. whenever, being, one

   d. in addition, is, with

TEXTBOOK SELECTION

Read the following selection from a textbook. Underline and label the thesis statement, and then underline and label the major details. The topic sentence in each paragraph will be a major detail for the thesis statement. Then, answer the questions that follow.

1 Many theme restaurants are a combination of a sophisticated specialty and several other types of restaurants. They generally serve a limited menu but aim to wow the guests by the total experience.

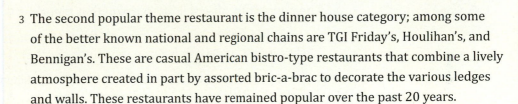

2 Of the many popular theme restaurants, two stand out. The first highlights the nostalgia of the 1950s, as exemplified in the T-Bird and Corvette diners. These restaurants serve all-American food such as the perennial meatloaf in a fun atmosphere that is a throwback to the seemingly more carefree 1950s. The mostly female food servers appear in short polka-dot skirts with gym shoes and bobby socks.

3 The second popular theme restaurant is the dinner house category; among some of the better known national and regional chains are TGI Friday's, Houlihan's, and Bennigan's. These are casual American bistro-type restaurants that combine a lively atmosphere created in part by assorted bric-a-brac to decorate the various ledges and walls. These restaurants have remained popular over the past 20 years.

4 People are attracted to theme restaurants because they offer a total experience and a social meeting place. This is achieved through decoration and atmosphere and allows the restaurant to offer a limited menu that blends with the theme. Throughout the United States and the world, numerous theme restaurants stand out for one reason or another. Among them are decors featuring airplanes, railway dining cars, rock and roll, 1960s nostalgia, and many others.

QUESTIONS

1. What is the topic of this selection?

    a. American restaurants   **c.** theme restaurants

    b. nostalgia restaurants   **d.** dinner houses

2. What is the topic sentence of paragraph 2?

    a. Of the many popular theme restaurants, two stand out.

    b. The first highlights the nostalgia of the 1950s, as exemplified in the T-Bird and Corvette diners.

    c. These restaurants serve all-American food such as the perennial meatloaf in a fun atmosphere that is a throwback to the seemingly more carefree 1950s.

    d. The mostly female food servers appear in short polka-dot skirts with gym shoes and bobby socks.

3. What is the topic sentence of paragraph 3?

   a. The second popular theme restaurant is the dinner house category; among some of the better known national and regional chains are TGI Friday's, Houlihan's, and Bennigan's.

   b. These are casual American bistro-type restaurants that combine a lively atmosphere created in part by assorted bric-a-brac to decorate the various ledges and walls.

   c. These restaurants have remained popular over the past 20 years.

   d. American bistro-type restaurants

4. What is the topic sentence of paragraph 4?

   a. People are attracted to theme restaurants because they offer a total experience and a social meeting place.

   b. This is achieved through decoration and atmosphere and allows the restaurant to offer a limited menu that blends with the theme.

   c. Throughout the United States and the world, numerous theme restaurants stand out for one reason or another.

   d. Among them are decors featuring airplanes, railway dining cars, rock and roll, 1960s nostalgia, and many others.

5. What is the main idea of the entire selection (the thesis)?

   a. Many theme restaurants are a combination of a sophisticated specialty and several other types of restaurants.

   b. They generally serve a limited menu but aim to wow the guests by the total experience.

   c. Of the many popular theme restaurants, two stand out.

   d. People are attracted to theme restaurants because they offer a total experience and a social meeting place.

U-Review

THINK, PAIR, SHARE

First, answer the following questions to yourself. Then, pair up with a partner and ask each other the questions, taking turns.

1. What are supporting details, and what are their functions?

....

2. What does a major detail do?

....

3. What does a minor detail do?

....

4. What are transitions, and how do they help readers?

....

Objective 2 CONCEPT MAPPING

Concept mapping is a way to show relationships among the ideas in a reading selection—for example, among the main idea, the major details, and the minor details. There are many different styles of concept maps, and you have probably seen them in your textbooks.

The following is a concept map of the passage you read earlier about Bianca's travel agency.

Topic

> Bianca's Travel Agency Business

Topic Sentence

> Bianca wants to own her own travel agency for several reasons.

Major Supporting Details

She would like to be independent and not have to worry about relying on an employer for her income.	She would like to have the opportunity to make as much money as she wants and not be limited to an hourly wage.	She wants flexible hours that let her decide when she wants to work.

Minor Supporting Details

If things slow down in the travel industry, she could be laid off.	Instead of making just a weekly salary, she wants to get commissions from every booking she makes.	With a child at home and another one on the way, she would like to work at her home computer and on the phone.

Another style of concept mapping is to place the topic and topic sentence in the center of your page, and then add the major details and minor details around it:

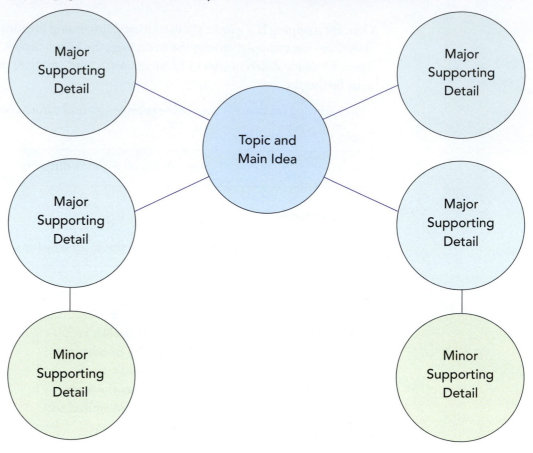

It is important to keep the major details attached to the center circle because they support the main idea. Minor details are attached to the major details that they support. Here is another example of a concept map for the earlier paragraph about the hospitality industry:

Topic: The Hospitality Industry

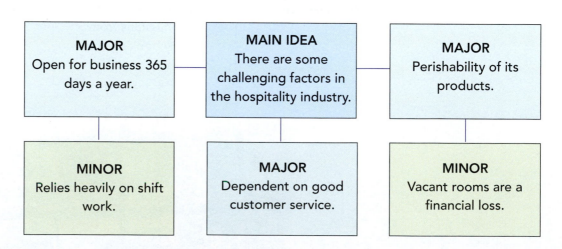

Practice

1. Read the following paragraph. Underline the main idea and major details. Then, fill in the missing information in the concept map that follows.

Recreation in the Hospitality Industry

Recreation has become an important segment of the hospitality industry. More hotels and tour companies are expanding their programs for recreation. Golf has long been a popular form of recreation at many resorts and hotels. Resorts also have featured tennis courts and swimming pools. Now hotels are including jogging and biking trails, rock climbing, and boating. The tourist industry also includes ecotourism with trips to observe wildlife in their natural habitats in rainforests, mountains, and waterways.

Topic: Recreation in the Hospitality Industry

Topic sentence: Recreation has become an important segment of the hospitality industry.

Golf at many	Swimming and	.... and biking trails	.... climbing and	Ecotourism trips

Rainforests .... and ....

Practice

2. Read the following paragraph. Underline the main idea and major details. Then, fill in the missing information in the concept map that follows.

The Theme Park Industry

One of the most popular tourist destinations around the world is theme parks. They first began with Hershey's Chocolate Company, which opened a leisure park in 1907. Walt Disney opened Disneyland in California in 1955 as a park for children "of all ages." Twenty-eight years later, Walt Disney World, much like Disneyland, opened in Florida. Following Disney's lead, Universal Studios opened its own theme parks in Florida and California. Parks that originally began as animal attractions, such as Sea World, soon expanded to include many theme park features including thrill rides, entertainment, and restaurants. Theme parks are now on all major continents across the world.

Topic: ....

Topic sentence: ....
....

1907 Hershey's	in California	in Florida	Florida and California	

Practice

3. Read the following paragraph. Underline the main idea and major details. Then, fill in the missing information in the concept map that follows.

According to the International Ecotourism Society, ecotourism is responsible travel to natural areas that conserve the environment and improve the well-being of the local people. Ecotourism is a popular form of tourism where tourists can visit a natural area to help make a difference in the environment and the economy. Tourists who sign up for ecotours are expected to help build environmental awareness and respect. Ecotours also must provide a positive experience for both the traveler and the local people. Another purpose of ecotourism is to provide financial benefits for the conservation of natural resources. Ecotourists visit unusual places and help to make improvements in the areas they visit.

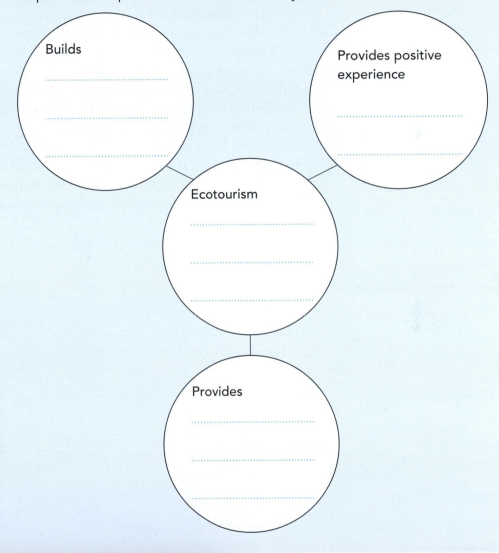

TEXTBOOK SELECTION

Read the following selection using the four-step reading process. Underline the main idea and major details. Then, fill in the missing items in the concept map that follows.

Social Events

Social function planners and managers work on a broad variety of events. This category of event planning includes weddings, engagement parties, birthday parties, anniversary parties, holiday parties, graduation parties, military events, and all other social gatherings or events. A social event planner is usually responsible for selecting the venue, determining any themes or design schemes, ordering and planning decorations, arranging for catering and entertainment, and having invitations printed and sent out.

Weddings are the most widely recognized social event. Wedding planners are a key player in the social event category. The title seems glamorous and has a certain perception that most of us will hold; yet the management involved in planning a wedding involves strict attention to detail. Don't forget that the planner is responsible for creating what is considered to be the most important day of a couple's life. "Realize this is a business," says Gerard J. Monaghan, president of the Association of Bridal Consultants. "A fun business to be sure, but a business nonetheless." Effective wedding planners will have formed contacts with a variety of services and venues, such as hotels, wedding locations, decorating companies, catering companies, bridal shops, musicians, photographers, florists, and so forth.

```
┌─────────────────────────────────────────────────┐
│                                                 │
│  .............................................  │
└─────────────────────────────────────────────────┘
                         │
┌─────────────────────────────────────────────────┐
│  Topic Sentence:                                │
│  .............................................  │
└─────────────────────────────────────────────────┘
           │                          │
┌────────────────────┐      ┌────────────────────┐
│  Includes weddings,│      │  Wedding planners are a │
│                    │      │                    │
│  ................. │      │  ................. │
│                    │      │                    │
│  ................. │      │  ................. │
│                    │      └────────────────────┘
│  ................. │                │
│                    │      ┌────────────────────┐
│  ................. │      │  Involves strict attention to │
│                    │      │                    │
└────────────────────┘      │  ................. │
                            └────────────────────┘
```

U-Review

Fill in each box below with the correct letter to show the structure of a concept map. Some answers will be used more than once.

A. topic
B. main idea
C. major detail
D. minor detail

199

Reading 1 Vocabulary Preview

The following vocabulary words are from the article "Let's Talk About Your Life, Son." With a partner or in a team, choose the correct meanings of the underlined words in the following sentences. Use context clues (LEADS), word part clues, and parts of speech to help you figure out the meanings.

1. Deciding to adopt a child is a serious commitment (kom-MIT-ment) and a huge responsibility.
   a. group
   b. obligation
   c. career
   d. visit

2. Manuel is very unfocused (un-FO-kusd) when he does his homework because he is distracted by the phone and TV.
   a. inattentive
   b. out of focus
   c. unhappy
   d. friendly

3. Even though I was upset by the professor's remark, I acted nonchalantly (non-cho-LONT- lee), as if it didn't bother me.
   a. in an upset manner
   b. carefully
   c. seriously
   d. in a carefree manner

4. Getting a good grade in algebra was gratifying (GRAT-i-fy-ing) after I struggled so hard in that course.
   a. frustrating
   b. unimportant
   c. rewarding
   d. impossible

5. The investigator found tangible (TAN-ji-ble) proof that the crime had occurred in the kitchen. There was blood on the floor, chairs were knocked over, and there was broken glass.
   a. suggested
   b. solid
   c. uncertain
   d. energetic

6. My best friend has such a <u>buoyant</u> (BOY-ant) personality that everyone loves being around her.

   a. depressing

   b. loud

   c. floating

   d. cheerful

7. Even the most <u>mundane</u> (mun-DANE) cooking-school tasks—like "turning" vegetables, or paring them into perfect, uniform shapes—started to seem kind of interesting.

   a. ordinary

   b. exciting

   c. difficult

   d. happy

8. Johnathan was known as one of the most <u>inventive</u> (in-VEN-tiv) chefs around, always creating new dishes and experimenting with unusual combinations of foods.

   a. ideal

   b. creative

   c. best

   d. insane

9. Andy is so <u>passionate</u> (PASH-on-it) about music that he plays four to five hours a day—every day.

   a. having a great love for something

   b. practical

   c. annoying

   d. perfect

10. As a <u>sous-chef</u> (SUE-shef) at the restaurant, Rachael is second in command and only takes orders from the head chef.

   a. cook

   b. waitress

   c. assistant to the head chef

   d. hostess

Reading 1 What Do You Already Know?

1. What are your favorite places to eat? What are some of your favorite dishes and foods?

2. If you were a chef and wanted to open a restaurant, what kind of restaurant would it be?

3. What do you know about Bobby Flay?

> Directions: As you read this article, practice the four-step reading process. Preview the article, and then write on the following lines one or two questions that you would hope to have answered.
>
> ....
>
> ....
>
> ....
>
> ....

As you read, answer the questions in the margins to check your comprehension.

"Let's Talk About Your Life, Son"

BY BOBBY FLAY

From *Guideposts* June 2008. Copyright © 2008 by Bobby Flay. Reprinted by permission of the author.

Bobby Flay is a famous chef, restaurant owner, popular TV show host, author of eight books on cooking, and winner of nine culinary arts awards. In this article, Flay tells about his past, when he had dropped out of high school and had no goals for his life. Read how he turned his life around when he discovered his passion for food.

1   Awhile back I took on a big commitment. I committed to a year volunteering at a public vocational high school in Queens, New York. I went every week to teach a class, and just cooked with the kids. It was a pretty amazing experience. I saw myself in a lot of them. The uncertainty, the insecurities were all there. These kids were a lot like me. Maybe that sounds surprising, coming from someone who's been a success in the restaurant business. Let me tell you more.

Finding Myself

2   Growing up, I never really thought about becoming a chef—much less owning restaurants or being on TV. The truth is, I didn't really have any goals. I didn't like school. I was unfocused. Most of all, I liked hanging out with my buddies on the corner of Lexington Avenue and 84th Street, on Manhattan's Upper East Side, where I was born and raised, just shooting the breeze. That was the life I

Reading 1

imagined for myself when I dropped out of high school. But someone had other plans for me. I was lounging around at home one day, watching TV, when the phone rang. It was my dad. "Come to my office," he said. "We need to talk about your life."

3   My life? I was 17! Was I supposed to have it all figured out? It felt like being called to the principal's office—but worse. My dad is a great guy. He's also very scholarly, so my leaving school must have hit him hard. I didn't want to let him down. But it seemed that was exactly what I was doing. Part of me was scared. Part of me tried to play it cool: just dad being dad. I went down to his office at Joe Alien—a famous restaurant in the theater district that he was a partner in. "Go get a job," he said, "You can't just hang out with your friends on a street corner."

What was Bobby's situation at this point in his life?

4   "Okay," I said nonchalantly, shrugged my shoulders, and headed out to meet my friends. Where was I going to find a job?

5   The next day, Dad called again. He sounded exasperated. I guess he figured out that my hunt hadn't just been a bust, but a complete nonevent.

6   "The busboy had to leave to take care of his grandmother. You're going to fill in." Dad didn't ask me; he told me. "And don't forget; no special treatment. Because you're my son, you better work harder than anyone else. Put your head down, do your job and don't aggravate anybody—including me."

7   I had my marching orders, and showed up at the restaurant the next day, and the day after that. I didn't have much interest in the business, but I didn't want to upset Dad. I showed up late sometimes—only to spot Dad waiting for me, eyes on his watch—but I did my job.

8   It wasn't so bad. I was clearing tables and setting tables. Two weeks went by pretty fast. Now what? I wondered. "Do you want a job?" the chef asked me as I was walking out of the kitchen. I think the guy took pity on me. "Sure," I said.

9   He had me start in the pantry. That's when my career really began. I stocked the pantry, washed dishes, and learned how to clean lettuce. I used a knife. I made salad dressing. I didn't think I had any natural skill, but it was gratifying to learn something. And my salads did taste pretty good.

Why did Bobby agree to take this job?

Opportunity Knocks

10   About six months into my job at Joe Alien, something unexpected happened. I remember waking up one morning, staring at the ceiling and saying to myself, "I'm really looking forward to going to work today." Where did that come from? Little things, I think, like learning new cooking techniques and watching my knife skills improve. From that point forward, I looked at work differently. I enjoyed it. I felt I was contributing. Slowly, I was shedding my irresponsible 17-year-old skin. I was prepping in the kitchen one day when my dad and his business partner—and the restaurant's namesake—Joe Alien, sauntered in. "We want to talk to Bobby about something," Joe said to the chef. Uh-oh. What had I done wrong? They took me up to the office.

11   "There's a new school opening," Joe said. "It's called The French Culinary Institute. Do you want to go?"

Describe in your own words how Bobby's life has changed and how this story might end.

12   "Nah," I said, "I don't think so." School and I didn't get along so well. In truth, I thought I wasn't good enough to go to cooking school. I had the idea in my head that, as a cook, you either had it or you didn't. It didn't come naturally to me. Cleaning produce was one thing. But if I didn't have "it" at 18, how could I ever possibly be a chef? But they talked me into it. I didn't want to let them down. I studied for my high school equivalency test—a requirement to enter culinary school—and passed. That felt good, like I'd achieved something tangible. To my surprise, I was looking forward to going back to school. It sounded like a great opportunity.

13   It was. The French Culinary Institute had just opened its doors. There were only nine students, but it was a mix of interesting people. I was the youngest by about six years. Our teacher was a great guy—an old-school, formally trained Alsatian chef named Antoine Shaeffers. He was obviously a terrific cook; he also had a wonderful, buoyant personality. Even the most mundane cooking-school tasks—like "turning" vegetables, paring them into perfect, uniform shapes— started to seem kind of interesting. But by then, anything having to do with food had become interesting to me. And since I was still working at the restaurant by night and going to school by day, food really took over my life, 24/7.

14   The culinary program lasted six months. It was intense, and I learned a lot. I went back to Joe Alien, thinking I'd move up the ranks in his restaurant. "Get out of here!" he said. "You're not gonna learn anything else here." *Wait a minute!* I thought. I finally got comfortable doing something I liked, and Joe and my dad were pushing me out? I couldn't believe it. "I want to stay," I pleaded. "I want to be the chef here someday. This is my career." Did I say career? I guess I had grown up, at least a little. They were unmoved. It was time for me to leave Joe Alien.

Why did Bobby want to stay, and do you think his father was right in making him go?

On My Own

15   I sent out resumés and pounded the pavement. I was hired as a sous-chef at a hot new restaurant on the Upper East Side. It was called Brighton Grill. They had hired a head chef from New Orleans.

16   Two days after the restaurant opened, I showed up at work (on time!) at 8:00 a.m.

17   "We've got a problem," one of the owners said to me. *Uh-oh,* I thought—again. But I knew I hadn't done anything wrong. It was the chef. "We found him passed out on the laundry bag. He apparently hit the tequila last night—and lots of it. He's fired. You're the head chef now." I was in shock. It was like I'd been the understudy in a Broadway show and was about to get my big break. But was I ready to perform? I could cook okay. I didn't have much of a repertoire yet. But somehow I managed. I stayed at the Brighton Grill for a year, learning every day. Then I was itching to move on, to try something new.

18   At The French Culinary Institute, I met a woman named Gail Arnold who was cooking in one of Jonathan Waxman's restaurants. Jonathan was known as one of the most inventive chefs around. I jumped at the chance to work at Bud's—his place on the West Side.

19   That's where I fell in love with the flavors of the southwest. Believe it or not, I'd never been to New Mexico, Arizona, or Texas. But there was something about this

food that I just instantly got and instantly loved. We were cooking on a high level at Bud's, with great ingredients. Things that I'd never tasted before—papayas and mangoes, chili peppers and blue corn tortillas. All that stuff was completely new to me. And it was awesome. And the crew was amazing—with energetic cooks eager to experiment. We all learned from each other. It was a rare, special, inspiring place. I wound up working at all three of Jonathan's restaurants. One was a tiny French bistro called Hulot's. But here's how passionate I'd become about cooking: another chef and I would get the keys from the manager and show up there on Sunday afternoons—when the place was closed—just to cook for fun. That's when I knew cooking was my life. I woke up every morning thinking about what I'd cook that day. I still do.

How did Bobby feel about cooking at this point in his life? What changed his attitude?

20 I worked in more kitchens. I kept learning and experimenting. Finally, I was feeling ready to open a place of my own that would feature the bold, southwest flavors I love. I wanted a bigger stage. Of course I talked to my dad about it. If he agreed I was ready to make this move, it would be my green light. By then I knew to trust his judgment better than my own! We started scouring the city for a good location. Then Jerry Kretchmer—who owned a famous restaurant called the Gotham Bar and Grill—came by to talk to talk to me about opening a place. "Do you want to open a southwestern restaurant with me?" he asked. That was a little awkward. I explained to him I'd been looking for a place with my dad. "Well, think about it," he said.

At this point in the story, do you think Bobby will be successful? Why or why not?

21 I went back to Dad. He actually seemed relieved. "Do it with him," he urged me. "That way you and I can just be father and son." Once again, wise counsel from my most trusted advisor. And soon my first restaurant, Mesa Grill, opened its doors.

22 That was more than 17 years ago. I still love every minute of it. I still wake up thinking about flavors, about new dishes to try. I still love the family atmosphere in the kitchen. I'm still amazed I was once that confused kid, without any clear sense of direction—and that there'd been a time when I worried I wasn't good enough to go to culinary school. Do I ever have doubts? You bet.

Giving Back

What did Bobby do for the high school students in Queens?

23 It's hard for me to think of myself as a great chef. I think of myself as someone who's always learning, always wanting to cook better, more delicious food. And that's what I saw in those kids I met at the public high school in Queens—a desire to learn, a commitment to give it their best. At the end of the year, thanks to The French Culinary Institute, I was able to give one of them a scholarship. It was too hard to pick one kid. There was some real talent there. I narrowed it down to five and came up with a plan to secure scholarships for all five of them. Sure, they're a little rough around the edges and have a long way to go, just like I did when I was their age. But in my dad and his partner, Joe, I was blessed with supportive—and demanding—mentors who not only helped turn my life around, but also helped me find my passion. I can't think of a better way to pay them back than to encourage other young people to find their passion too.

1,850 words divided by _____ minutes = _____ words per minute

Thinking About What You Read

It's a good habit to summarize everything you read to strengthen your comprehension.

Directions: On the following lines, write a two- or three-sentence summary of the article "Let's Talk About Your Life, Son." In your own words, describe what the article was about and why the author wrote it.

....

....

....

....

Comprehension Questions

The following questions will help you to recall the main idea and the details of "Let's Talk About Your Life, Son." Review any parts of the article that you need to find the correct answers.

LITERAL
COMPREHENSION

1. **What is the topic of this article?**

   a. learning about cooking   **c.** Bobby Flay

   b. becoming a chef   **d.** Bobby Flay's restaurant

MAIN IDEAS

2. **What is the main idea of the article?**

   a. The restaurant business is a fun way to make a living.

   b. Bobby Flay found his passion in cooking and learned how to become a great chef.

   c. Bobby Flay made a big commitment.

   d. It's important to give back to others what you have learned.

3. **What is the topic sentence of paragraph 14?**

   a. The culinary program lasted six months.

   b. This is my career.

   c. I guess I had grown up, at least a little.

   d. It was time for me to leave Joe Alien.

4. **What is the topic of paragraph 19?**

   a. Bobby discovers southwest cooking.   **c.** cooking in Jonathan's restaurants

   b. Bud's restaurant   **d.** Bobby cooks for fun.

Reading 1

SUPPORTING DETAILS

5. According to the article, Bobby was hired at his father's restaurant when:

   a. he applied for a job there as a server.

   b. he was told by his father to take the place of the busboy who couldn't come in to work.

   c. he asked the chef to teach him how to cook.

   d. the chef was found drunk.

6. After Bobby was hired as a sous-chef at the Brighton Grill, he was told that:

   a. he would be working with the servers.

   b. he would be getting a big break on Broadway.

   c. the head chef had been fired for getting drunk on tequila, and now Bobby was head chef.

   d. he would be cooking southwest-style dishes.

7. According to the article, which of these statements is not true?

   a. Bobby opened his own restaurant with Jonathan Waxman and called it Hulot's.

   b. Bobby's father was relieved that he didn't have to be Bobby's partner in a restaurant.

   c. Bobby gave five high school students scholarships to the French Culinary Institute.

   d. Bobby wants to help other young people find their passion.

DRAWING CONCLUSIONS

8. With which of these statements do you think Bobby would disagree?

   a. Finding your passion in life sometimes happens when you start out at the bottom in the lowest paying job.

   b. We should listen to the advice of someone who has more experience in our chosen careers.

   c. When your passion is your job, work seems more like fun than work.

   d. If you're not good at something in the beginning, you should probably quit because you have no talent for it.

VOCABULARY IN CONTEXT

Using context clues and word part clues, determine the best meaning for the underlined word in each of these sentences. If necessary, use a dictionary.

9. We started <u>scouring</u> the city for a good location.

   a. scrubbing

   b. searching

   c. arranging

   d. finding

10. When Bobby's father learned that his son hadn't even tried to find a job, be was <u>exasperated</u>.

   a. frustrated

   b. sad

   c. amused

   d. worried

Reading 1 Vocabulary Practice

Use the vocabulary words from the Word Bank to complete the following sentences. Write the words into the blanks provided.

> **WORD BANK**
> commitment   unfocused   nonchalantly   gratifying   tangible
> buoyant   mundane   sous-chef   inventive   passionate

1. Danny is such a(n) .... chef that he keeps coming up with new ideas for recipes.

2. If Sam does a favor for you, don't be surprised if he expects some type of .... reward, like cash or free tickets to a game!

3. Martina finds that working with handicapped children at the summer camp is very ....

4. Yun Ling is absolutely........................... about animals. She has three dogs and two cats, and plans on becoming a veterinarian.

5. Heather was hired as a(n) .... but soon became the head chef at the restaurant.

6. Omar has such a(n) .... personality that everyone wants to hang out with him.

7. Owning a puppy is a big .... because you are responsible for feeding it, training it, and taking it to the veterinarian regularly.

8. People who are .... often do not have any motivation to succeed in life.

9. When Rick asked me if I would like to go out with him, I answered ...., "I guess so."

10. Instead of writing a(n) ....story for her English Composition class, Maria decided to write about an exciting adventure she had while she was in Puerto Rico.

Reading 1 Questions for Writing and Discussion

Review any parts of the article you need to answer the following questions.

1. What kind of relationship did Bobby Flay have with his father?

   ....

   ....

   ....

2. Why did Bobby's father push him into getting a job at his restaurant? Do you think he should have done that, or do you think he should have let Bobby decide what he wanted to do? Explain your answer.

   ....

   ....

   ....

3. If Bobby had chosen to ignore the advice of his father and Joe Alien, how might his life have been different?

   ....

   ....

   ....

4. Based on what you read in this article, why do you think Bobby Flay achieved so much success?

   ....

   ....

   ....

5. In what ways are Taryn Rose (from Chapter 4) and Bobby Flay alike in terms of their attitudes and skills?

   ....

   ....

   ....

Reading 1 Vocabulary Practice—Speed Quiz

Get together in groups of four or five people. Each group should create a set of vocabulary cards according to the following directions.

In this activity, you will be given 60 seconds to give the correct definitions to five vocabulary words. You earn 2 points for each correct answer. Read through all of the directions before you begin.

1.

Fold a sheet of notebook paper into 10 sections. Tear the sections into 10 individual pieces. Give each team member 2 or more pieces to copy some of the words and definitions from the list below onto the squares. Upon completion, all 10 words and definitions will be copied onto the 10 squares.

2.

Put all 10 squares together in a pile and shuffle them face down.

3.

Divide your team into two opposing teams, team A and team B.

4.

Deal out 5 squares to each team, but do not look at your words until it is time to start, and keep them covered.

5.

One person on team A and one person on team B will be the clue givers. When it is time to start, the clue giver on team A will read the words one at a time to team B. Team B has 60 seconds to give the correct definitions to all 5 words. If a team can't remember the definition, they may say "Pass" and go to the next word. If they complete the remaining words before the 60 seconds are up, they may go back to the ones they passed and try them again. The first answer given by a team is the one that counts–no second attempts are allowed.

6.

One person on team A and one person on team B will be the score keepers. The scorekeeper on team A will keep track of correct responses for team B and give them 2 points per correct answer.

7.

When time is called, both teams must stop. The score for team A is totaled and they are told the answers to any words they couldn't define.

8.

Next the play will be repeated and team B will give the clues to team A, who will have 60 seconds to define the 5 words they are given.

9.

When time is called, the score will be totaled by the scorekeeper on team B.

10.

The team with the highest score wins.

1. commitment: obligation
2. unfocused: inattentive
3. nonchalantly: in a careless manner
4. gratifying: rewarding
5. tangible: solid
6. buoyant: cheerful
7. mundane: ordinary
8. inventive: creative
9. passionate: having a great love for something
10. sous-chef: assistant to the head chef

Reading 1 Supporting Details Chart

With your team, fill in the details for each of the topic sentences from "Let's Talk About Your Life, Son." Only list the details that explain, prove, or illustrate the main idea. There may be only one detail, or there may be two or more details. You may refer back the article to refresh your memory, but try to write the details in your own words. The first one is done for you.

MAIN IDEAS	SUPPORTING DETAILS
1. As a teenager, Bobby Flay had no plan for his future.	• He dropped out of high school and didn't graduate. • He didn't have a job. • He had no goals.
2. Bobby's father and the chef at his restaurant gave him jobs to do.	
3. Bobby got an opportunity to go back to school.	
4. Bobby had to go out on his own to earn a living.	
5. Bobby now gives back to others.	

Reading 2 Vocabulary Preview

The following vocabulary words are from the article "Where Wishes Come True." With a partner or in a team, choose the correct meanings of the underlined words in the following sentences. Use context clues (LEADS), word part clues, and parts of speech to help you figure out the meanings.

1. As a successful <u>entrepreneur</u> (on-tra-prah-NOOR), Mr. Lewis owns several businesses that he started himself.

    a. someone who works with a mentor to learn a trade

    b. executive

    c. someone who creates a new business

    d. someone who works for someone else

2. Ever since Robert lost his own parents, he has more <u>empathy</u> (EM-path-ee) for others who have lost theirs too.

    a. space

    b. understanding for the feelings of others

    c. orphan

    d. grief

3. In the courtroom, the defendant looked at her attacker with <u>contempt</u> (kon-TEMPT).

    a. understanding

    b. indifference

    c. carelessly

    d. hatred

4. During World War II, the Nazis imprisoned people in <u>concentration camps</u> under very harsh conditions.

    a. resort camps

    b. prison camps

    c. a place where soldiers live

    d. conservation crew quarters

5. When we returned home after our vacation, we found some moldy, <u>rancid</u> (RAN-sid) food in the refrigerator.

    a. rotten

    b. delicious

    c. frozen

    d. uneaten

6. In many old ships and prisons, people became ill with <u>typhus</u> (TIE-fus), which was spread by bacteria on rats and lice.

   a. seasickness

   b. homesickness

   c. a disease

   d. food poisoning

7. The bricks in the wall were held together with <u>mortar</u> (MOR-tar).

   a. paste

   b. glue

   c. cement

   d. rockets

8. During his POW imprisonment, Sergeant Morris had to <u>endure</u> (en-DO-ER) terrible conditions and harsh treatment.

   a. bear

   b. enjoy

   c. create

   d. witness

9. Putting the plant in the sun and giving it fertilizer helped it to <u>thrive</u> (THRIVE).

   a. die

   b. become weakened

   c. grow stronger and bigger

   d. wither

10. After the <u>massacre</u> (MASS-a-ker), the Nazis buried the bodies in a large grave and covered them with earth.

   a. defeat

   b. mass killing

   c. rubbing muscles

   d. loss of soldiers

Reading 2 What Do You Already Know?

1. What was your most memorable vacation? Where did you stay?

2. What do you know about Nazi Germany and World War II?

> **Directions:** As you read this article, practice the four-step reading process. Preview the article, and then write on the following lines one or two questions that you would hope to have answered.
>
> ....
>
> ....
>
> ....
>
> ....

As you read, answer the questions in the margins to check your comprehension.

"Where Wishes Come True"

BY CORINNE FENNESSY

One little girl's dream was the beginning of an incredible journey for one man. Henri Landwirth suffered through the worst inhumanity to humankind, but his pain led him to reach out to others in need and to build "Give Kids the World," a special resort near Orlando, Florida, for seriously ill children.

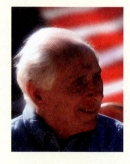

1　Six-year-old Amy, dying of cancer, wanted to meet Mickey Mouse. But while waiting for her dream to come true, she passed away. After learning this, Henri Landwirth, a hospitality <u>entrepreneur,</u> vowed that no child should ever have to die waiting for a last wish to be granted.

2　Henri was born in Belgium, before the Second World War, in a time of peace. He lived with his parents and twin sister in a family strengthened by love. He remembers that his parents loved to dance, and his twin sister and he were very close. They played together, and his parents often entertained guests in the evening. His life was peaceful in a loving family.

3　Then one day in 1939, a group of Nazi soldiers broke into their home, looking for valuables. Later that same year, another group of Nazis came and arrested their father. His only crime was his religion, and because he was Jewish, they threw him into prison.

4　The family began to suffer without their father's love and support. Food became scarce, and fear filled the city as more arrests were made. Soon, the Nazis came back for the rest of Henri's family. Along with all the other Jewish people, they were herded

Reading 2

How did Henri's life change after the Nazis took over?

like cattle into a ghetto and they were imprisoned there, with barely enough food to survive. During this time, no one was allowed to worship, to attend school, or to do any type of group activity. The Nazis treated them with contempt.

5   One day, Henri; his sister, Margot; and his mother were herded onto a train with thousands of others. They were jammed into a crowded boxcar and taken to a concentration camp in Poland. In the camps, they suffered cold, hunger, and thirst. Their daily ration of food was two slices of dry bread and one half cup of rancid, watery soup. It was a slow starvation that turned humans into walking skeletons. The men and women were separated, and Henri was taken from his family and put in another section. One day they were all forced to stand in line to receive a tattoo—a number on the forearm for identification. Soon after, Henri contracted typhus and became very sick, like many others in the camp. Death was everywhere, but Henri feared most for his mother and sister. He was alone and afraid, cut off from the people he loved and who loved him.

6   Henri remembers the kindness of the prisoners who reached out to one another, and he credits his survival to them. But other prisoners thought only of themselves and would do anything to stay alive. Henri and others were beaten for small offenses. His worst beating came when a crust of bread was found hidden in his clothing. And even though the air was filled with the stench of burning bodies as the Nazis cremated them, people still had hope that the war would end and that they would be saved. Hope was the only thing keeping them alive.

What was life like in the concentration camp for Henri?

7   One night toward the end of the war, he and a group of other men were taken to the forest to be shot, but by some miracle, he and a few others escaped through the woods. With open wounds, bleeding from his legs and skull, Henri ran and ran, stopping only to rest briefly. In the weeks that followed, he kept going, and his wounds became badly infected. One morning as he lay dying in a barn, he was found by an elderly couple who saved his life.

How did Henri escape the concentration camp?

8   It was the goal of the Nazis to completely destroy the Jewish people, but it only gave them strength. Henri says, "Pain and suffering become like mortar to those who have endured it together, and we are all held by it, joined in a common way, one to another, by the burden of having shared the same pain." Millions died in the Holocaust—not just Jews but also those who suffered a physical disability, or were Polish, non-white, or homosexual.

9   In the years after the war, Henri learned that his mother had drowned in a prison ship. His father had been killed in a Nazi massacre, but his sister was still alive. He found her, and they returned to Belgium to try to put their lives back together. Henri became an apprentice diamond cutter and soon learned the trade. But the horrible memories of war would not fade. He needed a fresh start, and he decided he would go to America.

10   After the war, America was a beacon of hope for the people of the world. It had not been scarred by war, and it held the promise of a new life. With Henri came millions of others who could not speak English and were hoping for a new beginning. Life in New York City was very difficult, but he found a job and a place to live. A few years later, he was drafted into the U.S. Army and served two years. After that, he began working in

Reading 2

hotels, first as a bellhop and other jobs, then at the night desk. Henri used his veterans' benefit to enroll in the New York Hotel Technology School, where he learned about the hotel business.

11   Two years later, Henri was married and managing a hotel in Miami Beach. There he learned about every aspect of the hotel business, including the restaurant. He was later offered the job as manager of a new hotel, The Starlight Motel. It was built to provide hotel rooms for the growing space industry in Cocoa Beach, Florida. Astronauts and famous news personalities came to stay at the Starlight, and Henri became good friends with many of them. Under his management, the Starlight was a huge success and a favorite hangout of everyone at Cape Canaveral, in the heart of the space industry.

12   Years later, Henri was offered the job as manager of the new Holiday Inn in Cocoa Beach. The hotel thrived under Henri's management. Then another opportunity came along, and Henri went into business with a new hotel. His years of experience in the hotel business paid off. He also expanded into the restaurant business, which led to more opportunities and success.

How did Henri learn the hotel business?

13   Remembering what it was like to suffer hardship, Henri began to use his gifts to help others, and he became involved with children's charities. He helped many children with special needs, and learned how to get others to help donate their goods and services. In 1980, he started the Fanny Landwirth Foundation, named after his mother, to help needy children. Henri's childhood experiences gave him empathy and a desire to help others in need. "Find someone who needs a lift up, who needs a little help. Offer him your hand. Once you experience the pleasure of helping others, many of your other problems will go away," Henri says.

14   When little six-year-old Amy wanted to see Mickey Mouse, her parents contacted Henri's foundation and made the arrangements to go to Disney World. But it took so long that Amy died before her wish was granted. When Henri found out, he was devastated. He learned that it took six to eight weeks to process an application for granting a sick child's wish. Many children with terminal illnesses didn't have that long to live.

15   Henri decided to do something about it. He contacted Disney World and presented a proposal for the children to come to Disney World before it was too late. He laid out his plans to build a village for sick children and their families. He expected that he would be sent away with the usual, "We'll think it over and get back to you." But instead, the executives agreed to help immediately. Henri was amazed when Disney promised to do more than he asked for.

16   Henri was so excited he drove straight to Sea World and made the same proposal to them. They, too, agreed immediately to be a part of his new plan. Henri needed money for his project, and he turned to his old friends, the NASA Mercury astronauts and friends in the news business, hoping some would help him. They all did—every single one—and Holiday Inn donated a million dollars. The ball was rolling on this exciting new project, and Henri's dream of being able to grant wishes to sick children was on its way.

How did Henri get Give Kids the World Village started?

17   Today, Give Kids the World Village is located in Kissimmee, Florida, near the theme parks. "The whole village has been built on handshakes. There were no contracts

216

Reading 2

The Gingerbread House at Give Kids the World Village.

whatsoever," says Henri. It has hundreds of corporate sponsors that give millions of dollars without asking for any credit or advertising.

The Amberville train station at Give Kids the World Village.

18   This magical place is spread over 70 acres. Accommodations for nearly 150 families are home-like villas in a beautifully landscaped park. Families check into the House of Hearts. Guests are welcomed by a six-foot rabbit, Mayor Clayton, who holds a birthday party every Saturday night and goes to the villas to tuck the children in at night. There is a wheelchair-accessible pool for children and their families. The Ice Cream Palace serves free ice cream every day. There is also a video game arcade. And no one pays for this dream vacation; it is all entirely free.

19   Children from 50 states and 50 countries have stayed at the village. Families who stay at the village are given annual passes to all of the local theme parks, including Disney World, Sea World, Universal Orlando, and others. The special children also receive gifts. More than 3,000 volunteers provide services, along with a regular paid staff of more than 100 employees. Families who have been financially devastated by years of living with a seriously ill child can have a vacation that they would never be able to afford on their own. It is the fulfillment of a dream for every family who comes to the village.

20   In his book, *Gift of Life*, Henri writes, "I see the connections now. I can draw a link from the past to the present. From the desperation of my own childhood grew the empathy to serve children facing their own desperate circumstances. From survival as a child, to fighting to help other children survive, my life has come full circle." Henri's dream has become his promise: that no child in need will ever be turned away.

1,730 words divided by .... minutes = ... words per minute

Reading 2 Thinking About What You Read

It is a good habit to summarize everything you read to strengthen your comprehension.

Directions: On the following lines, write a two- or three-sentence summary of the article "Where Wishes Come True." In your own words, describe what the article was about and why the author wrote it.

....

....

....

Comprehension Questions

The following questions will help you to recall the main idea and the details of "When Wishes Come True." Review any parts of the article that you need to find the correct answers.

LITERAL COMPREHENSION

1. **What is the topic of this article?**

   a. World War II

   b. Nazi concentration camps

   c. Henri Landwirth

   d. Give Kids the World Village

MAIN IDEAS

2. **What is the main idea of the article?**

   a. Henri Landwirth is a successful hotel manager.

   b. Give Kids the World Village is a resort for seriously ill children.

   c. Although the Nazis tried to kill Henri Landwirth, he survived and came to America.

   d. Henri Landwirth's life experiences led him to build Give Kids the World Village.

3. **What is the main idea of paragraph 4?**

   a. The family began to suffer without their father's love and support.

   b. Soon, the Nazis came back for the rest of Henri's family.

   c. During this time, no one was allowed to worship, to attend school, or to do any type of group activity.

   d. The Nazis treated them with contempt.

Reading 2

SUPPORTING DETAILS

4. According to the article, Henri's father:

    a. joined the Nazis and left the family.

    b. was killed when the Nazis broke into their home.

    c. was taken away by the Nazis and killed in a massacre.

    d. went with the family to the concentration camp.

5. According to the article, Henri's mother and sister:

    a. left the concentration camp and went to Belgium.

    b. were separated from Henri at the concentration camp.

    c. were sent to another concentration camp.

    d. stayed with Henri during his years at the concentration camp.

6. Henri was able to escape when:

    a. he dug a tunnel out of the concentration camp.

    b. he became sick and was taken to a hospital.

    c. the war ended.

    d. he was taken to the forest to be shot but instead escaped through the woods.

7. According to the article, which of the following is not true?

    a. Disney World and Sea World were both eager to help build the village.

    b. The Mercury astronauts all contributed to the village.

    c. The families only have to pay for their meals.

    d. The village was built with handshakes and not contracts.

8. Label the following sentences from paragraph 13 with "T" for topic, "TS" for topic sentence, "MA" for major detail, and "MI" for minor detail.

    .... Henri Landwirth

    .... He helped many children with special needs and learned how to get others to help donate their goods and services.

    .... In 1980, he started the Fanny Landwirth Foundation, named after his mother, to help needy children.

    .... Remembering what it was like to suffer hardship, Henri began to use his gifts to help others, and he became involved with children's charities.

DRAWING CONCLUSIONS

9. Henri came to America because:

    a. he wanted to escape the Nazis.

    b. he wanted to forget his past and make a fresh start.

    c. he had a dream to build a village for sick children.

    d. there were many other people from Europe coming here.

Reading 2

VOCABULARY IN CONTEXT

10. Use context clues, word part clues, and parts of speech to determine the meaning of the underlined word in the following sentence: It is the <u>fulfillment</u> of a dream for every family who comes to the village.

   a. idea

   b. achievement

   c. experience

   d. filling

Vocabulary Practice

Use the vocabulary words from the Word Bank to complete the following sentences. Write the words into the blanks provided.

WORD BANK				
entrepreneur	empathy	contempt	concentration camps	rancid
typhus	mortar	endure	thrive	massacre

1. The building was so old that much of the .... had fallen out from between the bricks and needed to be replaced.

2. Having had a serious illness herself, Sonia has more .... for other sick people.

3. During World War II, more than 2 million Soviet prisoners of war died in the ....

4. In 2007, the shooting of 32 people at Virginia Tech by a student gunman became known as the Virginia Tech ....

5. As a(n) .... , Bobby Flay has opened his own restaurants, has written seven successful cookbooks, and has his own cooking show on TV.

6. It's difficult to .... a boring class in the middle of the afternoon when I always feel tired.

7. When the economy is good, the unemployment rate is low, people have money to spend, and many businesses ....

8. Jessie treats his ex-girlfriend with such .... that it's hard to believe they once loved each other.

9. After the house was abandoned, the food left in the pantry began to grow ....

10. Antibiotics are used to treat people who have been infected with ....

Reading 2 Questions for Writing and Discussion

Review any parts of the article you need to answer the following questions.

1. If Henri had not decided to "do something" when he found out that Amy had died, what might have been the outcome?

   ....

   ....

   ....

2. Sometimes bad experiences in life can teach us important lessons. What lessons do you think that Henri learned from other people, both good and bad, in his life?

   ....

   ....

   ....

3. There is an old expression that says, "It takes a village to raise a child." Explain how you think this relates to Henri's life and the creation of Give Kids the World Village.

   ....

   ....

4. Explain what you think Henri means by saying, "Pain and suffering become like mortar to those who have endured it together, and we are all held by it, joined in a common way, one to another, by the burden of having shared the same pain."

   ....

   ....

   ....

5. Anti-Semitism (ant-eye-SEM-it-ism) means prejudice against Jews. The Nazis had tried to eliminate the entire race. Anti-Semitism still exists today. Why do you think some people have this prejudice, and what do you think can be done to eliminate it?

   ....

   ....

221

Reading 2 Vocabulary Practice—Crossword

The following vocabulary words are from the article "Where Wishes Come True."

How to Play:
One member of the team will be the clue giver and scorekeeper. The other members will be the players.

1.

The clue giver calls on one member to pick a word box number, such as "2 Across."

2.

The clue giver reads the clue to the player; the player has 10 seconds to give the correct answer. Only one answer is allowed.

3.

If the answer is correct, the word is filled in on the player's crossword puzzle, and the player receives points based on the number of letters in the word. If incorrect, the player receives no points, and the next player is called.

4.

The clue giver calls on the next player and asks for a word box number. Play continues until all the words have been completed.

5.

The player with the most points is the winner.

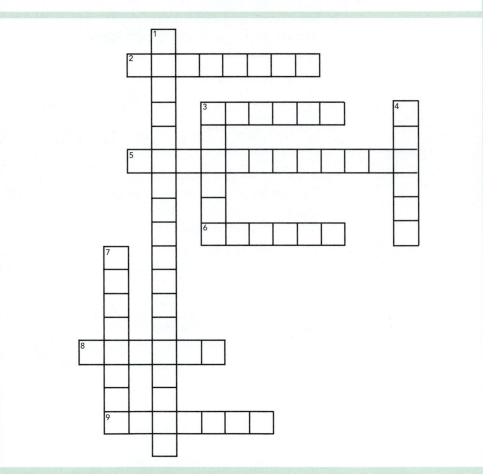

WORD BANK

endured	contempt	rancid	entrepreneur	thrive
massacre	mortar	concentration camps	empathy	typhus

CLUES

ACROSS
2. hatred
3. a disease
5. a person who starts businesses
6. to bear
8. rotten
9. understanding the feelings of others

DOWN
1. prisons (two words)
3. to grow bigger and stronger
4. cement
7. mass killing

Chef Nora Galdiano

How did you get into cooking?
I loved cooking when I was growing up. There were five kids in my family, so I helped my mother in the kitchen a lot. My older brother was a cook in a restaurant. I used to watch him, and I was impressed by his knife skills and wanted to learn how to use a knife like that.

What is your training?
I knew what I wanted to do with my life, and I set goals for myself. I graduated from Kapiʻolani Community College in Hawaii, where I grew up, and then attended the Culinary Institute of America in Hyde Park, New York. After graduation, I moved to Florida and worked for the Hyatt Corporation, at the Grand Cypress Resort and later at the Hyatt Airport Hotel, both in Orlando, Florida. Then four years ago I started at Isleworth Golf and Country Club as the executive sous-chef. I am also working on my bachelor's degree in hospitality management. I am a Certified Executive Chef (C.E.C.) through the American Culinary Federation. When you are a chef, you have to keep studying and learning. You need to keep up with changes in the industry such as standards, trends, and technology. Learning is a lifelong journey.

What's it like cooking for celebrities and millionaires?
It's similar to cooking for the hotel industry but on a much smaller scale, and more personal. Being in a country club is unique. You are expected to maintain good relationships with the members you are cooking for and know their food preferences. They all have specific wants. We go out into the dining room and talk to the members all the time, and you have frequent personal contact with the members.

What do you like about your job?
I love to cook, of course, and I like being able to get to know the people I'm cooking for. Also I like creating new dishes and working with a diverse staff. Each person has something to contribute. I have a great relationship with my supervisor who is a Certified Master Chef (C.M.C.).

What do you dislike about your job?
I don't focus on the negative aspects of the job. I try to always look at the positive aspects and how to improve them. When something negative happens, fix it right away and move on.

What advice do you have for someone who is interested in a career as a chef?
First, get some experience to find out what it's like working in a production kitchen. Do your research, and talk to successful people in the business to get guidance and advice. You have to be in good physical health because you're on your feet all day and the job requires lifting and other strenuous tasks. Really find out what it's like before committing to going to a culinary school. Many culinary students don't realize that you need the hands-on experience to improve your skills and to work your way up the ladder.

VIEWPOINT: Ecotourism

Read the following letters to the editor about whether ecotourism helps or hinders the environment. Then, answer the questions that follow.

Ecotourism is the term for visiting a place that is wild and undeveloped, with rare species of plants and animals. Tourists view natives' lifestyles and cultures. Examples of ecotours would be those to the jungles of Indonesia, the rain forests of Central America, or the mountains of South America.

Dear Editor:

More and more people are traveling to faraway areas to observe endangered wildlife and habitats. In many places, such as the Galapagos Islands, species that can only be found in one place on Earth have been disturbed by the arrival of tourists. New roads and hotels were constructed, polluting the land and water of these endangered species. Tourists mean more trash, more carbon dioxide in the air, and more cruise ships dumping garbage in the ocean. In many places no one is making sure that these companies are being as Earth-friendly as they claim to be. I say we should make laws to stop ecotourism into environmentally sensitive areas. Tourists should stay home and watch endangered animals on television!

Signed,

Mr Green

Dear Editor:

Ecotourism is one of the most unique and exciting ways to vacation. Instead of seeing the same places that everyone else sees, or going to theme parks, we can enjoy nature. Being able to visit remote places and explore new cultures is educational. Learning about endangered species of animals and plants by seeing them in their natural habitat is important for conservation. This sparks interest and support for groups who are trying to save the environment and endangered species, such as the World Wildlife Fund. Also, the local people in these faraway places are often poor, and they benefit from tourism. They sell their goods and services to the tourists, and it helps them. Ecotourism is a great way to vacation, and both tourists and the local economies benefit from this experience.

Signed,

Nature Lover

Critical Thinking

1. *A point of view* is the author's opinion about a topic. To find the author's point of view, ask yourself, "How does this author feel about this issue?" What is the author's point of view about ecotourism in the first letter?

   ....

   ....

2. What is the author's point of view about ecotourism in the second letter?

   ....

   ....

3. Which letter do you agree with, and why?

   ....

   ....

4. What could be the consequences of allowing ecotourism in certain areas where endangered species live?

   ....

   ....

5. What could be the consequences of not allowing ecotourism or severely limiting it?

   ....

   ....

WRITE YOUR THOUGHTS

Write a letter to the editor stating your own feelings about ecotourism. Use a separate sheet of paper.

Health Insurance Policy

The following is an excerpt from a health insurance policy. Preview the selection first, and then read it and answer the questions that follow.

Calendar Year Deductible[1] Requirement

1. Individual Calendar Year Deductible Requirement

This requirement must be satisfied by each Covered Plan Participant each Calendar Year before any payment will be made for any claim. Only those charges indicated on claims received for Covered Services will be credited toward the Individual Calendar Year [1]Deductible and only up to the Allowed Amount.

[1] Deductible: an amount deducted from the total medical costs that will first be paid by the insured customer. For example, if you have a $500 deductible listed on your insurance policy and your first medical bill comes to $700, you must pay $500 once, and after that, everything else will be covered for the rest of the year according to the terms of the policy.

2. Family Calendar Year Deductible Requirement Limit

Once the Covered Employee's family has reached such limit, no Covered Plan Participant in that family will have any additional Calendar Year Deductible responsibility for the remainder of that Calendar Year.

3. Prior Coverage Credit for Deductible

a. A Covered Plan Participant shall be given credit for any Deductible met by such Covered Plan Participant under a previous insurance policy maintained by HLP, which is replaced by this Group Health Plan. This provision only applies if the insurance policy was in effect immediately before the Effective Date of the Group Health Plan.

b. Each Covered Plan Participant is responsible for providing any information necessary to apply this previous coverage credit.

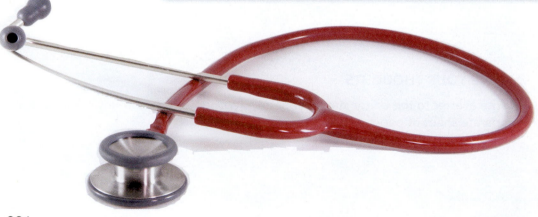

Questions

On the lines provided, write whether the following statements are true or false. If the statement is false, correct it on the space provided.

1. Before the insurance company will pay you for medical costs, every individual must first satisfy a Calendar Year Deductible.

2. A deductible is an amount deducted from the total medical costs that will first be paid by the insurance company.

3. Once the Covered Employee's family has reached such limit, no Covered Plan Participant in that family will have any additional Calendar Year Deductible responsibility for the remainder of their lives.

4. Participants in the Group Health Plan will be given credit for any deductibles they have met under a previous health insurance policy maintained by HLP.

5. Each Covered Plan Participant is responsible for providing any information necessary to apply a previous coverage credit.

TEXTBOOK GRAPHIC AIDS

Read the following chart, and then answer the questions that follow.

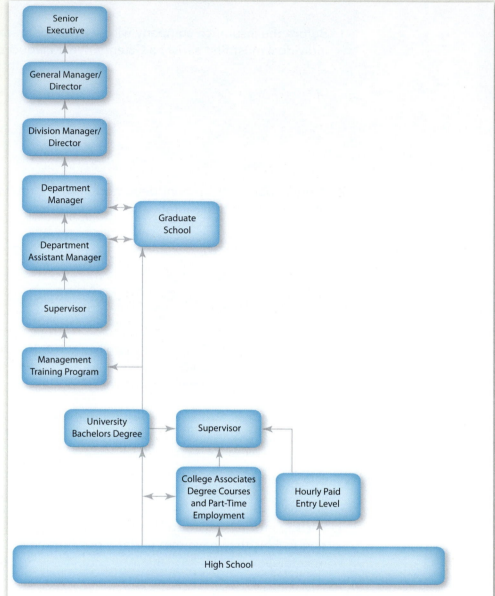

Figure 1.1 A Likely Career Path in the Hospitality Industry. Is Education Worth it? You Bet! Just Think— the Difference is Salary Over a Career Between an Associate's and a Bachelor's Degree is $500,000. Yes, That's Half a Million Bucks! (Source: U.S. Census Bureau Average Lifetime Earnings— Different Level of Education)

(From *Introduction to Hospitality*, 5th Ed. by John Walker. Copyright © 2009 by Pearson Education, Inc., Upper Saddle River, NJ. Reprinted with permission.)

1. **What is the topic of this chart?**
   a. management jobs
   b. a likely career path in the hospitality industry
   c. degrees and jobs
   d. the hospitality industry

2. **What type of job is offered to someone with a high school diploma and nothing more?**
   a. senior executive
   b. department manager
   c. management training program
   d. hourly paid entry level

3. What type of education would be required for someone to become a division manager?

   a. high school

   b. associates' degree

   c. bachelor's degree

   d. graduate school

4. What type of jobs would be offered to someone with a bachelor's degree? (Circle all that apply.)

   a. general manager/director

   b. supervisor

   c. division manager

   d. department assistant manager

5. Which of these jobs requires a graduate school degree? (Circle all that apply.)

   a. division manager/director

   b. department assistant manager

   c. senior executive

   d. general manager/director

BUILDING VOCABULARY

Throughout this course, you will be introduced to word parts that make up many words in the English language. Study the following word parts, and then answer the questions that follow.

Prefixes	Roots	Suffixes
inter- *between*	sect- *part, section*	-ion *action, state of**
bi- *two*	-ject- *to throw*	
re- *again**	-cess- *to stop, cease*	
in- *into**		*Word parts from previous chapters

1. What English words can you create from these word parts?

....

....

....

....

Using a dictionary, look up the meanings of any of the words you wrote that you can't define. Use one of the words you wrote in a sentence that reveals its meaning with a context clue:

....

....

....

CHAPTER REVIEW PRACTICE #1

Read the following paragraph, and underline the main idea and major details. Then, answer the questions that follow.

When Emeril Lagasse graduated from high school in Fall River, Massachusetts, he was offered a full music scholarship to the New England Conservatory of Music as a percussionist. Instead, he decided to become a professional chef and enrolled at Johnson and Wales University in Providence, Rhode Island. While he was in college, Emeril worked in restaurants. He also studied culinary arts in Paris and Lyon, France. After working in many restaurants, he was offered the job as executive chef at Commander's Palace, a famous restaurant in New Orleans. After achieving success there, he left to open his own restaurant, Emeril's, in New Orleans. A few years later, he began hosting his own TV show, cooking with his own special spice blends that now sell in supermarkets. Emeril has published eight best-seller cookbooks and has opened 10 Emeril's restaurants around the country. Each restaurant has a different style of cuisine, but all of them feature his special blends of bold spices, which he adds with a "Bam!" Emeril has made a successful career as a professional chef and restauranteur.

1. What is the topic?

   a. Emeril's restaurants

   b. Emeril Lagasse

   c. becoming a professional chef

   d. Emeril's cooking

2. What is the topic sentence of this paragraph?

   a. When Emeril Lagasse graduated from high school in Fall River, Massachusetts, he was offered a full music scholarship to the New England Conservatory of Music as a percussionist.

   b. Instead, he decided to become a professional chef and enrolled at Johnson and Wales University in Providence, Rhode Island.

   c. Emeril has made a successful career as a professional chef and restaurateur.

   d. Each restaurant has a different style of cuisine, but all of them feature his special blends of bold spices, which he adds with a "Bam!"

3. **Which of the following is not a major detail?**

   a. Instead, he decided to become a professional chef and enrolled at Johnson and Wales University in Providence.

   b. After working in many restaurants, he was offered the job as executive chef at Commander's Palace, a famous restaurant in New Orleans.

   c. Emeril has published eight best-seller cookbooks and has opened 10 Emeril's restaurants around the country.

   d. Each restaurant has a different style of cuisine, but all of them feature his special blends of bold spices, which he adds with a "Bam!"

4. **Which minor detail tells more about the sentence, "Instead, he decided to become a professional chef and enrolled at Johnson and Wales University in Providence, Rhode Island"?**

   a. While he was in college, Emeril worked in restaurants.

   b. After working in many restaurants, he was offered the job as executive chef at Commander's Palace, a famous restaurant in New Orleans.

   c. A few years later he hosted his own TV show, cooking with his own special spice blends that now sell in supermarkets.

   d. Emeril has made a successful career as a professional chef and restaurateur.

5. **Identify the best meaning for the underlined word in the following sentence: "Emeril has made a successful career as a professional chef and restauranteur."**

   a. someone who goes to restaurants

   b. a restaurant owner

   c. a chef

   d. an investor

CHAPTER REVIEW PRACTICE #2

Read the following paragraph, and underline the main idea and major details. Then, complete the concept map that follows, entering information in the order it is presented in the paragraph.

Mega events are major entertainment productions. Most of these are sporting events that bring in millions of dollars to the production companies and local economies. The biggest sporting event is the Olympic Games, which attracts more than 6 million people to its host city. The competition to host an Olympic Games event is very tough, and countries are willing to spend millions to accommodate this event because of the economic benefits. The World Cup event is the final competition for the best soccer teams in the world. It also draws millions of people during the three years of competition for the championship. The Super Bowl football game is the biggest American sporting event held annually. The halftime entertainment has become as big as the championship itself, featuring spectacular shows. Oddly enough, the commercials produced for this event are as much a part of the event as the entertainment. Other mega events include the World Series baseball championship and the Masters Golf Tournament. One of the most famous sailing races held every year is the America's Cup. Working at any one of these mega events is an exciting and challenging job, and thousands of people are needed to plan, coordinate, and produce these mega events.

Topic: ....

Main Idea: Mega events ....

Olympic	World	....	World	....	America's

Attracts ....

Halftime ....

and ....

CHAPTER REVIEW PRACTICE #3

Read the following paragraph, and underline the main idea and major details. Then, complete the concept map that follows, entering information in the order it is presented in the paragraph.

A concierge (kon-see-AIRJ) is a hotel employee whose job is to make the guests' stay as enjoyable as possible. The use of the concierge is free and includes a wide variety of services such as obtaining reservations to restaurants in town. They can sometimes get a reservation even when the restaurant tells other guests that there are none available. They also help the guests plan what to do and how to get to the local activities, attractions, and entertainment. They will also make airline reservations or confirm flights and obtain tickets for theater or concert performances. They suggest stores for shopping. They will also sometimes perform unusual services for their guests. One concierge in Madrid helped a guest find a bull to ship home to Japan. Another concierge in London took the place of the best man who was unable to come to a wedding. The job of a concierge is one that is unpredictable and perfect for people who like helping others to enjoy their visit.

Topic: ....

Main Idea: ....

....

Obtains	Helps guests plan	Makes	Suggests stores	Performs unusual services.
....	....	.... obtains tickets.	....	

Can get reservations				One found a bull in Madrid. Another was a best man.
....				

TEXTBOOK PRACTICE

Read the following textbook selection, and underline the main idea and major details. Then, complete the concept map that follows.

The Brewing Process

Beer is brewed from water, malt, yeast, and hops. The brewing process begins with water, an important ingredient in the making of beer. The mineral content and purity of the water largely determine the quality of the final product. Water accounts for 85 to 89 percent of the finished beer.

Next, grain is added in the form of malt, which is barley that has been ground to a course grit. The grain is germinated, producing an enzyme that converts starch into fermentable sugar. The yeast is the fermenting agent. Breweries typically have their own cultured yeasts, which, to a large extent, determine the type and taste of the beer. Mashing is the term for grinding the malt and screening out any bits of dirt.

The malt then goes through a hopper into a mash tub, which is a large stainless steel or copper container. Here the water and grains are mixed and heated. The liquid is now called wort and is filtered through a mash filter or lauter tub. This liquid then flows into a brewing kettle, where hops are added and the mixture is boiled for several hours. After the brewing operation, the hop wort is filtered through the hop separator or hop jack. The filtered liquid then is pumped through a wort cooler and flows into a fermenting vat where pure-culture yeast is added for fermentation. The brew is aged for a few days prior to being barreled for draught beer or pasteurized for bottled or canned beer.

(From *Introduction to Hospitality*, 5th ed. by John Walker. Copyright © 2009 by Pearson Education, Inc., Upper Saddle River, New Jersey. Reprinted with permission.)

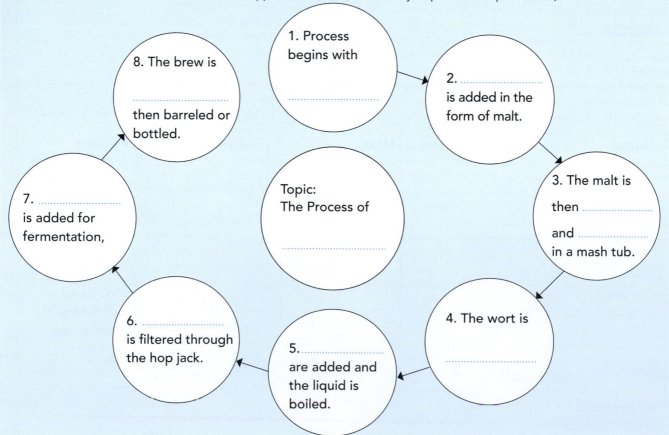

8. The brew is .... then barreled or bottled.

1. Process begins with ....

2. .... is added in the form of malt.

7. .... is added for fermentation,

Topic: The Process of ....

3. The malt is then .... and .... in a mash tub.

6. .... is filtered through the hop jack.

5. .... are added and the liquid is boiled.

4. The wort is ....

STUDY SKILL CHAPTER REVIEW

Concept maps are a helpful tool for reviewing chapter material or for planning essays or research papers.

Complete the following concept map for the content covered in this chapter.

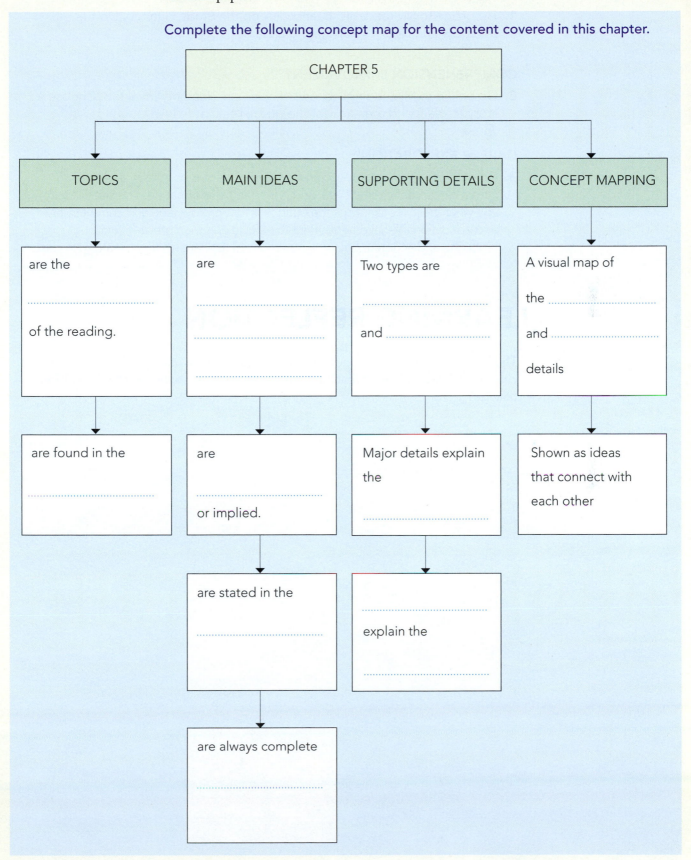

READING LAB ASSIGNMENTS

REVIEW PRACTICE

1. Go online to MyReadingLab, and click on the Study Plan tab. Do the practices and tests for Supporting Details.

COMPREHENSION IMPROVEMENT

2. Go online to MyReadingLab, and click on the Reading Level tab. Choose a story to read, and then answer the questions that follow.

CAREER EXPLORATION

3. Go online to www.bls.gov/oco and explore careers in hospitality and tourism. Find a career that interests you, and print out the information. This site will tell you what the job is like, what the outlook is for employment, and current salary and educational requirements. Print the article and then preview, read, highlight, and annotate one or two sections of it. Share what you learned in class.

LEARNING REFLECTION

Think about the skills and concepts in this chapter. What have you learned in this chapter that will help your reading comprehension and enable you to do well in college?

SELF-EVALUATION CHECKLIST

Rate yourself on the following items, using the following scale:

1 = strongly disagree   4 = agree

2 = disagree   5 = strongly agree

3 = neither agree nor disagree

1. I completed all of the assigned work on time. ....

2. I understand all of the concepts in this chapter. ....

3. I contributed to teamwork and class discussions. ....

4. I completed all of the assigned lab work on time. ....

5. I came to class on time. ....

6. I attended class every day. ....

7. I studied for any quizzes or tests we had for this chapter. ....

8. I asked questions when I didn't understand something. ....

9. I checked my comprehension during reading. ....

10. I know what is expected of me in the coming week. ....

11. Are you still on track with the goals you set in Chapter 1?

....

What changes can you make to improve your performance in this?

....

....

....

....

For support in meeting this chapter's objectives, go to the Study Plan in MyReadingLab and select Supporting Details. Read and view the resources in the Review Materials section, and then complete the Recall, Apply, and Write exercises in the Activities section. Check your results by clicking on Gradebook.

STUDY SKILL: METACOGNITION

According to researcher David A. Sousa, metacognition (met-ah-cog-NISH-un) is the awareness one has of his or her own thinking processes. It means that, as a student, you should know not only what you are learning but also how you are learning it and if your learning processes are successful or not. If they're not successful, you should think about why they aren't and what you should do to fix the problem. Students who are successful use metacognitive strategies regularly.

Metacognition involves several steps:

1.
Look at what you are trying to learn, and describe it in your own words by asking yourself, "What is my learning objective?"

2.
With your personal learning style in mind, choose an appropriate learning strategy that will help you to learn the objective or material. For example, will you practice something, make note cards, make a recording to listen to, work with a study partner, or watch a video?

3.
Use the strategies that you have chosen to study. Practice every day.

4.
Monitor your learning by using self-testing or other means. Go back to analyze your errors, and figure out why you made them.

5.
Decide if you have successfully learned the material, and, if you haven't, make changes in your learning strategies to accomplish your goal. Then try again.

Knowing your learning style strengths would be important for deciding what strategies to use to learn something. Here's an example of how one student uses metacognition:

Keisha, a visual and kinesthetic learner, was trying to learn to solve equations for a math exam. Her learning strategy was to study some examples of equations in her text and practice some of these problems. She spent a few hours doing this, and then took the quiz at the end of the chapter and checked her answers. Half of them were wrong, and she wondered why. She looked at the ones she missed and compared them to the ones she got correct. The problems she missed all included division as one of the steps. She looked "division" up in her textbook and read all the references to it. She discovered that multiplication comes before division in the order of operations, not after it as she had thought. She then again worked the problems that she had missed and got them all correct. Keisha learned that, in the order of operations, multiplication always comes before division. On her math exam, she earned a 95 percent and was pleased with her results.

1. What was Keisha's learning objective?

....

2. How did Keisha monitor her learning?

....

3. What did Keisha do that enabled her to be successful on her second try?

....

....

4. What changes did Keisha make to her learning strategies that enabled her to succeed?

....

....

5. If she had been unable to figure out why she missed half of the questions, what could she have done to reach her learning objective?

....

....

U-Review

With a partner, take turns asking each other the following questions. You may look up the answer if needed.

1. What is metacognition?

....

2. What is the first step you should do?

....

3. What is the second step?

....

4. What is the third step?

....

5. What is the fourth step?

....

6. What is the fifth step?

....

....

CHAPTER 6 PATTERNS OF ORGANIZATION—PART 1

LEARNING OBJECTIVES

IN THIS CHAPTER, YOU WILL:

Objective 1 identify different patterns of organization and indicate why they are important to comprehension.

Objective 2 recognize relationships within and between sentences.

FOCUS ON SPORTS AND FITNESS

There are many talented athletes who enter college with a scholarship and establish themselves on college sports teams. Only a small percentage of these hundreds of thousands of students will go on to play in professional sports.

There are many exciting and rewarding careers in fitness and sports, even if you are not an athlete. Many of these careers offer the opportunity to work with professional athletic teams. There is also a great deal of variety in the environments in which you may work: high schools, colleges, universities, cruise ships, exclusive vacation resorts, or health clubs, to name a few. Sports-related job opportunities are also available in the retail business selling sporting equipment. Outdoor sports are becoming increasingly popular, and you can enjoy activities like mountain climbing or skiing as an instructor or guide. Whatever your particular interests in sports and fitness, you can find a satisfying career in this field.

Objective 1 ▸ PATTERNS OF ORGANIZATION

Look at the following lists, and try to memorize the numbers in 60 seconds:

LIST 1

| 2, 4, 6, 8, 10, 12, 14 |

LIST 2

| 1, 5, 13, 90, 515, 267, 301 |

After the minute is up, turn the page so you're not looking at the numbers, wait one minute, and then try to recite or write the lists by memory. When you are ready, turn back to see how well you did. Which list was the most difficult to remember? You probably thought list 2 was the most difficult, because it consisted of random numbers, and you probably were able to repeat list 1 without any trouble.

The reason you probably had all of the numbers in list 1 right is because you recognized a familiar pattern. You could probably also predict what numbers would come next in the sequence because, once the brain recognizes a pattern, it starts to look for other pieces that fit the pattern. Our brains seek to find organization in what we observe or do. We are wired to understand information better when it is presented in an orderly way. We can also recall it more easily, as we saw with list 1. Similarly, knowing the common patterns of organization in writing and reading will not only improve your comprehension, but it will also improve your thinking and writing skills.

Patterns of organization, or thought patterns, are the way that writers arrange details in a sentence, a paragraph, or an essay. We will be looking at patterns at all three levels.

To determine the pattern of a paragraph, you must first determine the topic and find the topic sentence. Often, the topic sentence will give a clue as to the pattern of organization. Also, ask yourself, "What are most of the major supporting details showing me?" Next, think of the patterns of organization and ask yourself, "Which type of relationship is the author showing?"

> **Patterns of organization,** or thought patterns, are the ways that writers arrange the details in a sentence, a paragraph, or an essay.

TRANSITION WORDS

As you may recall from Chapter 5, transitions are words or phrases that signal an idea, such as a supporting detail. They also signal the author's train of thought. For example:

First, finish your homework. *Next*, go to the sports center, and *then*, go shoot some hoops.

In this sentence, the transition words indicate a specific order of ideas. Notice how the transition words in each pattern are very similar in that they all indicate *when* something happens.

241

One way to figure out the relationship within a sentence is to look for clues such as transition words. Learning the transition words for each pattern can help you determine the relationship of ideas being shown in the sentence. However, *some sentences do not have transitions*, or the transitions you see may *not signal the actual pattern*. In these cases, you need to rely on the details in the sentence, instead of transition words, to help you figure out the relationship. The more you practice looking for relationships and thinking about the ideas in sentences, the easier it will be for you to determine them.

For example:

> Body fat usually increases with age.

This sentence has no transitions, but the relationship being shown is one of cause and effect. Age is the cause, and increased body fat is the effect.

Objective 2 — RELATIONSHIPS WITHIN AND BETWEEN SENTENCES

As you learn the following patterns of organization, determine which patterns are used within or between the sentences that you are reading.

Definition Pattern

A definition pattern is easy to spot because it defines a word or term. The term may be shown in bold or italics, though not always. Definitions are often set off by commas, dashes, brackets, or parentheses. Use the definition transitions in the next box to complete the sentences that follow. There may be more than one transition that can complete a sentence correctly.

DEFINITION TRANSITIONS

are	are known as	defined	definition
describes	is	is known as	means
refers to	is (are) called	that is	

1. Meditation .... a state of complete mental and physical relaxation.

2. Abnormally high blood pressure .... hypertension.

3. Carbohydrates .... sugars that are a source of energy for the body.

4. The basic substances found in foods that your body needs to maintain health .... nutrients.

5. LBP.................... low back pain, a condition associated with a lack of exercise.

Listing Pattern

The listing pattern, also known as *simple listing*, presents a random list of ideas. The order of the ideas is not important. Use the listing transitions in the next box to complete the sentences that follow. There may be more than one transition that can complete a sentence correctly.

LISTING TRANSITIONS

one	final	furthermore	third
finally	last	then	also
and	in addition	moreover	besides
another	next	first	second
for one thing			

1. Three types of joints found in the human body are the ball and socket, the hinge joint, ...the pivot joint.

2. To maintain a healthy body weight, *first*, you should exercise; ...., eat healthy foods that are low in fat; and ...., drink plenty of water.

3. .... exercise, it is .... important to provide the body with enough rest.

4. Smoking can increase the risk of stroke, ...it can increase heart rate and blood pressure.

5. When training for her marathons, Karen runs 8 kilometers, rides 20 kilometers on her bike, ... swims 10 kilometers at least twice a week.

243

Cause-and-Effect Pattern

The cause-and-effect pattern shows the causes and/or the effects of one or more actions. It can also show how one effect can have several causes or how several causes can have several effects. Use the cause-and-effect transitions in the next box to complete the sentences that follow. There may be more than one transition that can complete a sentence correctly.

The word **affect** is a verb, meaning "to cause or influence." The word **effect** is a noun, meaning "a result."

CAUSE-AND-EFFECT TRANSITIONS

Cause Transitions			Effect Transitions		
affect	due to	lead to	as a result	consequently	result
cause	because	reason	consequence	effect	so
since	if...then	explanation	therefore	thus	

1. A lack of exercise can .... obesity.

2. *If* weight-bearing exercise is increased, ... the muscle fibers will increase in size.

3. Another.. of regular exercise is improved mental health because the brain releases chemicals during exercise that cause a sense of well-being.

4. Anabolic steroids, substances taken to increase muscle mass, can .... serious physical and mental health risks.

5. One .... of strength training is that it can reduce or eliminate lower back pain.

Compare-and-Contrast Pattern

The compare-and-contrast pattern shows how things are alike or different. When you compare things, you examine their similarities. When you contrast things, you examine their differences. Authors sometimes use only one of these patterns or both together, so this pattern is referred to as "compare and contrast" or "compare and/or contrast." Use the compare-and-contrast transitions in the next two boxes to complete the sentences that follow. There may be more than one transition that can complete a sentence correctly.

COMPARISON TRANSITIONS (show similarities)

alike	as	both	in the same way	same
in a similar	way	like	likewise	similar

1. When beginning a weight-training program, women achieve strength .... quickly as men do.
2. The human brain stores information .... a computer.
3. The brain works... as a shipping company, carrying loads of information to long-term storage.
4. American soccer and British football are very............................. .
5. .... aerobic exercises and swimming can improve heart function and fitness.

CONTRAST TRANSITIONS (show differences)

although	as opposed to	but	contrast	contrary to
differ	different	even though	however	
instead	in spite of	less than	more than	nevertheless
rather than	than	unlike	while	
yet	on the other hand	on the contrary		

1. People at their recommended body weight are likely to live longer ....those of people who are overweight and obese.
2. ....overweight individuals, people who maintain a healthy weight have fewer health, skeletal, and joint problems.
3. ....too much stored fat is not healthy, you would never want to eliminate it from your diet.
4. Salt is a necessary nutrient for the body; ...., most people eat much more salt than they should, which increases their blood pressure.
5. Controlling your weight means permanently changing the way you eat by choosing low-fat and low-calorie foods .... high-fat and high-calorie foods.

Than is used for comparison. **Then** signifies time order.

Practice

1. In the following sentences, choose the correct type of relationship that is being shown within or between the sentences.

1. To stay healthy, you should *include* vegetables, fruits, and whole grains in your daily diet.

   a. definition

   b. listing

   c. cause and effect

   d. compare and/or contrast

2. Don't drink soda with your meals because it's high in calories and sodium. *Instead*, have a glass of milk, soy milk, or water.

   a. definition

   b. listing

   c. cause and effect

   d. compare and/or contrast

3. As people age, they become weaker and can develop osteoporosis. Osteoporosis is *defined* as a bone disease in which the mineral content of the bone is reduced and the bone is weakened.

   a. definition

   b. listing

   c. cause and effect

   d. compare and/or contrast

4. Some fruits and vegetables can lose some of their vitamins during cooking. *Therefore*, it is best to eat them raw or only slightly cooked.

   a. definition

   b. listing

   c. cause and effect

   d. compare and/or contrast

5. Avoid processed meats even if they are "low-fat." The *reason* for this is that most of these have large amounts of salt.

   a. definition

   b. listing

   c. cause and effect

   d. compare and/or contrast

Practice

2. Read the following paragraph, and underline the main idea and major details. Then, identify the relationships in the questions that follow.

THE PARALYMPICS

Talented athletes who have physical disabilities are able to compete internationally like nondisabled athletes in the International Paralympic Games. The word "paralympic" means "with the Olympics." Disabled athletes compete in many of the same events as the regular Olympics. They compete in swimming, skiing, basketball, and many other sports. Because of the athletes' disabilities, many of the games have been modified. Ice hockey is played on small sledges, and many games, such as curling and basketball, are played in wheelchairs. Like the regular Olympics, the athletes are awarded bronze, silver, and gold medals. The idea of having athletic competitions for disabled athletes started in England in 1948 with wheelchair races. In 1952, games for the disabled were held along with the Olympics. The first official Paralympics started in 1960 when 400 athletes represented 23 countries. Now they are held every four years in the same city as the regular Olympic Games.

1. Talented athletes who have physical disabilities are able to compete internationally *like* nondisabled athletes in the International Paralympic Games.
   - **a.** definition
   - **b.** listing
   - **c.** cause and effect
   - **d.** compare and/or contrast

2. The word "paralympic" *means* "with the Olympics."
   - **a.** definition
   - **b.** listing
   - **c.** cause and effect
   - **d.** compare and/or contrast

3. They compete in swimming, skiing, basketball, and many other sports.
   - **a.** definition
   - **b.** listing
   - **c.** cause and effect
   - **d.** compare and/or contrast

4. *Like* the regular Olympics, the athletes are awarded bronze, silver, and gold medals.
   - **a.** definition
   - **b.** listing
   - **c.** cause and effect
   - **d.** compare and/or contrast

5. *Because of* the athletes' disabilities, many of the games have been modified.
   - **a.** definition
   - **b.** listing
   - **c.** cause and effect
   - **d.** compare and contrast

Practice

3. Read the following paragraphs, and underline the main idea and major details. Then, answer the questions that follow.

WIND SPRINTS

Wind sprints are short bursts of high-intensity exercise that increase your fitness level by forcing your body to adapt to a higher level of intensity. During the lower-intensity phase, your body builds fat-burning enzymes (substances your body makes). These enzymes help you handle the stress of the high-intensity sprint. This also increases your fat-burning ability. A person of average fitness who is not an athlete can do this during a 30-minute walk. Begin with a 5- to 10-minute warm-up. Next, sprint (run) for 30 seconds. Then, walk as you normally would for 1 minute. Repeat the sprint-and-walk pattern 3 times. In the second phase, walk for 5 minutes at normal speed. In the third phase, sprint for 1 full minute, and then walk for 1 minute. Repeat this pattern 3 times. In the last phase, return to your regular walking pace to warm down for the remaining time.

It is not necessary to go extremely fast when you run, but just fast enough to feel winded. There are other ways to do wind sprints, and they are described in various fitness articles found on the Internet. Just search for "wind sprints" to find the one that is right for you.

1. What is the topic sentence of this selection?

   a. Wind sprints are short bursts of high-intensity exercise that increase your fitness level by forcing your body to adapt to a higher level of intensity.

   b. During the lower-intensity phase, your body builds fat-burning enzymes (substances your body makes).

   c. It is not necessary to go extremely fast when you run, but just fast enough to feel winded.

   d. Just search for "wind sprints" to find the one that is right for you.

2. What is the meaning of the word "enzyme" as it is used in the second sentence?

   a. a type of exercise

   b. a level of exercise

   c. a substance that is produced by the body

   d. a drug

3. Identify the relationship within the following sentence: Wind sprints are short bursts of high-intensity exercise that increase your fitness level by forcing your body to adapt to a higher level of intensity.

   a. definition

   b. listing

   c. cause and effect

   d. compare and/or contrast

Practice

4. Identify the relationship between the following sentences: During the lower-intensity phase, your body builds fat-burning enzymes (substances your body makes). These enzymes help you handle the stress of the high-intensity sprint.

   a. definition

   b. listing

   c. cause and effect

   d. compare and/or contrast

5. Identify the relationship within the following sentence: It is not necessary to go extremely fast when you run, *but* just fast enough to feel winded.

   a. definition

   b. listing

   c. cause and effect

   d. compare and/or contrast

TEXTBOOK SELECTION

Read the following selection, and underline the main idea and major details. Then, answer the questions that follow.

Selecting Activities

Every exercise prescription includes at least one mode of exercise—that is, a specific type of exercise to be performed. For example, to improve cardiorespiratory—heart and respiration—fitness, you could select from a wide variety of activities, such as running, swimming, or cycling. To ensure that you'll engage in the exercise regularly, you should choose activities that you will enjoy doing, that are available to you, and that carry little risk of injury.

Physical activities can be classified as being either high impact or low impact, based on the amount of stress placed on joints during the activity. Low-impact activities put less stress on the joints than high-impact activities. Because of the strong correlation between high-impact activities and injuries, many fitness experts recommend low-impact activities for fitness beginners or for people susceptible to injury (such as people who are older or overweight). Examples of low-impact activities include walking, cycling, swimming, and low-impact aerobic dance. High-impact activities include running, basketball, and high-impact aerobic dance.

Swimming and volleyball are both excellent for the cardiovascular system. Swimming puts less stress on the joints and is considered a low-impact activity, whereas volleyball puts more stress on the joints and is considered a high-impact activity.

(From *Total Fitness and Wellness*, 5e by Scott K. Powers and Stephen L. Dodd. Copyright © 2009 by Scott K. Powers and Stephen L. Dodd. Reprinted by permission of Pearson Education, Inc., Upper Saddle River, NJ.)

QUESTIONS

1. What is the topic of this selection?

   a. high- and low-impact activities

   b. modes of exercise

   c. cardiorespiratory fitness

   d. selecting activities

Identify the relationships within the following sentences.

2. Every exercise prescription includes at least one mode of exercise—that is, a specific type of exercise to be performed.

   a. definition

   b. listing

   c. cause and effect

   d. compare and/or contrast

3. To ensure that you'll engage in the exercise regularly, you should choose activities that you will enjoy doing, that are available to you, and that carry little risk of injury.

   a. definition

   b. listing

   c. cause and effect

   d. compare and/or contrast

4. Low-impact activities put less stress on the joints than high-impact activities.

   a. definition

   b. listing

   c. cause and effect

   d. compare and/or contrast

5. Because of the strong correlation between high-impact activities and injuries, many fitness experts recommend low-impact activities for fitness beginners or for people susceptible to injury (such as people who are older or overweight).

   a. definition

   b. listing

   c. cause and effect

   d. compare and/or contrast

U-Review

Use the patterns listed below to answer the following questions. When you have finished, pair up with another person to check your answers.

definition

listing

cause and effect

compare and/or contrast

1. If you were trying to explain the outcome of an experiment you performed in a science lab, what pattern would you choose and why?

....

....

....

2. If you were taking notes at a lecture on the characteristics of a democracy, which pattern would you use?

....

....

....

3. If you wanted to buy a car but hadn't yet decided which one to buy, which pattern would you use to help you decide, and why?

....

....

....

4. If you were trying to explain to your study group what marsupials are, which pattern would you use, and why?

....

....

....

RECOGNIZING OVERALL PATTERNS OF ORGANIZATION

Recognizing overall patterns means looking at the whole paragraph instead of just a sentence or two to determine the pattern. As you are reading, look specifically at the major supporting details and ask yourself, "How are the supporting details organized?" The topic sentence can often give you a clue as to the paragraph's overall pattern of organization. For example, if the topic sentence contrasts two items, then it is likely the rest of the paragraph will give details about how the two items differ from one another. Note that the overall pattern of organization may differ from the patterns shown within or between sentences.

As you read the following paragraph, think about the topic, the main idea, and the major details.

The Benefits of Rest

Exercise causes muscle tissue breakdown, energy loss, and fluid loss. Getting enough rest after exercising or training is very beneficial to the body. One benefit of rest is that it allows the body to renew its energy, like a rechargeable battery renews its charge. Another effect is that it allows the body to repair damaged tissues. Resting also allows time for the body to remove chemicals that build up in the body during exercise.

Topic: The benefits of rest

Main idea: Getting enough rest after exercising or training is very beneficial to the body. (To find the major details, ask, "What are the benefits of getting enough rest?")

Major detail #1: One benefit of rest is that it allows the body to renew its energy.

Major detail #2: Another effect is that it allows the body to repair damaged tissues.

Major detail #3: Resting also allows time for the body to remove chemicals that build up in the body during exercise.

> **How are the major details organized?**
> **a.** a definition of a term
> **b.** a list of ideas in no particular order
> **c.** showing the effects of an action
> **d.** comparing things that are alike or contrasting things that are different

In a paragraph that lists the effects of something, you may think that it is a listing pattern—answer (b). But remember that the main idea is "Getting enough rest after exercising or training is very beneficial to the body." In this case, the author intends to show the *effects* of resting after exercise, so the correct answer would be (c). You should always go back to the main idea to look for clues as to what the author intended to show with the supporting details.

Practice

1. Read the following paragraph, and determine the overall pattern of organization. Underline the main idea and major supporting details, and then answer the questions that follow.

WARM-UPS

¹It's always tempting to begin a game or an exercise and skip over the warm-up, such as stretching. ²But warm-ups are an important part of training and exercise with several advantageous effects. ³First, after doing a warm-up routine, muscles that are warmed will perform better and increase strength and speed. ⁴Second, a warm-up will raise the body's temperature and improve the flexibility of the muscles, reducing the risk of injury. ⁵Third, the blood vessels will grow larger, increasing blood flow and reducing the stress on the heart. ⁶Also, your body will increase its production of hormones for energy, which will increase your endurance. ⁷Finally, a good warm-up will help you to focus mentally on the exercise or the game.

1. What is the main idea?

   a. It's always tempting to begin a game or an exercise and skip over the warm-up, such as stretching.

   b. But warm-ups are an important part of training and exercise.

   c. But warm-ups are an important part of training and exercise with several advantageous effects.

   d. Finally, a good warm-up will help you to focus mentally on the exercise or game.

2. Which sentences give the major details?

   a. sentences 1, 4, 5, and 6   **c.** sentences 5, 6, and 7

   b. sentences 1, 2, and 3   **d.** sentences 3, 4, 5, 6, and 7

3. Which of the following transitions are found in the major supporting details?

   a. another, also, additionally, and   **c.** but, is, means, always

   b. first, second, third, also, finally   **d.** but, however, in contrast, differently

4. How are the major details organized?

   a. They define what a warm-up is.

   b. They compare different types of warm-ups.

   c. They explain the causes of warm-ups.

   d. They describe the beneficial effects of warm-ups.

5. What is the overall pattern of organization?

   a. definition   **c.** cause and effect

   b. listing   **d.** compare and/or contrast

Practice

2. Read the following paragraph, and determine the overall pattern of organization. Underline the main idea and major supporting details, and then answer the questions that follow.

ERGOGENIC AIDS

¹Ergogenic (er-go-JEN-ik) aids are substances, drugs, procedures, or devices that improve athletic performance. ²These can be legal or illegal and are used by many athletes both amateur and professional. ³Some of these ergogenic aids have been banned by sporting authorities because they are unsafe and give players an unfair advantage. ⁴One is ephedrine (eff-FED-drin), which is a stimulant, meaning it increases the heart rate, raises blood pressure, and can cause death if too much is taken. ⁵Others are anabolic (an-a-BOLL-ik) steroids (STAIR-oids), which are various chemicals made in a laboratory to increase muscle mass. ⁶They delay fatigue and give players a false feeling of well-being. ⁷But the side effects of these drugs are often severe and cause serious damage to the body and mind with long-term use.

1. What is the main idea?

   a. Ergogenic (er-go-JEN-ik) aids are substances, drugs, procedures, or devices that improve athletic performance.

   b. These can be legal or illegal and are used by many athletes both amateur and professional.

   c. Some of these ergogenic aids have been banned by sporting authorities because they are unsafe.

   d. But the side effects of these drugs are often severe and cause serious damage to the body and mind with long-term use.

2. Which sentences give the major details?

   a. sentences 1, 2, and 3   **c.** sentences 2, 4, and 6

   b. sentences 3, 4, 5, and 6   **d.** sentences 4 and 5

3. Which of the following transitions are found in the <u>major</u> supporting details?

   a. is, are   **c.** both, because

   b. also, but   **d.** another, but

4. How are the major details organized?

   a. They provide a list of ergogenic aids

   b. They define two ergogenic aids.

   c. They compare ergogenic aids.

   d. They contrast ergogenic aids.

5. What is the overall pattern of organization?

   a. definition   **c.** cause and effect

   b. listing   **d.** compare and/or contrast

Practice

3. Read the following paragraph, and determine the overall pattern of organization. Underline the main idea and major supporting details, and then answer the questions that follow.

NUTRITION

[1]Good nutrition is following a diet that supplies all of the body's needs for good health. [2]Not eating enough of the right foods can lead to poor nutrition and health problems. [3]For example, not getting enough vitamin C can lead to scurvy, a disease that causes swelling and bleeding. [4]An iron deficiency will lead to anemia, causing fatigue. [5]Diets that are high in fat or sugar can cause many different types of health problems, including diabetes, obesity, cardiovascular disease, and certain types of cancer. [6]Therefore, to maintain good health, it is important to have good nutrition by following the dietary guidelines given by the Food and Drug Administration.

1. What is the main idea?

   a. Good nutrition is following a diet that supplies all of the body's needs for good health.

   b. Not eating enough of the right foods can lead to poor nutrition and health problems.

   c. Diets that are high in fat or sugar can cause many different types of health problems, including diabetes, obesity, cardiovascular disease, and certain types of cancer.

   d. Therefore, to maintain good health, it is important to have good nutrition by following the dietary guidelines given by the Food and Drug Administration.

2. Which sentences give the major details?

   a. sentences 2 and 6   **c.** sentences 1 and 6

   b. sentences 1, 2, and 3   **d.** sentences 3, 4, and 5

3. Which of the following transitions are found in the major supporting details?

   a. for example, lead to   **c.** lead to, therefore

   b. is, therefore,   **d.** lead to, for example

4. How are the minor details organized?

   a. They explain the definition of good nutrition.

   b. They list examples of good nutrition.

   c. They show the effects of poor nutrition.

   d. They compare foods that are nutritious to poor foods.

5. What is the overall pattern of organization?

   a. definition   **c.** cause and effect

   b. listing   **d.** compare and contrast

TEXTBOOK SELECTION

Read the following textbook selection, and determine the overall pattern of organization. Underline the main idea and major supporting details, and then answer the questions that follow.

Personality Behavior Patterns

[1]People's different reactions to the same stressful situation can be due to personality differences and how they have learned to respond. [2]There are many different ways to describe personalities and behavior patterns.

[3]People who exhibit Type A behavior pattern (TABP) are highly motivated, time conscious, hard driving, impatient, and sometimes hostile, cynical, and angry. [4]They have a heightened response to stress, and their hostility and anger, especially if repressed, place them at a greater risk for heart disease. [5]Individuals with Type B behavior pattern are easygoing, non-aggressive, and patient, and they are not prone to hostile episodes like their TABP counterparts. [6]People with Type B behavior pattern are less likely to perceive everyday annoyances as significant stressors and are at low risk for heart disease from stress. [7]People with Type C behavior pattern have many of the positive qualities of TABP; they are confident, highly motivated, and competitive. [8]However, individuals with Type C behavior pattern typically do not express the hostility and anger seen with TABP, and they use their personality characteristics to maintain a constant level of emotional control and to channel their ambition into creative directions. [9]As a result, individuals with Type C behavior pattern experience the same low risk for stress-related heart disease as do those with Type B behavior pattern. [10]Similar to those with Type A behavior pattern, individuals with Type D behavior pattern are also considered to be at greater risk for stress-related disease. [11]These individuals are prone to worry and anxiety and also tend to be socially inhibited and uneasy when interacting with others.

(From *Total Fitness and Wellness*, 5e by Scott K. Powers and Stephen L. Dodd. Copyright © 2009 by Scott K. Powers and Stephen L. Dodd. Reprinted by permission of Pearson Education, Inc., Upper Saddle River, NJ.)

QUESTIONS

1. What is the main idea?

   a. People's different reactions to the same stressful situation can be due to personality differences and how they have learned to respond.

   b. There are many different ways to describe personalities and behavior patterns.

   c. People who exhibit Type A behavior pattern (TABP) are highly motivated, time conscious, hard driving, impatient, and sometimes hostile, cynical, and angry.

   d. These individuals are prone to worry and anxiety and also tend to be socially inhibited and uneasy when interacting with others.

2. Which sentences give the major details?

   a. sentences 3, 4, 5, and 6

   b. sentences 3, 5, 7, and 10

   c. sentences 3, 7, 9, and 10

   d. sentences 3, 5, 10, and 11

3. Identify the relationship within the following sentence: As a result, individuals with Type C behavior pattern experience the same low risk for stress-related heart disease as do those with Type B behavior pattern.

a. definition

c. cause and effect

b. listing

d. compare and/or contrast

4. Identify the relationship between sentences 8 and 9.

a. definition

c. cause and effect

b. listing

d. compare and contrast

5. How are the major details organized?

a. They define the different types of behavior patterns while at the same time comparing and contrasting the different types.

b. They show the causes of different behavior patterns.

c. They show the effects of different behavior patterns.

d. They give examples of different behavior patterns.

U-Review

On the following lines, write whether the statements are true or false. If the statement is false, correct it to make it true on the lines provided.

1. When looking for a paragraph's overall pattern, you should look at the minor supporting details.

2. The main idea will often give a clue to the paragraph's pattern of organization.

3. Sometimes the transitions in the sentences do not match the overall relationship being shown in a paragraph.

4. You should ask yourself, "How are the major supporting details organized?"

5. Every sentence in the paragraph will have the same pattern of organization as the whole paragraph.

Reading 1 Vocabulary Preview

The following vocabulary words are from the article "Winter Dreams." With a partner or in a team, choose the correct meanings of the underlined words in the following sentences. Use context clues (LEADS), word part clues, and parts of speech to help you figure out the meanings.

1. Training for the Olympics was <u>consuming</u> (kon-SOO-ming) all of Vonetta's time.
   a. eating
   b. enlarging
   c. endangering
   d. using up

2. Tanika never had much <u>ambition</u> (am-BISH-un) until she discovered she was talented in gymnastics. Now she practices three hours every day.
   a. a desire to succeed
   b. a career
   c. intelligence
   d. limitation

3. After the Hawks made two goals in a row, the players became <u>supercharged</u> (SOO-per-charj'd), and no one on the opposing team could keep up with them.
   a. restless
   b. full of energy
   c. interesting
   d. talented

4. Rocky loved <u>flexing</u> (FLEKS-ing) his muscles in the gym in front of all the ladies.
   a. bending and contracting
   b. rubbing
   c. showing off
   d. tearing

5. In track and field, Lakeisha was such a good <u>sprinter</u> (SPRIN-ter) that she ran the 200-meter race faster than most men.
   a. someone who jumps over bars
   b. someone who runs fast over short distances.
   c. a device for springing off the ground
   d. someone who runs long distances

6. I was not surprised to hear that Mohammad became a professional athlete. He always showed great <u>potential</u> (po-TEN-shel) in high school soccer.
   a. activity
   b. interest
   c. ability to achieve
   d. fondness

Reading 1

7. The coach noticed that Su Ling walked with a spring in her <u>stride</u> (STRIDE).
   a. back
   b. shoes
   c. steps
   d. neck

8. After Ricky tore his <u>hamstring</u> (HAM-string), he had to drop out of the race.
   a. a tendon at the back of the knee
   b. a string lace for a running shoe
   c. a muscle
   d. a bone

9. The whole team felt <u>devastated</u> (DEV-a-stated) when they lost the championship.
   a. somewhat disappointed
   b. very disappointed; crushed
   c. sorry
   d. unaware

10. The couple decided to <u>rededicate</u> (re-DED-i-kate) their marriage on their 10th anniversary.
    a. undo
    b. celebrate
    c. remember
    d. dedicate again; renew a commitment

Reading 1 What Do You Already Know?

1. Have you ever competed in a sport or contest? Did you win or lose? How did you feel? In what ways did your experience help you to grow as a person?

2. Have you ever watched bobsledding live or on screen? Describe what you saw.

> **Directions: As you read this article, practice the four-step reading process. Preview the article, and then write on the following lines one or two questions that you would hope to have answered.**
>
> ....
>
> ....
>
> ....
>
> ....

As you read, answer the questions in the margins to check your comprehension.

"Winter Dreams"

BY VONETTA FLOWERS

From *Guideposts*, February 2006. Copyright © 2006 by Vonetta Flowers. Reprinted by permission of *Guideposts*.

"When life hands you lemons, make lemonade!" This old saying has never been better illustrated than in this article. Vonetta Flowers was the first black athlete (male or female)—from any country—to win an Olympic Winter Games gold medal. She describes her journey to success in her book, *Running on Ice*.

1   The time had come. I'd trained for this moment since the age of nine. All along the race route, fans jumped up and down, waved American flags, and cheered. I stood beside my bright red 2002 U.S. Olympic team bobsled. My heart pounded. Jill Bakken, my teammate, looked me straight in the eye. "Let's do it," she said. Two years earlier I'd failed in my second attempt to make it as a long jumper on the U.S. Olympic track and field team. Making the team had been my all-consuming ambition. Now, through a series of what seemed like miracles, I was representing my country at the Salt Lake City Winter Olympics.

2   I breathed deeply. We took our positions, with Jill next to me on the starting block near the rear of the sled. My job was to give us a supercharged running push start. "Back set," I said, flexing my legs into position. This was it; our shot at the gold.

3   "Front set," said Jill. "Ready … Go!" I threw my body against the bobsled as hard as I could and grunted. I ran as fast as I could. We exploded out of the starting gate.

Reading 1

4   It seems like I've been running all my life. From the time I was little, I'd race the boys down the street outside our house in Birmingham, Alabama, and beat most of them. But I didn't know how fast I really was until third grade. That's when Coach Thomas, of the local Marvel City Striders track team, came to my elementary school to time kids in the 50-yard dash—and to invite the fastest runners to join his squad. He must have time-tested dozens of runners at our school that day. I was the fastest. That night he called my parents and asked if I could report to the Striders' practice the next day.

5   "Who are you?" Coach Thomas asked the next day. He seemed surprised to see me.

6   "Vonetta Jeffrey," I said.

7   Coach Thomas looked me over. I was small for my age. Was he thinking that he'd made a mistake? "Okay. Let's see you run again." He put me against his best female sprinter. He blew his whistle, and I leaped out of the blocks. I beat her. It seemed my feet barely touched the ground.

8   Coach Thomas took me aside. "You can be a great runner, Vonetta, maybe even the next Jackie Joyner-Kersee." I didn't know then that Jackie was America's greatest female track and field star. But I knew Coach Thomas had trained lots of local athletes who'd gone on to compete in college, even in the pros. "But it takes more than just running fast. It takes commitment. It takes believing in yourself and your potential," he said.

9   *Potential.* I loved hearing that word. Track became my life after that; meets in the spring, practice all summer, cross country in the fall, and more training in the winter. I grew strong and tall. "I'm going to compete in the Olympics," I promised myself. I knew I had the potential.

10   One day when I was 11, Coach Thomas pulled me aside. "Vonetta, your legs are so powerful, and you have such spring in your stride. I want you to try the long jump." I fell in love with it. What an incredible feeling, taking off from the runway board, and then soaring through the air. I'd never felt so free. The long jump became my specialty. By high school I didn't have time for much else. The night of my prom, I competed in the state championship track meet. Sprinting down the runway, I thought, "Winning might get me a college scholarship, the next stop toward my Olympic dream."

11   I won an athletic scholarship to the University of Alabama at Birmingham. My goal was to compete in the 1996 Summer Games. By my senior year in 1996, I was a seven-time All-American. At the time I was ranked among the top five female long jumpers in the country. "I feel like my time has come," I confided to my boyfriend Johnny.

12   Then in May, two months before the Olympic Trials, I was running wind sprints in practice. Racing down the track, I felt something rip in my thigh. I'd torn my left hamstring. It's just about the worst thing that could happen to a track and field athlete. There was no way could I recover in time. Still, I went

How did Vonetta become involved in track and field?

261

Reading 1

How do you think Vonetta was feeling at this point?

to the Trials. "Who knows?" I said to Johnny. Johnny was a former track star turned coach, and my biggest fan. "Maybe I can pull off a miracle."

13   When my turn came Johnny knew how tough that would be. But he also knew how determined I was to make the U.S. Olympic Team. I sprinted hard down the runway. Everything felt good. "Maybe I can do it," I thought. I hit the takeoff board and jumped as far as I could. Nothing. I finished 13th. Only the top three finishers qualified for the team.

14   I went off with Johnny. I didn't want anyone else to see how devastated I was. I didn't go to church much as a child, but since meeting Johnny I'd found faith. Now I turned to God. "Why?" I asked him. "Why did this happen? I've worked my whole life for this goal!"

15   "Your time will come," a voice answered, sure and strong. Not a thought, a voice. I snapped to. Yes, I'd rededicate myself. The 2000 Olympics were four years away. I'd be 26, still young enough to compete. "Okay," I decided. "I'm not finished!" Johnny and I had talked about marrying and starting a family, but now I put everything outside of training on hold. "We'll have to wait," I said. I moved from Birmingham to Tuscaloosa, Alabama, to train during the week with my new coach. I worked harder than ever. Johnny and I got married in 1999. We still planned to wait on kids till after the Games.

16   One morning I was out on the track taking practice jumps. I hit the board and soared high into the air. I came down and hit the sand off balance. My ankle rolled. It swelled almost immediately. I iced it for a while, and then tried another jump. Sprinting down the runway felt fine, but when I pushed off to jump, a wave of pain shot through me, so I went to see my doctor. "You've torn a ligament," he said. "You're going to need surgery."

Why did Vonetta do so poorly at the Olympic trials? What do you think will happen next?

17   *No*! I'd never get back in shape by the trials in July. This time I didn't ask why. Instead, in utter desperation, I prayed for understanding, for acceptance. Everything I'd worked for was gone. All that potential—all for nothing. "Your time will come," the same voice assured me. But how? There was no way could I hang on four more years, until the 2004 Games. I'd be 30 and over the hill. Johnny and I were ready to start a family.

18   We flew out to Sacramento, California, for the Olympic Trials. They went about as I'd expected. I finished 12th. "Seventeen years. That's how long I've chased my dream," I told Johnny, with tears filling my eyes, "And now it's over."

19   "Maybe not," he said. He told me about a flyer he'd seen at our hotel—a special invitation for athletes registered for the trials. "A driver for one of the two-women Olympic bobsled teams is looking for a new partner for the 2002 Winter Games," Johnny said. "I think you should try out."

20   I just laughed. I didn't even know what a bobsled looked like. Winter Games? I was used to running in hot weather with as little clothing as possible. I grew up down South. We barely had winter. "Really, I'm serious," Johnny said. "The main requirements are speed and strength. You've got those."

Reading 1

Why didn't Vonetta want to agree with Johnny's suggestion?

Which person, Vonetta or Johnny, do you think has the better attitude about the situation, and why?

21   "Forget it. It's crazy," I said.

22   Johnny stared at me. "You want to compete in the Olympics or not?" Then he said, "I'll try out for the men's bobsled team. We can be the first husband-and-wife team to compete in the Winter Olympics."

23   I had to laugh. Johnny hadn't competed in three years, and he was no Winter Olympian either. But he insisted. Finally I agreed to try out with him. But I wasn't serious. I showed up with my long-jump spikes. I was one of a dozen athletes there. I had no idea what to expect. As I laced up my spikes, I had second thoughts. What was I getting into? How fast does a bobsled go? Was it dangerous?

24   I knew Johnny was watching. He'd already tried out. He'd pulled a hamstring and hadn't made the team. I spotted him on the sidelines, giving me a thumbs-up and an encouraging smile. "Go for it," I told myself. I blasted off the starting line. For the rest of the tryout I never stopped. Johnny kept cheering me. I breezed through the competition. A month later, Bonny, the bobsled captain, called. "I want you to go to Germany with me to train."

25   Johnny sat me down. "This is going to be tough on us," he said. "It means putting off starting our family. It means time apart from each other. But this is what you've prayed for all your life. This is your chance—your chance to make the Olympics."

26   Over the next two years I trained like never before. Shortly before the trials, Bonny and I had a falling out, and Jill Bakken asked me to be her brake person. We went to the trials as total underdogs, and we made it.

27   Now here we were, poised at the starting gate in Salt Lake City for the 2002 Winter Games. "Ready…Go!" We pushed off. Jill jumped into the sled. I kept pushing, building up speed, driving my legs, and then jumping into the sled just as we hit the first steep incline. It was a record start time—5.31 seconds—and our ride just built from there. There were 15 turns, and we navigated each of them perfectly, racing at an average speed of 82.3 mph. We crossed the finish line in 48.81 seconds, a new track record. There are two heats in Olympic bobsled, and our second one later that night was nearly as fast. I looked at our time: 48.95 seconds. Jill and I got out of our sled after that second heat. All around us, people were cheering. Suddenly, I was in Johnny's arms. "You did it, Baby!" he yelled. Our combined time—1:37.76—was good enough for the gold medal.

Vonetta Flowers (right) and Jill Bakken (left) celebrate their victory.

28   You know something? Potential is a funny thing. We all have it. But we can never be sure exactly how we will achieve it. Look at me. All my life I wanted to win gold, and I did. Just not in a way I could have imagined.

1,730 words divided by _____ minutes = _____ words per minute

Thinking About What You Read

It is a good habit to summarize everything you read to strengthen your comprehension.

> Directions: On the following lines, write a two- or three-sentence summary of the article "Winter Dreams." In your own words, describe what the article was about and why the author wrote it.
>
> ....
>
> ....
>
> ....
>
> ....

Comprehension Questions

The following questions will help you to recall the main idea and the details of the "Winter Dreams." Review any parts of the article that you need in order to find the correct answers.

LITERAL COMPREHENSION

1. **What is the topic of this article?**
   a. bobsledding
   b. 2002 Winter Olympics competition in bobsledding
   c. Vonetta Flowers wins an Olympic gold medal.
   d. dealing with disappointment

MAIN IDEA

2. **What is the main idea of the article?**
   a. Vonetta Flowers succeeded in winning an Olympic gold medal in bobsledding.
   b. You should never give up too soon.
   c. Since the age of nine, Vonetta Flowers trained to be an Olympic athlete.
   d. Vonetta Flowers is the first African American to win a gold medal in the Winter Olympics.

SUPPORTING DETAILS

3. **How many attempts did Vonetta make for the U.S. Olympic team as a long jumper?**
   a. one
   b. two
   c. three
   d. four

Reading 1

4. What was the first goal that Vonetta accomplished?

    a. She got onto the Olympic track team as a long jumper.

    b. She made the trials for the Olympic bobsled team.

    c. She traveled to Germany to train for the Olympics.

    d. She won an athletic scholarship.

DRAWING CONCLUSIONS

5. What does the author mean by the sentence, "I breezed through the competition"?

    a. She found the competition easy.

    b. She failed in the competition.

    c. She was blown away by the other competitors.

    d. She disliked the competition.

6. Which of the following conclusions would be most appropriate for this story? (Check all that apply.)

    a. You should always look before you leap.

    b. Every cloud has a silver lining.

    c. If at first you don't succeed, try and try again.

    d. Time waits for no one.

PATTERNS OF ORGANIZATION

7. Identify the relationship within the following sentence: There are two heats in Olympic bobsled, and our second one later that night was nearly as fast.

    a. definition

    b. listing

    c. compare and/or contrast

    d. cause and effect

8. Identify the relationship between the following sentences: "You've torn a ligament," he said. "You're going to need surgery."

    a. definition

    b. listing

    c. compare and/or contrast

    d. cause and effect

9. Identify the relationship between the following sentences: Track became my life after that; meets in the spring, practice all summer, cross country in the fall, and more training in the winter.

    a. definition

    b. listing

    c. compare and/or contrast

    d. cause and effect

VOCABULARY IN CONTEXT

10. Identify the meaning of the underlined word in the following sentence: We went to the trials as total underdogs, and we made it (paragraph 25).

    a. acting like dogs

    b. people who bring their dogs

    c. people who are not expected to win

    d. training like a dog

265

Reading 1 Vocabulary Practice

Use the vocabulary words from the Word Bank to complete the following sentences. Write the words into the blanks provided.

> **WORD BANK**
>
> consuming   ambition   supercharged   flexing   sprinter
> potential   stride   hamstring   devastated   rededicate

1. After the coach's pep talk, the team was so .... that they exploded onto the field.

2. .... your muscles slowly is an important part of a warm-up before intense exercise.

3. Vonetta was a great .... because of her fast starts and strong legs.

4. Talking on the phone was .... so much of Sophia's time that she never completed all of her homework.

5. Someone who is driving under the influence of alcohol has a greater .... for having an accident.

6. Johnny pulled his .... when he tried out for the bobsled team and couldn't finish the race.

7. When Marlon's team lost the championship, he felt ....

8. It takes a lot of .... to succeed at anything.

9. After failing to succeed, Vonetta decided to .... herself to achieving her goal.

10. Vonetta had such spring in her .... that her coach felt she would make a good long jumper.

Reading 1 Questions for Writing and Discussion

Review any parts of the article you need to answer the following questions.

1. Why did Vonetta feel that she was destined to become an Olympic athlete all during her young life?

2. In what ways did Johnny help Vonetta to achieve her dream?

3. Vonetta could have given up after her first two unsuccessful attempts in the trials to qualify for the Olympics. Why do you think Vonetta was willing to try again, despite her previous failures?

4. When Vonetta had her second injury and came in 12th in the Olympic trials for track and field, she then tried out for the bobsled team and won. What does this tell us about failure and perseverance?

5. Do you think that some nations place too much importance on winning competitions? Is this good or bad for the sport and for the athletes?

Reading 1 Vocabulary Practice—Concentration Game

Teams or pairs of students will take turns matching vocabulary words with their definitions. The object of the game is to match up as many correct words with their definitions as possible.

1.

Use index cards or fold 2 sheets of notebook paper into 10 squares on each page and tear them into 20 pieces of somewhat equal size.

2.

Teams will write 1 vocabulary word or 1 definition from the list below on the right each of the 20 cards.

3.

Shuffle the cards and lay them face down in even rows.

consuming	ambition	flexing	sprinter
sprinter	potential	stride	hamstring
devastated	rededicate	using up	a desire to succeed
full of energy	bending and contracting	someone who runs fast in short distances	the ability to achieve
a person's step	the tendon behind the knee	very disappointed; crushed	to dedicate again; renew a commitment

CONSUMING

USING UP

4.

The first player turns over any two cards. If the two cards match (the word and the correct definition) the player picks up the cards and keeps them. If the two cards do not match, the player turns the cards face down again in the same spots. Memorize the positions of the cards that have been shown so that you may find them on your turn.

5.

The next player turns over any two cards and plays according to step 4. The player with the most matching cards at the end is the winner.

Reading 2 Vocabulary Preview

The following vocabulary words are from the article "Most Valuable Player." With a partner or in a team, choose the correct meanings of the underlined words in the following sentences. Use context clues (LEADS), word part clues, and parts of speech to help you figure out the meanings.

1. Despite the <u>adverse</u> (add-VERS) conditions of playing in a snowstorm and freezing temperatures, the New York Giants defeated the Green Bay Packers.

   a. cold

   b. unfavorable

   c. neglectful

   d. slippery

2. Our grueling training had a positive <u>impact</u> (IM-pakt) on the team because we started winning games.

   a. effect

   b. decision

   c. drive

   d. to cement in

3. The colonel led his <u>battalion</u> (bat-TAL-yen) into the war zone, knowing that many would not come back alive.

   a. an army

   b. a military vehicle

   c. a group of soldiers

   d. an unmanned plane

4. The doctors tried to save Anita's leg when she had cancer, but they had to <u>amputate</u> (AM-pyu-tate) it to save her life.

   a. enlarge

   b. operate

   c. shorten

   d. cut off

5. The quarterback was <u>sidelined</u> (SIDE-lined) for the rest of the football season because he tore a ligament in his leg.

   a. used as a backup player

   b. played along the sides

   c. taken out of play

   d. sent to the hospital

Reading 2

6. After <u>intercepting</u> (in-ter-SEP-ting) a pass from quarterback Brett Favre, Corey Webster gave the ball to Greg Gadson.

    a. interacting

    b. capturing

    c. tackling

    d. receiving

7. Even though Jackie Robinson faced tremendous <u>adversity</u> (add-VERS-it-tee), he still overcame prejudice to become one of baseball's greatest legends.

    a. endurance

    b. contempt

    c. empathy

    d. difficulty

8. The school board passed a new law that made random drug testing <u>compulsory</u> (kom-PUL-sor-ree) for all school sports teams.

    a. rancid

    b. required

    c. holistic

    d. forlorn

9. After losing his leg in a car accident, John learned to walk again wearing a <u>prosthetic</u> (pros-THET-ik) leg.

    a. imitation

    b. potential

    c. injured

    d. orthopedic

10. Because of his contributions to the nation, former President Bill Clinton has received five <u>honorary</u> (ON-or-air-ee) doctorate degrees.

    a. earned

    b. given in honor of

    c. indulged

    d. high ranking

Reading 2 What Do You Already Know?

1. What makes a great team? How do you think it gets that way?

2. Have you ever missed out on an activity that you really wanted to be a part of? Describe the situation.

> **Directions:** As you read this article, practice the four-step reading process. Preview the article, and then write on the following lines one or two questions that you would hope to have answered.
>
> ....
>
> ....
>
> ....
>
> ....

As you read, answer the questions in the margins to check your comprehension.

"Most Valuable Player"

BY W. HODDING CARTER

From *Reader's Digest*, May 2008. Copyright © 2008 by The Reader's Digest Association. Reprinted with permission.

An injured Iraq war veteran led the New York Giants to a Super Bowl victory without ever setting foot on the field. He was voted 2008 Hero of the Year.

1   Greg Gadson, a lieutenant colonel in the Army's Warrior Transition Brigade, is a natural leader—the kind of guy you'd be looking for on the battlefield. He's also the kind of guy Mike Sullivan (wide receivers coach for the New York Giants) thought could make a difference to his losing football team. The two men had gone to West Point together but hadn't been in touch much afterward, until Sullivan walked into Gadson's hospital room at Walter Reed Army Medical Center, outside Washington, D.C., last June. Friends had told Sullivan that his former Army football teammate had suffered serious injuries in Iraq—resulting in both of Gadson's legs being <u>amputated</u> above the knee.

2   "This man had suffered so much," Sullivan recalls, "yet he was so happy to see me." The coach watched as Gadson interacted with the other patients and the doctors and nurses, encouraging them all. "To see the <u>impact</u> he had on these people—the look in his eyes and how they responded—was overwhelming and inspirational." Sullivan couldn't help but be impressed by Gadson's enthusiasm

Reading 2

Why was Sullivan so impressed by Gadson?

and lack of self-pity. "He was bragging about me and talking about the Giants, and I was like, 'Hell, I want to talk about you. How are you doing?'"

3   When the Giants were scheduled to play the Redskins in Washington three months later, Sullivan sent his friend tickets, along with a request: Would Gadson speak to the team before they took the field? Having lost the first two games of the season, the Giants had already given up 80 points and, worse, seemed to be playing with no heart. The coach felt that Gadson was the perfect person to tell the players something they needed to hear about commitment, about perseverance, about teamwork. "A lot of the guys were frustrated and searching for answers," Sullivan says. "And I thought, 'This is someone who knows about pressure and sacrifice when it's life and death, not just a game.'"

4   Teamwork was everything to Gadson. He had played football at Indian River High School in the Tidewater region of Virginia and gone on to become a starting linebacker for West Point from 1986 to 1988, despite his relatively slight build of 190 pounds on a 5-foot-11 frame. Following his graduation, Gadson planned to serve his compulsory five years and get out. But after tours in the Balkans and Afghanistan, he found himself hooked. "Serving my country is important," he says, "but for me it's about being a soldier, being there for each other in the biggest sense of the word. I love being part of that team."

5   Last May, in Baghdad, Gadson was returning from memorial services for two soldiers from his battalion when a bomb tore apart the truck he was riding in, knocking him clear of the vehicle and leaving him on the side of the road, bleeding and slipping in and out of consciousness. He awoke 10 days later at Walter Reed Hospital. A week later, after complications, his left leg was amputated, then his right. "I knew what had to be done even before the doctors told me," he says.

How did Gadson become a double amputee?

6   The night before the Redskins game, Gadson spoke from his heart with no script. "You have an obligation not only to your employer but to each other to do your best," he told the Giants. "You're playing for each other. When you find a way to do things greater than you thought you could, something you couldn't do as an individual, a bond is formed that will last forever." He told the team how much it had meant to him when his friends from West Point rallied around him in the hospital, and reminded them how powerful a team really is and how much stronger adversity would make them. "It's not about what happens to you in life," he said. "It's about what you do about it. It's about making the most of all your opportunities because I'm here to tell you, it can end in a flash."

7   When he finished speaking, the room was silent. "You could hear a pin drop," Sullivan says. And then it erupted in a standing ovation.

8   "You see a guy go through the things that he has, and he's in such good spirits," says Giants wide receiver Plaxico Burress. "I've never met somebody like that. I was like, 'Wow, I just have a little ankle injury. I have to go out there and give it my best.'"

Reading 2

9   The Giants invited Gadson to watch the game from the sidelines the next day. When Burress scored the winning touchdown, he ran to Gadson and placed the ball in his lap. "All I thought about when I made that touchdown was that I wanted to find him and give him that football," Burress says.

10   The Giants went on to win their next 10 road games. Gadson joined up with the team at the playoffs in Tampa, and again, they won. Later, at the NFC championship game against Green Bay as honorary co-captain, Gadson sat on the sidelines in the subzero weather instead of in the heated box seat reserved for him. This time, it was Corey Webster who gave Gadson a football, after intercepting a pass from star Packers quarterback Brett Favre near the end of the game. The Giants won in overtime, 23–20, and the ball wound up becoming a piece of history. It turned out to be the last NFL pass Favre threw before he announced his retirement in March.

How did the members of the team show Gadson their appreciation for his help?

11   The Super Bowl was next, and the team flew Gadson; his wife, Kim; and their two children, Gabriella, 15, and Jaelen, 14, to Phoenix for the game against the New England Patriots, who'd had an undefeated season and were widely favored to win. The night before the contest, Gadson again addressed the players. And for the crowning touch on what became a legendary season, the Giants won, 17–14, their first Super Bowl victory in more than a decade. "He is a powerful man with a powerful spirit," says Giants head coach Tom Coughlin. "And that is really what he gave us: the idea that the spirit rises above all these adverse conditions."

12   Physically, Gadson is making remarkable progress. He spends four hours a day in rehabilitation, learning, among other things, to use prosthetic legs equipped with Bluetooth technology. Computer chips in each leg send signals to motors in Gadson's artificial joints so his knees and ankles move in a coordinated fashion. He is one of only two double amputees to use this technology, which was designed for single amputees. He uses a wheelchair or two canes most of the time but can also walk without support for short distances.

How does Gadson get the courage to keep on trying to walk again?

13   His family helps him remain upbeat. "I take great inspiration from my wife and kids," he says. "I don't always feel good, but I owe it to them to keep on trying."

14   Gadson isn't sure whether his role with the Giants will continue next season. He hasn't been discharged from the military, and his only official duty is to focus on his rehab. The soldier says he'd like to be there when his battalion comes home.

15   "I'm living the journey right now," Gadson says, reflecting on all that's happened to him in the past year. "I've come a long way, and I still have a long way to go. I don't believe you ever really arrive in life. You live life." And who knows where that will take you? If you are Lt. Col. Greg Gadson, you could go from the battlefields of Iraq all the way to the Super Bowl alongside the New York Giants—in a wheelchair, but never, ever sidelined.

1,242 words divided by _____ minutes = _____ words per minute

Reading 2 Thinking About What You Read

It's a good habit to summarize everything you read to strengthen your comprehension.

Directions: On the following lines, write a two- or three-sentence summary of the article "Most Valuable Player." In your own words, describe what the article was about and why the author wrote it.

....

....

....

Comprehension Questions

The following questions will help you to recall the main idea and the details of "Most Valuable Player." Review any parts of the article that you need to find the correct answers.

MAIN IDEA

1. **What is the main idea of the article?**

   a. The New York Giants won the Super Bowl.

   b. A soldier who lost his legs in the war in Iraq has helped others.

   c. Lt. Col. Greg Gadson has taught the New York Giants players how to change their attitudes and win football games.

   d. Greg Gadson, a lieutenant colonel in the Army's Warrior Transition Brigade, is a natural leader—the kind of guy you'd be looking for on the battlefield.

SUPPORTING DETAILS

2. **According to the article, which of the following statements is true?**

   a. The New York Giants hired Gadson as a motivational speaker when the team was losing.

   b. The New York Giants were losing games until Gadson came to speak to them.

   c. Gadson asked the coach of the New York Giants if he could speak to the team to encourage them.

   d. Gadson played with the New York Giants before he went into the army.

DRAWING CONCLUSIONS

3. **Gadson taught the Giants players each of the following except:**

   a. They owed it to the team to play their best for each other.

   b. As a team, they would find a way to do something greater than they could have achieved individually.

   c. Life is about what you do with what you are given.

   d. If they worked together, they could win the Super Bowl.

Reading 2

4. From the article, you can conclude that (choose all that apply):

    a. Gadson will continue to help the Giants and other teams to win games.

    b. Mike Sullivan was so impressed by Gadson's impact on other people that he asked him to come and speak to his team.

    c. Gadson will not let anything defeat him.

    d. The Giants were just being lazy before Gadson spoke to them.

5. From the article, you can conclude that:

    a. Before his injury, Gadson had wanted to complete his tour of duty and then go back to playing football.

    b. The Giants had never won a Super Bowl before this.

    c. The Giants team members admire Gadson.

    d. Coach Tom Coughlin didn't think that Gadson would have any impact on the Giants.

PATTERNS OF ORGANIZATION

6. What is one of the patterns of organization that is used throughout this article?

    a. cause and effect

    b. listing

    c. compare and/or contrast

    d. definition

7. Identify the relationship within the following sentence: Last May, in Baghdad, Gadson was returning from memorial services for two soldiers from his battalion when a bomb tore apart the truck he was riding in, knocking him clear of the vehicle and leaving him on the side of the road, bleeding and slipping in and out of consciousness.

    a. comparison

    b. contrast

    c. cause and effect

    d. listing

8. Identify the relationship between the following sentences: Following his graduation, Gadson planned to serve his compulsory five years and get out. But after tours in the Balkans and Afghanistan, he found himself hooked.

    a. comparison

    b. contrast

    c. cause and effect

    d. listing

VOCABULARY IN CONTEXT

9. Identify the best meaning of the underlined word in the following sentence: The coach watched as Gadson <u>interacted</u> with the other patients and the doctors and nurses, encouraging them all.

    a. argued

    b. negotiated

    c. neglected

    d. communicated

10. Identify the best meaning of the underlined word in the following sentence: The coach felt that Gadson was the perfect person to tell the players something they needed to hear about commitment, about <u>perseverance</u>, about teamwork.

    a. determination

    b. perspective

    c. winning

    d. fitting in

Reading 2 Vocabulary Practice

Use the vocabulary words from the Word Bank to complete the following sentences. Write the words into the blanks provided.

WORD BANK

adverse	impact	battalion	compulsory	adversity
honorary	intercepting	prosthetic	sidelined	amputate

1. In most places, attending school is .... for students between ages 5 and 16.

2. After learning to use her .... arm, Davina was able to do many of the same activities she did before she lost her arm in an accident.

3. We elected Bryan our .... chairman because he accomplished more for our organization than our official one.

4. When you teach others to read and think, you never know the .... it will have upon their lives.

5. The soldier knew that the doctors would probably have to .... his leg after he was badly injured.

6. The instructor was known for .... notes from students who tried to pass them in her class.

7. Despite all the ....Greg Gadson has had to face, he remains an inspiration to others.

8. Our best linebacker was .... after being knocked unconscious during the game.

9. The entire .... was welcomed home by a large crowd at the airport.

10. Drinking alcohol while you are taking medications can cause........................... reactions.

Reading 2 Questions for Writing and Discussion

Review any parts of the article you need to answer the following questions.

1. Why do you think Greg Gadson believes that teamwork is important?

2. Why did coach Mike Sullivan believe that Gadson might be able to help his team?

3. Do you think the Giants could have won the Super Bowl without Gadson's help? Why or why not?

4. What important lessons do you think the Giants learned from Gadson?

5. What do you think Gadson means when he says, "I don't believe you ever really arrive in life. You live life"?

Reading 2 Vocabulary Practice

Use the vocabulary words from the Word Bank to complete the following sentences. Write the words into the blanks provided.

> **WORD BANK**
>
> adverse   impact   battalion   compulsory   adversity
>
> honorary   intercept   prosthetic   sidelined   amputated

"CHAMPION WARRIORS"

I was with the Fifty-First .... when I had my first real battle. The enemy was hiding somewhere in the woods ahead, and we were facing .... conditions in fog and rain. Throughout our .... training, we learned how to .... enemy messengers and find out where their unit was hiding. I was chosen as the .... captain because our real one was .... with a bad injury. But I doubted that his leg would be .... or that he would need to walk with a(n) .... leg the rest of his life. We found the enemy on the other side of the hill and surprised them with an ambush. The .... of our surprise helped us defeat them in a short but hostile attack. Despite having to face .... , we won the battle and are now the Paint Ball Champions of Johnson City!

ON THE JOB INTERVIEW

Rick Muhr,
Coach and Consultant

What is your career, and how did you become interested in coaching?

For 12 years I was head coach for Team in Training, sponsored by the Leukemia and Lymphoma Society, to help prepare people for running marathons. During those years, I was able to help others and raise money for an important cause. I also coached track and cross country at Worcester State College in Massachusetts. I am now an independent consultant and coach for many organizations and individuals. I've always been a runner, and I carried the Olympic Torch in St. Louis in 2004. A life-changing event occurred when my mother died of leukemia, and I made a promise to her that I would do something significant with my life to make her proud and to help others.

What is your training and education?

I graduated from college with a degree in business, and this has enabled me to work with a variety of businesses and organizations and to run my own business as a consultant and coach. I became certified in the areas of exercise and physiology, but most of my knowledge has been acquired through my own study.

Did you ever consider quitting?

I am not a quitter, so that wasn't something I would consider. Even when I ran a marathon of 117 miles in 24 hours, I never considered giving up. Once you have experienced running in a marathon like that, when you cross the finish line, you realize what you are capable of, and you appreciate the small things in life more. I have learned more from failure and disappointment than anything else in life. So quitting is not an option.

Where do you work now, and what do you like about your job?

I am now an independent coach and consultant. What I love most about my job is helping all kinds of people and inspiring them to become whole in body, mind, and spirit. I love connecting to people on a personal level and being able to help others achieve a sense of being whole.

What do you dislike about your job?

There is nothing I really dislike about my job. It's my passion, and I love what I do.

If you could give college students one piece of advice, what would it be?

Believe in yourself. Be open minded to different ideas and possibilities. Get comfortable being uncomfortable – meaning, go outside of your comfort zone to discover your capabilities. Work hard, learn from your failures, and give praise and credit to others. Take a challenging class, or get a college degree, or a better job. Think about your legacy early in life, and do whatever it takes to achieve it. Follow your passion!

VIEWPOINT:
Performance-Enhancing Drugs

Read the following letters to the editor debating whether it is the government's or the sports league's responsibility to test professional athletes for steroids. Then, answer the questions that follow.

Dear Editor:

I am shocked by the widespread use of steroids and performance-enhancing drugs by professional athletes. These athletes are regarded as role models by many young people, and by using drugs to improve their abilities, they are cheating in competitive sports. Is this the message we want to send to our youth? As a result of steroid use in professional sports, now many high school and middle school athletes are using them. They see that using drugs will help them achieve success or gain admission to a college or win an athletic scholarship. Anabolic steroids cause serious physical and mental health problems. Sports leagues are driven by money from fans and advertisers. The more successful the teams are, the more money they earn. Can we trust them to police themselves? I think not. We should urge our government representatives to propose laws to regulate testing in all sports leagues, both professional and amateur.

Signed,

Concerned Fan

Dear Editor:

Sports leagues are supported financially by the people who invest in them and fans who buy the tickets. They are a private enterprise and should not be subject to federal laws regarding drug testing. Each league should be allowed to make its own decisions, not the federal government. And random testing on players is a violation of their privacy. No one should be forced to be drug tested in order to play. The individual leagues who are paying the bills should be the ones to decide how testing will be done. And what if the drug testing is not accurate? Careers could be ruined by one or two bad tests. The federal government should keep its nose out of sports. Let the leagues regulate themselves. They'd probably do a better job and do it a lot cheaper than the government ever could.

Signed,

Fed Up with Feds

Critical Thinking

1. A *point of view* is the author's opinion about a topic. To find the author's point of view, ask yourself, "How does this author feel about this issue?" What is the author's point of view about performance-enhancing drugs in the first letter?

   ....

   ....

2. What is the author's point of view in about performance-enhancing drugs in the second letter?

   ....

   ....

   ....

3. Which letter do you agree with, and why?

   ....

   ....

   ....

4. What could be the consequences of allowing sports leagues to make their own rules for drug testing?

   ....

   ....

5. What could be the consequences of having the government regulate drug testing?

   ....

   ....

WRITE YOUR THOUGHTS

Write a letter to the editor stating your own feelings about government regulations for drug testing in sports. Use a separate sheet of paper.

Refund and Repayment Policy

Read the following "Refund and Repayment Policies," taken from a university catalog. Then, working with your team, answer the questions that follow.

REFUND AND REPAYMENT POLICIES

Students should be aware that if they withdraw from the University after having received financial assistance, they may have to repay a portion of that assistance. Students who received **Federal Stafford Loans** should also know that the Student Financial Assistance Office is required to notify lenders of student withdrawals.

REFUNDS

Financial assistance recipients planning to withdraw from the University should first consult the University's Withdrawal Policy published under Academic Policies and Procedures in the University Catalog.

If the student is due a refund according to this policy, the financial assistance program(s) from which the student received assistance will first be reimbursed. Any remaining balance after refunding all appropriate assistance programs will be refunded to the student.

In no case will the amount refunded to the assistance program exceed the amount paid to the student.

REPAYMENT

If a student withdraws on or before the midterm point in the time of the period of enrollment, calculated using calendar days, a portion of the total Title IV funds awarded a student must be returned according to the provisions of the Higher Education Amendments of 1998.

The calculation of the return of these funds may result in the student owing a balance to the University and/or the federal government. This calculated amount will be returned to the Title IV programs in the following order:

1) Unsubsidized Federal Stafford loans
2) Subsidized Federal Stafford loans
3) Federal Perkins loans
4) Federal PLUS loans
5) Federal Pell Grants
6) Federal SEOG
7) Other grant or loan assistance authorized by Title IV of the HEA
8) State aid
9) Institutional aid
10) Other

Students should schedule an appointment with or come to the Student Financial Assistance Office prior to withdrawing from classes to confirm the consequences of that withdrawal.

Questions

On the lines provided, write whether the following statements are true or false. If the statement is false, change it to make it true.

1. If a student who receives financial assistance withdraws from a course, he or she may have to repay a part of that loan.

....

....

....

2. If a student withdraws, he or she will receive a refund, and then the lender will be refunded.

....

....

....

3. All of the lenders who gave the student financial aid will be refunded in a specific order before the student is refunded.

....

....

....

4. Federal PLUS loans will be refunded before institutional aid.

....

....

....

5. If a student withdraws on or before the midterm point, the student will not have to pay back any of the money that he or she was loaned.

....

....

....

....

BUILDING VOCABULARY

Study the following word parts, and then answer the questions that follow.

Prefixes	**Roots**	**Suffixes**
con-, com- *with, together*	-struct- *to build*	-er, -or *one who**
im- *into*	-pose- *to place, to put*	-ive-*a state or quality**
in- *into**	* Word parts from previous chapters	

What English words can you create from these word parts?

....

....

....

....

Using a dictionary, look up the meanings of any of the words you wrote that you can't define. Use one of the words you wrote in a sentence that reveals its meaning with a context clue:

....

....

....

....

....

TEXTBOOK GRAPHIC AIDS

Examine the following maps, and then answer the questions that follow.

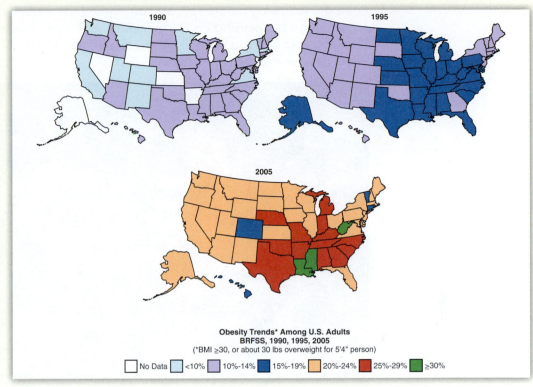

Obesity Trends* Among U.S. Adults
BRFSS, 1990, 1995, 2005
(*BMI ≥30, or about 30 lbs overweight for 5'4" person)

☐ No Data ☐ <10% ☐ 10%-14% ■ 15%-19% ☐ 20%-24% ■ 25%-29% ■ ≥30%

(From *Total Fitness and Wellness*, Brief Edition, 3rd, by Scott K. Powers and Stephen L. Dodd. Copyright © 2009. Printed and Electronically reproduced by permission of Pearson Education, Inc., Upper Saddle River, NJ.)

1. According to the Obesity Trends maps, in 1990, how many states had less than 10% of their population as obese adults?

   a. no states

   b. 1–5 states

   c. 6–11 states

   d. 12 or more states

2. In 1995, what was the obesity rate of most of the western states?

   a. less than 10% of the population

   b. 10%–14% of the population

   c. 15%–19% of the population

   d. more than 30% of the population

3. By 2005, which region of the country had the highest obesity rates?

   a. Northwest

   b. Southwest

   c. Northeast

   d. Southeast

4. By 2005, how many states had an obesity rate of more than 30% of the population?

   a. 28 states

   b. 3 states

   c. 16 states

   d. 30 states

5. By how much did the obese population change in the state of Alaska between 1995 and 2005?

   a. It increased by 25–29%.

   b. It decreased by 20–24%.

   c. It increased by 15–19%.

   d. It increased by 5–9%.

CHAPTER REVIEW PRACTICE #1

Read the following paragraph, and determine the overall pattern of organization by focusing on the main idea and major supporting details. Remember to ask yourself, "How are the supporting details organized?" Then, answer the questions that follow.

In soccer, each player has a specific role in helping the team score goals. First, there are **forwards**, also known as **attackers** and **strikers**. They play nearest to the other team's goal and are responsible for making the most goals. Most teams have one to three forwards. The center forward is the principal goal-scorer of the team. The **wingers** are stationed near the touchlines. Wingers must try to beat defenders from the other team. **Defenders**, or **backs**, are the players responsible for providing support to the goalkeeper and keeping the other team from scoring. The **center backs**, or **central defenders**, have the job of stopping the opposing team's strikers. One of these center backs is the **sweeper**, who sweeps up the ball if the opponent breaks through the team's defense. The **fullbacks** prevent the opposing players from getting the ball into the penalty area, and they support other positions. There are also various types of **midfielders**, who play between the strikers and defenders. Their main job is to keep possession of the ball from the opposing team's players.

1. What is the topic of this selection?
   a. soccer
   b. how to play soccer
   c. soccer positions
   d. scoring goals

2. Which sentence states the main idea?

    a. In soccer, each player has a specific role in helping the team score goals.

    b. First, there are forwards, also known as attackers and strikers.

    c. Most teams have one to three forwards.

    d. Their main job is to keep possession of the ball from the opposing team's players.

3. According to the passage, what are "backs"?

    a. They are responsible for making the most goals.

    b. They have the job of stopping the opposing team's strikers.

    c. They are the principal goal-scorers of the team.

    d. They are responsible for providing support to the goalkeeper and keeping the other team from scoring.

4. Identify the relationship within the following sentence: Defenders, or backs, are the players responsible for providing support to the goalkeeper and keeping the other team from scoring.

    a. definition

    b. listing

    c. cause and effect

    d. compare and/or contrast

5. What is the overall pattern of organization used in this paragraph?

    a. definition

    b. listing

    c. cause and effect

    d. compare and/or contrast

CHAPTER REVIEW PRACTICE #2

Read the following paragraph, and determine the overall pattern of organization by focusing on the main idea and major supporting details. Remember to ask yourself, "How are the supporting details organized?" Then, answer the questions that follow.

Recreational therapists are trained therapists who help people with disabilities or illnesses by using games or other techniques to improve their physical and mental health. They help patients to recover basic motor skills and flexibility. They also help people to improve their social skills. Recreational therapists work in hospitals, nursing homes, schools, or patients' homes. They assess the patient's needs and plan programs to help the individual or group, and then they work on the specific skills. Some recreational therapists specialize in art therapy or aquatic therapy. Most recreational therapists have an associate's or a bachelor's degree in recreational therapy. However, a few hold master's or doctoral degrees. Some require certification by the National Council for Therapeutic Recreation. A good recreational therapist is one who enjoys working with other people, likes to play, has good communication skills, and is patient.

1. What is the topic of this passage?

    a. recreational therapy
    b. recreational therapists
    c. helping people with disabilities
    d. therapists

2. What is the main idea of this passage?

    a. Recreational therapists are trained therapists who help people with disabilities or illnesses by using games or other techniques to improve their physical and mental health.

    b. Recreational therapists work in hospitals, nursing homes, schools, or patients' homes.

    c. They assess the patient's needs and plan programs to help the individual or group, and then work on specific skills.

    d. A good recreational therapist is one who enjoys working with other people, likes to play, has good communication skills, and is patient.

3. Identify the relationship within the following sentence: Recreational therapists work in hospitals, nursing homes, schools, or patients' homes.

    a. definition
    b. listing
    c. cause and effect
    d. compare and/or contrast

4. Identify the relationship between the following sentences: Most recreational therapists have an associate's or a bachelor's degree in recreational therapy. However, a few hold master's or doctoral degrees.

    a. definition
    b. listing
    c. cause and effect
    d. compare and/or contrast

5. What is the overall pattern of organization used in this passage?

    a. definition
    b. listing
    c. cause and effect
    d. compare and/or contrast

CHAPTER REVIEW PRACTICE #3

Read the following paragraph, and determine the overall pattern of organization by focusing on the main idea and major supporting details. Remember to ask yourself, "How are the supporting details organized?" Then, answer the questions that follow.

TYPES OF EXERCISE

[1]There are two different forms of exercise that can improve muscular strength. [2]Isotonic (eye-so-TON-ik) exercise involves contracting the muscles against a moving load, such as a weight machine. [3]Different muscles are used when lifting the weight than when lowering the weight. [4]To increase muscle mass, a person would increase the amount of weight and the number of lifts. [5]In contrast, isometric (eye-so-MET-trik) exercises involve moving muscles against a nonmoving load at a fixed angle. [6]An example would be to get into a push-up position and hold it for 10 seconds. [7]Increasing the amount of time would lead to improved strength over a period of time. [8]There are two important differences between isotonic and isometric exercise. [9]First, in isometric training, the range of motion is limited. [10]Second, during isometric exercises, people have a tendency to hold their breath, which can reduce blood flow to the brain and cause dizziness or fainting. [11]During both types of exercise, it is necessary to continue breathing.

1. What sentence states the main idea of this passage?

   a. There are two different forms of exercise that can improve muscular strength.

   b. Isotonic (eye-so-TON-ik) exercise involves contracting the muscles against a moving load, such as a weight machine.

   c. In contrast, isometric (eye-so-MET-trik) exercises involve moving muscles against a nonmoving load at a fixed angle.

   d. During both types of exercise, it is necessary to continue breathing.

2. Which sentences provide the major details?

   a. sentences 2 and 3

   b. sentences 2, 3, 4, and 5

   c. sentences 9 and 10

   d. sentences 2 and 5

3. Identify the relationship within the following sentence: Second, during isometric exercises, people have a tendency to hold their breath, which can reduce blood flow to the brain and cause dizziness or fainting.

   a. definition

   b. listing

   c. cause and effect

   d. compare and/or contrast

4. Identify the relationship between sentences 9 and 10.

   a. definition

   b. listing

   c. cause and effect

   d. compare and/or contrast

5. What is the overall pattern of organization used in this passage?

   a. definition

   b. listing

   c. cause and effect

   d. compare and/or contrast

TEXTBOOK PRACTICE

Read the following selection, and determine the overall pattern of organization by focusing on the main idea and major supporting details. Remember to ask yourself, "How are the supporting details organized?" Then, answer the questions that follow.

WHAT ARE THE GUIDELINES FOR A HEALTHY DIET?

Nutrition may seem like a complex subject, but the basics of consuming a healthy diet are fairly simple: balance the calories, eat a variety of foods, and consume unhealthy foods only in moderation. Additionally, everyone should strive to be physically active.

To make these points more clear, and to provide specific guidance in these areas, several national health agencies have suggested guidelines for healthy diets. For instance, the United States Department of Agriculture (USDA) released its latest version of the Dietary Guidelines for Americans in 2005.

Among its key points of advice:

- Consume adequate nutrients within energy needs: choose foods that limit the intake of saturated and trans fats, cholesterol, added sugars, salt, and alcohol.

- Balance energy intake with energy expended.

- Engage in regular physical activity.

- Consume sufficient amounts of fruits, vegetables, and whole grains while staying within energy needs.

- Consume less than 10% of energy intake from saturated fats and less than 300 mg per day of cholesterol; consume as little trans fat as possible.

- Choose fiber-rich fruits, vegetables, and whole grains often; choose and prepare foods and beverages with little added sugars or caloric sweeteners.

- Consume less than 1 tsp of salt per day.

- If you choose to drink alcohol, do so only in moderation.

- Take proper food safety precautions.

(From *Total Fitness and Wellness*, 5e by Scott K. Powers and Stephen L. Dodd. Copyright © 2009 by Scott K. Powers and Stephen L. Dodd. Reprinted by permission of Pearson Education, Inc., Upper Saddle River, NJ.)

1. What sentence states the main idea of this passage?

   a. Nutrition may seem like a complex subject, but the basics of consuming a healthy diet are fairly simple: balance the calories, eat a variety of foods, and consume unhealthy foods only in moderation.

   b. Additionally, everyone should strive to be physically active.

   c. To make these points more clear, and to provide specific guidance in these areas, several national health agencies have suggested guidelines for healthy diets.

   d. For instance, the United States Department of Agriculture (USDA) released its latest version of the Dietary Guidelines for Americans in 2005.

2. Identify the relationship within the following sentence: To make these points more clear, and to provide specific guidance in these areas, several national health agencies have suggested guidelines for healthy diets.

   a. definition

   b. listing

   c. cause and effect

   d. compare and/or contrast

3. Identify the relationship between the following sentences:
   • Consume adequate nutrients within energy needs: choose foods that limit the intake of saturated and trans fats, cholesterol, added sugars, salt, and alcohol.
   • Balance energy intake with energy expended.
   • Engage in regular physical activity.

   a. definition

   b. listing

   c. cause and effect

   d. compare and contrast

4. According to the selection, about how much salt should a person consume in one day?

   a. 1 tablespoon

   b. 1 teaspoon

   c. 300 mg

   d. less than 1 teaspoon

5. What is the overall pattern of organization used in this passage?

   a. definition

   b. listing

   c. cause and effect

   d. compare and contrast

STUDY SKILL CHAPTER REVIEW

Fill in the missing information in the following concept map about the four patterns of organization that you have learned in this chapter. Then, complete the summary that follows about the patterns of organization.

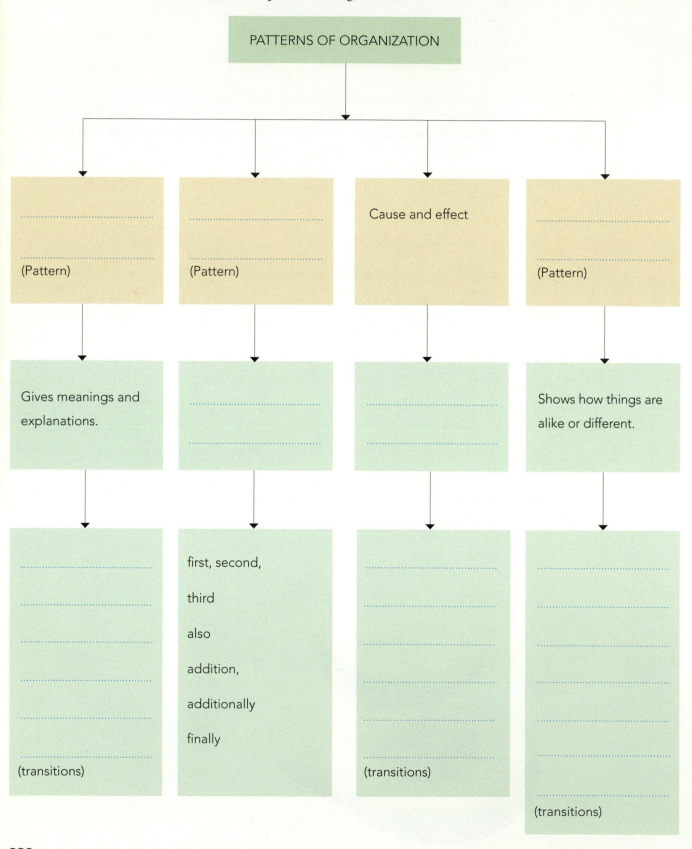

PATTERNS OF ORGANIZATION

(Pattern)

(Pattern)

Cause and effect

(Pattern)

Gives meanings and explanations.

Shows how things are alike or different.

first, second,

third

also

addition,

additionally

finally

(transitions)

(transitions)

(transitions)

Summary: Patterns of Organization

Patterns of organization are

....

....

....

Some patterns studied so far are

....

....

....

Transitions are

....

....

....

READING LAB ASSIGNMENTS

SKILL REVIEW

Skill practices in MyReadingLab are located at the end of Chapter 7, "Patterns of Organization—Part 2."

COMPREHENSION IMPROVEMENT

1. Go online to MyReadingLab and click on the Reading Level tab. Choose two stories to read, and then answer the questions that follow.

CAREER EXPLORATION

2. Go online to www.bls.gov/oco and explore careers in sports, fitness, and recreation. Find a career that interests you, and print out the information. This site will tell you what the job is like, what the outlook is for employment, educational requirements, and current salary. Print the article, and then preview, read, highlight, and annotate one or two sections of it. Find three examples of relationships within and between sentences using the patterns you have learned so far. Underline and label the sentences with the correct type of relationships shown.

SKILL APPLICATION

3. Using your textbooks for other classes or articles in newspapers or magazines, look for examples of the patterns of organization that you have learned so far. Explain how knowing the pattern helps your comprehension of the material.

LEARNING REFLECTION

Think about the skills and concepts in this chapter. What have you learned in this chapter that will help your reading comprehension and enable you to do well in college?

SELF-EVALUATION CHECKLIST

Rate yourself on the following items, using the following scale:

1 = strongly disagree

2 = disagree

3 = neither agree nor disagree

4 = agree

5 = strongly agree

1. I completed all of the assigned work on time. ....

2. I understand all of the concepts in this chapter ....

3. I contributed to teamwork and class discussions. ....

4. I completed all of the assigned lab work on time. ....

5. I came to class on time. ....

6. I attended class every day. ....

7. I studied for any quizzes or tests we had for this chapter. ....

8. I asked questions when I didn't understand something. ....

9. I checked my comprehension during reading. ....

10. I know what is expected of me in the coming week. ....

11. Are you still on track with the goals you set in Chapter 1? ....

12. What changes can you make to improve your performance in this course? ....

For support in meeting this chapter's objectives, go to the Study Plan in MyReadingLab and select Patterns of Organization. Read and view the resources in the Review Materials section, and then complete the Recall, Apply, and Write exercises in the Activities section. Check your results by clicking on Gradebook.

STUDY SKILL: PARAPHRASING

Paraphrasing: restating sentences or quotes to make them shorter and to the point, and saying them in your own words

Paraphrasing means restating sentences or quotes to make them shorter and to the point, and saying them in your own words. You may paraphrase whenever you want to state someone else's idea more clearly by using language that your audience will be able to understand more easily. When paraphrasing, the trick is to say the sentence or paragraph in a more direct way without leaving out important information.

Paraphrased Sentences

Read the following quotations, and then read the example paraphrases that follow.

> "Due to the overwhelming popularity of weight-loss products, the FDA has cracked down on pharmaceutical companies for producing products with dangerous side effects, such as Fen-phen."

Paraphrase:
The FDA has cracked down on companies producing weight-loss products with dangerous side effects.

> "In unicellular organisms, a single cell is required to carry out all the normal functions for survival, even those that require most or all of the cell's capacities."

Paraphrase:
Single-celled organisms must carry out all the survival functions, including those that require most of the cell's capacities.

Paraphrase the following sentences in your own words.

1. Maintaining flexibility is important and requires a commitment to regularly performing exercises, such as stretching. To make the stretching workouts more enjoyable, try doing them along with music.

....

....

....

....

2. It was believed that muscle cramping during exercises was due to dehydration or electrolyte imbalances. Recent studies have shown, however, that cramping risk factors include fatigue and poor stretching before exercising. Additional factors include age, family history of cramping, and a higher body mass index.

....

....

....

....

3. To get the most from your workouts, it's important to keep breathing and not hold your breath. Do not stretch to the point of pain, or overstretch. Forceful extensions of the knee, neck, back, or spine should also be avoided.

....

....

....

....

CHAPTER 7 PATTERNS OF ORGANIZATION—PART 2

LEARNING OBJECTIVES

IN THIS CHAPTER, YOU WILL:

Objective 1 identify more patterns of organization and explain why they are important to comprehension.

Objective 2 distinguish different relationships within and between sentences.

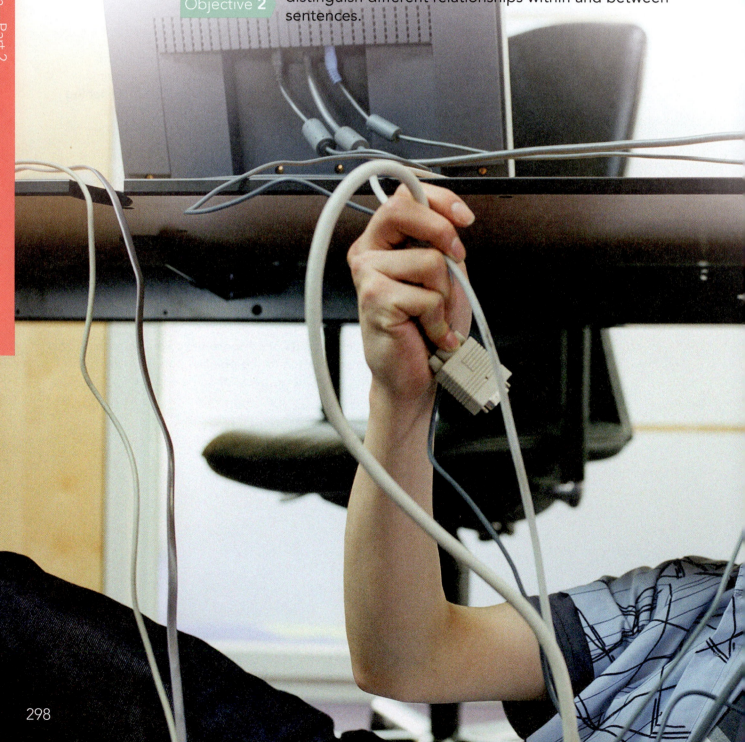

PATTERNS OF ORGANIZATION:

ORDER

CLASSIFICATION

EXAMPLE

ADDITION

Objective 1 ▸ # MORE PATTERNS OF ORGANIZATION

Patterns of organization, or thought patterns, are the ways that writers arrange supporting details in a sentence, a paragraph, or an essay.

You learned about four common **patterns of organization** in Chapter 6: definition, listing, cause and effect, and compare and/or contrast. You also learned that recognizing patterns in reading and writing helps you to remember what you read and helps you to better comprehend the material. This chapter teaches you four more patterns that authors commonly use when organizing their supporting details.

Remember that each pattern uses transitions that help the readers see the relationships between ideas. Learning the transitions for each of the patterns can often help you identify the pattern. Also remember from Chapter 6 that the author's main idea, or topic sentence, will often give you a clue as to the overall pattern of organization. It can also help to ask yourself, "What are most of the major supporting details showing me?"

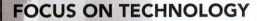

FOCUS ON TECHNOLOGY

One of the most exciting aspects of technology is its rapid growth, with new applications and devices entering the market on a daily basis. Technology is a large part of most jobs in nearly every industry—even in fields like theater and art. The skills needed for many careers in technology can be achieved with a two-year technical degree.

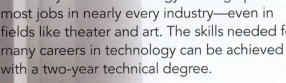

Order Patterns

Time Order (Chronological Order) Pattern

The time order pattern shows ideas in the order in which they happened in a chain of events. The transitions for this pattern answer the question, "When?" In addition to the transitions listed in the following box, dates are also considered signals of the time order pattern when they are given in chronological order. Use the transitions in the next box to complete the sentences that follow. There may be more than one transition that can complete a sentence correctly.

TIME ORDER TRANSITIONS				
as	current(ly)	later	over time	third
after(ward)	during	meanwhile	previous(ly)	until
before	finally	next	second	when
begin	first	now	start	while
beginning	last	often	then	

1. Classes started .... the Labor Day holiday weekend.

2. To create a basic Web page, you must .... choose a template with the format you would like to use.

3. .... Mr. Simon's lecture, he went online to show us several examples of well-designed Web sites.

4. I will be working .... late this evening.

5. .... Abdul turned in his final project, he saved a copy of it on his flash drive.

The Process Pattern

The process pattern is similar to the time order pattern, but it is used to show steps, stages, or instructions. The transitions are the same as those in the time order pattern, but the details focus on *how* and *when* something happens. Use the time order transitions to complete the following sentences. There may be more than one transition that can complete a sentence correctly.

1. The .... step in creating a graphic design is to open the right software program.

2. .... set up your screen to show how large you want your final image to be.

3. .... you are creating your design, remember to save your work often.

4. The process of making a digital movie .... with loading your video clips onto your computer.

5. .... you have loaded your video clips, ...
decide in which order you will place them to tell your story.

Space Order Pattern

Details arranged in space order (spatial order) show locations. The transitions for this pattern answer the question, "Where?" Use the transitions in the next box to complete the sentences that follow. There may be more than one transition that can complete a sentence correctly.

SPACE ORDER (SPATIAL ORDER) TRANSITIONS

adjacent to	beside	from	on	south
along	between	front	outer	through
around	beyond	inner	outside of	top
at	bottom	left	over	under
back	center	next to	parallel to	west
beneath	east	north	right	within

1. The fax machine is located on the desk .... the computer.

2. Most of your computer's software programs are visible .... the desktop.

3. You can find the new computer store just .... of Highway 429, *on* Keller Boulevard.

4. At the .... of your computer monitor, you can find the model number.

5. Plug your power cable into the .... of the computer, *next to* the monitor cable.

Classification Pattern

The classification pattern organizes details into groups or categories that share similar characteristics. Use the transitions in the next box to complete the sentences that follow. There may be more than one transition that can complete a sentence correctly.

CLASSIFICATION TRANSITIONS

categories	category	class	classification	classify
group	kind(s)	type		

---

1. .... of muscle cars include the 1969 Pontiac GTO and the 1971 Mustang Cobra Jet.

2. There are two .... of sports car racing: Sports Prototype and Grand Touring.

3. In the sports car .... , the Chevrolet Corvette is considered one of the most popular.

4. The latest sports car design and cutting-edge technology are featured in the Sports Prototype ....

5. In Sports Prototype cars, there are two .... , ... the P1 and the P2.

Practice

1. As you read the following paragraph, underline the main idea and transitions that help you to determine the overall pattern of organization. Then, answer the questions that follow.

In 1867, an American named Sylvester Howard Roper created a bicycle that was powered by steam. The Daimler-Maybach motorcycle, invented in Germany in 1885, was the first fuel-powered bike. Later, more motorcycles appeared with internal combustion engines, and by World War I, the Indian was the largest motorcycle manufacturer in the world. By 1920, Harley-Davidson took first place with dealers in 67 countries. After World War II, the BSA Group became the largest motorcycle producer. From the 1950s through the 1990s, small-engine motorcycles were popular worldwide. Today there are hundreds of different types of motorcycles manufactured throughout the world. The history of motorcycles is one filled with variety and innovation.

1. What is the topic?

   a. motorcycles

   b. the history of motorcycles

   c. Sylvester Howard Roper

   d. the variety of motorcycles

2. What is the topic sentence of this paragraph?

   a. In 1867, an American named Sylvester Howard Roper created a bicycle that was powered by steam.

   b. Later, more motorcycles appeared with internal combustion engines, and by World War I, the Indian was the largest motorcycle manufacturer in the world.

   c. Today there are hundreds of different types of motorcycles manufactured throughout the world.

   d. The history of motorcycles is one filled variety and innovation.

3. What is the overall pattern of organization used in this paragraph?

   a. time order   **c.** space order

   b. process   **d.** classification

4. Identify the relationship within the following sentence: After World War II, the BSA Group became the largest motorcycle producer.

   a. time order   **c.** process

   b. classification   **d.** space order

5. Identify the meaning of the underlined word in the following sentence: The history of motorcycles is one filled variety and <u>innovation</u>.

   a. variety   **c.** new ideas

   b. ideas   **d.** manufacturing

Practice

2. As you read the following paragraph, underline the main idea and transitions that help you to determine the overall pattern of organization. Then, answer the questions that follow.

There are several types of satellites, each have a different function. Astronomical satellites, like the Hubble, are used by astronomers to study the planets, galaxies, and other heavenly bodies. Another group of satellites are biosatellites, which carry living organisms for scientific experiments. Communication satellites are used in telecommunications, such as with cell phones. Navigational satellites use radio time signals for GPS systems. Another category of satellite is the reconnaissance satellite, which is mostly used by governments and militaries for obtaining information. Weather satellites are used to monitor Earth's changing weather and climates. With so many kinds of satellites orbiting the Earth, it is surprising that there are not more collisions in outer space.

1. What is the topic?

   a. satellites

   b. who uses satellites

   c. communication satellites

   d. types of satellites

2. What is the topic sentence of this paragraph?

   a. With so many categories of satellites orbiting the Earth, it is surprising that there are not more collisions in outer space.

   b. Astronomical satellites, like the Hubble, are used by astronomers to study the planets, galaxies, and other heavenly bodies.

   c. There are several types of satellites, which each have a different function.

   d. Communication satellites are used in telecommunications, such as with cell phones.

3. What is the overall pattern of organization for this paragraph?

   a. time order

   b. process

   c. space order

   d. classification

4. Identify the relationship within the following sentence: Astronomical satellites, like the Hubble, are used by astronomers to study the planets, galaxies, and other heavenly bodies.

   a. time order

   b. process

   c. space order

   d. listing

5. Identify the relationship within the following sentence: Another kind of satellite is the reconnaissance satellite, which is mostly used by governments and militaries for obtaining information.

   a. time order

   b. process

   c. space order

   d. classification

Practice

3. As you read the following paragraph, underline the main idea and transitions that help you to determine the overall pattern of organization. Then, answer the questions that follow.

The new Ford Shelby GT500 Coupe Convertible features a new headlight cluster and a larger grille opening out front. At the rear, the spoiler is covered with a Gurney flap and a new rear diffuser below. This gives the car more stability at higher speeds. Under the hood is an amazing 540 horsepower engine with improved air flow, resulting in a "significant improvement in performance," according to Ford. The model features new wheels: 18s on the convertible and 19s on the coupe. Each wheel sports a 225 mm Goodyear Eagle F1 Supercar tire. The exterior paint schemes can be "mild" or "wild," like the Superman paint job with bright red racing stripes over light blue paint. Owners can go for an edgy look or a classic street racing style. The beautiful interior and exciting exterior features of this car will not disappoint owners.

1. What is the topic?

   a. why you should buy a Ford Shelby GT500

   b. features of the Ford Shelby GT500 Coupe Convertible

   c. racing cars

   d. the Ford Shelby GT500

2. What is the topic sentence?

   a. The new Ford Shelby GT500 Coupe Convertible features a new headlight cluster and a larger grille opening out front.

   b. Under the hood is an amazing 540 horsepower engine with improved air flow, resulting in a "significant improvement in performance," according to Ford.

   c. Owners can go for an edgy look or a classic street racing style.

   d. The beautiful interior and exciting exterior features of this car will not disappoint owners.

3. What is the overall pattern of organization?

   a. listing   **c.** classification

   b. space order   **d.** time order

4. Identify the relationship within the following sentence: Under the hood is an amazing 540 horsepower engine with improved air flow, resulting in a "significant improvement in performance," according to Ford.

   a. compare and/or contrast   **c.** listing

   b. cause and effect   **d.** process

5. Identify the relationship within the following sentence: Owners can go for an edgy look or a classic street racing style.

   a. compare and/or contrast   **c.** time order

   b. cause and effect   **d.** process

TEXTBOOK SELECTION

Read the following textbook selection, and underline the main idea and the transitions that help you to determine the overall pattern of organization. Then, answer the questions that follow.

In 1964, track and cross-country coach Bill Bowerman formed a partnership with one of his former student-athletes, Phil Knight, to sell custom-designed shoes. Two years earlier, Knight had formed Blue Ribbon Sports to sell track shoes and later changed its name to Nike. In 1971, Bowerman was testing various sole patterns for running shoes for greater cushioning of the athlete's foot and gripping the ground firmly. While eating a waffle one morning, he realized that the waffle's form could be the very sole pattern for which he had been searching. He poured **urethane** into the waffle iron and then cut the resulting waffle pattern into the shape of a sole. Further testing proved the value of this sole pattern; the University of Oregon's cross-country team won that year's NCAA championship with the waffle soles. The following year, the waffle pattern was introduced to the public, and, thus, Bill Bowerman became the inventor of an improved running shoe.

(From *Engineering by Design*, 2e by Gerard Voland. Copyright © 2004 by Gerard Voland. Reprinted by permission of Pearson Education, Inc., Upper Saddle River, NJ.)

urethane
(YUR-a-thane): a compound used in making rubber soles.

QUESTIONS

1. What is the topic?
   a. Bill Bowerman
   b. the University of Oregon's championship
   c. the invention of waffle-pattern soles
   d. how to make running shoes

2. What is the topic sentence?
   a. Bill Bowerman served as coach for NCAA championship teams in both track and cross-country at the University of Oregon.
   b. In 1964, he formed a partnership with one of his former student-athletes, Phil Knight, to sell custom-designed shoes.
   c. Further testing proved the value of this sole pattern; the University of Oregon's cross-country team won that year's NCAA championship with the waffle soles.
   d. The following year, the waffle pattern was introduced to the public, and, thus, Bill Bowerman became the inventor of an improved running shoe.

3. What are the overall patterns of organization?
   a. cause and effect and time order
   b. compare and/or contrast
   c. time order and process
   d. process and cause and effect

4. Identify the relationship within the following sentence: While eating a waffle one morning, he realized that the waffle's form could be the very sole pattern for which he had been searching.

   a. space order

   b. time order

   c. process

   d. listing

5. Identify the relationship within the following sentence: Further testing proved the value of this sole pattern; indeed, the University of Oregon's cross-country team won that year's NCAA championship with the waffle soles.

   a. process

   b. cause and effect

   c. compare and/or contrast

   d. space order

U-Review

Decide which of the patterns described thus far in this chapter you would use in each of the following situations. Check your answers with a partner or in your teams.

1. Which pattern would you use to show how to use a new software program for a computer class?

   ....

2. Which pattern would you use to describe the history of the automotive industry?

   ....

3. Which pattern would you use to show the location of the different parts of a computer?

   ....

4. Which pattern would you use to describe the different types of motor vehicles?

   ....

5. Which pattern would you use to show how to insert a new graphics card into your computer?

   ....

   ....

The Example (Illustration) Pattern

Often an author will try to illustrate an idea by providing one or more examples. The example pattern is often used with definitions or main ideas. Use the transitions in the next box to complete the sentences that follow. There may be more than one transition that can complete a sentence correctly.

EXAMPLE (ILLUSTRATION) PATTERN TRANSITIONS

example	exemplify	for example	for instance
illustration	such as	to illustrate	

1. The Japanese motorcycle manufacturers, ... Honda, Kawasaki, Suzuki, and Yamaha, dominate the industry worldwide.

2. In many countries, motorcycles are more common than automobiles. .... , in Taiwan, there are twice as many motorcycles as automobiles on the roads.

3. Other companies— .... BMW, KTM, Triumph, Aprilia, Moto-Guzzi, and Ducati—are becoming more popular in the U.S. market.

4. Motorcycles have a higher number of fatal accidents than cars. .... this point, the number of fatal crashes in the United States for motorcycles is four times higher than for automobiles.

5. There are several types of motorcycles: street, off-road, and dual purpose. A chopper would be one .... of a street bike.

The Addition Pattern

When authors want to add more information, they will sometimes use the addition pattern. The following exercise will help you learn some transitions for the addition pattern. Use the transitions in the next box to complete the sentences that follow. There may be more than one transition that can complete a sentence correctly.

ADDITION PATTERN TRANSITIONS

additionally	also	and	another
furthermore	in addition	moreover	

---

1. In the street types of motorcycles, you will .... find cruisers and sports bikes.

2. Sports bikes designed for racing are fast, sleek, and lightweight. ...., the rider's seat is tipped forward for an aerodynamic riding posture.

3. Touring motorcycles are designed for comfort .... have larger fuel tanks for long-distance travel.

4. Off-road bikes include motocross and supermoto machines. They are mostly used on racing circuits. They .... can be used for recreational riding, or "mudding."

5. Motorcycles have 65 percent lower carbon emissions than cars. ...., they are more fuel efficient than automobiles.

309

Practice

1. As you read the following selection, underline the main idea and transitions that help you determine the overall pattern of organization. Then, answer the questions that follow.

Nearly everything we do involves technology of some kind, such as phones, televisions, or computers. Computer support specialists provide technical assistance to workers, customers, and others who have computer or software needs. They may work in an office as a help desk technician or out in the field servicing computer systems in businesses, hospitals, schools, or factories. Network systems analysts are responsible for maintaining local and wide area networks, Internet connections, and other similar systems. Furthermore, they monitor and adjust these networks to meet future needs. Another computer expert is a Web developer, who creates Web sites and monitors them to make sure they work correctly and achieve the sponsor's goals. Many people employed in these industries work from home.

1. What is the topic?

   a. computers

   b. computer support specialists

   c. technology

   d. network systems analysts

2. What is the topic sentence?

   a. They may work in an office as a help desk technician or out in the field servicing computer systems in businesses, hospitals, schools, or factories.

   b. Many people employed in these industries work from home.

   c. Computer support specialists provide technical assistance to workers, customers, and others who have computer or software needs.

   d. Another computer expert is a Web developer, who creates Web sites and monitors them to make sure they work correctly and achieve the sponsor's goals.

3. What is the overall pattern of organization?

   a. space order

   b. classification

   c. addition

   d. cause and effect

4. Identify the relationship within the following sentence: Nearly everything we do involves technology of some kind, such as phones, televisions, or computers.

   a. example

   b. definition

   c. compare and/or contrast

   d. classification

5. Identify the relationship between the following sentences: Network systems analysts are responsible for maintaining local and wide area networks, Internet connections, and other similar systems. Furthermore, they monitor and adjust these networks to meet future needs.

   a. addition

   b. listing

   c. classification

   d. definition

Practice

2. As you read the selection, underline the main idea and the transitions that help you determine the overall pattern of organization. Then, answer the questions that follow.

On January 27, 1967, three astronauts—"Gus" Grissom, Edward H. White, and Roger B. Chafee—were testing inside the *Apollo 1* spacecraft command module during a routine ground test. The spacecraft had nearly 12 miles of electrical wire in a pure oxygen environment. During the testing, a spark ignited a fire, which spread rapidly. Furthermore, there was no fire extinguisher on board, and the astronauts couldn't open the escape hatch because of the internal pressure of the capsule. Emergency crews were not on full alert because this was only a test and not an actual flight. All three *Apollo 1* astronauts died within minutes in a fire resulting from a faulty electrical system. Since then, hundreds of modifications have been made to make space flight safer for astronauts.

1. What is the topic?

   a. spaceflight

   b. *Apollo 1*

   c. the *Apollo 1* tragedy

   d. making spaceflight safer

2. What is the topic sentence of this passage?

   a. On January 27, 1967, three astronauts—"Gus" Grissom, Edward H. White, and Roger B. Chafee—were testing inside the *Apollo 1* spacecraft command module during a routine ground test.

   b. The spacecraft had nearly 12 miles of electrical wire in a pure oxygen environment.

   c. All three *Apollo 1* astronauts died within minutes in a fire resulting from a faulty electrical system.

   d. Since then, hundreds of modifications have been made to make space flight safer for astronauts.

3. What is the overall pattern of organization?

   a. cause and effect

   b. time order

   c. process

   d. addition

4. Identify the relationship within the following sentence: On January 27, 1967, three astronauts—"Gus" Grissom, Edward H. White, and Roger B. Chafee—were testing inside the *Apollo 1* spacecraft command module during a routine ground test.

   a. cause and effect

   b. addition

   c. space order

   d. time order

5. Identify the relationship between the following sentences: During the testing, a spark ignited a fire, which spread rapidly. Furthermore, there was no fire extinguisher on board, and the astronauts couldn't open the escape hatch because of the internal pressure of the capsule.

   a. listing

   b. addition

   c. time order

   d. example

Practice

3. As you read the following selection, underline the main idea and transitions that help you determine the overall pattern of organization. Then, answer the questions that follow.

Drafters are people who prepare technical drawings and plans for many different types of projects, big and small. They use their knowledge and training to construct the final drawing on a computer. Most drafters usually work in one specialty area. Aeronautical drafters prepare engineering drawings for aircraft and spacecraft. Another type of drafter is the architectural drafter, who specializes in drawing buildings and other structures. Mechanical engineering drafters produce drawings for manufactured products, such as cars and motorcycles. Electrical drafters design wiring and layout diagrams for equipment in buildings. Electronic drafters draw wiring diagrams for the circuit boards used in electronic devices. Civil drafters draw plans and maps for the construction of highways, bridges, pipelines, and sewage systems.

1. What is the topic?

   a. drafters

   b. mechanical engineering

   c. aeronautical drafters

   d. architectural drafters

2. What is the topic sentence?

   a. Drafters are people who prepare technical drawings and plans for many different types of projects, big and small.

   b. They use their knowledge and training to construct the final drawing on a computer.

   c. Drafters are given rough drawings showing the shapes and sizes of the object to be drawn.

   d. Most drafters usually work in one specialty area.

3. What is the overall pattern?

   a. listing   **c.** compare and/or contrast

   b. classification   **d.** example

4. Identify the relationship within the following sentence: Civil drafters draw plans and maps for the construction of highways, bridges, pipelines, and sewage systems.

   a. compare and/or contrast   **c.** listing

   b. example   **d.** cause and effect

5. Identify the relationship within the following sentence: Another <u>type</u> of drafter is the architectural drafter, who specializes in drawing buildings and other structures.

   a. cause and effect   **c.** example

   b. listing   **d.** classification

TEXTBOOK SELECTION

As you read the following textbook selection, underline the main idea and the transitions that help you determine the overall pattern of organization. Then, answer the questions that follow.

voltage (VOL-taj): a measurement of electrical power.

1 Spacecraft *Apollo 13* was 205,000 miles from Earth when the crew noticed a sudden drop in the electrical **voltage** of one of their two power-generating systems. They also heard a loud banging sound. The voltage then rose to normal. Even as Duty Commander John L. Swigert Jr. reported these observations to NASA control in Houston, the voltage in the Main B system dropped to zero, and the voltage in Main A began to fall.

2 The astronauts were in deadly danger. Without power, *Apollo 13* would become their tomb in space. The engineers in Houston, realizing that action would need to be taken immediately in order to prevent a tragedy, began to evaluate what was known (for example, voltage drops, a loud noise) as they collected further information from the crew. Then, only 13 minutes after the first voltage drop, Commander Swigert reported that their number 2 oxygen tank was reading empty and that the ship appeared to be leaking gas into space. Moreover, the ship's other tank also was losing oxygen.

phenomena (fen-NOM-men-ah): odd or unusual things happening.

3 The Houston engineers quickly determined that a rupture in the number 2 oxygen tank would explain all of the observed **phenomena**. A loud noise, such as that first heard by the astronauts, would accompany a rupture in the tank. Furthermore, the gas being leaked into space could be the lost oxygen from the tank (as well as that from the damaged number 1 tank). Once the situation was understood, appropriate actions could be taken to preserve the remaining oxygen and conserve electrical power, thereby allowing the crew of *Apollo 13* to return safely to Earth.

(From *Engineering by Design*, 2e by Gerard Voland. Copyright © 2004 by Gerard Voland. Reprinted by permission of Pearson Education, Inc., Upper Saddle River, NJ.)

QUESTIONS

1. What is the topic of this textbook selection?

   a. *Apollo 13* spacecraft   c. the crew of *Apollo 13*

   b. the near tragedy of *Apollo 13*   d. the dangers of spaceflight

2. What is the topic sentence of paragraph 3?

   a. The Houston engineers quickly determined that a rupture in the number 2 oxygen tank would explain all of the observed phenomena.

   b. A loud noise, such as that first heard by the astronauts, would accompany a rupture in the tank.

   c. Furthermore, the gas being leaked into space could be the lost oxygen from the tank (as well as that from the damaged number 1 tank).

   d. Once the situation was understood, appropriate actions could be taken to preserve the remaining oxygen and conserve electrical power, thereby allowing the crew of *Apollo 13* to return safely to Earth.

3. What is the overall pattern of organization for paragraphs 1 and 2?

    a. space order

    b. time order

    c. process

    d. example

4. Identify the relationship within the following sentence: Without power, *Apollo 13* would become their tomb in space.

    a. process

    b. compare and/or contrast

    c. cause and effect

    d. time order

5. Identify the relationship between the following sentences: Then, only 13 minutes after the first voltage drop, Commander Swigert reported that their number 2 oxygen tank was reading empty and that the ship appeared to be leaking gas into space. <u>Moreover,</u> the ship's other tank also was losing oxygen.

    a. time order

    b. space order

    c. cause and effect

    d. addition

U-Review

Choose one of the following activities:

1. Create a short TV commercial using one of the following patterns of organization. Read it to the class, and have them guess which pattern you used and explain how they determined the pattern.

definition	cause and effect	listing
compare and/or contrast	time order	process
space order	classification	addition
example		

2. In your team, draw a large concept map or a chart showing each of the patterns listed in activity 1. Describe each pattern, and give some examples of transitions that go with each pattern.

3. Split up the list of patterns in activity 1 among your team members. Write down what each pattern is, how you determine this type of pattern, and some transitions that go with it. Share your findings with your team.

Reading 1 Vocabulary Preview

The following vocabulary words are from the article "Game Master." With a partner or in a team, choose the correct meanings of the underlined words in the following sentences. Use context clues (LEADS), word part clues, and parts of speech to help you figure out the meanings.

1. The best graphic designs are those that have <u>simplicity</u> (sim-PLI-city) rather than too many details and elements.

   a. the quality of being complicated

   b. the quality of being easy

   c. the quality of being uncomplicated

   d. the quality of being sophisticated

2. The <u>gallant</u> (GAL-ant) young man rescued the princess from her evil stepmother.

   a. unlikely   **c.** brave

   b. happy   **d.** devastated

3. The quality of the jewelry made here is <u>unparalleled</u> (un-PAIR-a-lell'd) by anywhere else in the world.

   a. unmatched

   b. similar to

   c. not straight

   d. not as beautiful

4. Ricardo's serious music practicing accounts for the <u>consumption</u> (kon-SUMP-shun) of most of his free time.

   a. eating

   b. using up

   c. wasting

   d. direction

5. <u>Amid</u> (a-MID) all the confusion when we left home for the airport, I forgot my passport.

   a. coming from

   b. after

   c. because of

   d. in the middle of

6. With the introduction of cell phones, the communications industry was <u>reinvented</u> (re-in-VEN-ted).

   a. increased

   b. created

   c. refreshed

   d. made over again in a new way

Reading 1

7. The cell phones built in Germany <u>rivaled</u> (RY-val'd) those produced in Japan last year.

   a. were equal to

   b. were better than

   c. were worse than

   d. defeated

8. As an <u>aspiring</u> (as-PIRE-ing) artist, Jamal hopes his musical career will be very successful.

   a. hoping to become

   b. unemployed

   c. consuming

   d. conscientious

9. The National Guard was <u>deployed</u> (de-PLOY'd) to the areas of greatest need during the disaster.

   a. employed

   b. taken to

   c. put into a position ready to act

   d. driven

10. In the eighteenth century, the idea of using hot air balloons to travel was so <u>revolutionary</u> (rev-o-LOO-shun-air-ee) that large crowds gathered to see one of them launched.

    a. causing upset

    b. causing the collapse of a government

    c. going against the law

    d. a new and unique idea

Reading 1

What Do You Already Know?

1. Do you play video games? If not, why? If you do, which games are your favorites and why?

2. If you could invent a video game, what would it be?

> **Directions:** As you read this article, practice the four-step reading process. Preview the article, and then write on the following lines one or two questions that you would hope to have answered.
>
> ....
>
> ....
>
> ....
>
> ....

As you read, answer the questions in the margins to check your comprehension.

"Game Master"

BY SETH SCHIESEL

From "Resistance Is Futile" by Seth Schiesel from *The New York Times*, May 25, 2008. Copyright © 2008 by Seth Schiesel. Reprinted by permission of *The New York Times*.

Shigeru Miyamoto (she-GER-roo my-a-MO-toe) is the mastermind of Nintendo and the world's most influential video-game designer. His creative ideas and team leadership gave birth to the most popular games and characters in gaming history. His team's latest innovation was the development of the Wii entertainment system.

1　　When Disney died in 1966, Shigeru Miyamoto was a 14-year-old schoolteacher's son living near Kyoto, Japan's ancient capital. An aspiring cartoonist, he adored the classic Disney characters. When he wasn't drawing, he made his own toys, carving wooden puppets with his grandfathers' tools or devising a car race from a spare motor, string and tin cans.

2　　Even as he has become the world's most famous and influential video-game designer as the father of Donkey Kong, Mario, Zelda and, most recently, the Wii, Mr. Miyamoto still approaches his work like a humble craftsman, not as the celebrity he is to gamers around the world. As the creative mastermind at Nintendo for almost three decades, Mr. Miyamoto has unleashed mass entertainment unmatched since Walt Disney's famous career.

3　　By way of comparing Walt Disney's role in the larger brand with his, he said, "What's important is that the people that I work with are also recognized

How did Miyamoto show his creativity as a boy?

317

Reading 1

Why did Miyamoto become so famous?

and that it's the Nintendo brand that goes forward and continues to become strong and popular. And if people are going to consider the Nintendo brand as being on the same level as the Disney brand, that's very flattering and makes me happy to hear," he added, through an interpreter.

4   Mario, the mustached Italian plumber he created almost 30 years ago, has become by some measures the planet's most recognized fictional character, rivaled only by Mickey Mouse. As the creator of the Donkey Kong, Mario and Zelda series and the person who ultimately oversees every Nintendo game, Mr. Miyamoto may be personally responsible for the consumption of more billions of hours of human time than anyone around. In *Time* magazine's 100 online poll conducted this spring, Mr. Miyamoto was voted the most influential person in the world.

5   But it isn't just traditional gamers who are flocking to Mr. Miyamoto's latest creation, the Wii. Eighteen months ago, just when video games were in danger of losing popularity, Mr. Miyamoto and Satoru Iwata, Nintendo's chief executive, practically reinvented the industry. Their idea was revolutionary in its simplicity. Rather than create a new generation of games that would please serious players, they developed the Wii as an easy-to-use, inexpensive entertainment for families, with a particular appeal to women. So far the Wii has sold more than 25 million units, besting the competition from Sony and Microsoft.

6   In an effort to build on this success, Nintendo released its Wii Fit system in North America, a device that hopes to make doing yoga in front of a television screen almost as much fun as driving, throwing, jumping or shooting in a traditional game, such as baseball or basketball.

7   "Without Miyamoto, Nintendo would be back making playing cards," said Andy McNamara, editor in chief of *Game Informer*, referring to Nintendo's original business in 1889. "He probably inspires 99 percent of the developers out there today. You can even say there wouldn't be video games today if it wasn't for Miyamoto and Nintendo. He's the granddad of all game developers, but the funny thing is that, for all of the memorable characters he's designed and created, he is still pushing the limits with things like Wii Fit."

What training and experience did Mr. Miyamoto have that helped him to develop his talent?

8   Mr. Miyamoto graduated from the Kanazawa College of Art in 1975 and joined Nintendo two years later as a staff artist. The original Donkey Kong was a prime force in gaming's early surge of popularity, along with arcade classics like Space Invaders, Asteroids and Pac-Man.

9   He rose quickly at the company, and his name has been synonymous with Nintendo since the 1980s, when the original Mario Bros. games helped save the industry after the collapse of Atari, maker of the first broadly popular home console. When Atari failed amid many unpopular games, Nintendo renewed its faith in home gaming systems. The Nintendo Entertainment System, released in the West in 1985, became the best-selling console of its era.

10   Since then Mr. Miyamoto has been directly involved in the production of at least 70 games, including recent hits like Mario Kart Wii, Super Smash Bros. Brawl, Super Mario Galaxy and The Legend of Zelda: Twilight Princess. Mr. Miyamoto supervises about 400 people, including contractors, almost

entirely in Japan. The popular new versions of classic games have maintained his credibility among serious gamers even as he has reached out to new audiences with mass-market products like the Wii.

11   Through all his games, his designs are marked by an accumulation of care and detail. There is nothing obvious about why a goofy guy in blue overalls like Mario should appeal to so many, just as there is nothing obvious in how Disney could have built a company on talking animals. Rather, the reason I stood in line at a pizzeria more than 20 years ago to play Super Mario Bros. is that his games have some irresistible appeal that inspires you to drop just one more quarter (or, these days, to stay on the couch, just one more hour).

12   Just as a film is not measured by the quality of its special effects, a game is not measured merely by its graphics. This concept is lost on many designers, but not on Mr. Miyamoto. Even Mr. Miyamoto's earliest games hold up as worthy entertainment. (The story of two men battling for the world record in Donkey Kong was made into a film, "The King of Kong.")

13   "There are very few people in the video game industry who have managed to succeed time after time at a world-class level, and Miyamoto is one of them," said Graham Hopper, executive vice president and general manager of Disney Interactive Studios. "The level of creative success that he has achieved over a sustained period is probably unparalleled."

14   Given that its roster of characters includes not only Mario and Donkey Kong but also Princess Peach, Zelda, Bowser and Link, it's easy to imagine that Mr. Miyamoto designs his games around those characters. The truth is exactly the opposite. According to Mr. Miyamoto, game-play systems and mechanics have always come first, while the characters are created and deployed in the service of the overall design.

15   "I feel that people like Mario and people like Link and the other characters we've created not for the characters themselves, but because the games they appear in are fun," he said. "And because people enjoy playing those games first, they come to love the characters as well."

16   "I would say that over the last five years or so, the types of games I create has changed somewhat," he said. "Whereas before I could kind of use my own imagination to create these worlds or create these games, I would say that over the last five years I've had more of a tendency to take interests or topics in my life and try to draw the entertainment out of that."

17   It has proved the perfect strategy as Nintendo reaches out to non-gamers who may not care to understand why this frantic plumber keeps jumping on top of turtles, or why that gallant fellow in green has to keep rescuing the same princess over and over. At this moment, when consumers crave the ability to shape and become a part of their entertainment, the latest star in Nintendo's stable of characters is you. Mr. Miyamoto remains the game master and continues to strive for entertainment that is interactive and fun. When it comes to the Walt Disney of the digital generation, no one knows fun better.

Why are the games that Miyamoto and his team produce so successful?

1,251 words divided by .... minutes = ... words per minute

Thinking About What You Read

It is a good habit to summarize everything you read to strengthen your comprehension.

Directions: On the following lines, write a two- or three-sentence summary of the article "Game Master." In your own words, describe what the article was about and why the author wrote it.

....

....

....

....

....

....

Comprehension Questions

The following questions will help you to recall the main idea and the details of "Game Master." Review any parts of the article that you need to find the correct answers.

FINDING THE TOPIC

1. **What is the topic of this article?**
   a. video games
   b. the world of Nintendo
   c. Shigeru Miyamoto's video game legacy
   d. the most popular video games

MAIN IDEAS

2. **What is the main idea of the entire article?**
   a. When Disney died in 1966, Shigeru Miyamoto was a 14-year-old school teacher's son living near Kyoto, Japan's ancient capital.
   b. Through all his games, his designs are marked by an accumulation of care and detail.
   c. "The level of creative success that he has achieved over a sustained period is probably unparalleled."
   d. Mr. Miyamoto remains the game master and continues to strive for entertainment that is interactive and fun.

Reading 1

3. What is the topic sentence of paragraph 5?

   a. But it isn't just traditional gamers who are flocking to Mr. Miyamoto's latest creation, the Wii.

   b. Eighteen months ago, just when video games were in danger of losing popularity, Mr. Miyamoto and Satoru Iwata, Nintendo's chief executive, practically reinvented the industry.

   c. Their idea was revolutionary in its simplicity.

   d. Rather than create a new generation of games that would please serious players, they developed the Wii as an easy-to-use, inexpensive entertainment for families, with a particular appeal to women.

SUPPORTING DETAILS

4. According to the article, which of the following statements is false?

   a. Miyamoto designs his games around his characters.

   b. The Nintendo Entertainment System was released in the West in 1985.

   c. Miyamoto has led the development of games such as Mario Kart Wii, Super Smash Bros. Brawl, and Super Mario Galaxy.

   d. The new Wii entertainment system has attracted more non-gamers than previous entertainment systems.

VOCABULARY IN CONTEXT

5. Identify the meaning of the underlined word in the following sentence: He rose quickly at the company, and his name has been synonymous with Nintendo since the 1980s, when the original Mario Bros. games helped save the industry after the collapse of Atari, maker of the first broadly popular home console.

   a. famous

   b. known as

   c. like the same thing as

   d. popular

PATTERNS OF ORGANIZATION

6. What is the overall pattern of organization in paragraph 3?

   a. time order

   b. listing

   c. cause and effect

   d. compare and/or contrast

7. What is the overall pattern of organization in paragraphs 8 and 9?

   a. process

   b. time order

   c. listing

   d. compare and/or contrast

8. Identify the relationship within the following sentence: I feel that people like Mario and people like Link and the other characters we've created not for the characters themselves, but because the games they appear in are fun.

   a. cause and effect

   b. compare and/or contrast

   c. listing

   d. time order

Reading 1

DRAWING
CONCLUSIONS

9. According to the article, how have the Nintendo Company's games changed over the past few years?

   a. They include more characters like Mario and Princess Peach.

   b. They have added more detailed graphics to the games.

   c. They have made games that appeal to a wider audience.

   d. The mechanics and game-playing technology has improved.

10. How has Miyamoto influenced the success of video games? (Select all that apply.)

   a. Without his games and characters, the video gaming industry would not have been as successful as it is.

   b. He makes the decisions about how the Nintendo Company will be run.

   c. He has inspired most of the game developers working today.

   d. Nintendo has become one of the most valuable companies in Japan.

Vocabulary Practice

Use the vocabulary words from the Word Bank to complete the following sentences. Write the words into the blanks provided.

WORD BANK

amid	aspiring	consumption	deployed	gallant
reinvent	revolutionary	rival	simplicity	unparalleled

1. There's no reason to .... the design. We can use the existing one as it is.

2. The new model of this American sports car will .... any foreign sports car on the market.

3. If you are concerned about getting enough miles per gallon from your car's engine, measure its .... of gas each week and compare it to the number of miles you drove.

4. As a(n) .... architect, Danny hopes his ideas win approval at the next architecture competition.

5. The popularity of this motorcycle is .... ; no other models on the market can match it.

6. The police were .... to the college campus when the student demonstration became violent.

7. Using a cell phone as a GPS device was a(n) .... idea in 2007.

8. Evelyn dreamed about marrying a(n) .... man someday who would protect her from all harm.

9. Several cash registers were robbed .... the confusion of all the customers exiting the store during the power outage.

10. Rather than having a detailed design for their new cell phone, the designers created one with more ....

Questions for Writing and Discussion

Review any part of the article you need to answer the following questions.

1. Why do you think Shigeru Miyamoto's games have become so popular and have remained popular over three decades?

....

....

....

....

2. What kind of training and education did Miyamoto have that prepared him for a career in video game development?

....

....

....

....

3. What kinds of skills or specific talents are needed to become a game developer?

....

....

....

....

Reading 1

4. How has Miyamoto's game development changed over time?

....

....

....

....

5. Many software companies are now developing online courses that teach academic subjects in the form of video games. What would be the advantages and disadvantages of teaching students in this way?

....

....

....

....

Reading 1 Vocabulary Practice—Word Maze

To work through the word maze below, read the clues in the far left column. Then, find the word in that row that best fits the clue and circle the answer. When you have finished, check your answers to see if you made it through the word maze correctly (each box you circled should touch another circled box).

For fun, try competing against your team members to see who can complete the maze the fastest.

START

Clues	Answer A	Answer B	Answer C	Answer D
Soldiers, for instance	amid	sustained	deployed	aspiring
among	rival	amid	deployed	aspiring
plain	revolutionary	credibility	simplicity	unparalleled
using up	simplicity	amid	radiated	consumption
a rookie player	rivaled	deployed	aspiring	reinvented
teams in a championship	sustained	revolutionary	rival	unparalleled
a hero	aspiring	gallant	amid	unparalleled
remake	radiate	unparalleled	reinvent	deployed

FINISH

Reading 2 Vocabulary Preview

The following vocabulary words are from the article "Bionic Soldiers." With a partner or in a team, choose the correct meanings of the underlined words in the following sentences. Use context clues (LEADS), word part clues, and parts of speech to help you figure out the meanings.

1. After Nadiya lost her leg in a car accident, she soon learned to walk normally with a prosthetic (pros-THET-tic) leg.
   a. a stronger leg
   b. an artificial limb
   c. a brace
   d. a missing leg

2. Dr. Patel works at the army hospital, treating amputees (am-pyoo-TEEZ), who must learn to adjust to a missing limb.
   a. people who work with patients who have lost a limb
   b. people who make prosthetic devices
   c. people who have lost a limb
   d. a prosthetic device

3. The birth of the Ortiz's fourth child necessitated (ness-SESS-it-tated) an additional part-time job for the husband to supplement his income.
   a. made necessary
   b. encouraged
   c. something done for extra money
   d. adjusted

4. Strangely, even though many people survive an amputation (am-pue-TA-shun), for a long while they still can feel the missing limb.
   a. injury from an accident or war
   b. treatment
   c. surgery
   d. removal of a limb

5. In the laboratory, the prosthetist (pros-THET-ist) first creates a mold for the socket of the missing limb and then adjusts it to fit the amputee's leg.
   a. a person with a missing limb
   b. someone who wears a prosthetic device
   c. someone who creates artificial limbs
   d. someone who helps amputees learn to use prosthetic limbs

6. When a sheet of plastic is heated, it becomes so pliable (PLY-a-ble) that it can be molded into different shapes.
   a. stiff
   b. flexible
   c. small
   d. durable

Reading 2

7. The prosthetic leg must be fitted over the <u>residual</u> (re-ZID-u-al) limb until it fits comfortably and snugly.

   a. the remaining part

   b. the missing part

   c. living in

   d. amputee's

8. Electrical <u>impulses</u> (IM-pul-ses) in the brain signal the muscles to move.

   a. driving forward

   b. on the spur of the moment

   c. acting without thought

   d. short surges in electrical energy

9. In the Army, we often had to drive our <u>Humvee</u> (HUM-vee) off roads and over rough terrain to reach a remote destination.

   a. tractor

   b. motorcycle

   c. a large, heavily secured truck

   d. a tank

10. When George joined the Army, he became a <u>paratrooper</u> (PAIR-a-troop-er) because he loved the idea of flying weightlessly through the air.

    a. an Army soldier

    b. a naval officer

    c. a pilot

    d. someone who jumps from a plane using a parachute

Reading 2 What Do You Already Know?

1. Have you ever known anyone with a disability? Describe how this person coped with the disability and any technology he or she used for assistance.

2. Do you know anyone who has served or is serving in the military? What did (does) this person do? Was this person ever involved in a war? Share what you know.

> **Directions:** As you read this article, practice the four-step reading process. Preview the article, and then write on the following lines one or two questions that you would hope to have answered.
>
> ....
>
> ....
>
> ....
>
> ....

As you read, answer the questions in the margins to check your comprehension.

"Bionic Soldiers"

BY CORINNE FENNESSY

With advanced technology, amputees who have lost limbs in battle are now able to regain mobility through the use of advanced, highly technical artificial limbs. This article illustrates how amputees are benefiting from this amazing technology.

1   George Perez, a Puerto Rican paratrooper from the 82nd Airborne Division, remembers traveling on a road outside of Fallujah, Iraq. When a bomb blasted their Humvee, he flew through the air and hit the ground. Then he tried to get up and saw that his left foot was folded backward onto his knee and his combat boot stood in the road a short distance away—still laced.

2   George Perez is determined to regain the strength and abilities he had before losing his leg to the roadside bomb in Iraq. "I'm not ready to get out of the Army yet," he says. "I'm not going to let this little injury stop me from what I want to do." Perez is one of at least four amputees from the 82nd Airborne Division who decided to re-enlist. With a new carbon-fiber prosthetic leg, Perez intends to show that he can still run,

jump out of a plane, and pass all of the other challenging paratrooper tests so he can go back to active duty next year.

3   Surgeons tried to save part of his leg, but an infection necessitated the amputation of his leg just below the knee joint. After he recuperated and received his prosthetic leg, Perez asked a visiting general if he could stay in the army. "They told me, 'It's all up to you, and how much you want it,'" he says. "If I could do everything like a regular soldier, I could stay in."

4   Perez has worked hard to become accustomed to his prosthetic leg. He began exercising by doing push-ups in bed. Soon he was walking, and then running. Perez gets his inspiration from other paratroopers in the 82nd Division who have lost limbs in combat and have re-enlisted.

5   Due to advances in prosthetic technology, many soldiers are able to live their lives normally after losing one, two, or more limbs. Some have chosen to return to active duty wearing a prosthetic leg or arm.

6   The process of creating a prosthetic limb begins at the Walter Reed Hospital's **Orthotics** and Prosthetics laboratory. First, a custom-fit socket is made for the prosthetic. Each one is made to fit the individual amputee. The prosthetist creates a mold for a socket in about 20 minutes. Next, a sheet of plastic is heated until it is pliable, and then it is formed over the foam mold. It is trimmed and sanded, and then the amputee is given a fitting. They continue to make adjustments until it fits snugly and comfortably over the residual limb.

7   Next, the amputees move into occupational and physical therapy. Amputees who have lost arms are fitted with three different new arms: a computer-programmed myoelectric (my-oh-e-LEK-trik) arm, a body-powered arm, and a cosmetic arm. The myoelectric arm gives effortless movement, whereas the body-powered is more durable and can get wet without damage. The myoelectric arm uses the electrical impulses from the muscle tissue to control the prosthetic limb. The body-powered limb is controlled by body movements. A cable is attached to a harness system worn on the shoulders or chest, and the cable operates the arm and hand. The cosmetic arm is created to look identical to the other arm and is used when appearance is more important than function.

8   Amputees who have lost legs have a choice of several styles of feet. They can also choose a special style of creative artwork for the socket. Styles have included flags, NASCAR logos, unit patches, or their own design—such as the soldier who has pink Playboy bunnies on a black background.

9   The technology of prosthetic limbs has been making huge strides with the introduction of motorized joints with computer processors. Some prosthetic legs, for example, can determine their resistance

How did George Perez lose his leg?

orthotics

(or-THOT-ix): the branch of medicine dealing with prosthetic aids.

What are three types of prosthetic arms each amputee must learn to use?

How does Bluetooth technology work in prosthetic limbs?

with the ground based on the angle of the leg to the floor. This gives the amputee better balance and a steadier, more natural gait. But the newest technology in prosthetic limbs uses Bluetooth wireless technology.

10   Iraq war veteran Marine Lance Cpl. Joshua Bleil lost both of his legs in a roadside bombing. Bluetooth computer chips located in each artificial leg send signals to the motors in the joints so his ankles and knees move in a coordinated manner. This allows him to walk longer and with less effort. The only disadvantage to Bluetooth prosthetics is that they must be recharged—just like a cell phone.

11   Perez is back in uniform, looking like the same paratrooper he was before his injury. His maroon beret sits at an angle over one eye. His uniform pants have perfectly sharp creases, and his black boot gleams with a mirror shine. Before he is allowed to jump again, he will have to run two miles in just under 16 minutes, and do 42 push-ups and 53 sit-ups in two-minute stretches. In the meantime, he is working at the armory, maintaining weapons and grenade launchers. He wants to attend the Ranger School, a tough, grueling program at Fort Benning, Georgia. It's a real challenge even for soldiers with two normal legs, but that isn't stopping George Perez. Perez is a determined and strong soldier who works hard to overcome any obstacles.

12   "I've got a lot of things to do," he said. "I want to do as much as I can, and as much as they'll let me."

918 words divided by _____ minutes = _____ words per minute

Reading 2 Thinking About What You Read

It is a good habit to summarize everything you read to strengthen your comprehension.

> **Directions:** On the following lines, write a two- or three-sentence summary of the article "Bionic Soldiers." In your own words, describe what the article was about and why the author wrote it.

....

....

....

....

Comprehension Questions

The following questions will help you to recall the main idea and the details of "Bionic Soldiers." Review any parts of the article that you need to in order to find the correct answers.

FINDING THE TOPIC

1. What is the topic of this article?

   a. George Perez

   b. prosthetic devices

   c. bionic soldiers

   d. technology helping amputees

MAIN IDEAS

2. What is the main idea of the entire article?

   a. George Perez lost a leg in Iraq but is now re-enlisting in the 82nd Airborne Division.

   b. Many soldiers have lost limbs in war.

   c. New technology has improved the design and function of prosthetic limbs for soldier amputees.

   d. Perez is a determined and strong soldier who works hard to overcome any obstacles.

3. What is the topic sentence of paragraph 11?

   a. Perez is back in uniform, looking like the same paratrooper he was before his injury.

   b. It's a real challenge even for soldiers with two normal legs, but that isn't stopping George Perez.

   c. He wants to attend the Ranger School, a tough, grueling program at Fort Benning, Georgia.

   d. Perez is a determined and strong soldier who works hard to overcome any obstacles.

Reading 2

4. After losing his leg, what did George Perez decide to do?

   a. Retire from the Army and take a pension.

   b. Re-enlist and work hard to do all the same things that other soldiers do.

   c. Stay in the Army's Walter Reed Hospital to help other amputees learn to adjust.

   d. Become a prosthetist so he could help other amputees.

5. Identify the meaning of the underlined word in the following sentence: This gives the amputee better balance and a steadier, more natural <u>gait</u>.

   a. way of walking   c. appearance

   b. an entry   d. amputation

6. What is the overall pattern of organization for this article?

   a. compare and/or contrast   c. definition

   b. cause and effect   d. time order

7. Identify the relationship within the following sentence: Amputees who have lost arms are fitted with three different arms: a computer-programmed myoelectric arm, a body-powered arm, and a cosmetic arm.

   a. cause and effect   c. listing

   b. definition   d. process

8. Identify the relationship between the following sentences: The prosthetist creates a mold for a socket in about 20 minutes. Next, a sheet of plastic is heated until it is pliable, and then it is formed over the foam mold.

   a. process

   b. time order

   c. listing

   d. space order

9. From the article, you can conclude that:

   a. There are not many amputee soldiers who have been fitted with prosthetic devices.

   b. More soldiers will probably need prosthetic limbs if the war continues.

   c. Prosthetic devices can be operated easily.

   d. Soldiers who wear prosthetic limbs will want to re-enlist in the military.

10. According to the article, some of the amputees have regained their strength so that they could:

   a. re-enlist in the Army

   b. become prosthetists

   c. compete in the Paralympics

   d. get jobs outside of the military

Reading 2 Vocabulary Practice

Use the words from the Word Bank to complete the following sentences. Write the words into the blanks provided.

> **WORD BANK**
>
> prosthetic   amputees   necessitated   amputation   prosthetist
>
> pliable   residual   impulses   Humvee   paratrooper

1. Electrical.. from the brain signal the muscles to move.

2. A wet suit is made of material that is waterproof and.................................... so the swimmer can move his or her arms freely.

3. Sergeant Bonning was a(n).................................... whose parachute didn't open properly, and he broke his leg upon landing.

4. The.................................... at the military hospital are given artificial limbs as soon as they are well enough to wear them.

5. An artificial limb is known as a(n)....................................limb.

6. Losing her leg from a bomb blast.................................... Amita having to wear an artificial one.

7. The.................................... made several artificial legs for the amputee until he finally made one that fit comfortably and worked well.

8. The artificial leg is attached to the.................................... limb.

9. The Army unit was riding in a(n).................................... when the bomb exploded under them.

10. When the doctors could not save his leg, Sergeant Munoz was told he would need to have a(n).................................... .

Reading 2 Vocabulary Practice—Crossword

Use the words from the list to complete the following sentences. Write the answers in the crossword puzzle. Use context clues (LEADS), word part clues, and parts of speech to help you.

Humvee	amputation	prosthetic	amputees	pliable
necessitated	residual	prosthetist	paratrooper	impulses

CLUES

ACROSS

2. Most ____ are happy to get a prosthetic limb.

3. Losing my financial aid ___ my finding a part-time job while I was in college.

7. She wanted to be a(n) ___, so she joined the Army.

8. The prosthetic arm is fitted over the ___ limb.

9. An Army ___ transported soldiers to the battlefront.

DOWN

1. Electrical ___ signal the muscle to move the limb.

4. He did not allow the ___ of his legs to discourage him from walking again.

5. Learning to walk with a(n) ___ leg will take practice.

6. Mr. Hernandez is a(n) ___ who treats amputees.

7. This material is so ___ that it can be shaped and formed easily.

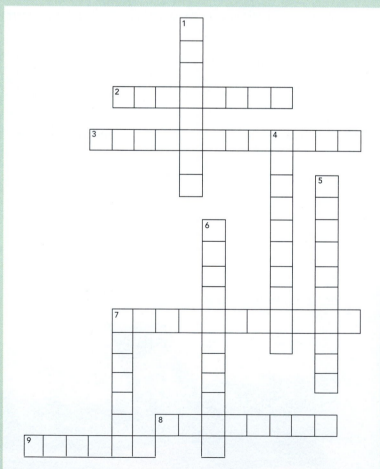

Reading 2 Questions for Writing and Discussion

Review any part of the article you need to answer the following questions.

1. How was George Perez able to re-enlist in the Army?

2. If new technology had not provided prosthetic limbs that could function almost as well as real ones, how would having an amputation be different?

3. What new advances in technology have helped people who are disabled?

4. If you had recently lost a limb in war, would you want to re-enlist? Why or why not?

5. Compare George Perez to one of the other people whom you have read about in previous articles. How are they alike, and how are they different?

VIEWPOINT: Copyright Infringement on the Internet

A copyright is a legal right of ownership to created materials such as music, books, films, or other materials. In October of 2007, Jammie Thomas was found guilty of posting 24 songs on the Internet service *Kazaa* without getting permission from the copyright holders. Thomas was fined $222,000 in damages to the Recording Industry Association of America (RIAA).

Read the following letters to the editor about copyrighted music, and then answer the questions that follow.

Dear Editor:

Suing someone for over $200,000 just because she copied a few songs from a CD onto the Internet is absurd! The Internet is supposed to be a place of sharing information and ideas. How can ideas be shared if people are sued every time they download something? It should be like an online library where everything can be shared for free. Most of the music being shared is done by musicians and singers who are well paid and should be willing to share. Besides, people who upload or download parts of TV shows don't always realize that they are breaking a law. Suing someone for $200,000 is too harsh. What's next, censorship?

Signed,

Free to Be Me

Dear Editor:

No one should upload copyrighted music, books, or films onto the Internet without getting the permission of the creators. Many people depend on the sales of their products to make a living. If their products are available free on the Internet, who will go out and buy them? Musicians, authors, artists, and filmmakers deserve to get paid for what they do. Stealing products off the Internet is no different than going into a store and stealing CDs, DVDs, or books off the shelves. Many people have invested their hard work, time, and money to produce these works. Giving them away for free is a form of theft. The only way to stop this kind of theft is to continue to issue harsh penalties to those who break copyright laws.

Signed,

Advocate for Artists

Critical Thinking

1. A *point of view* is the author's opinion about a topic. To find the author's point of view, ask yourself, "How does this author feel about this issue?" What is the author's point of view about copyright infringement in the first letter?

   ....

   ....

   ....

2. What is the author's point of view about copyright infringement in the second letter?

   ....

   ....

   ....

3. Which letter do you agree with, and why?

   ....

   ....

   ....

4. What could be the consequences of allowing people to upload copyrighted material onto the Internet without fear of being punished?

   ....

   ....

   ....

5. What could be the consequences of having harsh punishments for offenders who upload copyrighted materials?

   ....

   ....

WRITE YOUR THOUGHTS

Write a letter to the editor stating your own feelings about what should be done with people who upload copyrighted materials without permission. Use a separate piece of paper.

Following Instructions

Following instructions is one of the most important reading skills needed to survive in today's high-tech society. Read the following instructions on how to install memory into a portable computer, and then answer the questions that follow to check your comprehension.

INSTRUCTIONS

Replacing or upgrading the memory in your laptop computer involves removing the battery and putting it back in after installing the memory.

Installing Memory

1. Shut down your computer and disconnect the powercord, Ethernet cable, and any other cords connected to it, to prevent damage to the computer. If your computer was on, wait 10 minutes to let the internal components cool before proceeding.

2. Turn the computer over and remove the battery as shown in Figure 1.

3. Remove the screw(s) for the memory compartment and take off the cover. Note the location of any screws and keep them safe for replacement. To prevent harming the computer, do not touch any other internal components (Figure 2).

Figure 1

Figure 2

Figure 3

Figure 4

4. Touch a metal surface inside the computer to discharge any static electricity from your body. Avoid creating static electricity as you are working, such as standing on carpeted floors.

5. Press the pins on the sides of the memory away from the memory card. The memory card will pop up at an angle. Notice the slot where the memory was seated. (fig. 3)

6. Gently unplug the card at the same angle (fig. 4).

7. Align the new memory card with the slot at the same angle as the old one was removed.

8. Push the new card gently into the slot at an angle until it is in place, and then push it down until the pins on each side snap in place to hold it flat securely.

9. Replace the compartment cover and replace the screw(s). Install the battery and other cords before turning the computer back on.

Questions

1. What is the first thing you should do before you start to remove the old memory card from your computer?
   a. Take out the battery.
   b. Remove the screws from the memory compartment, and then remove the cover.
   c. Shut down the computer and let the components cool for 10 minutes before starting the installation.
   d. Discharge any static electricity that you may have by touching some thing metal inside the computer.

2. When removing the old memory card, what must you do?
   a. Press the pins at the sides of the memory card down.
   b. Press the pins at the sides away from the memory card.
   c. Use a small screwdriver to pry up the old card.
   d. Disconnect the Ethernet cable or any USB cables.

3. **What should you notice before taking out the old memory card?**

   a. Notice how many screws were used to secure the compartment cover.

   b. Notice the location of all the other screws on the back of the computer.

   c. Notice if there are any scorch marks on the old card.

   d. Notice the locations and angle of the slot that holds the old memory card.

4. **What's the first thing you must do when installing the new memory card?**

   a. Push the new card into the memory slot.

   b. Use two fingers with firm, even pressure to push down on the memory card.

   c. Align the new card with the slot at the same angle as the old card, and then push it into place until the pins snap in place to hold it securely.

   d. Hold the memory card by its edges without touching the connectors.

5. **Once the new memory card has been installed, what should you do?**

   a. Replace the compartment cover and screw(s) and reinstall the battery.

   b. Turn on the computer after plugging it into an AC outlet.

   c. Discharge any static electricity that you may have by touching some thing metal.

   d. Bend the pins down over the new memory card with a small screwdriver.

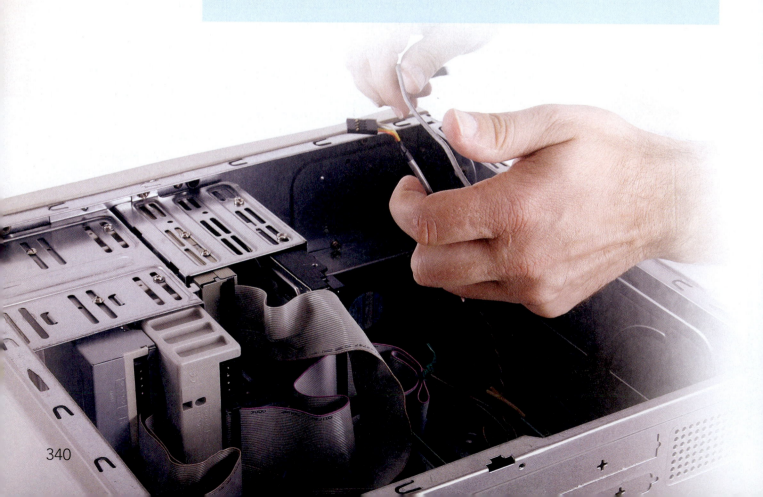

Kyle Williams, Show Systems Integrators in Orlando, Florida

What is your job description?

As a marketing manager, I have a very broad range of things I do at the company. I do marketing, sales, project management, and represent the company for the technical support systems for various projects. We have completed the Simpsons Ride for Universal theme parks in both Orlando and Los Angeles. For Six Flags theme parks, we developed the audio system for the new roller coaster. We're currently working on Universal's Rip Ride Rocket coaster here in Orlando.

What is your educational background and training?

I graduated from the University of Southern Mississippi with a degree in business administration and then got another degree in audio engineering from Full Sail in Orlando, Florida. I'm also a musician, and I play several instruments, but guitar is my favorite. I have a small home recording studio where I compose and record my own music. I have also played in bands throughout the years. So I have a musical and technical background.

What do you like about your job?

No one else does what I do. It's a unique blend of business and technology, where we get to be technically creative. This job is a perfect fit for my interests and my educational background.

How did you become interested in this job?

While I was attending school in Orlando, I worked at SSI part time and found my niche here. I was able to utilize my business training and my technical and audio interests.

What do you dislike about your job?

It can be stressful at times when there are deadlines and things don't go smoothly, which is to be expected when pushing the envelope and making technology work in new ways. I try to live and work by the Golden Rule, and maintain my values and ethics on the job, which can be challenging in some situations.

Did you have any particular difficulties in college?

I worked while going to school, so it was always a challenge to manage my time carefully. I wanted to be responsible and independent, and to help pay my way through school. The most difficult thing was moving 600 miles from home and family and being on my own.

If you could give college students some advice, what would it be?

Don't underestimate the curriculum that you are studying. Sometimes the things you're learning that may seem irrelevant or unimportant now turn up being extremely beneficial in your career. Also, I would say to treat others with respect, and you'll benefit from learning how to work with others. Teamwork is really important in most careers.

What plans do you have for the future?

I am committed to the company's welfare and would like to see it grow and succeed. I enjoy what I do and want to continue working and expanding into new projects and creating new opportunities for using technology. Otherwise, I'll just take life as it comes.

TEXTBOOK GRAPHIC AIDS

Use the following graphs to answer the questions that follow.

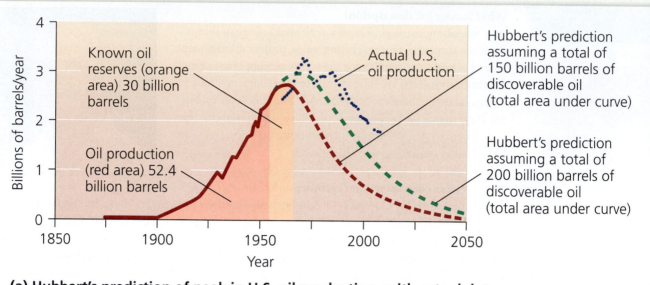

(a) Hubbert's prediction of peak in U.S. oil production, with actual data

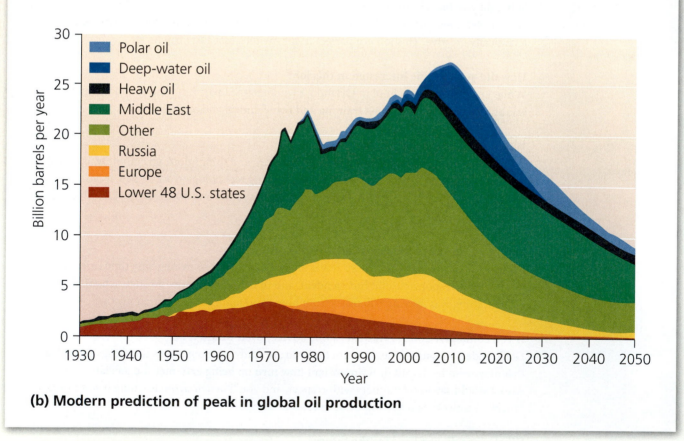

(b) Modern prediction of peak in global oil production

(From *Essential Environment: The Science Behind the Stories,* 3rd ed. by Jay Withgott and Scott Brennan. Copyright © 2009 by Pearson Education, Inc., Upper Saddle River, NJ. Reprinted with permission.)

1. **According to the first graph, which of the following is false?**

   a. Geologist M. King Hubbard predicted in the 1950s that the United States would reach its peak oil production before 1975.

   b. About 1970, the actual U.S. oil production reached more than 3 billion barrels.

   c. Actual U.S. oil production is less than both of Hubbard's predictions.

   d. Actual U.S. oil production was about 2 billion barrels in the year 2000.

2. **In the second graph, what is the data being shown?**

   a. how much oil the United States produces

   b. which locations have the most oil

   c. Hubbard's prediction of oil production

   d. a modern prediction of global oil production

3. **In the second graph, in roughly what year did the United States lower 48 states reach their peak oil production?**

   a. 1970

   b. 1985

   c. 2005

   d. 2010

4. **According to the second graph, about how much oil will the lower 48 U.S. states produce in 2020?**

   a. five billion barrels per year

   b. ten billion barrels per year

   c. less than one billion barrels per year

   d. fifteen billion barrels per year

5. **According to the second graph, what will happen to future oil production for all locations?**

   a. it will increase

   b. it will decrease

   c. it will remain the same

   d. the graph doesn't show this information

BUILDING VOCABULARY

Throughout this course, you will be introduced to word parts that make up many words in the English language. Study the following word parts, and then answer the questions that follow.

Prefixes
micro- *very small*
tele- *distant, far off*

Roots
-phone- *sound*
-scope- *to look*
-graph- *to write*

Suffixes
-ic *having to do with*

1. What English words can you create from these word parts?

....

....

....

....

Using a dictionary, look up the meanings of any of the words you wrote that you can't define. Use one of the words you wrote in a sentence that reveals its meaning with a context clue:

....

....

....

....

....

CHAPTER REVIEW PRACTICE #1

As you read the following selection, underline the main idea and transitions that help you determine the overall pattern of organization. Then, answer the questions that follow.

Being an engineer doesn't have to be all work. Kent Seko gets plenty of excitement and thrills as a roller coaster designer. After graduating from the University of Utah, Seko took a job as a drafter at Arrow Dynamics, one of the largest designers and manufacturers of amusement rides. During his years of employment at Arrow, Seko learned more about how to design thrill rides. When he began with the company 15 years ago, the company was designing roller coasters that were over 60 meters tall. Now the company is designing coasters over 90 meters tall. As a designer, Seko must create a ride that is exciting while still maintaining safety and operating within a budget. Numerous other team members help with the layout, structural support design, mechanics, electronics, and construction of the coaster. The most exciting part of his job is when he gets to ride the coaster for the first time.

1. What is the topic of this paragraph?
   a. designing roller coasters
   b. Kent Seko's career as a roller coaster designer
   c. how to become a roller coaster designer
   d. thrill rides

2. What is the topic sentence of this paragraph?
   a. Being an engineer doesn't have to be all work.
   b. Kent Seko gets plenty of excitement and thrills as a roller coaster designer.
   c. As a designer, Seko must create a ride that is exciting while still maintaining safety and operating within a budget.
   d. The most exciting part of his job is when he gets to ride the coaster for the first time.

3. What is the overall pattern of organization?
   a. listing   c. time order
   b. cause and effect   d. addition

4. Identify the relationship within the following sentence: Numerous other team members help with the layout, structural support design, mechanics, electronics, and construction of the coaster.
   a. listing   c. example
   b. cause and effect   d. addition

5. Identify the relationship between the following sentences: When he began with the company 15 years ago, the company was designing roller coasters that were over 60 meters tall. Now the company is designing coasters over 90 meters tall.
   a. cause and effect   c. contrast
   b. comparison   d. process

CHAPTER REVIEW PRACTICE #2

As you read the following selection, underline the main idea and transitions that help you determine the overall pattern of organization. Then, answer the questions that follow.

Ten years ago, the idea of wearing a rocket strapped to your back and jetting through the air only happened in animated films and James Bond movies. But today, a Swiss pilot named Yves Rossy has achieved the reality of sustained human flight using a jet-powered wing strapped to his back. Rossy began his career as a fighter pilot in the Swiss Air Force. He later flew Boeing 747s for Swissair and also worked as a pilot for Swiss International Airlines. Rossy developed a carbon-fiber wing and attached four model aircraft engines that he modified. Over the past several years, Rossy has experimented with several models of the jet-powered wing. In 2008 he flew across the English Channel in 9 minutes and 7 seconds. Later that same year, he flew over the Alps reaching speeds of 189 miles per hour.

(Adapted from Hagerman, Eric. Wingman. *Popular Science Magazine*. February 2009, 36–43.)

1. What is the topic?
   a. Yves Rossy's jet-powered wing   **c.** human jet-powered flight
   b. Yves Rossy   **d.** flying without a plane

2. What is the topic sentence of this paragraph?
   a. Ten years ago, the idea of wearing a rocket strapped to your back and jetting through the air only happened in animated films and James Bond movies.
   b. But today, a Swiss pilot named Yves Rossy has achieved the reality of sustained human flight using a jet-powered wing strapped to his back.
   c. Rossy has experimented with several models of the jet-powered wing.
   d. In 2008 he flew across the English Channel in 9 minutes and 7 seconds.

3. What is the overall pattern of organization?
   a. process   **c.** time order
   b. listing   **d.** cause and effect

4. Identify the relationship within the following sentence: He later flew Boeing 747s for Swissair and also worked as a pilot for Swiss International Airlines.
   a. cause and effect   **c.** classification
   b. space order   **d.** addition

5. Identify the relationship between the following sentences: Ten years ago, the idea of wearing a rocket strapped to your back and jetting through the air only happened in animated films and James Bond movies. But today, a Swiss pilot named Yves Rossy has achieved the reality of sustained human flight using a jet-powered wing strapped to his back.
   a. process   **c.** addition
   b. compare and/or contrast **d.** example

CHAPTER REVIEW PRACTICE #3

As you read the following selection, underline the main idea and transitions that help you determine the overall pattern of organization. Then, answer the questions that follow.

Robots may change the way we explore the universe. The National Aeronautics and Space Administration (NASA) is conducting research into creating robots that will build a space station on the moon. Robotic parts have been used successfully in previous space missions. One example was in 2008, when a robotic arm on the *Mars Lander* scooped soil from the surface for analysis. Two other examples of robots are in the Mars rovers, named *Opportunity* and *Spirit*. They have robotic parts that help them travel over the Martian surface and send data back to Earth. Also, on the International Space Station, a $200 million robot is used to handle maintenance outside of the station, so that fewer human space walks are needed. Robots have successfully demonstrated that they have an important role in future space explorations.

1. What is the topic?
   - **a.** robots
   - **b.** robots in space exploration
   - **c.** space technology
   - **d.** robots may change the way we explore the universe

2. What is the topic sentence?
   - **a.** Robots may change the way we explore the universe.
   - **b.** The National Aeronautics and Space Administration (NASA) is conducting research into creating robots that will build a space station on the moon.
   - **c.** Robotic parts have been used successfully in previous space missions.
   - **d.** Robots have successfully demonstrated that they have an important role in future space explorations.

3. What is the overall pattern of organization?
   - **a.** example
   - **b.** cause and effect
   - **c.** space order
   - **d.** definition

4. Identify the relationship within the following sentence: Also, on the International Space Station, a $200 million robot is used to handle maintenance outside of the station, so that fewer human space walks are needed.
   - **a.** compare and/or contrast
   - **b.** example
   - **c.** cause and effect
   - **d.** listing

5. Identify the relationship between the following sentences: They have robotic parts that help them travel over the Martian surface and send data back to Earth. Also, on the International Space Station, a $200 million robot is used to handle maintenance outside of the station, so that fewer human space walks are needed.
   - **a.** cause and effect
   - **b.** addition
   - **c.** example
   - **d.** process

TEXTBOOK PRACTICE

As you read the following textbook selection, underline the main idea and transitions that help you determine the overall pattern of organization. Then, answer the questions that follow.

Silver can be recovered from used photographic and x-ray plates by soaking these plates in a **cyanide** solution. Workers must wear protective clothing and use respirators in order to prevent contact with deadly cyanide gas.

Film Recovery Systems was one company that was active in this recovery work. Unfortunately, employees were not provided with respirators but only cloth gloves and paper face masks. Workers frequently became physically ill. Finally, an autopsy revealed that one employee had died of cyanide poisoning, leading the authorities to file murder charges against certain company executives.

The company president, the plant manager, and the plant foreperson were shown to be familiar with the hazards associated with cyanide and its use at their facility. In 1985, each was convicted of industrial murder, fined $10,000, and given a 25-year prison sentence. Although company officials knew the silver recovery process was toxic, they did not provide enough safety precautions, and, consequently, they committed industrial murder.

(From *Engineering by Design*, 2e by Gerard Voland. Copyright © 2004 by Gerard Voland. Reprinted by permission of Pearson Education, Inc., Upper Saddle River, NJ.)

cyanide (SY-a-nide): a poisonous chemical

1. What is the topic?
   a. cyanide
   b. Film Recovery Systems
   c. cyanide poisoning
   d. industrial murder

2. What is the topic sentence?
   a. Silver can be recovered from used photographic and x-ray plates by soaking these plates in a cyanide solution.
   b. Film Recovery Systems was one company that was active in this recovery work.
   c. Finally, an autopsy revealed that one employee had died of cyanide poisoning, leading the authorities to file murder charges against certain company executives.
   d. Although company officials knew the silver recovery process was toxic, they did not provide enough safety precautions, and, consequently, they committed industrial murder.

3. What is the overall pattern of organization?
   a. listing
   b. addition
   c. cause and effect
   d. space order

4. Identify the relationship within the following sentence: Finally, an autopsy revealed that one employee had died of cyanide poisoning, leading the authorities to file murder charges against certain company executives.

   a. cause and effect

   b. process

   c. example

   d. time order

5. Identify the relationship between the following sentences: The company president, the plant manager, and the plant foreperson were shown to be familiar with the hazards associated with cyanide and its use at their facility. In 1985, each was convicted of industrial murder, fined $10,000, and given a 25-year prison sentence.

   a. compare and/or contrast

   b. process

   c. listing

   d. time order

READING LAB ASSIGNMENTS

SKILL PRACTICES

1. Go online to MyReadingLab and click on the "Study Skills" tab. Next, click on "Patterns of Organization" and complete the practices and tests according to your instructor's directions.

COMPREHENSION IMPROVEMENT

2. Go online to MyReadingLab and click on the "Reading Level" tab. Choose two stories to read, and then answer the questions that follow.

CAREER EXPLORATION

3. Go online to www.bls.gov/oco and explore careers in technology. Find a career that interests you, and print out the information. Print the article, and then preview, read, highlight, and annotate one or two sections of it. Find three examples of relationships within and between sentences using the patterns of organization you studied in Chapters 6 and 7. Underline the sentences, and label them with the type of relationships shown.

SKILL APPLICATION

4. Using your textbooks for other classes or newspaper articles, look for examples of the patterns of organization that you have learned in Chapters 6 and 7. How does knowing the pattern help you understand the material? Share your findings with your team.

STUDY SKILL CHAPTER REVIEW

Outlines are useful for studying the main concepts and major details of topics that you have learned in your college courses. Complete the following outline for patterns of organization using information from Chapters 6 and 7.

PATTERNS OF ORGANIZATION

Definition of Patterns of Organization: ....

....

I. DEFINITION PATTERN

    A. Defines the word or term. This pattern may use:

        1. ....   **3.** ....

        2. dashes   **4.** ....

II. LISTING PATTERN

    A. Presents ideas ....

III. CAUSE AND EFFECT PATTERN

    A. Shows ....

IV. COMPARE AND/OR CONTRAST PATTERN

    A. Comparison shows .... and .... shows differences

V. .... **PATTERN**

    A. A chain of events

VI. .... **PATTERN**

    A. Shows how something is done

VII. SPACE ORDER PATTERN

    A. Shows details according to ....

VIII. .... **PATTERN**

    A. Organizes details into groups or categories

IX. .... **PATTERN**

    A. Provides illustrations

X. .... **PATTERN**

    A. Gives additional information about the topic

LEARNING REFLECTION

Think about the skills and concepts in this chapter. What have you learned in this chapter that will help your reading comprehension and enable you to do well in college?

....

....

SELF-EVALUATION CHECKLIST

Rate yourself on the following items, using the following scale:

1 = strongly disagree   4 = agree

2 = disagree   5 = strongly agree

3 = neither agree nor disagree

1. I completed all of the assigned work on time.   ....

2. I understand all of the concepts in this chapter.   ....

3. I contributed to teamwork and class discussions.   ....

4. I completed all of the assigned lab work on time.   ....

5. I came to class on time.   ....

6. I attended class every day.   ....

7. I studied for any quizzes or tests we had for this chapter.   ....

8. I asked questions when I didn't understand something.   ....

9. I checked my comprehension during reading.   ....

10. I know what is expected of me in the coming week.   ....

11. Are you still on track with the goals you set in Chapter 1?   ....

12. What changes can you make to improve your performance in this course?   ....

For support in meeting this chapter's objectives, go to the Study Plan in MyReadingLab and select Patterns of Organization. Read and view the resources in the Review Materials section, and then complete the Recall, Apply, and Write exercises in the Activities section. Check your results by clicking on Gradebook.

STUDY SKILL: OUTLINING

Outlining is a very efficient way to take notes. Like concept maps, outlines provide the major and minor details in a paraphrased form. Formal outlines follow a specific sequence in their format. But for your own purposes, you may use a simpler format that is easy to remember.

When making an outline, use the following guidelines:

1. Use phrases, not sentences.
2. Use paraphrasing to state a general idea.
3. Work from most general to most specific, indenting to show the relationships of more specific ideas:

Main idea (most general)

    Major details (more specific)

        Minor details (most specific)

Read the following paragraph, and then look at the sample outline that follows.

Leonardo da Vinci (1452–1519) is the artist who painted the *Mona Lisa* and *The Last Supper*, two of the world's most treasured paintings. But da Vinci also had another talent as an inventor. His notebooks and journals are filled with ideas for inventions; everything from flying machines to weapons. He designed machines to do mechanical work and for military use. Some of his designs included a winch for lifting heavy loads, a lathe for drilling holes, a cutting machine, and a heat-powered rotisserie for roasting meat. His weapon designs included a giant crossbow, a mechanical rapid-firing arrow machine, rapid-firing cannons, and artillery guns that could fire multiple rounds at once. Leonardo da Vinci is admired not only because he was a talented artist but also because of his ability to create in so many different fields.

Outline of the Paragraph

Topic: Leonardo da Vinci (1452–1519)

(Main Idea)   I. da Vinci was a talented artist and inventor.

(Major Detail)   A. Painted *Mona Lisa* and *The Last Supper*

(Major Detail)   B. Designed machines for mechanical work

(Minor Details)
     1. Winch for lifting loads
     2. Lathe for drilling holes
     3. Cutting machine
     4. Heat-powered rotisserie

(Major Detail)   C. Designed weapons

(Minor Details)
     1. Giant crossbow
     2. Rapid-firing arrow machine
     3. Artillery guns firing multiple rounds

Practice Outlining

Read the following selection, and then complete the outline that follows.

Leonardo da Vinci was also an inventor of musical instruments. He designed mechanical drums that were attached to wagon wheel axles and played automatically as an army marched into battle. He also invented a stringed instrument that could be played with a keyboard, called the "viola organista." He sketched ideas for flutes and keyboards for wind instruments. He invented a pipe instrument that was played with a mechanical **bellows** that provided a continuous movement of air. He designed organs and even a portable organ that could be carried and played. Another of his interests was bells, and he spent considerable time on experimenting with casting bronze bells.

bellows: a device for pumping air

Topic: Leonardo da Vinci

Main Idea: I. ....

Major Detail: A. Mechanical drums

Minor Detail: 1. ....

....

Major Detail: B. Viola organista

Major Detail: C. Flutes and ....

Minor Detail: 1. ....

Major Detail: D. Organs

Minor Detail: 1. ....

Major Detail: E. ....

Minor Detail: 1. Experimented with casting bronze bells

DRAWING CONCLUSIONS

LEARNING OBJECTIVES

IN THIS CHAPTER, YOU WILL:

Objective 1   learn how to draw logical conclusions

FOCUS ON SOCIOLOGY AND EDUCATION

People who choose careers in sociology and education often find their greatest satisfaction by helping others improve their lives through better living conditions, improved health, and education. Some opportunities begin with a two-year college degree, and others may require a bachelor's or master's degree. In education, you might enjoy teaching a specific subject, such as sports, technology, or theater. People who work in sociology often help others obtain housing, welfare, health care, and other social services. Some people work directly with clients while others help set up programs and run them.

Objective 1 ▸ DRAWING CONCLUSIONS

Drawing conclusions is something we all do daily. For example, when a family member gives you a certain look, you know exactly what he or she is thinking. If someone smiles at you, you understand the message being communicated. As a reader, you interpret similar messages. Authors frequently imply an idea by providing you with enough information to draw your own conclusions.

Good readers examine the details and facts and draw logical conclusions. Drawing good, logical conclusions is a skill, like determining the meaning of an unfamiliar word. However, be careful not to assume more than the details tell you. An assumption is something you guess to be true but is not supported by details in the passage. If there is no evidence to prove your conclusion, it is not a valid conclusion.

> A **conclusion** is an idea that is based on facts and observations, determined by using inductive reasoning.

Drawing logical **conclusions** is a higher-level thinking skill than finding the stated main idea or recognizing supporting details. It requires *inferential thinking*, which means you have to look beyond the words on the page and think about what is implied. Inferential thinking is a necessary skill in reading comprehension. When you use information to arrive at a conclusion, you are using a method of thinking called *inductive reasoning*.

Drawing Conclusions from a Photo

It is said that a picture is worth a thousand words. Look closely at the following photo, and try to draw as many conclusions as you can from the photo. Remember to stick to the facts shown in the photo.

Write your conclusions on the following lines.

....

....

....

....

355

How to Draw Logical Conclusions

When drawing logical conclusions, you need to think like a detective. Just as you used LEADS to determine the meanings of unfamiliar words, you can use "CLUES" to reach logical conclusions:

C = **Check your comprehension** of the passage. State the topic and main idea.

L = **Look closely at the supporting details**, both major and minor ones.

U = **Use only the facts** in the details to draw conclusions.

E = **Examine the facts**. When you have made your conclusion, examine the facts to see if they support it. Don't assume more than what is in the passage, even though the conclusion might be something that everyone would agree with.

S = **Support your conclusion** with the facts that prove it.

EXAMPLE #1:

Students who did not complete high school or a certificate program (such as the GED) for the years 1972, 1998, and 2006

Year	Total % of students who dropped out	Race: white	Race: black	Race: Hispanic
1972	14.6%	12.3%	21.3%	34.3%
1998	11.8%	7.7%	13.8%	29.5%
2006	9.3%	5.8%	10.7%	22.1%

(Source: http://nces.ed.gov)

Using the information in this table, identify the following statements as "T" for true or "F" for false.

1. The total percentage of students who dropped out of high school was less in 2006 than in 1972. ....

2. The percentage of black students who dropped out in 2006 was about half the percentage in 1972. ....

3. High school students were smarter in 2006 than in 1972. ....

4. There were fewer Hispanic students in high school in 1972 than in 2006. ....

5. The percentage of students dropping out of high school has decreased for all races from 1972 to 2006. ....

Some of these statements are false because the table does not provide the facts that you need to decide whether the answer is true or false. For example, for the statement, "There were fewer Hispanic students in high school in 1972 than in 2006," this would be false. Nothing in the table tells you how many students are represented. If something is not represented in a table, or discussed in a passage, do not assume it is true. If there is no supporting information for your conclusion, then it is not a logical conclusion.

Beware of Absolutes

Always be cautious of reaching conclusions that are absolute statements, which use words such as "all," "everyone," "no one," "none," "always," and "never." Rarely are these statements supported. Unless an idea is *directly stated* in the passage using one of the absolute words or phrases listed here, don't assume that it is true.

Practice

1. Read the following passage, and then answer the questions that follow. Remember to follow the CLUES.

Teen pregnancy continues to be a serious issue in the United States. Pregnancies among teens between the ages of 15 and 19 are at nearly 1 million per year in the United States. This is the highest rate of all the developed countries in the world and twice the rate of Canada. Teen pregnancies are more common in dysfunctional families and low-income families. Having unplanned pregnancies increases the likelihood that the teen mother will not finish high school and will spend her life in poverty. Although the teens are physically mature enough to conceive, they do not yet have the emotional maturity to understand the difficult consequences of teen pregnancy.

(From *Society: The Basics* by John J. Macionis. Copyright © 2007 by John J. Macionis. Reprinted by permission of Pearson Education, Inc., Upper Saddle River, NJ.)

1. What is the topic?

   a. pregnancy in the United States

   b. teen pregnancies in the United States

   c. why teens become pregnant

   d. what happens to pregnant teens

2. What is the topic sentence of this paragraph?

   a. Teen pregnancy continues to be a serious issue in the United States.

   b. Pregnancies among teens between the ages of 15 and 19 are at nearly 1 million per year in the United States.

   c. Although the teens are physically mature enough to conceive, they do not yet have the emotional maturity to understand the difficult consequences of teen pregnancy.

   d. Teen pregnancies are more common in dysfunctional families and low-income families.

Identify the following statements as "T" for true or "F" for false. Underline the sentences in the passage that provide the support for the true statements.

3. .... Fewer teens become pregnant in Canada than in the United States.

4. .... All teens who become pregnant will spend their lives in poverty.

5. .... Teen girls are more likely to drop out of high school if they have unplanned pregnancies.

Practice

2. Read the following passage, and then answer the questions that follow. Remember to follow the CLUES.

Two out of every three crimes committed are drug related. The effects of drug abuse have also increased medical costs nationally, creating a burden on the economy. Because of drug use and drug marketing, the need for more law enforcement both locally and federally continues to increase. Drug users who can no longer work because of their addictions are more dependent upon social services than non-users. This has increased the need for additional social services. Courts are filled with drug-related cases, and the number of cases continues to rise yearly. As a result of drug abuse, the number of prisons and corrections officers has grown significantly but cannot keep up with the demand. Clearly, the effects of drug abuse have a major impact on our society.

1. What is the topic?

   a. drug abuse

   b. increased need for law enforcement

   c. crimes and drug abuse

   d. the effects of drug abuse on society

2. What is the topic sentence of this paragraph?

   a. Two out of every three crimes committed are drug related.

   b. The effects of drug abuse have also increased medical costs nationally, creating a burden on the economy.

   c. Courts are filled with drug-related cases, and the number of cases continues to rise yearly.

   d. Clearly, the effects of drug abuse have a major impact on our society.

Identify the following statements as "T" for true or "F" for false. Underline the sentences in the passage that provide the support for the true statements.

3. .... Drug abuse is the fastest growing crime in the nation.

4. .... Drug abuse has resulted in hiring and training more corrections officers.

5. .... Drug abuse had caused an increase in homelessness.

Practice

3. Read the following passage, and then answer the questions that follow. Remember to follow the CLUES.

The United States has the highest divorce rate in the world. One of the reasons is that individualism is a trait of many Americans. This means that people are less connected to family members and more concerned with their own individual goals and happiness. Couples who marry young because of an unexpected pregnancy are the most likely to divorce. Another key factor in divorce is addiction to alcohol, drugs, or gambling. If one of the partners has an addiction, the marriage often becomes unstable. Also, if one or both marriage partners have a demanding or highly successful career, they face a higher risk for divorce. People who divorce are more likely to divorce again. For many reasons, divorce has become an acceptable course of action in American society.

(From *Society: The Basics* by John J. Macionis. Copyright © 2007 by John J. Macionis. Reprinted by permission of Pearson Education, Inc., Upper Saddle River, NJ.)

1. **What is the topic?**

   a. reasons for divorce in the United States

   b. getting divorced

   c. society's view of divorce

   d. the U.S. divorce rate

2. **What is the topic sentence of this paragraph?**

   a. The United States has the highest divorce rate in the world.

   b. One of the reasons is that individualism is a trait of many Americans.

   c. People who divorce are more likely to divorce again.

   d. For many reasons, divorce has become an acceptable course of action in American society.

Identify the following statements as "T" for true or "F" for false. Underline the sentences in the passage that provide the support for the true statements.

3. .... Young couples who marry because of an unplanned pregnancy are at increased risk for divorce.

4. .... If a marriage partner is addicted to alcohol, the couple is more likely to divorce.

5. .... Many Americans are individualistic and focused more on their own happiness than on others'.

TEXTBOOK SELECTION

Read the following textbook selection, and then answer the questions based on the information in the passage and in the graph.

Census 2000: Minorities Now a Majority in the Largest U.S. Cities

The 2000 U.S. census reported that minorities—Hispanics, African Americans, and Asians—are now a majority of the population in 48 of the 100 largest U.S. cities, up from 30 in 1990. What accounts for the change? The reason is that large cities have been losing their non-Hispanic white populations. For example, by 2000, Santa Ana, California, had lost 38 percent of the white population it had in 1990; the drop was 40 percent in Birmingham, Alabama, and a whopping 53 percent in Detroit, Michigan. The white share of the population of the 100 largest cities fell from 52.1 percent in 1990 to 43.8 percent in 2000.

But perhaps the biggest reason for the minority–majority trend is the increase in immigration. Immigration, coupled with higher birth rates among new immigrants, resulted in a 43 percent gain in the Hispanic population (almost 4 million people) of the largest 100 cities between 1990 and 2000. The Asian population also surged by 40 percent (more than 1.1 million people). The African American population remained steady over the course of the 1990s.

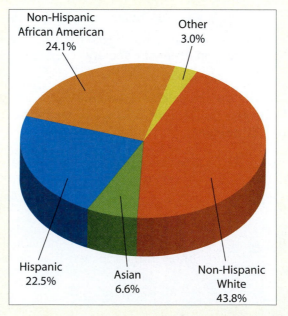

Population Profile for the 100 Largest U.S. Cities, 2000
Racial and ethnic minorities make up a majority of the population of this country's 100 largest cities. *Source: Based on U.S. Census Bureau (2001).*

QUESTIONS

1. What is the topic?

   a. minorities

   b. racial and ethnic populations

   c. minority populations of U.S. cities

   d. minorities and immigration

2. What is the topic sentence of the first paragraph?

   a. The 2000 U.S. census reported that minorities—Hispanics, African Americans, and Asians—are now a majority of the population in 48 of the 100 largest U.S. cities, up from 30 in 1990.

   b. The reason is that large cities have been losing their non-Hispanic white populations.

   c. For example, by 2000, Santa Ana, California, had lost 38 percent of the white population it had in 1990; the drop was 40 percent in Birmingham, Alabama, and a whopping 53 percent in Detroit, Michigan.

   d. The white share of the population of the 100 largest cities fell from 52.1 percent in 1990 to 43.8 percent in 2000.

Identify the following statements as "T" for true or "F" for false. Underline the sentences in the passage that provide the support for the true statements.

3. .... The white share of the population is no longer the largest part of the population in 48 of the largest U.S. cities.

4. .... One reason for the increase in minorities is immigration.

5. .... Hispanics have a larger share of the population in these cities than non-Hispanic African Americans.

U-Review

With your team, answer the following questions. You may go back to review the information in the chapter if needed.

1. **What is a conclusion?**

   a. a guess about something

   b. a guess based on what you think about something

   c. an idea that is determined by looking at facts

   d. an assumption

2. **What does CLUES stand for?**

   a. comprehend, look at the details, use the facts at hand, explain your main idea, and support your conclusion with facts

   b. comprehend, look at the main idea, use the facts at hand, examine the details, and support your conclusion with facts

   c. check comprehension, look at the supporting details, use only the facts at hand, examine the facts, and support your conclusion with facts

   d. comprehending, logical thinking, understanding, explaining, and simplifying

3. **What is an assumption?**

   a. something you know to be true

   b. something you guess is probably true, but there are no facts in the passage to prove it

   c. something you do when you use all the facts in the passage

   d. making a conclusion based on the facts in the passage

4. **What should you do after you make your conclusion?**

   a. state the main idea

   b. support your conclusion by looking for the facts in the passage that prove it

   c. examine the details

   d. look for absolutes

5. **Which of the following statements is accurate regarding the words *all, none, no one, everyone, always*, and *never*?**

   a. Never draw a conclusions using one of those terms.

   b. You should not assume a conclusion using those terms is true unless the passage specifically states them.

   c. Those terms are always acceptable in logical conclusions.

   d. Never believe anything that uses these terms.

Reading 1 Vocabulary Preview

The following vocabulary words are from the article "College Drinking: Harmless Fun?" With a partner or in a team, choose the correct meanings of the underlined words in the following sentences. Use context clues (LEADS), word part clues, and parts of speech to help you figure out the meanings.

1. When Pedro first went to college, he joined a <u>fraternity</u> (fra-TERN-it-ee) in his freshman year.
   a. military group
   b. brotherly
   c. group of college men
   d. sports team

2. To join the fraternity each <u>pledge</u> (PLEJ) had to dress up like a woman and carry a sign with his phone number on it.
   a. to promise
   b. a person who is trying to become a member of a fraternity
   c. a type of contract
   d. to drench

3. After the big party, the fraternity house was <u>reeking</u> (REEK-ing) of smoke and beer.
   a. stinking
   b. disgusting
   c. distributing
   d. enveloping

4. Because my roommate had stayed out too late, I couldn't <u>arouse</u> (ar-OWS) her to get her to get up for class on time.
   a. interest
   b. awaken
   c. convince
   d. engage

5. Most hotels and restaurants now have portable <u>defibrillators</u> (de-FIB-rill-ate-ors) to shock the hearts of people in cardiac arrest.
   a. pills
   b. medics
   c. oxygen tanks
   d. medical devices that give electrical shocks

Reading 1

6. All of Georgina's efforts to lose weight seemed <u>futile</u> (FYOU-tal) because she never lost more than a pound before putting it back on.

   a. ineffective

   b. ridiculous

   c. ambitious

   d. hard-working

7. During the fire at the club, many people were killed because falling debris created an <u>obstruction</u> (ob-STRUCT-shun) in front of the main exit.

   a. overly large

   b. construction

   c. blockage

   d. opening

8. If a person gets a deep cut that bleeds heavily, you should apply pressure with a clean cloth to <u>stanch</u> (STANCH) the flow of blood.

   a. an odor

   b. hold back

   c. strengthen

   d. not firm

9. Anthony did not receive the scholarship he had wanted because his grades did not meet the required <u>criteria</u> (cry-TEER-ee-ya).

   a. failing

   b. understood

   c. standards

   d. documents

10. The elderly and very young children are more <u>vulnerable</u> (VUL-ner-a-bul) to disease because their immune systems are not as strong as those of healthy adults.

    a. open to

    b. original

    c. inborn

    d. healthy

Reading 1 What Do You Already Know?

1. Have you ever been to a party where there has been a lot of drinking? Describe the situation.

2. Have you or anyone you know ever been affected by someone else's excessive drinking? Describe the situation.

> Directions: As you read this article, practice the four-step reading process. Preview the article, and then write on the following lines one or two questions that you would hope to have answered.
>
> ....
>
> ....
>
> ....
>
> ....

"College Drinking: Harmless Fun?"

BY CORINNE FENNESSY

The most recent studies of college drinking show that it has increased in the past ten years. College drinking may seem like harmless fun to most students, but the truth of its effects is sobering.

1   Fraternities, sororities, spring break, Halloween, or St. Patrick's Day all have something in common at college: drinking. What may seem like harmless fun to most students has a darker side, one that many students ignore.

2   In 2004, a 19-year-old student who had consumed beer and vodka with her college classmates was put into a room to sleep it off and was found dead the next morning. At a fraternity party Adrian Heideman of Palo Alto, California died just by drinking too much blackberry brandy. Scott Krueger, a freshman pledge at M.I.T. with a bright future also died from drinking. He was just 18. What started as harmless fun ended in tragedy when these students overdosed on alcohol.

3   Approximately 1,400 college students die and over 500,000 are injured each year due to alcohol-related incidents, including car accidents. According to a government study, binge drinking and alcohol-related deaths are on the rise. Binge drinking (4 to 5 drinks at one sitting) has risen to 45% of college students, and 29% of students drive drunk. It's no surprise that the consequences of such heavy drinking are far-reaching.

Reading 1

4   One night at Louisiana State University in Baton Rouge what began as a fraternity keg party ended in disaster. Pledges began drinking at a local bar and continued later at a fraternity house. Donald Hunt Jr. and his best friend and roommate, Benjamin Wynne, were among the group of young men who were partying. By late evening, the pledges were vomiting and some were taken back to the fraternity house to sleep if off. Around midnight, someone called 911. When the paramedics arrived, they found over a dozen young men lying unconscious and reeking of alcohol. Medics began shaking them, trying to arouse them, shouting, "Can you hear me?" Four of them were unresponsive and one was in cardiac arrest—Benjamin Wynne.

5   Immediately the medics began CPR. They hooked him up to an I.V. and inserted an oxygen tube into his lungs. They shocked him with a defibrillator to restart his heart. He was rushed by ambulance to Baton Rouge General Hospital where tests showed his blood alcohol level was nearly 6 times the legal limit. After doctors' futile efforts to revive him, Benjamin Wynne was finally pronounced dead of acute alcohol poisoning. At the same time, other doctors and nurses worked frantically to save the lives of three other pledges, including Donald Hunt Jr., who also suffered alcohol poisoning and nearly died.

Why were the students hospitalized?

6   Even though most college drinking may not end like the party at Louisiana State, it does have widespread consequences in terms of assaults, rapes, accidents, unplanned pregnancies, sexually transmitted diseases, and academic failure. College drinking is a contributing factor in 70,000 rapes, and 70,000 assaults each year. In addition, about 400,000 students engaged in unprotected sex under the influence of alcohol. For example, five of the six college women raped at Daytona Beach, Florida, during spring break in 2010 were drunk or unconscious at the time.

7   A common occurrence resulting in death is that students will leave drunken friends to "sleep it off." "Alcohol kills when the person is too intoxicated to maintain his own airway. He then suffocates on his own vomit or an otherwise harmless obstruction, such as a pillow," says Robert Davis of *USA Today*.

8   Colleges nationwide have conducted alcohol abuse awareness programs and have imposed rigid zero tolerance policies on drinking on campus, but most of these efforts have been unable to stanch the problem. Some college administrators reason that lowering the drinking age from 21 to 18 might help reduce the amount of secret drinking that goes on, but others argue that it will only increase the problem.

What's the most common effect of college drinking?

9   College students drink for fun, to relieve stress, or to make socializing easier. "What you've got here are people who think they are having fun," Harvard's Henry Wechsler says, "You can't change their behavior by preaching at them or telling them they'll get hurt."

10   For regular college drinkers, the most common effects of frequent drinking are poor grades and dropping out. According to a recent study, one-fourth of the

college students who fail courses is a result of excessive drinking. The study also found that nearly a third of all college students met the criteria for alcohol abuse.

11   Recent studies show that drinking among college women is more serious than ever. Wendy Garcia, the director for the Drug and Alcohol Information Center at Florida State reports, "We're seeing more women participating in the drinking games and being competitive with men in the drinking games." One such drinking game involves rolling dice. When your number is rolled, others drink. Other games, like Quarters, require players to bounce quarters into beer glasses. If you succeed, others drink, but if you miss, you drink. Among the most popular drinking games today is Beer Pong. Players try to throw a ping-pong ball across a table and land it into a cup of beer and then must drink it.

12   A study at Columbia University showed that 90% of all reported campus rapes happened when either one or both partners were using alcohol. In addition, 60% of college women who became infected with sexually transmitted diseases including AIDS were drunk at the time.

13   Leslie Baltz, a senior at the University of Virginia, was killed when she drank too much and fell down a flight of stairs. A freshman at Indiana University, Lorraine Hanna, was found dead by her own twin sister after a college New Year's Eve party. Lorraine's blood alcohol level was four times the legal limit. Women tend to get drunk more easily due to a higher level of body fat than men, and their bodies process alcohol more slowly than men's, which makes them more vulnerable to its effects.

Why are women more vulnerable to alcohol?

14   Mindy Sommers was an 18-year-old freshman at Virginia Tech. Her dorm room on the 8th floor had a wide window that was level with her bed. One Friday night it was Halloween and there were parties all over campus. Mindy decided to check out a few, but not go overboard because her parents were coming to visit that weekend for her 19th birthday on Sunday.

15   After partying, she got back to her dorm at 3:00 AM and fell into bed, fully clothed and drunk. The window next to her bed was open, and somehow during the night she fell out of it. Mindy's body was discovered on the grass the next morning by a paperboy. At first he thought it was some kind of Halloween prank. But police and EMT's confirmed that Mindy had died of massive internal injuries from the fall. She had a blood alcohol level only twice that of the legal limit.

What programs have been tried on campuses to stop alcohol abuse?

16   Efforts to fight alcohol abuse on campus are largely ineffective. Educational programs and scare tactics don't work. "If parents speak with their college students about alcohol, students are less likely to have problems with drinking," says Scott Walters, associate professor of the University of Texas.

17   In the meantime, many colleges will continue to prohibit drinking on campus and offer counseling and support for students. But in the end, if a student really wants to get drunk, there is very little that any college can do to prevent it.

1,232 words divided by _____ minutes = _____ words per minute

Reading 1 Thinking About What You Read

It is a good habit to summarize everything you read to strengthen your comprehension.

Directions: On the following lines, write a two- or three-sentence summary of the article "College Drinking: Harmless Fun?" In your own words, describe what the article was about and why the author wrote it.

Reading 1 Comprehension Questions

The following questions will help you to recall the main idea and the details of "College Drinking: Harmless Fun?" Review any parts of the article that you need to in order to find the correct answers.

LITERAL COMPREHENSION

1. **What is the topic of this article?**

   a. underage drinking

   b. alcohol abuse

   c. women's drinking habits

   d. college students' alcohol abuse

MAIN IDEAS

2. **What is the main idea of the entire article?**

   a. College students drink to have fun.

   b. Fraternities, sororities, spring break, Halloween, or St. Patrick's Day all have something in common at college: drinking.

   c. But in the end, if a student really wants to get drunk, there is very little that any college can do to prevent it.

   d. Excessive drinking by college students has many negative effects.

3. **What is the topic sentence of paragraph 11?**

   a. Recent studies show that drinking among college women is more serious than ever.

   b. Wendy Garcia, the director for the Drug and Alcohol Information Center at Florida State reports, "We're seeing more women participating in the drinking games and being competitive with men in the drinking games."

   c. One such drinking game involves rolling dice.

   d. Among the most popular drinking games today is Beer Pong.

SUPPORTING DETAILS

4. **According to the story, which of the following statements is not true?**

   a. Donald Hunt Jr. and Benjamin Wynne were best friends and roommates.

   b. Mindy Sommers died after falling 8 stories from her dormitory room window.

   c. Both Donald Hunt Jr. and Benjamin Wynne died from alcohol poisoning.

   d. Most rapes, unwanted pregnancies and sexually transmitted diseases occurred when one or both partners were under the influence of alcohol.

DRAWING CONCLUSIONS

5. **Based on the facts in the story, which of the following statements would be a logical conclusion?**

   a. Alcohol abuse is not considered as serious as drug abuse.

   b. Students who abuse alcohol are more likely to fail and drop out of college.

   c. Students who abuse alcohol, will also abuse drugs.

   d. More educational programs about alcohol abuse should be taught in college.

Reading 1

6. Based on the facts in the story, which of the following statements would be a logical conclusion?

   a. Mindy Sommers was probably a regular drinker.

   b. Students in fraternities tend to drink more than sororities (college women's organizations).

   c. Nearly all students on college campuses have been drunk at one time or another.

   d. Efforts to stop excessive drinking among college students have not been successful.

PATTERNS OF ORGANIZATION

7. What is the overall pattern of organization in paragraphs 14 and 15?

   a. listing

   b. time order

   c. compare and/ or contrast

   d. space order

8. Identify the relationship within the following sentence: Women tend to get drunk more easily due to a higher level of body fat than men, and their bodies process alcohol more slowly than men's, which makes them more vulnerable to its effects.

   a. listing

   b. comparison

   c. contrast

   d. cause and effect

9. Identify the relationship between the following sentences: Alcohol kills when the person is too intoxicated to maintain his own airway. He then suffocates on his own vomit or an otherwise harmless obstruction, such as a pillow.

   a. cause and effect

   b. time order

   c. compare and/ or contrast

   d. space order

VOCABULARY IN CONTEXT

10. Identify the meaning of the underlined word in the following sentence: Colleges nationwide have conducted alcohol abuse awareness programs and have imposed rigid zero tolerance policies on drinking on campus, but most of these efforts have been unable to stanch the problem.

   a. liking

   b. acceptance

   c. importance

   d. strict

Reading 1 · Vocabulary Practice

Use the vocabulary words from the Word Bank to complete the following sentences. Write the words into the blanks provided.

WORD BANK

| fraternity | pledge | reeking | arouse | defibrillator |
| futile | obstruction | stanch | criteria | vulnerable |

1. Cathy's husband sleeps so soundly that she can't .... him even when the baby is screaming.

2. When a person is choking, first check to see if there is a (an) .... in the airway.

3. My grandmother has poor balance that makes her more .... to falls and broken bones.

4. The .... had to wash all his fraternity brothers' cars in one week as a condition of his membership.

5. Despite the company's efforts to .... the oil leak, it was unable to prevent major ecological damage along the coast.

6. .... parties often serve a great deal of alcohol, especially beer.

7. The firefighters made a .... attempt to stop the forest fire, but the high winds spread the fires quickly.

8. The medics tried to revive the man in cardiac arrest with a ....

9. After the poker game the hotel room was .... with smoke.

10. Not all of the candidates for the position of president met the .... established by the college.

Questions for Writing and Discussion

Review any part of the article you need to answer the following questions.

1. From the article, describe the example of the effect of drinking that you think is the most powerful.

....

....

....

....

Reading 1

2. What attempts have been made to curb college drinking and what do you think should be done?

3. Why do you think so many college students drink excessively even when they know the consequences can be serious?

4. If you were with a friend who was drinking more than he or she should, what would you do?

Reading 1 Team Activity—Speed Quiz

Get together in groups of four or five people. Each group should create a set of vocabulary cards according to the following directions.

1.

Fold a sheet of notebook paper into 10 squares, and tear into squares. Write the 10 vocabulary words from "College Drinking: Harmless Fun?" and their correct definitions from the "Reading 1 Vocabulary Preview" on the squares—one word and its definition on each square.

2.

Shuffle the squares, and then place them face down on the desk.

3.

Divide your team into two groups, so that there are two or three people in each group.

4.

Each group will choose one clue giver and one scorekeeper/timekeeper.

FRATERNITY Group of college men	AROUSE Awaken
REEKING Stinking	PLEDGE A person who is trying to become a member of a fraternity
FUTILE Ineffective	DEFIBRILLATORS Medical devices that give electrical shocks
OBSTRUCTION Blockage	STANCH Hold back
CRITERIA Standards	VULNERABLE Open to

Take 5 squares from the deck

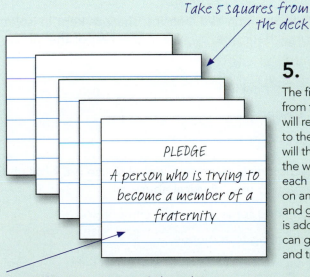

PLEDGE

A person who is trying to become a member of a fraternity

Read the definition and the other team has to guess the word.

5.

The first group will take five squares from the deck and, when told to start, will read the definitions, one at a time, to the second group. The second group will then have 60 seconds to try to give the word that matches the definition for each of the five words. If they get stuck on an answer, they should say "pass" and go on to the next question. If there is additional time left at the end, they can go back to the words they missed and try again.

6.

The scorekeeper will keep track of how many words the group answered correctly. When 60 seconds are up, the scorekeeper/timekeeper should write down the total number of correct answers given.

7.

Teams will then switch roles. When the cue to start is given, the second team will read the definitions on the remaining five cards to the first team, repeating steps 5 and 6. The team with the most correct answers is the winner.

Reading 2 Vocabulary Preview

The following vocabulary words are from the article "The Girl in the Garage." With a partner or in a team, choose the correct meanings of the underlined words in the following sentences. Use context clues (LEADS), word part clues, and parts of speech to help you figure out the meanings.

1. People living in <u>impoverished</u> (im-POV-er-ish'd) countries often make less than $1,000 a year in income.

   a. very poor   **c.** expensive

   b. wealthy   **d.** cheap

2. Luann's parents are both lawyers and have a very <u>posh</u> (POSH) home on a golf course in Naples, Florida, and a condo in New York City.

   a. small   **c.** bright

   b. luxurious   **d.** interesting

3. After Napoleon was defeated at Waterloo, he was taken prisoner and later <u>banished</u> (BAN-ish'd) forever to the island of St. Helena in the Atlantic Ocean.

   a. invited

   b. sent on holiday

   c. sent away somewhere as a punishment

   d. sailed

4. While Shannon had measles, she was kept in <u>isolation</u> (eye-so-LA-shun) in a small bedroom, away from the rest of the family.

   a. a small crib

   b. a hospital room

   c. suspense

   d. kept alone, away from others

5. Psychologists claim that <u>verbal abuse</u> (VER-bal uh-BYOUS) is often more damaging than physical abuse.

   a. striking someone as punishment

   b. listening to someone

   c. saying hurtful words intending to harm someone

   d. suffering

6. After we moved South, I had such a <u>longing</u> (LONG-ing) for my home up North that I became homesick.

   a. picture

   b. strong desire

   c. expectation

   d. transportation

Reading 2

7. The old man was so <u>shabbily</u> (SHAB-il-lee) dressed that no one knew he was in fact a millionaire.

   a. perfectly

   b. expensively

   c. without good taste

   d. raggedly

8. During the nineteenth century, women and children were <u>exploited</u> (ex-PLOY-ted) by factory owners who made them work long hours in unsafe and harsh conditions.

   a. taken advantage of

   b. treated

   c. beaten

   d. sold

9. We may go to Spain for our vacation, but we haven't decided yet, so our plans are still <u>tentative</u> (TEN-ta-tiv).

   a. certain

   b. not sure

   c. unhappy

   d. rude

10. The man who sold fake stock certificates to investors was given a prison sentence and forced to pay <u>restitution</u> (res-ti-TOO-shun) of $50,000.

    a. a prison sentence

    b. someone in the courts

    c. money paid for the harm done to someone

    d. a firm decision

Reading 2 What Do You Already Know?

1. How would you feel if your parents had sold you as a child to another family so that you could work for them? What would you have done?

2. Some immigrants are afraid to contact authorities when someone commits a crime against them. Why do you think they won't ask for help?

> Directions: As you read this article, practice the four-step reading process. Preview the article, and then write on the following lines one or two questions that you would hope to have answered.
>
> ....
>
> ....
>
> ....
>
> ....

As you read, answer the questions in the margins to check your comprehension.

"The Girl in the Garage"

BY MARY A. FISHER

(Adapted from "The Slave in the Garage," by Mary A. Fisher, *Reader's Digest*, May 2008 Copyright © 2008 by The Reader's Digest Association. Reprinted with permission.)

According to the Department of Health and Human Services, human trafficking is now the fastest-growing criminal industry in the world. The United States is a popular destination, with as many as 17,500 people brought in each year and exploited for sex or labor. Shyima Hall, no stranger to hardship, fell into the latter category.

1   Like a typical teen, Shyima Hall forgets to make her bed and groans when it's time to do her two chores—vacuuming the floor and cleaning the fishbowl. In the Orange County, California, home she shares with her adoptive parents and five brothers and sisters, the petite 18-year-old lounges on the couch, talking on her cell phone. Last May she went to her prom in a silky gown, her long dark hair worn up with a gardenia. She juggles a packed schedule—part-time job, homework, weekend camp—as if she's making up for lost time. And she is. In 2000, her impoverished parents sold her to a wealthy couple in Cairo, Egypt. When the pair moved to the United States, they arranged for Shyima to be brought illegally into the country, where she worked, day and night, in the family's posh home.

Reading 2

How was Shyima separated from her family?

2   One of 11 children born to desperately poor parents, Shyima grew up in a small one-bathroom house shared by three families. She and her parents and siblings slept in one room on blankets laid out on the floor. Her father was often gone for weeks at a time. "When he was home," says Shyima, "he beat us."

3   When she was eight, she went to live with another family. Shyima's older sister had worked as a maid for them, but the couple fired her, claiming she'd stolen cash. As a result, the couple made a deal with her parents, and Shyima was forced to replace her.

4   Two years later, her new family decided to move with their five children to start an import-export business. Shyima, 10 years old at the time, didn't want to go. The father, she says today, "told me I had no choice in the matter." She remembers standing outside the kitchen, overhearing her employers talk with her parents. "I heard them negotiate, and then my parents gave me away for $30 a month to these people," she says.

5   Shyima was brought into the United States on an illegally obtained six-month visitor's visa and settled into the couple's two-story Mediterranean-style house in a gated community in Irvine, California. When she wasn't working, she was banished to an 8-by-12-foot section of the garage with no windows and no air-conditioning or heat. Shyima says the family sometimes locked her in. Her furnishings: a dirty mattress, a floor lamp, and a small table. Shyima kept her clothes in her suitcase. Each day she rose at 6 a.m. with the couple's six-year-old twin boys. She took orders from everyone, including the twins' three sisters, 11, 13, and 15. She cooked, served meals, did the dishes, made beds, changed sheets, helped with laundry, ironed, dusted, vacuumed, swept, mopped, and washed the patios, and was often still doing chores at midnight. One day, when Shyima tried to do her own laundry, the mother stopped her. "She told me I couldn't put my things in the washing machine because they were dirtier than theirs." From then on, Shyima washed her clothes in a plastic bucket she kept by her mattress and hung them outside to dry on a metal rack, next to the garbage cans.

How was Shyima treated by the family who bought her?

6   Both parents hit Shyima, but the isolation and verbal abuse were worse. "They called me a stupid girl and a nothing," she says. "They made me feel less than them." She ate alone and wasn't allowed to attend school or leave the house without a parent escorting her. The couple warned her against telling anyone about her situation. "They threatened that the police would take me away because I was an illegal," Shyima says.

7   Though she never admitted longing for her mother, she cried openly when she came down with a bad flu. "They saw me suffering and didn't care," she says. "I still had to do my chores. They wouldn't even get medicine for me."

377

Reading 2

How do you think Shyima felt at this point in her life? Why?

8   At night, exhausted and lonely, she stared into the darkness. They had taken her passport, and she feared she would be held prisoner forever. When Shyima turned 12, there was no celebration. She spent her birthday doing housework.

9   Six months later, on the morning of April 9, 2002, Orange County Child Protective Services social worker Carole Chen responded to an anonymous caller (believed to be a neighbor) reporting a case of child abuse. The person said that a young girl was living in the family's garage, acting as a maid, and not attending school.

10   Chen, along with Irvine police investigator Tracy Jacobson, knocked at the front door. When the father answered, Jacobson asked who lived in the house. The father said his wife and five children.

11   "Are there other children?" the officer pressed. He admitted there was a 12-year-old girl. He claimed she was a distant relative.

12   "Can I talk to her?" Jacobson asked.

13   The father called to her in Arabic, telling her to come downstairs and deny that she worked for them. Shabbily dressed in a brown T-shirt and baggy pants, she hurried to the door.

14   Chen, who noticed that the girl's hands looked red and raw, called a translator on her cell phone. Shyima told him that she'd been in the country for two years and had never been to school.

15   Officer Jacobson promptly took the girl into protective custody. Riding in the backseat of the police car, headed to a children's group home where she would be temporarily placed, Shyima prayed she'd never have to face her captors again. "She was amazing, a very strong child," Jacobson recalls. "She never cried. Shyima liked being in protective custody, unlike other kids, because she felt safe."

16   A few hours later, Jacobson, armed with a search warrant, returned to the house with agents from the FBI and Immigration and Customs Enforcement (ICE). "Shyima lived in complete contrast to the rest of the family," says Jacobson. ICE agent Bob Schoch adds, "I've seen pets that are treated better."

How did Shyima escape from her situation?

17   The investigator arrested the parents and charged them with four counts of criminal offense. Immigration officials offered Shyima a choice: Return to Egypt or stay in America and live in a foster home. Nervous and tentative, Shyima phoned her father in Egypt and blurted out, "I want to stay here."

Reading 2

He was angry, but Shyima's mind was made up: she wanted to start a new, better life.

18 During the next two years, she lived with two foster families. In the first home, she learned to speak and read English. In the next one, after an argument, they dropped Shyima off at a local group home. "I just wanted to be a regular American teenager," she says.

19 She soon got her wish. Chuck and Jenny Hall, parents of two daughters and a son, had recently bought a four-bedroom house in Orange County and decided they had room for more children. At their first meeting with Shyima, "we all clicked," says Chuck, a uniform company service manager.

20 "The No. 1 rule: homework and school first," added Jenny, a youth counselor. "We'll treat you as our own daughter. You'll be part of our family."

21 By then 15, Shyima had blossomed into a beautiful young woman. But she brought more with her than her suitcase. "I had a whole lot of anger," she says. For the first six months, she had trouble sleeping and suffered from anxiety. She regularly saw a therapist and took medication for depression.

22 With time, she grew more self-confident. At school, she made friends, including a first boyfriend, and joined the track team. She got a part-time job and participated in church dinners and fundraisers. She even volunteered to be a counselor at a camp for children with low self-esteem.

23 Meanwhile, Shyima's captors accepted a plea bargain to avoid trial. At their October 2006 sentencing hearing, Shyima sat nervously in the courtroom, listening to their pleas for mercy. Unable to contain her outrage, Shyima asked to address the court. She spoke about her captors. "She is a grown woman, so she knows right from wrong," she said. "Where was their loving when it came to me? Wasn't I a human being too? I felt like I was nothing when I was with them. What they did to me is going to scar me for the rest of my life."

24 The father received a reduced sentence of three years in prison, and the mother got 22 months. The couple was also ordered to pay Shyima $76,137 as <u>restitution</u> for the work she did. Both will be deported to Egypt when they get out of jail.

25 As for the future, Shyima says she'd like to be a police officer so she can help other people. She also wants to return to Egypt one day to visit her brothers and sisters. For now, though, she's content, indulging the dream she never imagined would come true: life as a regular American teen.

How did Shyima feel about her years as a captive?

1,500 words divided by _____ minutes = _____ words per minute

Reading 2 — Thinking About What You Read

It's a good habit to summarize everything you read to strengthen your comprehension.

Directions: On the following lines, write a two- or three-sentence summary of the article "The Girl in the Garage." In your own words, describe what the article was about and why the author wrote it.

Comprehension Questions

The following questions will help you to recall the main idea and the details of "The Girl in the Garage." Review any parts of the article that you need to find the correct answers.

LITERAL COMPREHENSION

1. What is the topic of this article?
   a. human trafficking
   b. slavery
   c. Shyima Hall's captivity
   d. two social workers finding Shyima Hall living as a slave in Irvine, California

MAIN IDEAS

2. What is the main idea of the entire article?
   a. Shyima Hall was kept as a slave until a social worker discovered her and found her a new family.
   b. Life is not always fair.
   c. Shyima was paid restitution by the family who kept her captive.
   d. Shyima's parents sold her as a slave to another family.

3. What is the topic sentence of paragraph 18?
   a. During the next two years, she lived with two foster families.
   b. In the first home, she learned to speak and read English.
   c. In the next one, after an argument, they dropped Shyima off at a local group home.
   d. "I just wanted to be a regular American teenager," she says.

Reading 2

4. According to the article, which of the following statements is false?

   a. Shyima's new mom, Jenny Hall, is a youth counselor.

   b. Shyima had the chance to go back to her parents in Egypt but wanted to stay in the United States.

   c. Shyima later became a volunteer counselor at a children's camp.

   d. When she was a slave, Shyima was living in the United States as a legal alien.

SUPPORTING DETAILS

5. Identify the meaning of the underlined word in the following sentence: Six months later, on the morning of April 9, 2002, Orange County Child Protective Services social worker Carole Chen responded to an <u>anonymous</u> caller (believed to be a neighbor) reporting a case of child abuse.

   a. someone who tells on someone else

   b. someone who doesn't give his or her name

   c. annoyed

   d. suspicious

VOCABULARY IN CONTEXT

6. What is the overall pattern of organization in paragraph 3?

   a. process   c. cause and effect

   b. compare and/or contrast   d. listing

7. What is the overall pattern of organization for this article?

   a. time order   c. cause and effect

   b. compare and/or contrast   d. process

PATTERNS OF ORGANIZATION

8. According to the article, how long did Shyima work for the family?

   a. one year

   b. two years

   c. three years

   d. four years

DRAWING CONCLUSIONS

9. Who is responsible for saving Shyima from her captors? (Choose all that apply.)

   a. Shyima

   b. Carole Chen and Tracy Jacobson

   c. the anonymous caller who tipped off police

   d. Chuck and Jenny Hall

10. Human trafficking is increasing in the United States.

    a. true

    b. false

Reading 2 Vocabulary Practice

Use the vocabulary from the Word Bank to complete the following sentences. Write the words into the blanks provided.

> **WORD BANK**
>
> | impoverished | posh | banished | isolation | tentative |
> | --- | --- | --- | --- | --- |
> | verbal abuse | longing | shabbily | exploited | restitution |

1. The young couple was dressed so .... that the restaurant manager would not let them have a table.

2. Some spouses suffer from so much .... in their failed marriages that they lose their self-esteem.

3. My plans for spring break are still .... but I may go to Miami Beach.

4. Most .... people have few opportunities to escape their poverty other than through getting an education.

5. On their honeymoon, Jim and Natasha stayed at a very .... hotel on Miami Beach.

6. Seeing other people's dogs filled Mother with .... for the little dog that she had lost in an accident last year.

7. The judge ordered the youths who robbed the old couple to pay .... for their crime in addition to a prison sentence.

8. After being kept in .... at the hospital during his illness, Simon was glad to be home with his family again.

9. Roberto's mother warned him that if he didn't clean his room, he would be .... from the dinner table until it was cleaned.

10. The scam artist .... elderly people by selling them worthless land and taking their money.

Questions for Writing and Discussion

Review any parts of the article you need to answer the following questions.

1. Why do you think it is so difficult for social workers and immigration officials to find out about people who are being kept as slaves?

   ....

   ....

   ....

2. What might have happened if the anonymous caller had not reported the girl living in the garage?

   ....

   ....

   ....

3. Why didn't Shyima try to escape from her captors?

   ....

   ....

   ....

4. What role did the social worker have in releasing Shyima from her captors?

   ....

   ....

   ....

   ....

5. Do you think the parents who kept Shyima as a slave were punished fairly or unfairly for their crimes?

   ....

   ....

   ....

383

Reading 2 Vocabulary Practice—Bingo Game

The object of the game is to be the first person with five matching words in a row.

1. Fold two sheets of paper into 12 squares and tear them into pieces. Hand out one blank piece to each student. Some students may need to do more than one piece to complete all 24 pieces. Index cards may be used instead of paper.

2. Each student will write one of the definitions below on the square until all 24 definitions have been written on the squares. Collect the squares and shuffle them. One person will call out the definitions for the game.

3. For Bingo markers, use coins, paper clips, or pieces of paper cut into small squares.

4. Draw a bingo card on a sheet of paper, with five rows across and five rows down. Make the squares large enough to write a word in each one. Write "FREE" in the center space, and then write each of the following vocabulary words from Chapters 7

and 8 into the squares, scattering the words randomly throughout the card. Do not place them in the order they are listed, and do not write a word in the FREE space. You should use each word only once.

1. incomprehensible	13. impoverished
2. impulses	14. rein
3. savor	15. verbal abuse
4. gleefully	16. compelling
5. restitution	17. excerpt
6. emerge	18. tentative
7. protagonist	19. longing
8. banished	20. posh
9. persist	21. exploited
10. pliable	22. isolation
11. shabbily	23. dialogue
12. residual	24. prosthetic

5. One person will take the top card from the definitions pile and read the definition aloud. Find the word on your bingo card that matches the definition, and put a marker on the word.

incomprehensible	emerge	shabbily	verbal abuse	posh
impulses	protagonist	residual	compelling	exploited
savor	banished	FREE	excerpt	isolation
gleefully	persist	impoverished	tentative	dialogue
restitution	pliable	rein	longing	prosthetic

6. As soon as you have five markers in a row—horizontally, vertically, or diagonally—call out "Bingo!" Be prepared to read your list of words and give the matching definitions.

Definitions

1. not understood	9. happily	17. wishing for
2. a part taken from a whole	10. enjoy	18. something left behind
3. keep trying	11. made poor	19. in a shabby way
4. a good character	12. luxurious	20. temporary
5. to come out	13. taken advantage of	21. to pay back
6. forceful	14. forced to leave	22. signals
7. conversation	15. kept alone	23. flexible
8. restrain	16. saying harmful things	24. artificial limb

Kim Walter,
High School Chemistry Teacher

How did you become interested in teaching?
When I was young, I used to teach swimming lessons. I really enjoyed helping others learn how to swim. I also had wonderful elementary and high school teachers, so I decided I would go into teaching when I got older. I first wanted to be a physical education teacher; therefore, I had to take courses in anatomy and physiology. I discovered my love for science and decided to change my major to biology.

What is your training and background?
I graduated from State University of New York at Brockport with a bachelor of science degree in science with a major concentration in biology and minors in chemistry and secondary education. I went on to earn a master of science in education and a master of science in science education.

Did you ever consider quitting college?
No, because I knew I had to have a college education to have a successful future. I never thought about quitting.

Where do you work now?
I teach Regents chemistry at Churchville-Chili High School in upstate New York. It was a great honor to be recognized by my students when the National Honor Society chose me as Teacher of the Year. It reinforced the reason I am in this profession.

What do you like best about your job?
I love working with high school kids, and I learn new things every day working with them. Besides teaching them chemistry, I try to teach them things they need to be successful in life, like problem solving, staying organized, establishing good study habits, and working with others.

What do you dislike about your job?
I don't think any teacher likes having to discipline students. Some students don't have respect for education and take their opportunities to learn for granted. And there is a certain amount of politics in any school district that educators have to deal with.

What advice would you give to college students?
I think the best advice I would give them is to choose a career that allows them to do what they love to do. If you do what you love to do, you will always find enjoyment in your work.

What are your plans for the future?
My plans are to keep on teaching for another 10 to 15 years. I still feel enthusiastic about teaching and about my students. I hope to inspire them to become lifelong learners and to help them find joy in learning.

VIEWPOINT: Welfare Programs

In 1996, the federal government ended its public assistance program and turned the responsibility of caring for the poor over to the states' control. The new state-run welfare programs required people receiving welfare payments to work or get job training. Failure to do either of these would result in having their welfare cut off. Welfare programs are supposed to help support the poorest people in society until they can earn enough money to be independent. Read the following letters to the editor about welfare programs, and then answer the questions that follow.

Dear Editor:

Why shouldn't the poor receive financial assistance from the government—either the state or federal? Without welfare, some people would be forced into crime in order to feed themselves or their families. I should think that both the state and federal government would bend over backwards to help citizens who can't help themselves. What little money people receive from welfare is not enough to meet basic needs and wouldn't attract anyone who didn't need to take it. Welfare should be increased to really help poor people get out of the cycle of poverty they are in. Instead of cutting funds to welfare programs, state governments should be increasing them to provide more job training, more childcare assistance, and better health care for the poor.

Signed,

Brother's Keeper

Dear Editor:

Our governments—state or federal—cannot afford to support a large portion of the population over a sustained period of time. In addition, welfare has done nothing to eliminate poverty; it only encourages it. Young teenagers are having babies because they can get welfare payments for being single mothers, and the more children they have, the more money they get. If there was no welfare to support them, maybe they would stay in school and finish their education so they could contribute something to society instead of being a financial burden upon it. Unless someone is physically or mentally unable to work, he or she should be out earning a living instead of depending on taxpayers to feed them.

Signed,

Tired of Taxes

Critical Thinking

1. A *point of view* is the author's opinion about a topic. To find the author's point of view, ask yourself, "How does this author feel about this issue?" What is the author's point of view about welfare programs in the first letter?

   ....

   ....

   ....

2. What is the author's point of view about welfare programs in the second letter?

   ....

   ....

3. Which letter do you agree with, and why?

   ....

   ....

   ....

4. What could be the consequences of increasing welfare benefits?

   ....

   ....

   ....

5. What could be the consequences of reducing or eliminating welfare programs?

   ....

   ....

   ....

   ....

WRITE YOUR THOUGHTS

Write a letter to the editor stating your own feelings about what should be done with welfare programs. Should they be increased? Changed? Eliminated? Use a separate piece of paper.

Applying for Student Financial Aid

Use the following information from the U.S. Department of Education Web site to answer the questions that follow.

WHY FILL OUT A FAFSA?

The (*Free Application for Federal Student Aid*), or **FAFSA**, is the first step in the financial aid process. Use it to apply for federal student financial aid, such as the Pell Grant, student loans, and college work-study.

We enter your **FAFSA** responses into a formula (known as the Federal Methodology), which is regulated by the Higher Education Act of 1965, as amended. The result is your Expected Family Contribution, or **EFC**. The **EFC** is a preliminary estimate that measures your family's financial strength. It is subtracted from the Cost of Attendance at the school(s) you plan to attend to determine your eligibility for federal student aid.

HOW DO I FIND OUT WHAT MY EFC IS?

We will send you a report, called a *Student Aid Report* (**SAR**) by e-mail or by postal mail depending on the addresses that we have on file for you. The **SAR** lists the information you reported on your **FAFSA**. At the upper right of the front page of the **SAR**, you'll find a figure called the **EFC**.

HOW MUCH AID DO I GET?

Schools use your **EFC** to prepare a financial aid package (grants, loans, and/or work-study) to help you meet your financial need. Financial need is the difference between your **EFC** and your school's cost of attendance (which can include living expenses).

WHEN DO I GET THE AID?

Your financial aid will be paid to you through your school. Typically, your school will first use the aid to pay tuition, fees, and room and board (if provided by the school). Any remaining aid is given to you for your other expenses.

WHERE CAN I GET MORE INFORMATION ABOUT STUDENT AID?

The financial aid office at the school you plan to attend is the best place to get information about federal, state, school and other sources of student financial aid.

Information about other nonfederal assistance may be available from foundations, religious organizations, community organizations, and civic groups, as well as organizations related to your field of interest, such as the American Medical Association or American Bar Association. Check with your parents' employers or unions to see if they award scholarships or have tuition payment plans.

WARNING!

Be wary of organizations that charge a fee to submit your application, or to find you money for school. Some are legitimate and some are scams. Generally, any help that you pay for can be received free from your school or Federal Student Aid.

Questions

1. Why do you need to answer so many questions in order to get financial aid?

2. How is your EFC used to determine your financial aid?

3. If an organization asks you for money to apply for financial aid or a scholarship, what should you do?

4. Where is the financial aid sent, and what, specifically, can the financial aid be used for?

5. What are some other sources of financial aid for students?

BUILDING VOCABULARY

Study the following word parts, and then answer the questions that follow.

Prefixes
dis- *apart, away from*
in- *not*
ex- *out**

Roots
-able- *able to*
-tend- *to move*
-tinct- *to incite or to quench*
-tort- *to twist*

Suffixes
-ity *quality of*
-tion, -sion *action, state of**
-ive *a state or quality**

* Word parts from previous chapters

What English words can you create from these word parts?

....

....

....

....

....

....

Using a dictionary, look up the meanings of any of the words you wrote that you can't define. Use one of the words you wrote in a sentence that reveals its meaning with a context clue:

....

....

....

....

....

....

TEXTBOOK GRAPHIC AIDS

Use the following chart to identify the statements that follow as true or false.

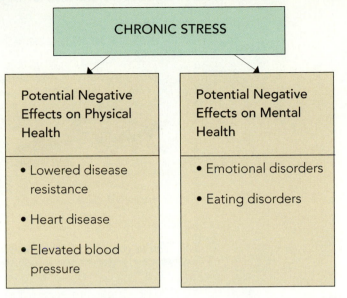

CHRONIC STRESS	
Potential Negative Effects on Physical Health	**Potential Negative Effects on Mental Health**
• Lowered disease resistance • Heart disease • Elevated blood pressure	• Emotional disorders • Eating disorders

(From *Total Fitness and Wellness*, Brief Edition, 3rd, by Scott K. Powers and Stephen L. Dodd. Copyright © 2009. Printed and Electronically reproduced by permission of Pearson Education, Inc., Upper Saddle River, NJ.)

1. .... Heart disease causes mental disorders.

2. .... There are potentially more negative effects of stress on physical health than on mental health.

3. .... Eating disorders may be caused by chronic stress.

4. .... Chronic stress can have an effect on your body's ability to fight off illness.

5. .... People who deal with chronic stress on a daily basis will have heart attacks.

CHAPTER REVIEW PRACTICE #1

Study the following cartoons, and then identify the statements that follow as true or false.

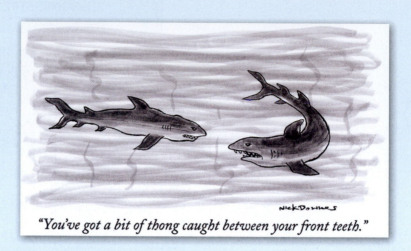

"*You've got a bit of thong caught between your front teeth.*"

1. .... The sharks are eating thongs.

2. .... One shark has eaten a swimmer who wore a thong.

3. .... The artist implies that like people, sharks care about their appearance.

"*We're saved! We're saved!*"

1. .... The aliens in the space ship think that the shark has come to help them.

2. .... The aliens have been to Earth before and know about sharks.

CHAPTER REVIEW PRACTICE #2

Study the following cartoons, and then identify the statements that follow as true or false.

"Poor old Stanley. He was only 3 months away from paying off his student loan."

(www.CartoonStock.com)

1. .... The man in the grave had been a college student at one time.

2. .... According to the cartoon, college loans are not difficult to pay back.

"I take it you didn't like my meatballs."

(www.CartoonStock.com)

1. .... The man in the cartoon thinks his wife is a good cook.

2. .... The cartoonist is implying that meatballs are terrible.

3. .... The meatballs the man had on his plate resembled golf balls.

CHAPTER REVIEW PRACTICE #3

Read the following paragraph, and then answer the questions that follow. Remember to use CLUES to help you make logical conclusions.

In the days of ancient Egypt, preserving the body after death was a religious practice that honored the dead. The wealthiest and most important Egyptians were cut open, and their internal organs were placed in clay jars. The brain was removed either through the nostrils or through an incision in the back of the skull. The body was then packed in natron, a natural salt. The mummy was then cleansed and bandaged, while priests recited prayers and applied oils and perfumes. A gold or silver mask was sometimes placed over the face. The mummy was placed into a wooden coffin, which was put into a larger, rectangular stone "sarcophagus" (sar-KOFF-a-gus). The priests performed a formal ceremony for last rites, and the sarcophagus was laid to rest in its own tomb, which was sometimes a giant pyramid.

1. **What is the topic of the passage?**

    a. mummies

    b. how ancient Egyptians preserved their dead

    c. ancient priests

    d. ceremonies for the dead

2. **What is the topic sentence of the passage?**

    a. In the days of ancient Egypt, preserving the body after death was a religious practice that honored the dead.

    b. The wealthiest and most important Egyptians were cut open, and their internal organs were placed in clay jars.

    c. The brain was removed either through the nostrils or through an incision in the back of the skull.

    d. The priests performed a formal ceremony for last rites, and the sarcophagus was laid to rest in its own tomb, which was sometimes a giant pyramid.

Identify the following statements as "T" for true or "F" for false.

3. .... The ancient Egyptians showed great respect for their dead.

4. .... The ancient Egyptians were religious.

5. .... Ancient Egyptians believed they needed their entire bodies after death.

TEXTBOOK PRACTICE

Read the following textbook selection, and then answer the questions that follow. Remember to use CLUES to help you make logical conclusions.

There may be no way to rid the world of dishonesty, but researchers have learned a great deal about how to tell when someone is lying. According to Paul Ekman, a specialist in analyzing social interaction, clues to deception can be found in four elements of a performance: words, voice, body language, and facial expressions.

1. Words. People who are good liars mentally go over their lines, but they may say something that is inconsistent, thereby suggesting deception.

2. Voice. Tone and patterns of speech contain clues to deception because they are hard to control. Especially when hiding a powerful emotion, a person cannot easily prevent the voice from trembling or breaking.

3. Body language. A "leak" conveyed through body language, which is also difficult to control, may tip off an observer to deception. Subtle body movements, sudden swallowing, or rapid breathing may show that the person is nervous.

4. Facial expressions. Because there are 43 different muscles in the face, facial expressions are more difficult to control than other body language.

Look at the two faces in the photos. Can you tell which is the lying face? It's the one on the left. A real smile is usually accompanied by a relaxed expression and lots of "laugh lines" around the eyes; a phony smile seems forced and unnatural, with fewer wrinkles around the mouth and eyes.

(From *Society: The Basics* by John J. Macionis. Copyright © 2007 by John J. Macionis. Reprinted by permission of Pearson Education, Inc., Upper Saddle River, NJ.)

1. **What is the topic of this selection?**

    a. clues to deception

    b. lying

    c. how lying harms society

    d. deception

2. **What is the main idea of the entire selection?**

    a. There may be no way to rid the world of dishonesty, but researchers have learned a great deal about how to tell when someone is lying.

    b. According to Paul Ekman, a specialist in analyzing social interaction, clues to deception can be found in four elements of a performance: words, voice, body language, and facial expressions.

    c. People who are good liars mentally go over their lines, but they may say something that is inconsistent, thereby suggesting deception.

    d. Especially when hiding a powerful emotion, a person cannot easily prevent the voice from trembling or breaking.

3. **According to the article, what is a "leak"?**

    a. A leak is something someone does that leads the observer to believe that a person is lying.

    b. A leak is when the liar gives out false information.

    c. A leak is saying something that is inconsistent with something said earlier.

    d. A leak is a phony smile.

4. **According to the article, if someone's voice is trembling, what does it mean?**

    a. It indicates that the person is lying.

    b. It indicates that the person is nervous.

    c. It indicates that the person is hiding a powerful emotion.

    d. It indicates that the person is upset.

5. **How can a person tell if someone is probably lying?**

    a. if the person is smiling a lot

    b. if the person is revealing clues through words, voice, body language, and facial expressions

    c. when the person smiling is thinking the opposite of what the person is saying

    d. if the person smiling is actually sad or angry

STUDY SKILL CHAPTER REVIEW

Creating flow charts is an easy way to remember the steps in a process. Fill in the following flow chart for the steps you learned in this chapter that help you draw logical and valid conclusions.

C: ....

....

L: ....

....

U: ....

....

E: ....

....

S: ....

....

READING LAB ASSIGNMENTS

SKILL PRACTICES

1. Go online to MyReadingLab and click on the "Study Skills" tab. Next, click on "Inferences " and complete the practices and tests according to your instructor's directions.

COMPREHENSION IMPROVEMENT

2. Go online to MyReadingLab and click on the Reading Level tab. Choose two stories to read and answer the questions that follow.

CAREER EXPLORATION

3. Go online to www.bls.gov/oco and explore careers in sociology or education. Find a career that interests you and print out the information. Print the article, and then preview, read, highlight, and annotate one or two sections of it. Write two conclusions you can draw about the job (for example, whether it would be a good job for you and why you think this job is important).

SKILL APPLICATION

4. Go online to www.bls.gov/oco and explore careers in sociology or education. Find a career that interests you and print out the information. Print the article, and then preview, read, highlight, and annotate one or two sections of it. Write two conclusions you can draw about the job (for example, whether it would be a good job for you and why you think this job is important).

LEARNING REFLECTION

Think about the skills and concepts in this chapter. What have you learned in this chapter that will help your reading comprehension and enable you to do well in college?

SELF-EVALUATION CHECKLIST

Rate yourself on the following items, using the following scale:

1 = strongly disagree

2 = disagree

3 = neither agree nor disagree

4 = agree

5 = strongly agree

1. I completed all of the assigned work on time. ....

2. I understand all of the concepts in this chapter. ....

3. I contributed to teamwork and class discussions. ....

4. I completed all of the assigned lab work on time. ....

5. I came to class on time. ....

6. I attended class every day. ....

7. I studied for any quizzes or tests we had this for chapter. ....

8. I asked questions when I didn't understand something. ....

9. I checked my comprehension during reading. ....

10. I know what is expected of me in the coming week. ....

11. Are you still on track with the goals you set in Chapter 1? ....

12. What changes can you make to improve your performance in this course? ....

For support in meeting this chapter's objectives, go to the Study Plan in MyReadingLab and select Inferences. Read and view the resources in the Review Materials section, and then complete the Recall, Apply, and Write exercises in the Activities section. Check your results by clicking on Gradebook.

STUDY SKILL: CORNELL NOTES

Cornell Notes are very popular among college students everywhere because they are a good way to take notes during a lecture or from a reading assignment, and they can be an efficient way to study for tests. They were created by Walter Pauk at Cornell University in the 1950s and remain popular today. Here are the steps to take Cornell Notes:

Question / Cue	Notes
	In 2005, women earned less money than men for the same jobs—earning 77 cents for every dollar earned by a man.
	At top of pay scale, men were 2 1/2 times more likely to earn more than $75,000.
	Gender compensation inequality: when one gender is not paid equally for the same job as the other gender

Step 1: Divide your notebook paper into two columns, with the left column one-third of the width of the paper.

Step 2: The column on the left is the "Cue" or "Question" column. The column on the right is where you take your notes. As you listen to a lecture or read, write brief notes in the right column.

Question / Cue	Notes
How do women's earnings compare to men's?	In 2005, women earned less money than men for the same jobs—earning 77 cents for every dollar earned by a man.
	At top of pay scale, men were 2 1/2 times more likely to earn more than $75,000.
What is "gender compensation inequality"?	Gender compensation inequality: when one gender is not paid equally for the same job as the other gender

Step 3: Later, during your study time, read through the notes you took in the right column. Think of them as answers to key questions. Then, write those questions or topics in the left column to match the notes on the right.

Summary of topic	
	Women do not receive equal pay to men, known as gender compensation inequality, for many different reasons. Research shows that women receive less pay and have fewer opportunities to advance in their careers than men.

Step 4: At the end of the notes, write a short summary of the entire topic, based on your notes. Just mention the most important points in very general terms without being specific.

(Text excerpt "Study Skill: Cornell Notes" by Macionis, from *Society: The Basics*, pp. 162–163 and 280. Copyright © 2006 Prentice-Hall, Inc. Reproduced by permission of Pearson Education, Inc.)

USING YOUR CORNELL NOTES TO STUDY

Simply cover the right column with your hand or a sheet of paper. Read the questions in the left column and try to answer them without looking at the notes. Then, slide your paper down to see if you answered correctly. At the end, try to summarize the notes in your own words, and then read the summary to see if you remembered all the major points.

Read the following textbook excerpt, and underline the main idea and major details. Then, complete the Cornell Notes by filling in the missing information.

Date Rape

A common myth is that rape usually involves strangers. In reality, however, only about one-third of all rapes fit this pattern. Three of every four rapes involve people who know each other—more often than not, pretty well—and these crimes usually take place in familiar surroundings, such as the home or a college campus. The term "date rape," or "acquaintance rape," refers to forcible sexual violence against a person by someone he or she knows.

A second myth, often linked specifically to date rape, is the idea that a woman who has been raped must have done something to encourage the man and make him think she wanted to have sex. Perhaps the victim agreed to go out with the offender. Maybe she even invited him to her room. But, of course, such actions do not justify rape any more than they would justify any other kind of physical assault.

(From *Society: The Basics* by John J. Macionis. Copyright © 2007 by John J. Macionis. Reprinted by permission of Pearson Education, Inc., Upper Saddle River, NJ.)

Question / Cue	Notes
What is the first myth about rape?	One myth about rape is that ....
How and where	.... involve people who know each other.
....	They usually take place ....
....	Date rape, or "acquaintance rape," refers to ....
What is the second	A second myth ....
....	....
Summary of topic	....

CHAPTER 9 IMPLIED MAIN IDEAS AND CENTRAL POINT

LEARNING OBJECTIVES

IN THIS CHAPTER, YOU WILL:

Objective **1**   identify an implied main idea.

Objective **2**   describe the central point of a long passage.

FOCUS ON THE ARTS AND RELATED FIELDS

Many people have special talents and interests in art, music, filmmaking, theater, photography, digital media, and dance. Although job opportunities and the competition in these fields can be very stiff, anyone who is well prepared and committed to the craft can make a living in the arts—and perhaps a very good one. Jobs are found in theater, television, on cruise ships, resorts, theme parks, schools, private businesses, and studios. Many creative people are self-employed. There are unlimited opportunities to use your talents in these fields if you have good ideas and are dedicated.

Objective 1 IMPLIED MAIN IDEAS

An **implied main idea** is a main idea that is not stated but is suggested by the details. Using the details, you draw a logical conclusion about the author's most important point. As an active reader, you can figure out the author's main point by following three simple steps:

1. First, begin with the topic. Who or what is the passage about?

2. Second, find the major details.

3. Third, summarize what the author is saying about the topic in the major details Be sure to use very broad, general terms to describe the author's point. Ask yourself, "What are the major details telling me about the topic?" When you have formed your implied main idea, ask yourself, "Do the major details tell me more about this idea?" If they do, then you have an implied main idea that is general enough to include all the major points.

Read the following example paragraphs, and then answer the questions that follow. The major details have been underlined.

> A film director works with other creative members on the production team, such as the cinematographer, screenwriters, the visual effects supervisor, and others. He or she makes the decisions about how the film will be made to create a specific experience for viewers. Directors can have many different styles. Some directors welcome suggestions from production team members, while others prefer to make most of the decisions alone. Many directors also like to be involved with the film's editing, while others work more closely with the screenwriters. Directors work under producers, who set the budget and time limit for creating a movie.
>
> 1. What is the topic?
>   - **a.** directors and producers
>   - **b.** directing
>   - **c.** film directors
>   - **d.** styles of directing
>
> 2. What do the major details describe?
>   - **a.** how directors have many responsibilities
>   - **b.** how film directors have many different styles and work with various members of the production team
>   - **c.** why film directors are important
>   - **d.** why people want to be film directors
>
> **Complete the following implied main idea, beginning with the topic.**
>
> .... have many different .... of working
>
> with ....

Notice how the implied main idea in the preceding example is broad enough to include all of the major details. When choosing or writing an implied main idea, remember to summarize the author's most important point in very general terms.

Practice

1. Read the following paragraph, and underline the major details. Then, answer the questions that follow.

Walt Disney was born in 1901 and began taking night courses at the Chicago Art Institute when he was a freshman in high school. He was the cartoonist for his school newspaper until World War I broke out, when he was 16. He served three years in the war and then returned home and worked as an advertising artist with his brother. After an unsuccessful attempt with their own company, Walt went back into advertising where he met Fred Harman and began making animated cartoons in Kansas City. Although his animated cartoons were popular, this company also failed due to poor management. Next, Walt and Roy Disney moved to Hollywood to start the Disney Brothers Studio, where he began producing animated cartoons with characters. When they lost the rights to one of his most popular characters, Oswald the Rabbit, the Disney brothers found themselves once more at the bottom. But Walt put his pen to paper and, with the help of another animator, created Mortimer Mouse—later renamed Mickey Mouse. The rest is history.

1. What is the topic?
    a. Walt Disney's career beginnings
    b. Walt and Roy Disney
    c. Disney Brothers Studio
    d. animated cartoons

2. What do the major details describe?
    a. reasons why Walt Disney is successful
    b. the early influences on Walt Disney's art
    c. Walt Disney's background experience
    d. Disney's most memorable characters

3. What is the author's implied main idea? (What do the major details describe?)
    a. Never give up on your dreams.
    b. Walt Disney experienced failures before becoming successful.
    c. Walt Disney went to art school and started his own business.
    d. The Disney Brothers Studio created Mickey Mouse.

Practice

2. Read the following paragraph, and underline the major details. Then, answer the questions that follow.

After World War II, a Japanese artist named Tezuka Osamu was influenced by American cartoons, particularly those of Walt Disney. He brought his own artistic style to create *manga*, illustrated stories similar to American comic books. But Osamu created stories for all ages with themes of sorrow, anger, and hatred. In 1958, Osamu founded his own animation company and created the Mighty Atom character. When this character came to the United States in the 1960s, he became Astroboy, and the animé industry was born. Osamu's animé  style remains popular today, featuring characters with big eyes and rounded features. The success of animé sparked international interest, which soon brought more characters such as Pokemon, Speed Racer, and Akira to a worldwide stage. Animé is now one of the most popular forms of graphic novels in the world.

1. What is the topic?

   a. Tezuka Osamu

   b. manga

   c. the history of animé

   d. the comic industry

2. What do the major details describe?

   a. a list of animé characters

   b. how animé became popular internationally

   c. who started animé

   d. why animé is so popular

3. What is the author's implied main idea? (What do the major details describe?)

   a. The success of the Mighty Atom helped Tezuka Osamu to succeed in animé.

   b. Tezuka Osama was the father of modern manga and animé.

   c. Animé is now one of the most popular forms of graphic novels in the world.

   d. Internationally popular animé originated in Japan, with an artist named Tezuka Osamu.

Practice

3. Read the following paragraph, and underline the major details. Then, answer the questions that follow.

In the late 1800s, New Orleans was a thriving seaport that drew people from all around the world. Everywhere in the city was filled with many different styles of music from various cultures. Bands were very popular, and almost everyone played an instrument, even those who couldn't read music. Band music was one of the first musical influences on early jazz. Another popular style of music was "ragging." This means playing a melody in an off-beat style. Ragging had its roots in Africa and developed into "ragtime," another influence on early jazz. A third influence on jazz was the blues. The blues came from early African-American spiritual music and followed a simple four-chord pattern. Jazz developed from these three styles of music, using the off-beat rhythms of ragtime, the melodies and instruments of band music, and the feel of the blues.

1. What is the topic?

   a. music

   b. the blues

   c. influences on jazz

   d. jazz

2. What do the major details describe?

   a. the history of jazz

   b. why New Orleans is known for jazz

   c. music in New Orleans

   d. the styles of music that influenced jazz

3. What is the author's implied main idea? (What do the major details describe?)

   a. There are many styles of music in New Orleans.

   b. Jazz is a form of the blues.

   c. The history of jazz is interesting.

   d. The history of jazz shows that it developed from three styles of music.

TEXTBOOK SELECTION

Read the following textbook selection, and underline the major details. Then, answer the questions that follow.

genre (ZSHAN-rah): a type or variety of something.

The evolution of the horror film demonstrates how **genre** conventions change. Old conventions become exhausted, and filmmakers search for new ones in their never-ending challenge to retain the interest of the audience. Horror films of the 1930s and 1940s portrayed the monster using an actor in (often brilliant) makeup, whereas contemporary films often use computer-based special effects to visualize the creatures. Moreover, horror films during their golden age tended to end on a very comforting note. The monster was destroyed, and the romantic couple reached safety unharmed. Horror often was left to the viewer's imagination in contrast with the graphic gore of modern films, which use contemporary effects technology to visualize the elaborate violence that is now basic in the genre. (In this respect, *The Blair Witch Project* [1999], *The Sixth Sense* [1999], and *The Others* [2001], all of which work through suggestion rather than graphic violence, are a return to the golden age of horror.)

By the 1970s and 1980s, in such films as *Halloween* and the never-ending *Nightmare on Elm Street* and *Friday the 13th* series, the monster became indestructible and undefeatable. These monsters—Freddy, Jason, Michael Myers of the *Halloween* films, and the aliens in the *Alien* series—remain alive at the end of each episode, and viewers know they will come back again to haunt and terrify. Contemporary horror films, therefore, are more disturbing and unsettling than horror was in previous decades, when narrative traditions insisted that normality be restored and secure at film's end. The monsters today are everywhere, and they cannot be defeated, a perception that the narrative design of contemporary horror emphasizes.

QUESTIONS

1. **What is the topic?**
   a. horror films
   b. why horror films are popular
   c. the evolution of horror films
   d. famous horror films

2. **What do the major details describe?**
   a. a history of horror films
   b. the differences between horror films of the past and present
   c. famous monsters
   d. the best horror movies ever made

3. **What is the author's implied main idea? (What do the major details describe?)**
   a. Monsters in horror films are more frightening than ever before.
   b. The evolution of horror films has changed these movies into something more disturbing and uncertain.
   c. People want horror films to be scarier than they used to be.
   d. The evolution of the horror film demonstrates how genre conventions change.

407

U-Review

For each of the following sentences, write "T" if the statement is true or "F" if the statement is false. As you go over the answers with your team, discuss why the false statements were false.

1. .... Implied main ideas are usually found at the beginning of a paragraph.

2. .... Implied main ideas are found by looking for the idea most often repeated.

3. .... An implied main idea is not stated and must be formed by the reader.

4. .... To find the implied main idea, focus on the topic and major supporting details.

5. .... A question to ask when finding the implied main idea is, "What are the major details telling me about the topic?"

RECOGNIZING STATED MAIN IDEAS AND IMPLIED MAIN IDEAS

How do you know when an author has stated the main idea or implied it? To help you become more adept at knowing the difference, study the following examples.

Read the following paragraph, and then answer the questions that follow. The major details have been underlined.

Cubism is a form of modern art that is **abstract** and uses geometric shapes and forms. This form of art was introduced by Pablo Picasso and Georges Braque in Paris between 1907 and 1914. Picasso was influenced by the African art that he viewed in the Palais de Trocadero in Paris. The "cubes" in his paintings often represent figures, suggest a scene, or emphasize an emotion. The construction of a cubist painting is something like cutting up a traditional painting into geometric sections, and then reassembling it onto a canvas. Many other artists also adopted this style of modern art, which had a significant influence on 20th century art and sculpture.

What is the topic?

....

In your own words, what is the main idea?

....

....

....

....

....

Notice that the first sentence introduces the topic and defines the term cubism. All of the other sentences tell you more about the topic, so it is the topic sentence. It is broad and general enough to include all of the details that follow. In paragraphs where the details describe a term, the definition is often the topic sentence. As you read the next paragraph, look for a general statement that summarizes or makes a point about the topic (the major details have been underlined).

In New York City, Latino Americans and African Americans created a new style of music and dance that grew out of deejaying, called "hip hop." DJs created strong rhythms by moving a vinyl record back and forth on a turntable in a rhythmical beat. They also used microphones to accompany the beat with rhythmic rhymes, which became known as rapping. Rap developed in the street parties of the Bronx, and, by the late 1970s, rap gained media attention. It was popularized by rappers such as Kool Herc and The Furious Five. By the mid-1980s, rap music artists made social statements about poverty, violence, drugs, and sex. Hip hop is now a global culture, giving youth a voice to express their ideas and to challenge traditions and old ideas.

What is the topic?

....

Notice that the paragraph lacks a general statement that summarizes the details about the topic, hip hop. It begins with a major detail about how hip hop originated and moves to other details about how it grew to be a worldwide music style. Because no broad statement summarizes the topic or states an important general point about it, you must infer the main idea.

Which of these statements expresses the implied main idea?

- **a.** Hip hop became a famous cultural style of music in the 1970s.
- **b.** Hip hop was made popular by rappers.
- **c.** Hip hop music grew out of deejaying techniques.
- **d.** Hip hop began as a music and dance style that became a worldwide culture.

To determine if a sentence is a major detail or a topic sentence, ask yourself, "Does this provide a specific fact or detail, or is it a general description of the major details?" If the sentence provides a specific fact or detail about the topic, it is either a major or a minor detail. A general description or a general point about most of the major details is the topic sentence, or stated main idea.

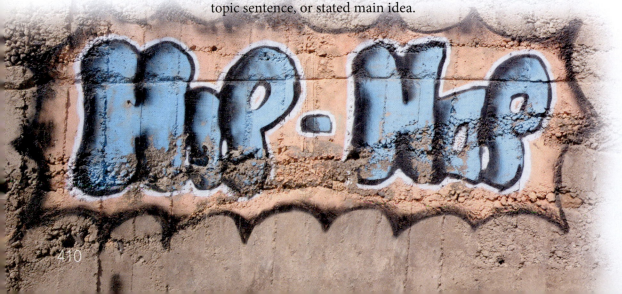

Practice

1. Read the following paragraph, and underline the major details. Then, answer the questions that follow.

prestigious
(pres-TEEJ-us):
highly respected;
honored

One of the world's most **prestigious** film festivals is the Cannes Film Festival, which is held every year in Cannes (pronounced "kan"), France. Each year, filmmakers from around the world submit their works to the judges at the festival, hoping to win a "golden palm" for the best film. Like the Oscars, the Cannes festival bestows awards in many different categories, such as Best Short Film, Best Director, and Best Student Film. For 13 days in May of each year, hundreds of films are shown. Many movie stars attend this famous event, taking time out to pose for photographers and reporters. Filmmakers hope that their films will not only win awards but be sold to distributors who will market their films all over the world.

1. What is the topic?
   a. Cannes
   b. Cannes Film Festival
   c. filmmakers hoping to win awards
   d. filmmakers

2. What do most of the major details describe?
   a. how filmmakers win awards at Cannes
   b. what kinds of awards are given at Cannes
   c. why filmmakers go to Cannes
   d. what the Cannes Film Festival is

3. Is the main idea stated or implied?
   a. stated
   b. implied

4. Which of the following sentences best states the main idea (either stated in the paragraph or implied)?
   a. One of the world's most prestigious film festivals is the Cannes Film Festival, which is held every year in Cannes, France.
   b. Each year, filmmakers from around the world submit their works to the judges at the festival, hoping to win a "golden palm" for the best film.
   c. Filmmakers hope that their films will not only win awards but be sold to distributors who will market their films all over the world.
   d. The Cannes Film Festival is attended by filmmakers and entertainers from all over the world.

Practice

documentary: a film that attempts to document, or record, a real event or subject

2. Read the following paragraph, and underline the major details. Then, answer the questions that follow.

Two University of Central Florida film school students decided to make a horror movie in a **documentary** style. Daniel Myrick and Eduardo Sanchez used their credit cards to finance the $22,000 project. Three unknown actors played college students who became lost in a Maryland woods while seeking the legendary Blair Witch. The murderous Blair Witch, which the audience never does get to see, lurks in the woods at night. The suspense and terror that the film created made this an amazingly compelling movie. *The Blair Witch Project* captured much attention at the Sundance Film Festival in Utah. Later, it was bought for $1.1 million. It soon became an international blockbuster, racking up $250 million in sales, making it the most profitable independent film in American history.

1. What is the topic?

    a. the legend of the Blair Witch

    b. *The Blair Witch Project* movie

    c. Daniel Myrick and Eduardo Sanchez

    d. the most profitable independent film in American history

2. What do most of the major details describe?

    a. how frightening the movie was

    b. why the movie was so successful

    c. how two film school students made a successful movie

    d. who made the movie

3. Is the main idea stated or implied?

    a. stated

    b. implied

4. Which of the following sentences best states the main idea (either stated in the paragraph or implied)?

    a. Two University of Central Florida film school students decided to make a horror movie in a documentary style.

    b. Three unknown actors played college students who become lost in a Maryland woods while seeking the legendary Blair Witch.

    c. It soon became an international blockbuster, racking up $250 million in sales, making it the most profitable independent film in American history.

    d. Two college film school students made a very successful horror movie, *The Blair Witch Project,* on a small budget.

Practice

3. Read the following paragraph, and underline the major details. Then, answer the questions that follow.

Vincent van Gogh (1853–1890)

At the age of 16, Vincent van Gogh (van-GO) worked for an art dealer and did sketching and watercolors as a hobby. Because he suffered from depression, he couldn't hold a job, so his brother Theo suggested that he take up a career in art. Van Gogh studied art and began painting in oils. Over the years, van Gogh fell deeper into mental illness and had hallucinations. During an argument with painter Paul Gauguin (go-GAN), he cut off part of his own ear. Van Gogh went into a mental hospital for treatment, and there he painted *The Starry Night*. Van Gogh began to receive recognition as a painter, but his success did not improve his mental condition. He committed suicide at the age of 37, leaving behind some of the most celebrated paintings in art history.

1. What is the topic?

   a. Vincent van Gogh's art

   b. how van Gogh lost his ear

   c. van Gogh's mental illness

   d. how van Gogh became an artist

2. What do most of the major details describe?

   a. the life of van Gogh

   b. the art of van Gogh

   c. van Gogh's mental illness

   d. why van Gogh was famous

3. Is the main idea stated or implied?

   a. stated

   b. implied

4. Which of the following sentences best states the main idea (either stated in the paragraph or implied)?

   a. Throughout his life, painter Vincent van Gogh struggled with mental illness.

   b. Because he suffered from depression, he couldn't hold a job, so his brother Theo suggested that he take up a career in art.

   c. Van Gogh was the painter who created *The Starry Night*.

   d. He committed suicide at the age of 37, leaving behind some of the most celebrated paintings in art history.

TEXTBOOK SELECTION

Read the following textbook selection, and underline the major details. Then, answer the questions that follow.

Frank Lloyd Wright remains one of the greatest American artists in any medium. His primary message stressed the relationship of architecture to its setting, a lesson that some modern architects seem to have forgotten. Wright's buildings appear to grow out of their environment.

One of his most inventive designs—the Kaufmann House, also known as "Falling Water," at Bear Run, Pennsylvania, built in 1936–1937—projects out over a waterfall with exciting, dramatic imagery. "Falling Water" erupts out of its natural rock site, and its beige concrete terraces blend tastefully with the colors of the surrounding stone. Wright has successfully blended two seemingly contrasting styles: the house stays a part of its environment, yet it has the rectangular design, which Wright usually opposed. He has taken those geometric boxes and made them harmonize with their natural surroundings. Wright's great asset and greatest fault was his insistence on using his own ideas. This meant he could work only with clients who would bend to his wishes. So, unlike many architects whose designs are influenced by the client, what Wright built remained Wright's, and Wright's only.

(From *Creative Impulse: An Introduction to the Arts,* 8e by Dennis J. Sporre. Copyright © by Dennis J. Sporre. Reprinted by permission of Pearson Education, Inc., Upper Saddle River, NJ.)

QUESTIONS

1. **What is the topic?**
   a. Falling Water
   b. Frank Lloyd Wright
   c. Frank Lloyd Wright's architecture designs
   d. architecture

2. **What do most of the major details describe?**
   a. Frank Lloyd Wright's life
   b. Frank Lloyd Wright's architectural style
   c. Falling Water
   d. how Frank Lloyd Wright became a famous architect

3. **Is the main idea stated or implied?**
   a. stated
   b. implied

4. Which of the following sentences best states the main idea (either stated in the paragraph or implied)?

a. Frank Lloyd Wright remains one of the greatest American architects in any medium.

b. Wright's buildings appear to grow out of their environment.

c. One of his most inventive designs—the Kaufmann House, also known as "Falling Water," at Bear Run, Pennsylvania, built in 1936–1937—projects out over a waterfall with exciting, dramatic imagery.

d. Wright has successfully blended two seemingly contrasting styles: the house stays a part of its context, yet it has the rectangular design, which Wright usually opposed.

THE CENTRAL POINT

> A **central point** is the main idea of a reading selection that is longer than one paragraph.

A **central point** is the main idea of a reading selection that is longer than one paragraph. A central point may also be called a *thesis statement* or a *central idea*. It's the most important point that the author makes about the topic. Like a main idea, the central point may be stated or implied. It is always a complete sentence and never a question. It usually names or refers to the topic and makes a broad, general point about it. To find the central point, first find the main idea of each paragraph. These will provide the main points the author is making in the essay as a whole. Sometimes the topic sentence of the first paragraph will also act as the central point of the entire reading selection. Read the following example paragraphs, and then see how they are broken down into their main ideas and central point.

> Reggae ("REG-gay") music started in Jamaica in the 1960s, and is characterized by its off-beat rhythms. It has its origins in rhythm and blues, jazz, blues, calypso, and other styles of music. Because of its themes of love, sexuality, social issues, and political issues, reggae soon became popular in other countries around the world. The word "reggae" comes from *regerege*, which means "rags" or "tattered clothing."
>
> The first reggae hit in America was American artist Johnny Nash's "Hold Me Tight" in 1968. The ever-popular British band the Beatles picked up on the reggae style and recorded their own song, "Ob-La-Di, Ob-La-Da." The most famous reggae band was The Wailers, featuring Bob Marley. Bob Marley became the most well-known reggae musician, earning 11 different awards, including a Grammy Lifetime Achievement Award, his name in the Rock and Roll Hall of Fame, and a star on the Hollywood Walk of Fame. In the United Kingdom, British rocker Eric Clapton recorded Bob Marley's song, "I Shot the Sheriff," which helped to bring reggae into popular music around the world.

Main idea of the first paragraph:
(implied) Reggae music started in Jamaica in the 1960s and soon became popular around the world.

Main idea of the second paragraph:
(implied) Notable musicians made reggae music popular worldwide.

Central point:
Jamaican reggae music owes its popularity to the musicians who made it famous worldwide.

Practice

1. Read the following paragraphs, underline the major details, and then answer the questions that follow.

Creative individuals who enjoy art may become graphic designers. Using art materials or computers, they illustrate ideas or objects. Graphic designers create visual images for publications or Web sites. Their goal is to make an idea or product look appealing and interesting to their audience.

Industrial designers make cars, tools, appliances, entertainment systems, and other devices more beautiful and practical to use. They choose the shape, style, and feel of objects to make them look as good as they work. Industrial designers work with engineers to create products that will function well and attract buyers.

Interior designers bring the elements of furniture, lighting, décor, and space together in a pleasing and functional way. Interior designers create not only home environments but also public spaces such as stores, airports, restaurants, hotels, and office buildings. Interior designers usually specialize in one type of environment, such as residential or commercial space. Good design has a powerful impact on humans, affecting the way they think and feel in an environment.

1. What is the topic?

   a. artists

   b. designers

   c. graphic designers

   d. creative individuals

2. What is the main idea of the first paragraph?

   a. Creative individuals who enjoy art may become graphic designers.

   b. Using art materials or computers, they illustrate ideas or objects.

   c. Graphic designers create visual images for publications or Web sites.

   d. Their goal is to make an idea or product look appealing and interesting to their audience.

3. What is the main idea of the third paragraph?

   a. Interior designers bring the elements of furniture, lighting, décor, and space together in a pleasing and functional way.

   b. Interior designers create not only home environments but also public spaces such as stores, airports, restaurants, hotels, and office buildings.

   c. Interior designers usually specialize in one type of environment, such as residential or commercial space.

   d. Good design has a powerful impact on humans, affecting the way they think and feel in an environment.

Practice

4. **What is the central point of the selection (either stated in the reading or implied)?**

   a. Creative individuals who enjoy art may become graphic designers.

   b. Industrial designers make cars, tools, appliances, entertainment systems, and other devices more beautiful and practical to use.

   c. Designers make images, objects, and living spaces more beautiful and functional.

   d. Good design has a powerful impact on humans, affecting the way they think and feel in an environment.

2. Read the following paragraphs, underline the major details, and then answer the questions that follow.

Each year, the members of the National Academy of Recording Arts and Sciences, also known as the Recording Academy, recognize individuals with an award known as "the Grammy." Throughout the year, record companies and members of the Recording Academy suggest names of people who they think should be considered for an award. There are more than 100 categories of awards given to musicians, producers, engineers, and recording professionals. The members of the academy select the winners based on their artistic achievement and excellence in the recording industry. The winners are not based on record sales or chart position in the top 100 songs of the year.

The Recording Academy originated in 1957 for the purpose of improving culture through music. There are now 12 chapters throughout the United States with thousands of members. To be considered for membership in the academy, an applicant must be credited on at least six tracks of any album. Applicants must also be recommended by two other voting members of the academy.

1. **What is the topic of the first paragraph?**

   a. the National Academy of Recording Arts and Sciences

   b. how to win a Grammy award

   c. the Grammy award

   d. the Recording Academy

2. **What do most of the major details in the first paragraph describe?**

   a. why Grammy awards are given

   b. who wins the Grammy awards

   c. what the Grammy award is

   d. where the Grammy award is given

3. **Is the central point of the entire reading stated or implied?**

   a. stated

   b. implied

4. What is the central point of the selection (either stated in the reading or implied)?

   a. The National Academy of Recording Arts monitors the quality of music.

   b. To be considered for membership in the academy, an applicant must be credited on at least six tracks of any album.

   c. Throughout the year, record companies and members of the Recording Academy suggest names of people who they think should be considered for an award.

   d. Each year, the members of the National Academy of Recording Arts and Sciences, also known as the Recording Academy, recognize individuals who have achieved the admiration of their peers and give them a very special award known as "the Grammy."

3. Read the following paragraphs, underline the major details, and then answer the questions that follow.

In the valley of the Vezere River in France, just outside of a small town, a group of children played among the caves. No one knew about the amazing treasures hidden in the Lascaux (lahs-KOE) caves until the children explored them in 1940 and discovered cave paintings on the walls. Archaeologists determined the ancient paintings were made in 14,000–16,000 B.C. The caves were sealed in 1963 to prevent damage to the paintings from the atmosphere. Visitors to the caves today are shown exact copies in a nearby quarry.

The images in the original paintings show running herds of bulls, horses, and deer. The paintings are up to 12 feet high, and the artists who made them demonstrate their artistic ability to show the animals in motion. The paintings were done in a 30- by 100-foot mural over a long period of time by many artists. It is interesting to imagine how these artists painted them with simple materials working under the light of a flickering torch.

The paintings tell us more about these artists than their admiration for the power and beauty of animals. The magnificent cave paintings at Lascaux reveal the mind and soul of these people, who not only possessed artistic skill but the desire to create an image that would communicate the sights and sounds of the thundering herds.

(From *Creative Impulse: An Introduction to the Arts,* 8e by Dennis J. Sporre. Copyright © by Dennis J. Sporre. Reprinted by permission of Pearson Education, Inc., Upper Saddle River, NJ.)

1. What is the topic?
   a. the cave paintings at Lascaux
   b. ancient artists
   c. Lascaux, France
   d. animal paintings

Practice

2. **What is the topic sentence of the first paragraph?**

   a. In the valley of the Vezere River in France, just outside of a small town, a group of children played among the caves.

   b. No one knew about the amazing treasures hidden in the Lascaux (lahs-KOE) caves until the children explored them in 1940 and discovered cave paintings on the walls.

   c. Archaeologists determined the ancient paintings were made in 14,000–16,000 B.C.

   d. The caves were sealed in 1963 to prevent damage to the paintings from the atmosphere.

3. **What is the topic sentence of the second paragraph?**

   a. The images in the original paintings show running herds of bulls, horses, and deer.

   b. The paintings are up to 12 feet high, and the artists who made them demonstrate their artistic ability to show the animals in motion.

   c. The paintings were done in a 30- by 100-foot mural over a long period of time by many artists.

   d. It is interesting to imagine how these artists painted them with simple materials working under the light of a flickering torch.

4. **What is the central point of the selection?**

   a. In 1940, some children discovered ancient paintings on the walls of the caves of Lascaux, France.

   b. The paintings on the walls of the caves in Lascaux, France, were done by many artists more than 16,000 to 18,000 years ago.

   c. The magnificent cave paintings at Lascaux reveal the mind and soul of these people, who not only possessed artistic skill but the desire to create an image that would communicate the sights and sounds of the thundering herds.

   d. The paintings in the caves at Lascaux, France, are still on the walls and sealed from the damaging atmosphere.

TEXTBOOK SELECTION

Read the following selection, underline the topic sentences and major details, and then answer the questions that follow.

Pyramid building (circa 2,700 B.C.) produced the most remarkable structures of Egyptian civilization. Egypt's pyramids, the oldest existing buildings in the world, also rank among the world's largest structures. The largest stands taller than a 40-story building and covers an area greater than that of 10 football fields. More than 80 pyramids still exist, and their once smooth limestone surfaces hide secret passageways and rooms. The pyramids of ancient Egypt served a vital purpose: to protect the pharaohs' bodies after death. Each pyramid originally held not only a pharaoh's preserved body but also all the goods he would need in his life after death.

Egyptian pyramids typically contained a temple that was constructed a short distance from the pyramid and connected by a causeway. The most elaborate example of the temple appears at Giza (GEE-za), with the pyramids of three kings built close together. Beginning in the 10th century, the entire Giza **complex** served as a source of building materials for the construction of Cairo. As a result, all three pyramids were stripped of their original smooth outer facing of limestone.

The three pyramids at Giza have a carefully planned layout. Each stands along the north–south line of longitude, with the faces of the pyramids pointing directly north, south, east, and west. The larger two rise neatly along a southwest diagonal, with the third slightly offset and smaller. Scholars assume that this peculiar layout was a deliberate choice made by the architects, but the reasons for such a choice (if one existed) remain mysterious.

(From *Creative Impulse: An Introduction to the Arts*, 8e by Dennis J. Sporre. Copyright © by Dennis J. Sporre. Reprinted by permission of Pearson Education, Inc., Upper Saddle River, NJ.)

complex (KOM-plex): a group of structures that have a common purpose

QUESTIONS

1. What is the topic?

    a. pyramids

    b. the pyramids of Giza

    c. Egyptian pyramids

    d. Egyptian architecture

2. What is the topic sentence of the second paragraph?

    a. Egyptian pyramids typically contained a temple that was constructed a short distance from the pyramid and connected by a causeway.

    b. The most elaborate example of the temple appears at Giza (GEE-za), with the pyramids of three kings built close together.

    c. Beginning in the 10th century, the entire Giza complex served as a source of building materials for the construction of Cairo.

    d. As a result, all three pyramids were stripped of their original smooth outer facing of limestone.

3. **What is the topic sentence of the third paragraph?**

   a. The three pyramids at Giza have a carefully planned layout.

   b. Each stands along the north–south line of longitude, with the faces of the pyramids pointing directly north, south, east, and west.

   c. The larger two rise neatly along a southwest diagonal, with the third slightly offset and smaller.

   d. Scholars assume that this peculiar layout was a deliberate choice made by the architects, but the reasons for such a choice (if one existed) remain mysterious.

4. **What is the central point of the selection?**

   a. Pyramid building (circa 2,700 B.C.) produced the most remarkable structures of Egyptian civilization.

   b. Egypt's pyramids, the oldest existing buildings in the world, also rank among the world's largest structures.

   c. The three pyramids at Giza have a carefully planned layout.

   d. Egyptian pyramids typically contained a temple that was constructed a short distance from the pyramid and connected by a causeway.

U-Review

Answer the following questions, and then check your answers with another student.

1. What is an implied main idea? ....

....

2. What do you focus on when trying to figure out the implied main idea?

....

3. What question should you ask yourself to find the implied main idea?

....

4. What is a central point?

....

5. What should you do first to find the central point?

....

Reading 1 Vocabulary Preview

The following vocabulary words are from the article "My Best Role Ever!" With a partner or in a team, choose the correct meanings of the underlined words in the following sentences. Use context clues (LEADS), word part clues, and parts of speech to help you figure out the meanings.

1. While waiting for the nurse to insert the IV into my arm, I steeled (STEEL'd) myself for the pain.

   a. rededicated

   b. encouraged

   c. resisted

   d. braced

2. Our high school history teacher would say it is irony (EYE-ron-ee) that Jan graduated from college with a degree in history since he always skipped his high school history class.

   a. a bad situation

   b. the opposite of what you expect

   c. an incomplete sentence

   d. good advice

3. The date of the historic home that had just been renovated was listed as "circa (SIR-ka) 1750."

   a. around

   b. over

   c. since

   d. late

4. When Juan saw how upset his wife was over denting the car, his anger dissipated (DIS-i-pay-ted).

   a. increased

   b. enraged

   c. disappeared

   d. tentative

5. When she stays at her brother's house, Julia sleeps on a small pallet (PAL-et) on the floor.

   a. chair

   b. pillow

   c. mattress

   d. footstool

Reading 1

6. I was <u>dumbfounded</u> (dum-FOUND-ed) when I discovered that I had the winning lottery ticket to the $100,000 jackpot.

   a. knocked down

   b. speechless

   c. distressed

   d. devastated

7. Knowing there were few <u>prospects</u> (PRAH-spekts) for acting jobs in a small town like Garland, Nebraska, Giovanni decided to move to Los Angeles.

   a. ideas

   b. restitution

   c. agents who hire actors

   d. opportunities

8. To soothe the frightened, injured rabbit, Jenny spoke to it in <u>dulcet</u> (DULL-sit) tones and stroked its fur.

   a. soft and gentle

   b. careful

   c. sad

   d. loud

9. Sandra took some medicine and laid down on the sofa for an hour to <u>alleviate</u> (a-LEEV-ee-ate) her migraine headache.

   a. to strengthen

   b. undermine

   c. radiate

   d. to lessen the severity of

10. Even though she was tired, Heather <u>reluctantly</u> (re-LUCK-tant-lee) agreed to work an extra shift at the restaurant to cover for her friend.

    a. happily

    b. eagerly

    c. unwillingly

    d. realistically

Reading 1   What Do You Already Know?

1. Have you ever performed on stage before an audience? What did you do? How did you feel about the experience?

2. Would you ever consider acting as a career? Why or why not?

> **Directions:** As you read this article, practice the four-step reading process. Preview the article, and then write on the following lines one or two questions that you would hope to have answered.
>
> ....
>
> ....
>
> ....
>
> ....

As you read, answer the questions in the margins to check your comprehension.

"My Best Role Ever!"

BY MARCIA GAY HARDEN

From *Guideposts*, March 2008. Copyright © 2008 by Marcia Gay Harden. Reprinted by permission of Schreck Rose Dapello Adams and Hurwitz LLP.

Academy Award winner Marcia Gay Harden says that acting is really about connecting with people and making the right choices. In her story, she describes the time when her big chance finally came along, and she had to make a difficult choice. Should she turn down the biggest break in her career or break her promise to a child?

1   Look up "struggling young actress" in the dictionary, and you might see a picture of me, circa 1982. I rushed to open casting calls in between waiting tables and always worried about how to pay the rent. I was based in Washington, D.C., where I was waiting to get my Screen Actors Guild Union card. When I did, then I'd make the big move to New York City.

2   It was an uncertain time in my life, but one thing I was certain of: acting meant everything to me. From the first part I'd played in high school there was a quality about acting that made me feel in touch with

425

Reading 1

something big and mysterious and meaningful. It may sound funny, but when I was playing a role I connected with, I got the feeling that God was using me for something good. I felt like I was doing something I was truly meant to do. Of course, most days found me hustling through a pair of swinging restaurant doors with a stack of hot plates on my arm. And that was fine too. I was paying my dues, doing what all young actors did.

What was Marcia looking forward to doing?

3   One day, as I was finishing up a long hard lunch shift, I found myself in a particularly upbeat mood. The famous director, Oliver Stone, was coming to town to do a casting call for his upcoming movie *Born on the Fourth of July*, the story of paralyzed Vietnam War veteran Ron Kovic. The call was just for crowd-scene extras, but I didn't care. The way I figured, Oliver Stone would notice me, pull me out of the lineup, and, lo and behold, I'd have my big break.

4   Two women came in, sat down at a table in my section and smiled like they knew me when I came up to take their order. And they did. "We saw your performance in a play last week. You were wonderful! We'd like to offer you a job." I asked what the part was.

5   "Probably not what you think," the other woman said. "Snow White."

6   "Snow White? Where's the production?" I asked.

7   "Georgetown University Hospital," the first woman said. "We're from the Make-A-Wish Foundation. A seven-year-old girl named Bonnie is dying of pediatric cancer. She doesn't have much more than a month to live. Our foundation grants wishes to terminally ill children, and Bonnie's wish is to meet Snow White." I promised them I'd be available the day they needed me. I'm not a big fan of irony. So you can imagine how I felt two days later when one of the Make-A-Wish ladies called to give me the date for my appearance at the hospital. You guessed it. The same date as my big casting call.

8   "Couldn't you make it another day?" I asked, panicked.

9   "I'm sorry," she said. "Bonnie's running out of time."

10   I hung up and called the casting agency in charge of Oliver Stone's visit, asking if I could audition on another day.

11   "Oliver's only in town for that day," the casting director told me. "Marcia, this is a great opportunity. Whatever conflicts you have on that date, I'd advise you to find a way to reschedule them."

What problem is Marcia facing at this point?

12   I didn't sleep a wink that night. I had to make a decision. What was

right for me? Success had to be priority number one. It was as simple as that. They could get another Snow White. I might not get another prospect like this. I'd call first thing in the morning and cancel the hospital job. Yet it just didn't feel right. I'd promised to make a sick little girl's wish come true. How could I put ambition above that?

13   The next day I called the agency and told them I couldn't make the casting call. "I have another engagement I can't back out of," I said reluctantly.

14   By the day of my performance as Snow White, I was as ready as I'd ever been for any role I'd played in my life. The only problem was I kept bursting into tears. I was positive the casting call would've been my big break—my one chance to make it. And I was letting it go.

15   I must have been a curious sight as I made my way to Georgetown University Hospital. How many times do you see a weeping Snow White at the wheel of a yellow convertible VW Bug? On top of everything else, traffic was horrible. I got to the hospital late and flew in—stopping only to make one last call to the casting director to beg once more for a chance to reschedule. "No, Marcia," the agent said. "This is it."

How was Marcia feeling about her situation?

16   I hung up, asked for directions at the information desk, and went running for the elevator. Down at the end of a long hallway, a woman and a girl were standing outside the hospital room: Bonnie's mother and 12-year-old sister. Bonnie's mom recognized me and greeted me with a big hug. Then she handed me a bag with some toys in it. "If you don't mind, I thought it would be nice if Snow White gave Bonnie some presents. She's having a bad day, but she's looking forward to this so much."

17   "Sure," I said, taking the bag of toys. Then I took a deep breath and steeled myself—the way I do before every performance—and walked into the room. What I found stopped me cold. All my qualms about whether this was the right thing to do dissipated. I'd been prepared to meet a sick girl. But the girl sitting on a pallet on the floor was so small and thin. I knew Bonnie was seven, but she barely looked five. Bonnie raised her eyes and stared at me. Her pale face lit up like a candy store. "Snow White!" she cried.

Why was Marcia shocked when she entered Bonnie's room?

18   I stood there dumbfounded. *Come on*, something inside me said, *pull it together. You know what you're here for*. Then something clicked. I wasn't just a struggling actress playing Snow White. I *was* Snow White.

19   "Hello, Bonnie!" I said in dulcet tones, "I'm so glad to see you! I'm

Reading 1

so sorry that Grumpy and Sneezy and Doc (I named all seven) weren't able to make it!" We talked for a while. I told her all about the handsome prince and gave her the gifts.

20   "Snow White?" Bonnie said, grabbing my hand.

21   "Yes, Bonnie?"

22   "When I die, will the prince kiss me and then I'll wake up again?"

23   The room fell silent. How do you answer a child's question like that? It had never struck me that Bonnie wanted to meet Snow White to answer a life-after-death question. What could I say to this brave, beautiful, honest girl? I closed my eyes for a second and tried to imagine what Bonnie must be feeling. How lonely it must be to be this young and this sick.

24   "No, Bonnie," I said, "it's even better. When you go to heaven, God will kiss you and then you'll wake up again."

25   You remember what I was saying earlier about how the real mystery of acting came when I was playing a role I knew I was meant to play? Well, at that moment in that hospital room with Bonnie, I got that feeling. I got it like I had never gotten it before in my life. I knew that I was exactly where I was meant to be, playing exactly the role I was meant to play.

What did Marcia learn from Bonnie?

26   Bonnie died just a week later. Was I able to <u>alleviate</u> her passing? Hopefully, I was part of that plan. And Bonnie was definitely part of the plan for me. She taught me that acting is about connecting, not about union cards and red carpets and ambition. Eventually I got my SAG card and moved up to New York City. After a couple more years of acting classes, waitressing, living in shoddy apartments and all the rest of that stuff, I got my big break. Two directors, Joel and Ethan Coen, cast me in their movie *Miller's Crossing*. I was on my way.

27   Later, I received an Academy Award for my work as the painter Jackson Pollock's wife, Lee Krasner, in Ed Harris's film *Pollock*. I also played the mother of Chris McCandless in the film *Into the Wild*. I had wonderful roles in wonderful movies. Roles that, while I was playing them, made me *know* I was where I was meant to be, and that all the struggle and uncertainty was for a reason. It's a wonderful feeling.

1,452 words divided by _____ minutes = _____ words per minute

Reading 1 Thinking About What You Read

It is a good habit to summarize everything you read to strengthen your comprehension.

Directions: On the following lines, write a two- or three-sentence summary of the article "My Best Role Ever!" In your own words, describe what the article was about and why the author wrote it.

....

....

....

....

....

....

429

Reading 1 Comprehension Questions

The following questions will help you to recall the main idea and the details of "My Best Role Ever!" Review any parts of the article that you need to find the correct answers.

LITERAL COMPREHENSION

1. What is the topic of this article?
   a. the best role an actress ever played
   b. Bonnie
   c. a tough decision actress Marcia Gay Harden had to make
   d. an actress's career

MAIN IDEA

2. What is the central point (main idea) of the entire article?
   a. An actress played Snow White for a dying girl.
   b. Marcia Gay Harden gave up an opportunity for a role in a movie to play Snow White to a dying girl.
   c. Marcia Gay Harden worked hard to become an actress and finally got her chance.
   d. Marcia Gay Harden worked her way up to become an Academy Award–winning actress.

SUPPORTING DETAILS

3. At the time of the story, why was Marcia waiting to move from Washington, D.C., to New York City?
   a. because there were no acting jobs available in New York City
   b. because she had family in Washington, D.C.
   c. because she was waiting to get her Screen Actors Guild Union card
   d. because she didn't have enough money to move to New York City

DRAWING CONCLUSIONS

4. Why was Marcia crying when she drove to the hospital to see Bonnie?
   a. because she wished that she had not agreed to play the part of Snow White
   b. because she feared that she would disappoint Bonnie
   c. because she felt she had given up her only chance to get a part in a movie with a famous director
   d. because she had lied to Bonnie's mother about wanting to play Snow White

5. Why did Marcia believe that she was meant to be an actress?
   a. After she performed in a high school play, her teacher and director told her she was meant to be on the stage.
   b. She always studied her part and was well prepared for her roles.
   c. Her parents had encouraged her to become an actress.
   d. She felt something special when she was playing a part that she knew she was meant to play.

Reading 1

6. What did Marcia mean when she said, "Then something clicked. I wasn't just a struggling actress playing Snow White. I was Snow White"?

   a. She believed that she was the real Snow White.

   b. To Bonnie, she was the real Snow White and knew she had to become that person for her.

   c. She wanted to be like the Snow White in the fairy tale.

   d. She turned into Snow White.

PATTERNS OF
ORGANIZATION

7. Identify the relationship within the following sentence: After a couple more years of acting classes, waitressing, living in shoddy apartments, and all the rest of that stuff, I got my big break.

   a. time order

   b. listing

   c. compare and/or contrast

   d. cause and effect

8. Identify the relationship between the following sentences: I'd call first thing in the morning and cancel the hospital job. Yet it just didn't feel right.

   a. time order

   b. spatial order

   c. compare and/or contrast

   d. cause and effect

9. What is the overall pattern of organization for the entire article?

   a. listing

   b. addition

   c. compare and/ or contrast

   d. time order

VOCABULARY IN
CONTEXT

10. Identify the meaning of the underlined word in the following sentence: All my qualms about whether this was the right thing to do dissipated.

   a. doubts

   b. potential

   c. suspicions

   d. intentions

Reading 1 Vocabulary Practice

Use the vocabulary words from the Word Bank to complete the following sentences. Write the words into the blanks provided.

> **WORD BANK**
>
> | irony | circa | steeled | dissipated | pallet |
> |---|---|---|---|---|
> | dumbfounded | prospect | dulcet | alleviate | reluctantly |

1. By finishing his degree, Sean felt he would have a better .... for getting the job he wanted.

2. Darla's hopes for getting a full scholarship .... when she saw her failing grade in algebra.

3. When my best friend confessed that she had secretly been dating my boyfriend, I was totally ....

4. The new mother held her baby snugly and, singing in a(n) .... voice, rocked him to sleep.

5. It was just .... that Wanda, who never really liked high school, became a high school teacher.

6. The ancient ruins were so old that no one had an exact date of their construction, but archaeologists believe they were built .... 100 B.C.

7. I .... agreed to babysit for my older sister's kids because I knew they could be difficult to handle.

8. Whenever we go to the mountains to camp, I usually sleep on a(n) .... made from a pillowcase stuffed with pine needles.

9. Sonia tried to .... her aunt's loneliness by visiting her at least once every week.

10. Jenny .... herself to face the possibility that she might not have gotten a part in the play.

Questions for Writing and Discussion

Review any parts of the article you need to answer the following questions.

1. What had led Marcia to believe that she was meant to be an actress?

Reading 1

2. Why do you think Marcia decided to go through with her decision to play Snow White?

....

....

....

....

3. Describe a time when you had to give up something you wanted to do in order to do something for someone else. How did you feel about it afterward?

....

....

....

....

4. Like many successful people, Marcia had "paid her dues" by working as a waitress for more than two years while trying to achieve success. Do you feel there is such a thing as an "overnight sensation" (meaning someone becomes instantly famous without first having to suffer disappointment and failure)? Why or why not?

....

....

....

....

5. Describe a time when you had to speak or perform in front of a crowd. What did you do? Were you nervous? Describe what happened.

....

....

....

....

Reading 1 Vocabulary Practice—Word Drawing Game

Get together in groups of four or five people.

1. Each group should write the following vocabulary words on 10 slips of paper. Fold them in half, and put them into an envelope or container. Mix them well.

irony	circa
steeled	dissipated
pallet	dumbfounded
prospect	dulcet
alleviate	reluctantly

2. Create two teams of people within each group, with at least two people on each team.

3. One person from each team will draw five slips of paper. Do not read them.

4. One person (the artist) on the first team will select one of the slips and draw a picture on a piece of paper to represent the idea or an example of the word on the slip. The artist may include a few words on the drawing, but no form of the word, definitions, or word clues to the definition may be used.

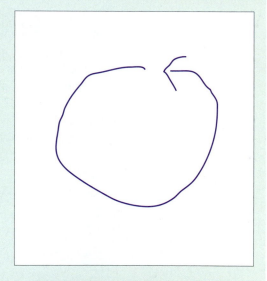

5. The person who draws the word will show the drawing to his or her partner. The partner has one minute to guess the word shown in the drawing. The other team will keep time and keep score.

6. If the partner correctly names the word, the team receives one point. If the answer is incorrect or not given by the time one minute is up, no points are awarded.

7. The second team will select a new slip of paper. The artist from that team will draw a clue, and the partner will try to guess it while the first team keeps time and the score.

8. Each of the members on a team should take turns being the artist.

9. When all of the words have been drawn, the team with the most points wins.

Reading 2 Vocabulary Preview

The following vocabulary words are from the article "The Many Miracles of Mark Hicks." With a partner or in a team, choose the meanings of the underlined words in the following sentences. Use context clues (LEADS), word part clues, and parts of speech to help you figure out the meanings.

1. At the end of the semester, a large portion of their grades in art class were based on the students' portfolios (port-FOL-ee-oes).
   a. essays
   b. notebooks
   c. collection of works
   d. artwork

2. A skiing accident made Shawna a quadriplegic (quad-rih-PLEE-gic), but she is determined to lead a productive life and keep a positive attitude, even without the use of any of her limbs.
   a. paralyzed in the legs
   b. paralyzed in the arms
   c. handicapped
   d. paralyzed from the neck down

3. I was intrigued (in-TREE-g'd) by Mr. Stone's offer to help me get my business started and wondered what he would do to help.
   a. made curious
   b. tricked
   c. suspicious
   d. excited

4. Shawna's spinal cord was severed (SEV-erd) when she skied into a tree and tumbled down the icy slopes.
   a. dented
   b. separated
   c. sprained
   d. twisted

5. The old man couldn't help but chuckle at the little girl's disarming (dis-ARM-ing) smile as she handed him a flower.
   a. causing friendliness
   b. removing danger
   c. resentful
   d. silly

Reading 2

6. At the campaign rally, Senator Johnson gave an <u>impassioned</u> (im-PASH-un'd) speech about the rights of every citizen to speak freely.

   a. romantic

   b. with love

   c. sexy

   d. showing strong feelings

7. Although the city had several million dollars in an account, those funds were <u>earmarked</u> (EER-mark'd) to build a new expressway.

   a. specially marked

   b. set aside for a purpose

   c. ragged

   d. put under

8. Gina helped Huang <u>transpose</u> (trans-POZE) her notes for her speech into a more logical order.

   a. to rearrange

   b. to edit

   c. to change from one language into another

   d. to transfer

9. The drowning victim had <u>aspirated</u> (AS-per-a-ted) so much water into his lungs that the EMTs didn't know if he would make it to the hospital alive.

   a. inspired

   b. absorbed

   c. expelled

   d. inhaled

10. At the art gallery, we purchased several signed <u>lithographs</u> (LITH-o-grafs) by Jan Stussy, and we donated them to the college library.

    a. paintings

    b. printed copies of artwork

    c. copies

    d. pages

Reading 2 What Do You Already Know?

1. Have you known anyone with a handicapping condition? Describe the challenges this person faced.

2. Describe something you tried to do that seemed impossible, and tell how you solved the problem.

> Directions: As you read this story, practice the four-step reading process. Preview the article, and then write on the following lines one or two questions that you would hope to have answered.
>
> ....
>
> ....
>
> ....
>
> ....
>
> ....

As you read, answer the questions in the margins to check your comprehension.

"The Many Miracles of Mark Hicks"

BY JAN STUSSY

From *Reader's Digest*, July 1980. Copyright © 1980 by the Reader's Digest Association, Inc. Reprinted by permission of *Reader's Digest*.

The author of the following article was a successful artist and professor of art at the University of California at Los Angeles. Then one day, a special student came into his class and changed his life. What important lesson did he learn from his most unforgettable student?

1   Eight years ago, I was reviewing the art portfolios of applying students in my studio classroom on the campus of the University of California at Los Angeles. My secretary approached me with a special request from a quadriplegic student who wished to join my class in life drawing. "He draws by holding the pencil in his teeth," she said.

2   "That's crazy!" I replied. "It's tough enough to learn with skilled hands, but to try to draw with your mouth is. . . impossible. My answer is *No*!"

437

Reading 2

3   When I turned back to the portfolios of the waiting students, accepting some and rejecting others on the merits of their ability as draftsmen, my secretary added another student's portfolio to the pile. The work was above average in skill, and the drawings intrigued me.

4   "Yes," I said, "I'll accept this student."

5   Before I could say another word, the quadriplegic flashed past me in his wheelchair, turned, and stopped—facing the suddenly quiet class and a red-faced professor.

6   I tried not to look at him as I explained to the class (but mostly to him) that the work was going to be very hard for all of them (especially him) and now was the time to withdraw if anyone (*anyone!*) had second thoughts. Two students left, but those serious eyes from the wheelchair didn't even blink. I dismissed the class and asked the young man to remain.

7   In a soft, quiet voice, 23-year-old Mark Hicks told me that when he was 12 he fell from a tree house in his back yard in Manhattan Beach, California. "It was nobody's fault," he said calmly. "I just fell." The accident severed his spinal column, causing permanent paralysis from the neck down.

8   Mark had drawn before his accident. Slowly, he began to sketch again, and later he taught himself to paint with oils by holding the tools clenched in his teeth. He developed very strong jaw muscles. "If all my muscles were as strong as my jaws," he remarked with disarming good humor, "I could lift up this building."

9   Perfecting his drawing, for Mark, was like learning to fly. Through it, he could escape from his body into the make-believe world of his mind. He worked with a tutor at home to complete high school and then went to a junior college to major in art and to develop his skill as a draftsman.

10   Mark did not think of himself as pitiful, so he was not embarrassed. He simply was what he was. He accepted his limitations and worked beyond his capacities, setting an example and inspiring other students. True, I was his teacher—but in a larger sense, he was mine.

11   His impact on me and the class was so dramatic and useful that I resolved to capture him on film. I wanted to show other people how courage and spirit can achieve great things in spite of all odds. I had never made a film, but if Mark could draw, I could make a movie.

12   I wrote an impassioned letter to my dean telling him how I wanted to make a short documentary so others could share what we found in Mark. The dean was so moved that he sent a check for $6000 from funds earmarked for special projects. It was the first of many unbelievable miracles.

Reading 2

13   Mark knew a student, John Joseph, in the UCLA cinema department, who wanted to make a film for his senior project. We joined forces. Four other talented students soon joined us. We rented cameras, tripods, sound equipment, and lights, and shot Mark as he lived his life. No real story, no firm plot. We filmed his father getting him out of bed, sitting him in his chair and brushing his teeth. We followed his mother cooking food and feeding it to him. We shot his attendant putting him into his van and driving him to school. We photographed him in my life-drawing class, going to exhibits, parties, and back to the hospital.

14   The high point of the movie came about when my gallery director—unaware that Mark made his pictures with his teeth—saw his paintings and offered to give Mark a one-man exhibition. We followed Mark's van to San Francisco and documented the opening of his show, the reception party, and the highly successful exhibit. Mark sat among his pictures enjoying one of the happiest moments of his life. "I reached my goal," he said. "And I did it sitting down."

What goal did Mark reach?

15   At that point we ran out of money and film. In our enthusiasm, we had spent the entire $6000 and had shot 64 rolls of expensive color film. Not a dime was left to develop it. It was excruciating to have that huge stack of film and not be able to see what we had done. It was, said Mark, "like being pregnant, forever."

16   Hat in hand and trembling nervously, I called on Paul Flaherty, chief executive at the Technicolor laboratory. When I told him about Mark and the film project, he offered to develop and print 15 rolls as a charitable gesture. So I sent 30. If the miracle was going to work, we might just as well go for 30.

17   About a month later, Flaherty called: "That film is very, very good. Can I meet Mark?"

18   We wheeled Mark in the next day. After 35 minutes of conversation, Flaherty promised to develop the remaining 34 rolls—again for free. The miracles were holding.

19   But we were still broke. We had editing to do and sound tapes to transpose and music to score and inserts and titles to make and a final print to get. We needed more money. I wrote a letter describing our project and offering one of Mark's lithographs for a $200 donation, or a set of one of his and one of mine for $500. I mailed it to everyone I ever knew. The money began to roll in, and we went back to work.

How were they able to raise the money they needed to finish the film?

20   When it came time for a title, we recalled a clever observation Mark made in the movie and chose *Gravity Is My Enemy*. It was perhaps the only enemy he ever had.

439

Reading 2

21   Then the money problem struck again. The rough cut was finished, but we needed a major miracle to get the final and expensive print and negative made. We had begged and borrowed from everyone. It looked like the miracles had finally run out.

22   At that dark moment, Mark died.

What happened to Mark? Would his film ever be completed?

23   He had <u>aspirated</u> some food into his lung while swallowing and was unable to cough it up. It could have happened a dozen times before. But it didn't happen until he had finished his film and seen a rough cut. Mark was gone, but we had come this far because of him and we could not stop now. We had to show others what he had been. About three weeks after Mark's funeral, I took our scratchy work print to Ray Wagner, then a vice president of MGM. Halfway through he turned on the lights and, with tears running down his face, told me he would make a free final print. Mark's miracles were still operating.

24   We sent the finished film to the prestigious San Francisco Film Festival. To our surprise, it took first place in the documentary-films competition, winning the Golden Gate Award, the top festival prize. This made it automatically eligible to be nominated for an Academy Award—and to our astonishment, it was. Yet another miracle!

How did the movie get to the Academy Awards?

25   Although we knew we hadn't a chance of winning the Oscar, it was well worth the price of our rented tuxedos for John Joseph and me to attend the glamorous Academy Awards. As I sat through the opening presentations my mind drifted back to Mark and how much I wished he could be sharing the nomination with us. Despite the realities, I really wanted that Oscar—for Mark and UCLA and for everyone who had made the film possible. Most of all, I wanted it to prove to other students who want to make movies that if you do it with feeling and honesty. . . you can win.

26   My mouth was dry as the moment approached for the presentation in our category. Time passed in slow motion as Kirk Douglas and Raquel Welch joked around before opening the envelopes. Then I heard Raquel say: "And the winner is—*Gravity*. . ."

27   I have no recollection of walking up that long aisle of applauding movie stars and reaching the podium. I meant to thank everyone, but I froze.

28   Then, as in a dream, I heard myself saying, "Just finishing our film was a miracle—and this award is another. But the greatest miracle of all was Mark Hicks. He showed us how to live life as a hero. It's Mark's film and his award. He can't be here tonight; he has left his wheelchair and is running free somewhere in God's Heaven." Then, I took the golden Oscar, held it over my head and concluded: "Mark, this is for you."

1,525 words divided by _____ minutes = _____ words per minute

Reading 2 Thinking About What You Read

It's a good habit to summarize everything you read to strengthen your comprehension.

Directions: On the following lines, write a two- or three-sentence summary of the article "The Many Miracles of Mark Hicks." In your own words, describe what the article was about and why the author wrote it.

....

....

....

....

Comprehension Questions

The following questions will help you to recall the main idea and the details of "The Many Miracles of Mark Hicks." Review any parts of the article that you need to find the correct answers.

LITERAL COMPREHENSION

1. **What is the topic of this article?**
   a. *Gravity Is My Enemy*
   b. Jan Stussy
   c. the trials and triumphs of making a film about Mark Hicks
   d. making an Oscar-winning film

MAIN IDEA

2. **What is the central point of the article?**
   a. Professor Jan Stussy made a film.
   b. Through his example, Mark Hicks taught others how to live.
   c. After overcoming many obstacles, a film about Mark Hicks won an Academy Award.
   d. Mark Hicks died while his professor was making a film about him.

SUPPORTING DETAILS

3. **How did Mark achieve his own goal?**
   a. He saw the rough-cut film about his life before he died.
   b. He had a one-man art exhibition of his work.
   c. He helped to raise money for his film.
   d. He inspired his professor to make a film about him.

Reading 2

4. Why did Professor Jan Stussy decide to make a film about Mark?

   a. He admired Mark's artistic talent.

   b. He felt sorry for Mark.

   c. He wanted to show other students how talented Mark was.

   d. He wanted to show others how Mark lived his life and achieved his dream despite many obstacles.

5. Why did the professor think that Mark shouldn't be in his class?

   a. He didn't think Mark had enough talent.

   b. He thought it would be impossible for him to do the difficult work his course required.

   c. He thought that teaching Mark would take too much of his time away from other students.

   d. He didn't want to have a quadriplegic in his class.

6. Why do you think they decided to call the movie *Gravity Is My Enemy*?

   a. Mark felt as if gravity was dragging him down.

   b. Gravity is a dangerous force.

   c. It was gravity that caused Mark's injury when he fell from a tree, and it kept him in a wheelchair.

   d. They named it this because Mark didn't have any real enemies.

7. Identify the relationship within the following sentence: When I told him about Mark and the film project, he offered to develop and print 15 rolls as a charitable gesture.

   a. cause and effect

   b. space order

   c. compare and/or contrast

   d. time order

8. Identify the relationship between the following sentences: We filmed his father getting him out of bed, sitting him in his chair and brushing his teeth. We followed his mother cooking food and feeding it to him. We shot his attendant putting him into his van and driving him to school.

   a. compare and/or contrast

   b. listing

   c. cause and effect

   d. process

9. What is the overall pattern of organization for the article?

   a. compare and/or contrast

   b. listing

   c. process

   d. time order

10. Identify the meaning of the underlined word in the following sentence: He accepted his limitations and worked beyond his <u>capacities</u>, setting an example and inspiring other students.

    a. abilities

    b. achievements

    c. strength

    d. fullness

Reading 2 Vocabulary Practice

Use the vocabulary words from the Word Bank to complete the following sentences. Write the words into the blanks provided.

WORD BANK

portfolio	quadriplegic	intrigued	severed	disarming
impassioned	earmarked	transpose	aspirated	lithographs

1. To decorate our apartment, we bought some .... at a local art show and hung them in frames.

2. Although Travis was seriously injured in an auto accident that left him a(n) .... , he continued to work for a charity organization for people with spinal cord injuries.

3. Miguel thought that the professor's grade for his drawing .... was too low, so he made an appointment to discuss it.

4. Eleanor gave a(n) .... performance as Juliet in the play "The Tragedy of Romeo and Juliet" at the college theater last night.

5. Catherine .... all relations with her ex-husband after their divorce.

6. Curtis made a sarcastic remark about the "fascinating poetry assignment" to Professor Simms. Not really angry, the professor just gave a(n) .... shrug and smiled, saying, "I'm glad you think that poetry is so interesting."

7. If we .... the second act of our play to make it the third act, I think it will be a much better ending.

8. I was .... by the many machines and inventions that Leonardo da Vinci made during his lifetime even though he was primarily an artist.

9. Amber refused to spend her savings on an expensive vacation for spring break because the funds were .... for college.

10. When her daughter .... a chunk of food into her windpipe, Marissa performed first aid and saved her daughter's life.

Reading 2 Questions for Writing and Discussion

Review any parts of the article you need to answer the following questions.

1. Jan Stussy wrote that he examined the students' portfolios, accepting some and "rejecting others on the merits of their ability as draftsmen." What did he mean by this, and why did he reject their work?

2. How did Mark feel about his disability?

3. Why do you think that art was so important to Mark?

4. Jan Stussy wrote that, although he was Mark's teacher, Mark taught him a valuable lesson. What lesson(s) do you think he learned?

5. Why do you think it was so important to Jan Stussy to complete the documentary film about Mark after he died?

Reading 2 Vocabulary Practice—Word Search

1.
In groups, divide into two teams, each with one to three people.

2.
One team will complete all of the odd-numbered Clue Questions. The other team will do the even-numbered questions. Answer the Clue Questions in the order they appear, taking turns.

3.
First, answer the Clue Questions by writing on the blank the correct answer from the Word Bank. Then, write the word anywhere on the grid, using one letter per square. Try to use letters that are already on the grid, including the letters in "Word Search."

4.
Teams get five points for each word they correctly answer. Each time you cross over another letter, you get one extra point. You may cross over as many other words as you can to earn points for each word you write, but the letters must match what is already there. You can go across, down, diagonally, or backwards.

5.
One person on each team should keep time. Each team has one minute to write a correct answer or lose their turn.

6.
All words must be spelled correctly. The team with the most points at the end is the winner.

```
        B
        L
S T E A (L)  ←——————
        E
        E
        D
```

The answer "steal" gets one extra point for crossing over "bleed."

WORD BANK

portfolio	impassioned
quadriplegic	earmarked
intrigued	transpose
severed	aspirated
disarming	lithographs

CLUE QUESTIONS

1. What might you do to change the order of something?
   ....

2. If you reserved something, what might you have done?
   ....

3. What would be something displayed on a wall? ....

4. If you wanted to know more, what might you be? ....

5. What might someone be who cannot swim? ....

6. How did some of Henry the Eighth's wives lose their heads?
   ....

7. If you wanted to calm someone down, what would you have to be?
   ....

8. If you felt deeply about something, what would you be? ....

9. If you choked on something, what have you done? ....

10. What might you show during a job interview? ....

Grid contains: **W O R D   S E A R C H**

VIEWPOINT FOR CRITICAL THINKING

VIEWPOINT: Television Standards

Read the following letters to the editor about whether there should be more government control over what is shown on television. Then, answer the questions that follow.

Dear Editor:

I am alarmed at the increase of violence and sex on television shows. What happened to the standards set by the FCC (Federal Communications Commission) which were supposed to keep our television shows from being too violent or sexually explicit? Parents cannot be there to watch everything their kids are seeing on TV. We rely on government agencies such as the FCC to keep broadcasting companies from putting smut on TV. Too much sex and violence on television is harming our nation's youth. We wonder why there is so much violence in society, but the answer is, that is what we are feeding our children every day from the TV set.

Signed,

Mad About TV

Dear Editor:

Some of your readers are opposed to the amount of violence and sex on television. Personally, I don't have a problem with it. I'm an adult, and I don't have any kids. It's a free country, and broadcasting companies have the right to free speech like everybody else. They should show whatever they want. If you have kids, turn off the television, use a V chip, or only let them watch it when you're watching the kids. I wouldn't want to see the FCC get so strict with the broadcasting companies that all the programming choices are only for kids or "family" entertainment. That would be totally boring to me and other adults.

Signed,

Liberty for All

Critical Thinking

1. A point of view is the author's opinion about a topic. To find the author's point of view, ask yourself, "How does this author feel about this issue?" What is the author's point of view about television standards in the first letter?

   ....

   ....

   ....

2. What is the author's point of view about television standards in the second letter?

   ....

   ....

   ....

3. Which letter do you agree with, and why?

   ....

   ....

   ....

4. What could be the consequences of allowing broadcasters to make their own decisions about what they show on television?

   ....

   ....

   ....

5. What could be the consequences of having the government enforce stricter standards on television broadcasting?

   ....

   ....

   ....

WRITE YOUR THOUGHTS

Write a letter to the editor stating your own feelings about regulating what is on television. Use a separate sheet of paper.

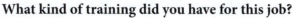

ON THE JOB INTERVIEW

Meaghan Girouard,
Graphic Artist

What kind of work do you do?
I work for a national trade show contractor company that designs trade shows. I work with 3D modeling programs, animation programs, and other graphics programs. I design the layout of the shows, the overall look of the shows, the decorating, and anything related to the show including logos and graphic design.

What kind of training did you have for this job?
I graduated from art school with a bachelor's in fine arts in visual communication and a minor in business, and I worked as a freelance designer before taking this job.

What do you like best about this job?
I enjoy collaborating with other people on projects. I like the variety of projects that we do, and the creativity that's involved. I love my job because it's a constant challenge, and there are always new projects to work on, and each one is different.

What do you dislike about your job?
Sometimes there isn't enough time to do all that I would like to do on a project. I sometimes must put in late hours to meet deadlines. And some people can be difficult to work with.

How did you become interested in this career?
I loved art in school and didn't want to become a painter, so graphic design was the perfect area for me.

When you were in college, did you have to overcome any obstacles to succeed?
I certainly did! I have dyslexia, which is a learning disability, so it was a real challenge for me to succeed. I had to work a lot harder than other students, but I knew my strength was in art, so I kept going even though many courses were difficult for me.

Did you ever think about giving up when you were in college?
There were times when everything seemed overwhelming. But I just kept my head down and worked through it. I just tried hard to do my best. I got a lot of help from teachers and classmates along the way. I didn't get where I am today without seeking out the support and guidance I needed to get through my schooling.

If you had any advice for college freshmen interested in graphic art, what would it be?
I would strongly suggest that they do whatever they can to get as much experience as possible. By that I mean do volunteer work, internships, or freelance work. Try to network with people in the business so that you can make the transition from college to the real world. Graphic design is a good career with plenty of opportunity and variety. But getting your foot in the door isn't always easy, so that's why networking and experience are helpful.

BUILDING VOCABULARY

Throughout this course, you will be introduced to word parts that make up many words in the English language. Study the following word parts, and then answer the questions that follow.

Prefixes	**Roots**	**Suffixes**
extra-, extro- *outside*	-vert-, -vers- *to turn**	-tion, -sion *action, state of**
in- *into**	-tract- *to draw, to drag*	-er, -or *one who*
con-, com- *with, together**		
ex- *out**		

* Word parts from previous chapters

What English words can you create from these word parts?

....

....

....

....

....

Using a dictionary, look up the meanings of any of the words you wrote that you can't define. Use one of the words you wrote in a sentence that reveals its meaning with a context clue:

....

....

....

....

449

Car Leasing Agreements

Leasing a car is like renting it long term. When you lease a car, you are renting it from a leasing company that owns the vehicle. You should be aware of some unfair deals that can happen with a lease. Use the four-step reading process as you read the following excerpt from a car leasing agreement, and then answer the questions that follow to check your comprehension.

Vocabulary Terms:

lessor: the person or company who leases the car to you

default: if you fail to do anything that is required in the agreement

Terms of Lease Agreement
VEHICLE MAINTENANCE You must maintain and service the Vehicle at your own expense, using materials that meet the manufacturer's specifications. This includes following the owner's manual and maintenance schedule, keeping records of maintenance performed, and making all needed repairs.
DAMAGE REPAIR You are responsible for repairs of all damage that is not a result of normal wear and use. Repairs must be made with original equipment manufacturer parts. Failure to do so will result in damage charges.
TERMINATION This lease will terminate (end) upon (a) the end of the term of this lease, (b) the return of the Vehicle to Lessor, and (c) the payment by you of all amounts owed under this lease. The Lessor may cancel this lease if you default. If you default, you may be required to pay damages to the Lessor.
RETURN OF VEHICLE If you do not buy the Vehicle at lease end, you must return it to the Lessor. If you fail to return the Vehicle, you must continue to pay the monthly payments plus other damages to the Lessor, including amounts payable under default, which can be up to 40% of the monthly payment. Payment of these amounts will not allow you to keep the Vehicle.
EXCESS WEAR AND USE You are responsible for all repairs to the Vehicle that are not the result of normal wear and use. If any such damage is found on the vehicle when it is returned, you will be charged for the repairs to such damage.

Questions

1. Which of the following is included in the required vehicle maintenance?

   a. following the owner's manual

   b. following the maintenance schedule

   c. keeping a record of maintenance performed

   d. all of the above

2. What happens if you repair a damaged part with one that is not an original manufacturer part?

   a. You will not be allowed to return the car.

   b. You will be charged extra in damage charges.

   c. You will have to buy the vehicle.

   d. It doesn't matter which kind of parts you use, so nothing happens.

3. What happens if you default?

   a. You must pay more money each month.

   b. You are given the option to buy the car.

   c. You may have to pay damages to the company, and you could lose the car.

   d. You are given a warning and a second chance to catch up on payments.

4. What happens if you don't return the vehicle at the end of the lease?

   a. You must continue to pay the monthly payments plus other damages, including amounts up to 40% of the monthly payment.

   b. You keep on paying for the car until it's paid for and you keep it.

   c. You will be charged with grand theft auto.

   d. Nothing will happen because the car dealers won't know about it.

5. What happens if you return the car with a large dent in the hood?

   a. The vehicle will be accepted.

   b. The repairs will be done by the dealership at no cost to you.

   c. You must pay for the repairs.

   d. You are charged a small Excess Wear and Use fee.

TEXTBOOK GRAPHIC AIDS

Study the following graph, and then answer the questions that follow.

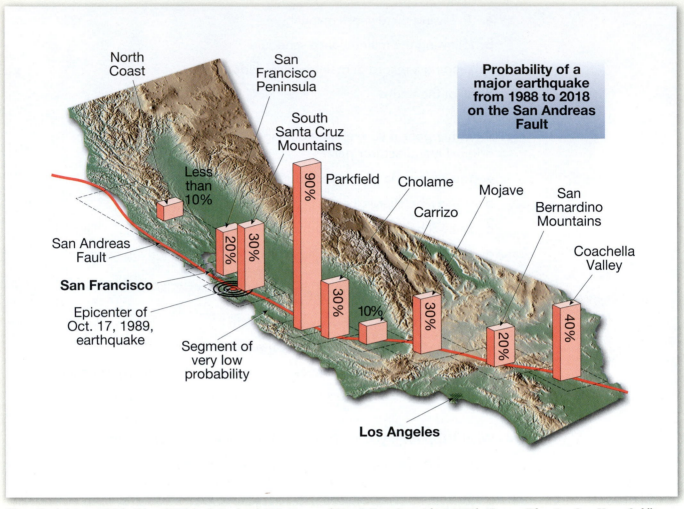

(From *Earth Science*, 12th by Edward J. Tarbuck, Frederick K. Lutgens, and Dennis Tasa. Copyright © 2009 by Pearson Education, Inc., Upper Saddle River, NJ. Reprinted with permission.)

1. **What does the graph show?**

    a. cities in California where earthquakes have occurred (1988–2018)

    b. locations in California that have had the most earthquakes

    c. the probability of major earthquakes along the San Andreas Fault (1988–2018)

    d. the percentage of earthquakes in various areas of California (1988–2018)

2. **Which city has the highest probability of a major earthquake by 2018?**

    a. Parkfield

    b. San Francisco

    c. San Andreas Fault

    d. Los Angeles

3. Which area has the lowest probability of a major earthquake before 2018?

   a. the area north of San Francisco

   b. San Francisco

   c. Carrizo

   d. Los Angeles

4. Which of the following conclusions can you draw from the graph?

   a. The probability of a major earthquake is high anywhere on the San Andreas Fault.

   b. The probability of a major earthquake is lower north of San Francisco.

   c. A major earthquake will destroy all the cities on the San Andreas Fault.

   d. The probability of a major earthquake along the San Andreas Fault is higher than in other parts of California.

5. According to the graph, the two largest cities shown, San Francisco and Los Angeles, have an equal probability of a major earthquake before 2018.

   a. true

   b. false

CHAPTER REVIEW PRACTICE #1

Read the following paragraph, underline the major details, and then answer the questions that follow.

Fashion designers are artists who create "art" to wear. They begin by studying art and design at a college, university, or private art and design school. Their training includes fashion history, design, drawing, pattern making, and using computer-aided design (CAD) programs. Besides having a foundation in art and design, designers must have a good sense of what is pleasing to the eye. They must understand how color, texture, and proportion play important roles in the overall look of a style. In addition to being creative, fashion designers must be able to communicate their ideas to others. Most fashion designers start out as sketching assistants or pattern makers for a professional designer or clothing label. After gaining experience and proving their talent, they can work their way up into higher positions as fashion designers. Teamwork skills are important since designers must work with many other people to achieve the final product.

1. **What is the topic?**
   a. fashion design
   b. fashion designers
   c. designing fashions for others
   d. art as fashion

2. **What do most of the major details describe?**
   a. how a person becomes a fashion designer
   b. how fashions are designed
   c. what is needed to be a fashion designer
   d. why fashion designers create designs

3. **Is the main idea stated or implied?**
   a. stated
   b. implied

4. **Which of the following sentences best states the main idea (either stated in the paragraph or implied)?**
   a. Fashion designers are artists who create "art" to wear.
   b. Besides having a foundation in art and design, designers must have a good sense of what is pleasing to the eye.
   c. Most fashion designers start out as sketching assistants or pattern makers for a professional designer or clothing label.
   d. Teamwork skills are important since designers must work with many other people to achieve the final product.

CHAPTER REVIEW PRACTICE #2

Read the following paragraphs, underline the major details, and then answer the questions that follow.

On October 28, 1886, the Statue of Liberty was dedicated to celebrate the signing of the Declaration of Independence 100 years prior. The statue was a gift from France to celebrate the friendship that had been established between the two countries during the American Revolution.

The famous statue is of a robed woman, wearing a crown and holding a torch, which is coated in gold leaf—a thin layer of gold. The statue is over 150 feet tall. The design of the statue is based on ancient Roman statues, and its features are symbols of freedom. By the statue's feet are broken chains, symbolizing America's freedom from Great Britain. The torch she holds represents wisdom and truth. The seven spikes on the crown she wears represent the seven seas and continents of the world. July 4, 1776, the date of America's Declaration of Independence, is written on the tablet she holds. Her location on Liberty Island in the New York Harbor welcomed visitors and immigrants to the United States who arrived by ships in earlier times.

1. What is the topic?
    a. construction of the Statue of Liberty
    b. the meaning of the Statue of Liberty
    c. the Statue of Liberty
    d. the location of the Statue of Liberty

2. What do most of the major details describe?
    a. why the statue was given to the United States and what it represents
    b. who designed the statue
    c. how the statue was constructed
    d. where the statue is located

3. Is the main idea stated or implied?
    a. stated
    b. implied

4. Which of the following sentences best states the main idea (either stated in the reading or implied)?
    a. On October 28, 1886, the Statue of Liberty was dedicated to celebrate the signing of the Declaration of Independence 100 years prior.
    b. The statue was a gift from France to celebrate the friendship that had been established between the two countries during the American Revolution.
    c. The Statue of Liberty, a gift from France, represents independence, truth, and freedom.
    d. The design of the statue is based on ancient Roman statues, and its features are symbols of freedom.

CHAPTER REVIEW PRACTICE #3

Read the following paragraphs, underline the major details, and then answer the questions that follow.

Designer Karim Rashid is a world-famous designer of things—everything from furniture and appliances to art. Rashid graduated from Carleton University in Ottawa, Canada, and did post-graduate studies in Italy. Although he was born in Cairo, Egypt, he now lives in New York City. Rashid holds honorary doctorate degrees from the Ontario College of Art & Design and the Corcoran College of Art & Design. His work has been featured in major magazines and newspapers worldwide.

Karim Rashid has designed thousands of items all over the world for major companies, including Prada and Umbra. He has earned numerous international awards, and his designs and sculptures are featured in art museums in several major cities around the world. His style is futuristic and modern, featuring smooth shapes and lines. His product designs are not only practical and comfortable, but they look like art. Rashid believes that practical products can also be designed to beautify the environment in which we live.

(From website by Karim Rashid. Copyright © 2010 by Karim Rashid. Reprinted with permission.)

1. What is the topic?

   a. the life of Karim Rashid

   b. Karim Rashid's art

   c. modern product design

   d. living in an artistic environment

2. What do most of the major details describe?

   a. why Rashid creates beautiful designs

   b. how Rashid became a designer

   c. how successful Rashid is

   d. Rashid's design background and his work

3. Is the main idea stated or implied?

   a. stated

   b. implied

4. Which of the following sentences best states the main idea (stated or implied)?

   a. Designer Karim Rashid is a world-famous designer of things—everything from furniture and appliances to art.

   b. He has designed thousands of items all over the world for major companies, including Prada and Umbra.

   c. His designs have earned him numerous international awards, and his designs and sculptures are featured in art museums in several major cities around the world.

   d. Rashid believes that practical products can also be designed to beautify the environment in which we live.

TEXTBOOK PRACTICE

Preview the following paragraphs, then read actively and answer the questions. Read the following textbook selection, underline the major details, and then answer the questions that follow.

American painter Georgia O'Keeffe (oh-KEEF), born near Sun Prairie, Wisconsin, grew up on her family's farm in Wisconsin. She spent 1904–1905 at the Art Institute of Chicago and 1907–1908 at the Art Students League of New York, and then supported herself by doing commercial art and teaching at various schools and colleges in Texas and the South. Her break came in 1916, when her drawings were discovered and exhibited by the famous American photographer Alfred Stieglitz, who praised and promoted her work vigorously. They maintained a lifelong relationship, marrying in 1924, and O'Keeffe became the subject of hundreds of Stieglitz's photographs.

Her early pictures lack originality, but by the 1920s she had developed a uniquely individualistic style. Many of her subjects include enlarged views of skulls and other animal bones, flowers, plants, shells, rocks, mountains, and other natural forms. Her images have a mysterious quality about them, with clear color washes and a suggestive, psychological symbolism that often implies eroticism. She created her best-known work in the 1920s, 1930s, and 1940s but remained active as a painter almost until her death in 1986. Her later paintings exalt the New Mexico landscape, which she loved.

(From *Creative Impulse: An Introduction to the Arts*, 8e by Dennis J. Sporre. Copyright © 2009 by Dennis J. Sporre. Reprinted by permission of Pearson Education, Inc., Upper Saddle River, NJ.)

1. What is the topic?

   a. Georgia O'Keeffe's art

   b. Georgia O'Keeffe

   c. the art of the 1920s to 1940s

   d. a famous woman painter

2. What is the main idea of the first paragraph (either stated or implied)?

   a. American painter Georgia O'Keeffe (oh-KEEF), born near Sun Prairie, Wisconsin, grew up on her family's farm in Wisconsin.

   b. Georgia O'Keeffe studied and taught art before her marriage to photographer Alfred Stieglitz, who praised her work vigorously.

   c. They maintained a lifelong relationship, marrying in 1924, and O'Keeffe became the subject of hundreds of Stieglitz's photographs.

   d. Her break came in 1916, when her drawings were discovered and exhibited by the famous American photographer Alfred Stieglitz, who praised and promoted her work vigorously.

3. **What is the main idea of the second paragraph (either stated or implied)?**

   a. Her early pictures lack originality, but by the 1920s she had developed a uniquely individualistic style.

   b. Many of her subjects include enlarged views of skulls and other animal bones, flowers, plants, shells, rocks, mountains, and other natural forms.

   c. O'Keeffe's beginning style of painting was not considered very good.

   d. She created her best-known work in the 1920s, 1930s, and 1940s but remained active as a painter almost until her death in 1986.

4. **What is the central point of the selection (either stated or implied)?**

   a. American painter Georgia O'Keeffe (oh-KEEF), born near Sun Prairie, Wisconsin, grew up on her family's farm in Wisconsin.

   b. After meeting Stieglitz, O'Keeffe spent most of her time in New York, with occasional periods in New Mexico, but she moved permanently to New Mexico after her husband's death in 1946.

   c. Her early pictures lack originality, but by the 1920s she had developed a uniquely individualistic style.

   d. Georgia O'Keeffe was an American painter who painted enlarged views of natural subjects in a unique, original style.

STUDY SKILL CHAPTER REVIEW

Cornell Notes are a style of note taking shown in the following example. Complete the Cornell Notes to review the concepts you learned in Chapter 8.

Cue/Question Column	Notes
What is the first step to finding an implied main idea?	First, ...
What is the second step to finding the implied main idea?	Second, ...
What is the third step to finding the implied main idea?	Third, ...
What question should you ask yourself to find the implied main idea?	Ask yourself, ...
What should you do to check your implied main idea?	When you have formed your implied main idea, check your answer by asking yourself,
What is a central point or thesis statement?	It is ....

READING LAB ASSIGNMENTS

SKILL PRACTICES

1. Go online to MyReadingLab and click on the "Study Skills" tab. Next, click on "Implied Main Idea" and complete the practices and tests according to your instructor's directions.

COMPREHENSION IMPROVEMENT

2. Go online to MyReadingLab and click on the Reading Level tab. Choose two stories to read and answer the questions that follow.

CAREER EXPLORATION

3. Go online to www.bls.gov/oco and explore careers in the arts. Find a career that interests you and print out the information. Print the article, and then preview, read, highlight, and annotate it. Write the main idea or central point for the article.

SKILL APPLICATION

4. Using your textbooks for other classes or newspaper articles, read a section and then state the implied main idea in your own words. Remember to focus on the major supporting details and summarize what the details are telling you in a general statement. Read an entire section under a heading and determine the central point by focusing on the main ideas for each paragraph. Then, state the author's central point in your own words.

LEARNING REFLECTION

Think about the skills and concepts in this chapter. What have you learned in this chapter that will help your reading comprehension and enable you to do well in college?

SELF-EVALUATION CHECKLIST

Rate yourself on the following items, using the following scale:

1 = strongly disagree

2 = disagree

3 = neither agree nor disagree

4 = agree

5 = strongly agree

1. I completed all of the assigned work on time. ....

2. I understand all of the concepts in this chapter. ....

3. I contributed to teamwork and class discussions. ....

4. I completed all of the assigned lab work on time. ....

5. I came to class on time. ....

6. I attended class every day. ....

7. I studied for any quizzes or tests we had for this chapter. ....

8. I asked questions when I didn't understand something. ....

9. I checked my comprehension during reading. ....

10. I know what is expected of me in the coming week. ....

11. Are you still on track with the goals you set in Chapter 1? ....

12. What changes can you make to improve your performance in this course? ....

For support in meeting this chapter's objectives, go to the Study Plan in MyReadingLab and select Implied Main Idea. Read and view the resources in the Review Materials section, and then complete the Recall, Apply, and Write exercises in the Activities section. Check your results by clicking on Gradebook.

STUDY SKILL: HOW TO SURVIVE A BORING CLASS

Boring class? Boring teachers? If you find that you are in boring classes with boring teachers, the best cure for this is to get busy!

Boredom is the result of inactivity and noninvolvement. People who sit back and expect to be entertained will always find life boring no matter what is going on around them. Using class time to sleep or socialize will only lead to failure. To eliminate boredom, you must be actively involved in what you are learning.

During class, try to take notes. Write down key points, and leave space to add your own details later. If the instructor discusses something in class, it may appear on a test. For this reason, you need to write down the subject, even if you don't understand it. You can get more information about it later.

FIRST

Take a close look at the course syllabus or outline. What is it you are expected to know by the end of the semester? This is your study plan.

SECOND

Create a notebook or computer file and fill it with key information about the topics for each chapter. Use your textbook as a reference guide. Using your personal learning style, do whatever you need to get the information into your brain. You can even use lecture time to do this if you feel the lectures are not helping you. Become your own instructor, as if you had to teach this course to someone else.

THIRD

Find a study partner or study group to work with outside of class. Begin to teach each other the concepts listed in the course syllabus. Help each other on difficult topics, and work together to find answers. If the study group begins to socialize too much, get them back on track. If the problem persists, drop them and find others who take their education seriously.

FOURTH

Use online resources, videos, and other materials that you can get for free at your college's library or on the Internet. Ask librarians for assistance in finding what you need. Take some of these resources to class for quick reference in case you need additional information. If your instructor catches you reading extra materials or the textbook for this class, he or she may even encourage you because you are showing an interest in the subject.

Students who take this active approach to learning will discover that it is possible to learn in spite of the "boring" course or the lackluster teacher. Learning is a lifelong skill, and by discovering how to become your own teacher, you will always succeed in school and in life. You may have boring classes and teachers, but you will never feel bored if you are actively involved in your own learning.

KEY POINTS
TO REVIEW

1. Why do some people feel bored all the time?

....

....

....

2. Why would sleeping or socializing in class not be a good use of time?

....

....

....

3. What can you do to eliminate boredom during class?

....

....

....

4. How can the syllabus or course outline be useful to you?

....

....

....

5. Paraphrase four ways that you can learn information on your own.

....

....

....

....

....

....

CHAPTER 10 CRITICAL READING AND THINKING

LEARNING OBJECTIVES

IN THIS CHAPTER, YOU WILL:

Objective 1 characterize the difference between fact and opinion.

Objective 2 explain the author's purpose and tone.

Objective 3 identify the intended audience.

Objective 4 recognize bias or point of view.

FOCUS ON SCIENCE

Are you a person who likes to know how things work, or why something happens? Do you like to explore new ideas and create? All of these are characteristics of a scientific mind. Crime scene investigators, medical researchers, and environmental biologists all strive to find answers to important questions. Some scientists work in laboratories at least part of the time, but many of them work outdoors observing, collecting samples, measuring, and conducting experiments. Some work in zero gravity in outer space while others explore our solar system from powerful telescopes on land. Some technicians' jobs may require only an associate's degree while others require higher degrees. For curious individuals, science can offer a world of exploration and discovery in many different areas.

CRITICAL READING AND THINKING

Being a critical reader and thinker means that you look beyond the words printed on the page, and you use what you know to make new connections and draw logical conclusions. Critical readers use facts and reasoning skills to evaluate an author's point. Critical readers and thinkers ask many questions, such as "Why did the author write this?" They analyze facts and interpret what they read. They recognize techniques that authors may use to persuade readers, and they detect any personal bias that an author may have. Critical readers and thinkers apply what they have learned to new situations to solve problems or create new ideas. Using some of the same critical thinking skills that scientists use, you can also become a critical thinker.

Objective 1 | # FACT AND OPINION

One of the most basic critical reading and thinking skills is being able to distinguish a fact from an opinion. Facts are provable, but opinions are not.

Examples of facts:

The Earth is approximately 4.5 billion years old.
The diameter of the Earth is about 8,000 miles (12,800 km).
This college has 10,000 students.

Examples of opinions:

Dr. Johnson is the best physiology instructor at the college.
He probably wishes that he had fewer classes to teach.
Dr. Johnson's students are lucky to be in his class.

Because facts are statements that can be proved as either *true or false*, a fact does not have to be true to remain a fact. It may be referred to as a "false fact." For example, the college mentioned in the third fact may only have 9,999 students, but it remains a fact because we can prove it as true or false. Facts can be proved by some observable or measurable means.

Incorrect statements that can be proved true or false are still facts. Through the centuries, our understanding of the world has evolved and changed. For instance, we recently considered it a fact that Pluto was a planet; now we know that Pluto is not a true planet but a dwarf planet. Future discoveries will continue to change our understanding of what is true and what is false. Facts will change, but they will remain facts—true or false—as long as they can be proved.

On the other hand, opinions are not provable and use words or phrases that imply judgment, such as "best" or "worst." Some opinions are very popular, and most people may agree with them, but they're still opinions. For example, many people agree that people should not pollute but it is still an *opinion*.

FACTS	OPINIONS
Facts can be proved true or false by some observable or measurable means.	Opinions cannot be proved as either true or false.
Quotations can be proved. Think of it this way: Can you prove that this person said this? Yes, so the quotation is a fact, even if what the quotation asserted is an opinion.	Opinions include feelings, attitudes, beliefs, and guesses.
	All future events, including predictions, are opinions (because they cannot be proved true or false with the information currently available to us).

Words That Signal Opinion

You can recognize opinions by words or phrases that suggest guesses or attitudes. Here are some examples:

it appears that	apparently	it seems that	believe
guess	surmise	presumably	in my opinion
in my view	it's likely that	possibly	this suggests
should	ought to	may	could

Keep in mind that the context of the word in the sentence is important to consider when deciding if a sentence is a fact or an opinion. Although the word "may" appears in both of the following sentences, one is a fact and one is an opinion. In such situations, ask yourself, "Can this be proved true or false?"

EXAMPLE:

1. Scientists *may* discover life on other planets in the universe. (Opinion: future event)

2. This rock cycle *may* occur either beneath the Earth's surface or on the Earth's surface. (Fact: The rock cycle can happen in two places—beneath the Earth's surface or on the Earth's surface.)

Judgment Words in Opinions

You can also identify opinions by looking for words that make judgments about something, such as:

worst	best	horrible	amazing
wonderful	awful	weird	troublesome

EXAMPLES:

Allowing our planet to become polluted is a *terrible* legacy to leave for the next generation.

The octopus is *amazingly* intelligent, and during experiments it performs many tasks that require thinking.

Sentences with Both Fact and Opinion

Occasionally you will see a sentence that has both fact and opinion. If you are offered the option of choosing "fact and opinion" on a test, that is the best description. But often, you are only offered two answer choices: fact or opinion. In this case, consider the entire sentence to be opinion if any portion of it is opinion.

EXAMPLE:

The production of carbon dioxide from human activities includes burning coal, gas, and oil, which *may* cause *serious* climate change on Earth. (The first half of this sentence is a fact, but the ending is an opinion because of the words "may" and "serious.")

Is It Wrong to Use Opinions in Writing?

Expect to find opinions in just about everything you read, including newspapers, textbooks, and reference materials. Opinions form a valuable part of our understanding of a subject, and they should not be excluded from writing. We cannot make important predictions about the future without stating opinions. We rely on experts who have knowledge and experience to give us their *expert opinions*, which give us insight to problems and solutions. For instance, meteorologists predict the weather every day, and most of the time they are correct.

467

Can It Be Proved?

Read the following statements, and decide if they can be proved. Ask yourself, "Can this be proved by some measurable means?" Write "Y" for yes or "N" for no on the lines provided. Underline any clues that helped you decide.

EXAMPLES:

........*Y*........ Jellyfish are meat eaters and feed on anything from small worms to large fish.

........*N*........ Bats are the <u>worst</u> mammals to encounter in the wild.

1. .... When volcanoes erupt, hot lava spreads down the sides.

2. .... Entire cities have been destroyed by volcanoes.

3. .... Volcanoes are the most dangerous natural disaster on Earth.

4. .... The seas cover about 72 percent of the Earth's surface.

5. .... There will be less land as the ocean levels rise higher in the next decades.

Read the following paragraph. Turn the sentences into facts by crossing out the words that make them opinions.

One of the most fascinating sharks in the sea is the goblin shark. It is the ugliest shark because it has a long pointed snout that sticks up above its mouth. Its strange pink and grey body is covered in soft, flabby flesh. It lives in the darkest and deepest level of the ocean, which is a good place for a goblin to stay.

Practice

1. Label each of the following sentences as fact (F) or opinion (O), and underline any words or phrases that signal an opinion.

1. .... The most beautiful sunsets can be seen in the Caribbean Sea.

2. .... The changing of the seasons is caused by the 23-degree tilt of the Earth on its axis.

3. .... The color of the sky is determined by the number of particles in the atmosphere.

4. .... The Northeast has the worst weather in the country.

5. .... In the coming decade, automobiles will use less energy and will cause less pollution.

2. Label each of the following sentences as fact (F) or opinion (O), and underline any words or phrases that signal an opinion.

1. .... It appears that global surface temperatures may have increased more rapidly over the past 10 years than in the past.

2. .... Global temperatures have increased more rapidly over the past 10 years than in the past.

3. .... Climate change has not been equal across all parts of the globe.

4. .... The most increasingly warming trend has occurred over North America and Eurasia.

5. .... Scientists have been keeping excellent records of the temperatures around the globe over the past century.

3. Read the following paragraph, and then label each sentence as fact (F) or opinion (O). Underline any words or phrases that signal an opinion.

[1]Scientists get their information about the Earth's climate from many natural sources. [2]Some data is found in tree rings, which can be seen when the trunk is cut in half and the rings are examined. [3]The difference in the size of some tree rings is interesting because it shows years of larger amounts of precipitation (rain or snow) and years of drought. [4]Wider rings mean that there was more growth during the season due to additional precipitation. [5]Using the data from tree rings and other natural sources, scientists are able to form some remarkable conclusions about the history of our planet's climate.

Sentence 1: ....   Sentence 4: ....

Sentence 2: ....   Sentence 5: ....

Sentence 3: ....

TEXTBOOK
SELECTION Read the following textbook selection, and then label each sentence as fact (F), opinion (O), or fact and opinion (F & O). Underline any words or phrases that signal an opinion.

Sea-Level Rise

[1]An important effect of human-caused global warming is a rise in sea level. How is a warmer atmosphere related to a global rise in sea level? [2]The most obvious connection is the melting of glaciers. [3]Also important is that a warmer atmosphere causes an increase in ocean volume of water due to expansion. [4]Higher air temperatures warm the upper layers of the ocean, which in turn causes the water to expand and sea level to rise. [5]Research indicates that sea level has risen between 10 and 25 centimeters (4 and 8 inches) over the past century, and that the trend will continue at an accelerated rate.

Sentence 1: .... Sentence 3: .... Sentence 5: ....

Sentence 2: .... Sentence 4: ....

U-Review

On a sheet of paper, make two columns. Label one column "facts" and the other column "opinions." Working with a partner or a team, you will be given a few minutes to write down everything you have learned about facts and opinions without looking in the text. When the paper is passed to each person, he or she must write and read one point about facts or opinions. When time is called, compare your team's list to others in the class. For each idea that you wrote that is not on another team's list, you earn one point. The team with the most points wins.

Objective 2 # AUTHOR'S PURPOSE

When authors write something, they always have a purpose in mind. Three basic reasons why authors write are to inform, persuade, and entertain. To learn the author's purpose, ask yourself, "Why did the author write this?" Consider the main idea or central point. An author's purpose is closely related to the author's main idea. Notice how the main idea gives a clue to the author's purpose in the following examples.

<u>To inform</u>: Here the author's purpose is to give information.

> The ocean tides are a result of the gravitational pull of the sun and moon.

<u>To persuade or convince</u>: An author uses persuasion to try to convince readers to accept his or her ideas or opinions. Look for phrases and judgment words that signal an opinion (see the lists of words under "Words That Signal Opinion," on page 466.)

> You *should not* swim in areas inhabited by sea lions and seals.

<u>To entertain</u>: This is when an author tries to convey a feeling, or an emotion.

> I'm on a "seafood" diet. I see food, and I eat it.

Read the following paragraphs to determine the author's purpose, and then answer the questions that follow.

Paragraph 1

Two students walked in late to a physics lecture, and, as they whispered to each other to find seats, several students told them to be quiet. One of the late students asked the other one, "Why do we have to be so quiet?" The other replied, "So we won't wake up the other students!"

What is the author's purpose? (Why did the author write this?)

   a. The author is trying to inform the reader.

   b. The author is trying to persuade the reader.

   c. The author is trying to entertain the reader.

Paragraph 2

A typical lightning bolt contains 1 billion volts of electrical current. A household electrical outlet typically carries 120 volts. The average lightning flash can light a 100-watt light bulb for 3 months.

What is the author's purpose? (Why did the author write this?)

   a. The author is trying to inform the reader about lightning.

   b. The author is trying to persuade the reader that lightning is dangerous.

   c. The author is trying to entertain the reader with a story about lightning.

Paragraph 3

Drinking alcohol can increase the risk of certain types of cancer. People who drink and smoke can double their risk of getting cancer. Reducing your risk of cancer can be as simple as following healthful eating habits. You should eat a low-fat, balanced diet that includes fruits and vegetables every day to reduce your risk factor.

What is the author's purpose? (Why did the author write this?)

   a. The author is trying to inform the reader about cancer.

   b. The author is trying to persuade the reader that healthful eating habits can reduce risk of cancer.

   c. The author is trying to entertain the reader with a story.

AUTHOR'S INTENDED AUDIENCE

Critical thinkers ask not only why an author wrote something but also for whom the selection was written. Knowing the intended audience can help you determine the author's purpose and tone. When trying to decide who the intended audience is, think about the source of the material. For example, the intended audience for a textbook is students. The intended audience for a medical journal is medical professionals.

As you read the following paragraphs, try to determine for whom these paragraphs were written. Then, answer the questions that follow.

Paragraph 1
The Great White shark is a powerful fish that can kill a person with a single bite. It eats other fish, sea turtles, birds, porpoises, seals, other sharks, and sometimes humans. When it charges to attack, its eyeballs roll back into its head for protection. Great White sharks are found throughout the world's seas and sometimes migrate over long distances.

The intended audience is:

- **a.** newspaper reporters
- **b.** biology students
- **c.** wildlife artists
- **d.** television producers

Paragraph 2
We must stop shark fishing on the Great Barrier Reef of Australia. The Australian government is allowing more than 70,000 sharks to be killed each year in this reef. This will contribute to the global decline of shark populations. Killing these sharks could have a terrible impact on the ecosystem of the reef. Protecting these sharks is necessary for protecting all marine wildlife living on the Great Barrier Reef.

The intended audience is:

- **a.** students
- **b.** tourists
- **c.** people who want to preserve nature
- **d.** news reporters

Paragraph 3
The Great Barrier Reef is one of Australia's most beautiful natural environments. The reef is made up of more than 3,000 reef systems and hundreds of tropical islands with sun-drenched white sandy beaches and turquoise water. You can explore the exotic islands in a boat, snorkeling, or scuba diving among the coral reefs, or simply lie on the beach enjoying the balmy soft ocean breeze.

The intended audience is:

- **a.** tourists
- **b.** environmentalists
- **c.** biology students
- **d.** writers

Notice how the first paragraph contains many facts about Great White sharks, whereas the second paragraph tries to convince the reader to stop shark fishing on the Great Barrier Reef. The third paragraph points out the most enjoyable features of the Reef.

AUTHOR'S TONE

Tone refers to the author's feelings about the topic. When trying to determine the author's tone, also consider the author's purpose and intended audience. Ask yourself, "What are the author's feelings or attitude about this topic?" Do not be influenced by your own attitude about the topic. Always begin by stating the topic and the main idea, and then consider the author's intended audience, the author's purpose, and the author's point of view about the topic. Look for words or phrases with positive or negative tones.

EXAMPLE:

> The Town Council members <u>have done it again.</u> They've voted to approve the building of shopping malls, car dealers, and small businesses on what is now prime farmland. These people <u>have no respect</u> for agriculture. Their <u>foolish</u> decision will affect the future of this town and change its traditions and character forever. There will be <u>more traffic, more pollution, and more crime</u> as shoplifters and thieves are drawn to this area. <u>We need to reverse this decision and stop further development</u> of farmland before there is no land left for growing crops.

Topic: developing farmland

Main idea: The town's farmland should be used for growing crops and not for development.

Intended audience: the people who live in the town

Author's purpose: to persuade readers that developing farmland is wrong

Author's tone: The author's tone is critical. Note the underlined words and phrases that reveal the author's concern about the topic.

1. What is the author's tone in paragraph 1 about the Great White shark?
   - **a.** happy
   - **b.** worried
   - **c.** factual
   - **d.** angry

2. What is the author's tone in paragraph 2 about shark fishing on the Great Barrier Reef?
   - **a.** concerned
   - **b.** excited
   - **c.** sad
   - **d.** careless

3. What is the author's tone in paragraph 3 about the features of the Great Barrier Reef?
   - **a.** frightened
   - **b.** serious
   - **c.** funny
   - **d.** positive

Tone Words

Following is a list of common tone words. There are many more words used to describe tone, but in this text, you will only use some of them. Neutral tone words state facts objectively, without opinion.

List of Common Tone Words

Positive Tone Words	Negative Tone Words	Neutral Tones Words
amused	angry	informative
cheerful	discouraging	factual
funny	critical	objective
excited	frustrated	neutral
joyful	hateful	straightforward
happy	harsh	unbiased
approving	disapproving	indifferent

Practice

1. Read the following paragraph, and underline the main idea (if stated) and the major details. Then, answer the questions that follow.

A black hole in space is a region where the gravity is so strong that nothing can escape its pull. The entrance to the black hole is called an *event horizon*. Objects, such as asteroids, can get pulled into the hole but never come out. They are called black holes because even light is pulled into the massive dark center. *Escape velocity*—the speed at which something must travel to escape being pulled into the black hole—exceeds the speed of light. There are different types of black holes according to their size. Some are as massive as a solar system. Once a black hole is formed, it can continue to grow in size by absorbing more matter. Astronomers believe that hundreds of massive black holes wander the galaxy. Fortunately, the nearest black hole to Earth is thousands of light years away.

1. What is the main idea?
   a. Black holes wander the galaxy.
   b. A black hole in space is a region where the gravity is so strong that nothing can escape its pull.
   c. They are called black holes because even light is pulled into the massive dark center.
   d. Fortunately, the nearest black hole to Earth is thousands of light years away.

2. What is the author's purpose?
   a. to inform readers about black holes
   b. to entertain readers with a story about black holes
   c. to persuade readers that black holes are dangerous
   d. to inform readers why black holes exist

3. Who is the intended audience?
   a. astronomers who study the universe
   b. people who want to know about black holes
   c. astronomy magazine advertisers
   d. newspaper reporters

4. What is the author's tone?
   a. humorous
   b. disapproving
   c. concerned
   d. informative

5. Determine whether the following sentence is a fact, an opinion, or both. Underline any words or phrases that signal an opinion. "Objects, such as asteroids, can get pulled into the hole but never come out."
   a. fact
   b. opinion
   c. fact and opinion

Practice

2. Read the following paragraph, and underline the main idea (if stated) and the major details. Then, answer the questions that follow.

On April 20, 2010 an explosion on an oil rig in the Gulf of Mexico killed 11 people and caused several pipe leaks about 50 miles off the coast of Louisiana. Oil poured out at a rate of up to 60,000 barrels a day, making it one of the worst environmental disasters in recent history. Oil drilling in the Gulf of Mexico was a disaster waiting to happen. A fragile marsh environment along Louisiana's coast serves as a buffer in storms. Damage to the salt marshes from an oil spill can cause major erosion from storm surge, and impact wildlife all along the southern coast. Offshore oil drilling is too dangerous. Instead of drilling for oil, our resources should be directed to developing cleaner and safer energy resources.

1. What is the main idea?

   a. There was a major oil spill in 2010 in the Gulf of Mexico.

   b. Louisiana will lose coastal land due to erosion and loss of marshes.

   c. Instead of drilling for oil, our resources should be directed to developing cleaner and safer energy resources.

   d. Oil drilling in the Gulf of Mexico was a disaster waiting to happen.

2. What is the author's purpose?

   a. to inform readers about the 2010 oil spill

   b. to persuade readers that offshore oil drilling is dangerous

   c. to persuade readers that instead of offshore oil drilling, our resources should be directed to developing cleaner and safer energy resources

   d. to entertain readers about offshore oil drilling

3. Who is the intended audience?

   a. people who work for the oil company

   b. people who care about the environment

   c. people who want lower gas prices

   d. people who own gas stations

4. What is the author's tone?

   a. critical   **c.** objective

   b. straightforward   **d.** approving

5. Determine whether the following sentence is a fact, an opinion, or both. Underline any words or phrases that signal an opinion. "Oil drilling in the Gulf of Mexico was a disaster waiting to happen."

   a. fact

   b. opinion

   c. fact and opinion

Practice

3. Read the following paragraphs, and underline the main idea (if stated) and the major details. Then, answer the questions that follow.

Birds fly from one place to another during their seasonal migrations to find food and breeding grounds. Some birds travel thousands of miles. For instance, the arctic tern flies about 18,600 miles each way—an incredible journey for any bird. Today scientists are able to track migrating birds with geo-locators similar to the GPS systems in cars. They were surprised to discover that songbirds fly more than 300 miles a day. In addition, more than half of the bird species they tracked show a shift in their migration patterns due to climate change. Another alarming trend is that nearly half of the migrating water birds are decreasing in number. Because of climate change, some birds must also fly farther than ever before to find certain types of habitats. This requires more energy and food sources than before and, unfortunately, may be a reason why some populations of birds are decreasing. Biologists are concerned about the negative effects of climate change on birds and will continue to study them closely.

1. What is the main idea of the selection?

    a. Because of geo-locators, scientists are learning about the trends in bird migration and population.

    b. Birds fly from one place to another during their seasonal migrations to find food and breeding grounds.

    c. Today scientists are able to track migrating birds with geo-locators similar to the GPS systems in cars.

    d. Biologists are concerned about the negative effects of climate change on birds and will continue to study them closely.

2. What is the author's purpose?

    a. to persuade readers to study birds

    b. to entertain readers about birds

    c. to describe different kinds of birds

    d. to inform readers about bird migrations and population trends

3. Who is the intended audience?

    a. anyone interested in birds   **c.** biologists

    b. retail managers   **d.** artists

4. What is the author's tone?

    a. objective   **c.** critical

    b. upset   **d.** concerned

5. Determine whether the following sentence is a fact, an opinion, or both. Underline any words or phrases that signal an opinion. "They were surprised to discover that songbirds fly more than 300 miles a day."

    a. fact   **c.** fact and opinion

    b. opinion

As you read the following textbook selection, circle the topic and underline the main idea (if stated) and the major details. Then, answer the questions that follow. Consider the source of the selection and the topic when answering the questions.

Historically, tigers roamed widely across Asia from Turkey to northeast Russia to Indonesia. Within the past 200 years, however, people have driven the majestic striped cats from most of their historic range. Today, tigers are exceedingly rare and are creeping toward extinction.

The Russians who moved into the region in the early 20th century hunted tigers for sport and hides, and some Russians reported killing as many as 10 tigers in a single hunt. Later, poachers (illegal hunters) began killing tigers to sell their body parts to China and other Asian countries, where they are used in traditional medicine. Meanwhile, road building, logging, and agriculture began to decrease the tiger's habitat and provide easy access for poachers. The tiger population dipped to perhaps 20 to 30 animals.

International conservation groups began to get involved, working with Russian biologists to try to save the decreasing tiger population. One such group was the Hornocker Wildlife Institute, now part of the Wildlife Conservation Society (WCS). In 1992 the group helped launch the Siberian Tiger Project, devoted to studying the tiger and its habitat.

Today, WCS biologists track tigers with radio collars, monitor their movements and health, determine causes of death when they die, and provide funding for local wildlife officials to stop and capture poachers. Thanks to such efforts, today, Siberian tigers in the wild number roughly 330 to 370, and about 1,500 more survive in zoos and captive breeding programs around the world.

(From *Essential Environment: The Science Behind the Stories,* 3e by Jay H. Withgott and Scott R. Brennan. Copyright © 2009 by Jay H. Withgott and Scott R. Brennan. Reprinted by permission of Pearson Education, Inc., Upper Saddle River, NJ.)

QUESTIONS

1. What is the central point of the entire selection?

   a. Historically, tigers roamed widely across Asia from Turkey to northeast Russia to Indonesia.

   b. Within the past 200 years, however, people have driven the majestic striped cats from most of their historic range.

   c. Although tigers were nearly hunted to extinction, due to conservation efforts, the number of tigers in the world has increased.

   d. The Russians who moved into the region in the early 20th century hunted the tigers until they were nearly extinct.

2. What is the author's purpose?

   a. to entertain readers with a story about tigers

   b. to persuade readers to contribute to tiger conservation groups

   c. to inform readers about how conservation helps tigers to avoid extinction

   d. to inform readers about the history of tigers

3. Who is the intended audience?

   a. biologists who work with tigers

   b. business managers

   c. biology students

   d. advertisers

4. What is the author's tone?

   a. straightforward

   b. frustrated

   c. upset

   d. discouraged

5. Determine whether the following sentence is a fact, an opinion, or both. Underline any words or phrases that signal an opinion. "Meanwhile, road building, logging, and agriculture began to decrease the tiger's habitat and provide easy access for poachers."

   a. fact

   b. opinion

   c. fact and opinion

U-Review

Complete the following sentences with a word or phrase from the list below.

author's purpose   author's tone   intended audience
fact   opinion

1. When thinking about whom something was written for, you are thinking about the ....

2. To find the ...., you should ask, "What is the author's attitude toward this topic?"

3. Something that cannot be proved true or false is a(n) ....

4. To find the ...., you should ask, "Why did the author write this?"

5. Something is a(n) .... if you can answer yes to the question, "Can this be proved true or false?"

DETECTING BIAS AND POINT OF VIEW

Bias: the author's attitude is revealed as for or against something.

When authors reveal their attitudes about a topic, they are showing readers their point of view—how they see an issue—from their own perspective. Sometimes authors may reveal an attitude about their topic that is positive or negative. *Bias* is present when an author reveals his or her opinion about something. We often refer to bias as a type of prejudice. For instance, someone preferring a BMW over a Mercedes shows bias.

When looking for bias, ask yourself, "What is the author's attitude about this topic?" If the author reveals a positive or negative attitude about the topic, or gives an opinion, then the author is showing bias. If the author is just presenting the facts in a balanced manner by showing the positive and negative sides about the topic, then the writing is **unbiased.** As you read the following sentences, look for bias.

1. Climate change is due to many factors, including the impact of humans on the environment.

2. Apathetic and selfish humans have had a negative impact on the environment and are responsible for climate change.

In the first sentence, it can be proved that climate change is due to many factors, including humans. Therefore, it is a fact. In the second sentence, the words "apathetic" and "selfish" are opinions, so it shows bias.

Often you will see opinions in biased writing, so be aware of opinion words and phrases. In the sentence, "Inhaling toxic substances will cause brain damage," there is no bias because the author doesn't reveal his or her opinion about the topic. However, in the sentence, "Companies that <u>dump</u> toxic materials into the environment <u>should be</u> severely punished," the author is stating his or her opinion about the topic, so this is a biased statement. When the author's attitude about the topic is not evident, the writing is *unbiased*.

Unbiased: when the author's opinion of the topic is not evident, the writing is unbiased.

Bias is present in many different situations and can even be found in textbooks. If you are able to recognize bias, then you will be aware when someone is trying to influence your thinking. Critical readers look for facts and make their own decisions about what they believe. Passive readers let other people do their thinking for them.

Are You Biased?

Everyone has some type of bias. We all have our favorite brands of clothing, cars, sports teams, or restaurants. Some bias is normal. However, we do not expect news to be biased; it should be factual, without showing reporters' personal attitudes about the topics. We also want our instructors to be fair and without bias toward all students. We expect our police to be unbiased, treating everyone the same. On the other hand, we expect advertisers to be biased in favor of their products and political candidates to be biased about their ability to lead. Bias is expected in some circumstances but not in others.

Read the following sentences. Which sentence is biased in favor of pesticides? Which one is biased against pesticides? Which one is unbiased?

1. Thanks to pesticides, crop losses have been significantly reduced.

2. Pesticides include insecticides but can also control fungi and bacteria.

3. Pesticides are harmful chemicals that can poison wildlife and birds, and they should not be used in agriculture.

When Bias Is Factual

Bias can be present even when an idea is presented entirely with facts. The bias comes into play when an author chooses to use only positive facts and to leave out the negative facts (or vice versa). Can you tell which of the following paragraphs is biased?

President Clinton was a well-liked politician. He made strides in revising the welfare system to reduce the number of years a person could receive benefits, and he remained popular until he left the White House.

President Clinton was successful in revising the welfare system but was unable to push his health insurance plan through Congress. He remained a popular president throughout his term in the White House despite a highly publicized extramarital affair.

The second paragraph shows both positive and negative facts about the topic and has no opinions, so it is the unbiased paragraph. Even though the first paragraph is factual, it left out the negative facts and therefore is biased.

481

Practice

1. Identify the following sentences as either biased (B) or unbiased (U). Underline any words or phrases that reveal the author's bias.

1. .... Hydrogen is the best fuel to use in motor vehicles because it doesn't pollute the air.

2. .... Hydrogen fuel is produced from water or other substances.

3. .... Hydrogen production is too expensive to do on a large scale.

4. .... Hydrogen fuel reduces the need for fossil fuels.

5. .... When compared with hydrogen-fuel engines, battery-operated engines cost less and are a better way to produce clean energy.

2. Identify the following sentences as either biased (B) or unbiased (U). Underline any words or phrases that reveal the author's bias.

1. .... Wolves are highly social animals that care for each other, hunt cooperatively, and mourn their dead.

2. .... In the 1920s, wolves were ruthlessly hunted until they were completely eliminated from Yellowstone National Park.

3. .... In the mid-1990s, wolves were reintroduced into Yellowstone National Park.

4. .... In a few years, the wolves strengthened the herds of elk by eliminating the weakest and sickest animals.

5. .... The entire park was greatly improved by the remarkable wolves who lived and hunted there.

3. In the following paragraph, identify which sentences are biased (B) or unbiased (U) by writing your answer on the spaces after each sentence. Underline any words or phrases that reveal the author's bias.

Dolphins are known for their high intelligence and social behavior. .... They are so gentle and kind that they will sometimes come to the aid of other dolphins, whales, and even humans. .... Dolphins have also been known to engage in aggressive behavior such as fighting and will mercilessly kill porpoises for no apparent reason. .... Some male dolphins have even killed their own babies. .... Dolphins break off sponges that grow in the sea and use them to cover their snouts for protection when looking for food. ....

TEXTBOOK SELECTION

As you read the following textbook selection, underline the main idea and major details. Then, answer the questions that follow.

As individuals, we each can help reduce agricultural water use by decreasing the amount of meat we eat, because producing meat requires far more water than producing grain or vegetables. In our households, we can reduce water use by installing low-flow faucets, showerheads, washing machines, and toilets. We can water lawns at night, when water loss from evaporation is minimal. Better yet, we can replace water-intensive lawns with native plants adapted to our region's natural precipitation patterns.

The quantity and distribution of fresh water pose one set of environmental and social challenges. Safeguarding the *quality* of water involves another set of environmental and human health issues. Developed nations have made admirable advances in cleaning up water pollution over the past few decades. Still, the World Commission on Water recently concluded that more than half the world's major rivers are seriously endangered and polluted, poisoning the surrounding ecosystems, and threatening the health and livelihood of people who depend on them. Meanwhile, the largely invisible pollution of groundwater has been termed a "covert crisis."

(From *Essential Environment: The Science Behind the Stories*, 3e by Jay H. Withgott and Scott R. Brennan. Copyright © 2009 by Jay H. Withgott and Scott R. Brennan. Reprinted by permission of Pearson Education, Inc., Upper Saddle River, NJ.)

QUESTIONS

1. What is the topic of the first paragraph?

   a. water pollution

   b. polluted ecosystems

   c. how individuals can reduce water use

   d. water for agriculture

2. What is the author's implied main idea the first paragraph?

   a. As individuals, we each can help reduce agricultural water use by decreasing the amount of meat we eat.

   b. We should limit water use by installing low-flow plumbing fixtures.

   c. Landscaping should be designed with plants that do not require much water.

   d. There are many ways that individuals can help reduce water use.

3. What is the topic of the second paragraph?

   a. reducing pollution

   b. water pollution

   c. polluted rivers

   d. saving water

4. **Which of the following sentences from the selection is biased?**

   a. Developed nations have made admirable advances in cleaning up water pollution over the past few decades.

   b. Still, the World Commission on Water recently concluded that more than half the world's major rivers are seriously endangered and polluted, poisoning the surrounding ecosystems, and threatening the health and livelihood of people who depend on them.

   c. We can water lawns at night, when water loss from evaporation is minimal.

   d. Safeguarding the *quality* of water involves another set of environmental and human health issues.

5. **In this selection, the author is:**

   a. biased against using water.

   b. biased against countries that pollute.

   c. biased in favor of saving water and cleaning up water pollution.

   d. biased against developing countries.

U-Review

For each of the following sentences, write "T" if the statement is true or "F" if the statement is false. As you go over the answers with your team, discuss why the false statements were false.

1. .... Authors are biased when they reveal their attitudes toward a subject.

2. .... Bias is never found in textbooks or newspapers.

3. .... Bias often contains opinion.

4. .... A paragraph that contains only facts is always unbiased.

5. .... If the author does not reveal an attitude in favor of or against something, the writing is unbiased.

Reading 1 Vocabulary Preview

The following vocabulary words are from the article "Shark!" With a partner or in a team, choose the correct meanings of the underlined words in the following sentences. Use context clues (LEADS), word part clues, and parts of speech to help you figure out the meanings.

1. The killer whales in the Sea World show raise their <u>flukes</u> (flooks) above the water and wave at the audience.

   a. heads

   b. tails

   c. snouts

   d. bellies

2. Whales in the wild live together in <u>pods</u> (pods) and communicate to each other through "songs."

   a. groups

   b. containers

   c. coverings for a pea or bean

   d. seas

3. The elephant pulled <u>strenuously</u> (STREN-you-us-ly) on the tree branch until it snapped off, and then he stripped off the leaves and ate them.

   a. easily

   b. carefully

   c. with great effort

   d. waving it

4. Skiing down the mountainside, Briana kept <u>traversing</u> (tra-VERS-ing) the slope until she reached the bottom.

   a. reversing

   b. studying

   c. aiming at

   d. crossing

5. When someone yelled "Shark!" at the beach, there was such <u>chaos</u> (KAY-os) that the children were lost in the crowds scurrying to shore.

   a. confusion

   b. crowded

   c. fear

   d. evil

Reading 1

6. The snow leopard can <u>catapult</u> (CAT-a-pult) himself over 50 feet to reach his prey.

   a. a weapon

   b. leap through the air

   c. run

   d. slide down

7. The habitat of the Japanese snow monkey is <u>encompassed</u> (en-COME-pass'd) by the mountains, but their favorite place to hang out is in the steamy water of the hot springs.

   a. directions

   b. identified

   c. surrounded by

   d. passed over by

8. The <u>ghoulish</u> (GOOL-ish) vampire bat gets its name because it feeds on the blood of mammals, such as cattle or deer.

   a. evil

   b. disgusting

   c. unusual

   d. monster-like

9. Some animals with high intelligence have the ability to feel <u>empathy</u> (EM-path-ee) for other beings.

   a. understanding of another's feelings

   b. dependent upon others

   c. helpless

   d. happiness

10. Steven's painful <u>encounters</u> (en-COUNT-ers) with jellyfish have taught him to be careful when swimming in the ocean.

    a. meetings

    b. injuries

    c. battles

    d. studies

Reading 1 What Do You Already Know?

1. Have you, or someone you know, ever been attacked by an animal? Describe what happened.

2. What do you already know about sharks and shark attacks?

> **Directions:** As you read this article, practice the four-step reading process. Preview the article, and then write on the following lines one or two questions that you would hope to have answered.
>
> ....
>
> ....
>
> ....
>
> ....

As you read, answer the questions in the margins to check your comprehension.

"Shark!"

BY CATHY FREE

In *Reader's Digest*, July 2008. Copyright © 2008 by The Reader's Digest Association, Inc. Reprinted by permission of *Reader's Digest*.

When a two-ton shark caught surfer Todd Endris in its jaws in Monterey Bay, an unlikely group of swimmers came to his rescue.

1   Silver fog blanketed California's Monterey Bay on a late August morning. For Todd Endris, it was a perfect end-of-summer day for surfing. The lanky 24-year-old aquarium technician zipped into his wet suit and headed to Marina State Beach, two miles from his apartment. As he waded into the surf, a <u>pod</u> of dolphins played in the waves just ahead of him. Other than a few dedicated surfers, the dolphins were the only creatures visible in the bay. Endris paddled <u>strenuously</u> and caught a wave in, then headed out to find another.

2   Resting on his board 75 yards from shore, he turned to watch his friend Brian Simpson glide under the curve of a near-perfect wave. Suddenly

Reading 1

What occurred when Todd Endris was surfing?

Endris was hit from below and catapulted 15 feet in the air. Landing headfirst in the water, he felt his pulse quicken. He knew only one thing could slam him with such force. Frantically paddling to the surface, he yanked at the surfboard, attached to his ankle by a leash, climbed on, and pointed it toward shore. But within seconds he was hit again. An enormous Great White shark had him in its jaws, its teeth dug into his back.

3   The vast aquatic wilderness known as the Monterey Bay National Marine Sanctuary stretches from Marin County, north of San Francisco, to the rugged Cambria coastline south of Big Sur, encompassing 5,322 square miles of ocean. One of the most diverse protected ecosystems in the world, it includes the Red Triangle, an area that earned its ghoulish nickname for its history of shark attacks, particularly in the period from late August through November, when Great Whites come to feed on young seals and sea lions.

4   Shark–human encounters make headlines, but they're rare; fewer than 50 people were attacked in the Red Triangle between 1959 and 2007. Humans may be mistaken for prey, but some experts say that Great Whites just don't care much what they eat. "Anybody who surfs or dives where seals and sea lions are **prevalent** could be asking for trouble," says George Burgess, director of the International Shark Attack File in Gainesville, Florida, a group that tracks shark incidents worldwide.

prevalent (PREV-a-lent): widespread

5   In Monterey Bay that August morning, the Great White dragged Endris below the surface. Attempting to force the shark to release him, the surfer slugged it on the snout over and over. "It was like punching a Chevy Suburban covered with sandpaper," he says. "I was getting nowhere."

6   The 16-foot shark had clamped down on his back with three rows of razor-sharp teeth. Endris felt no pain, only a tremendous pressure as the shark dipped him beneath the churning water and shook him back and forth in its powerful jaws.

7   A few feet away, Joe Jansen, a 25-year-old college student from Marina, California, was relaxing on his board when he heard a loud splash. Glancing over his shoulder, he spotted a gray creature rising 12 feet out of the water with Endris and a blue surfboard in its mouth. At first, Jansen thought the creature was a whale, "the biggest thing I'd ever seen." Then he heard Endris scream. "My immediate thought was to get the hell out of there," he says. He paddled as fast as he could toward shore, looking back every few seconds. When he made eye contact with Endris, he paused.

Reading 1

What was happening to Endris at this point?

"Help me!" yelled Endris, disappearing beneath the water again. The shark now had the surfer by the right thigh and appeared to be trying to swallow his leg whole.

8   Another 20 feet beyond the chaos, Wes Williams, a 33-year-old Cambria bar owner, stared from his surfboard in disbelief. Six bottlenose dolphins were leaping in and out of the water, stirring up whitecaps. When Williams saw Endris surface, he believed the dolphins were attacking him. "He was shouting like he was being electrocuted," he says.

9   Williams watched as the dolphin pod circled Endris, slapping their flukes in agitation. It was then that he saw the bright red ring of Endris's blood diffusing through the water. With a burst of adrenaline, Endris thrust his head above the surface, gasping for air. The Great White still had a hold on his upper thigh. "I figured my leg was gone," Endris says, "but I couldn't think about that right then." He used all his strength to kick the shark repeatedly in the face with his free leg. The Great White shot out of the water, thrashing Endris like a wet towel. The surfer swung his fists, hoping he'd get lucky and hit an eye. "Let me go!" he shouted. "Somebody, help me!"

What was Endris doing to try to get away?

10   He barely noticed the dolphins leaping over his head. Suddenly the shark released him. Fighting to stay afloat, Endris thought he saw the dolphins form a protective wall between him and the Great White.

11   Joe Jansen had paddled only 15 feet toward shore in his panic when he decided he couldn't live with himself if he didn't go back. He entered the pool of bloody water, half expecting to be attacked. "Quick! Get on your board!" he shouted to Endris. "C'mon, pal—it's behind you. Let's go!"

12   Less than a minute had passed since the shark had taken its first bite. Endris pulled his board close and crawled onto it. His skin was shredded to the bone. Jansen was horrified but stayed calm. "You can do it," he said. "There's a small swell coming. Let's take it in." Williams had also swum back to help. As soon as they reached the beach, they were joined by Simpson, who had been in shallow water when he saw his friend attacked. The three lifted Endris under his armpits and dragged him onto dry sand.

How did Endris escape from the shark?

13   "That's when the pain hit," recalls Endris. He cried out as the men positioned him facedown on a slope so that more blood would flow to his heart and head. While Endris's blood spurted from the gashes in his wet suit, somebody dialed 911. Endris closed his eyes and said a silent prayer over and over.

Reading 1

14   As it happened, Simpson, an X-ray tech at Salinas Valley Memorial Hospital, had witnessed his share of trauma cases. Working quickly, he wound a six-foot surfboard leash tightly around Endris's leg to help slow the bleeding. There wasn't much he could do for the 40-inch gash on his friend's back. A flap of skin was hanging from his body, exposing his spine and internal organs.

15   It took 10 minutes for a beach patrol crew, <u>traversing</u> the steep dunes in a four-wheel-drive pickup, to transport Endris to an ambulance. He was helicoptered to a trauma center in Santa Clara, where surgeons spent six hours putting him back together.

16   He had lost half of his blood and required more than 500 stitches and 200 staples to close the deep gashes. "His muscles were completely severed," says Dr. Allo. "It was hard to tell what belonged to what. It was tedious work, like doing a jigsaw puzzle."

What happened to Endris next?

17   Endris spent six days in the hospital, and his mom retired from nursing so she could take care of him. Over the next few months, Endris took to focusing on the positive view from that August day. "A lot of things came together to pull me through," he says. "The guys who rushed to help, the dolphins—they all saved my life."

18   Hoping to do his part to protect dolphins, Endris joined several organizations dedicated to their preservation. "I tell my story now to anybody who will listen because I want people to know how truly remarkable dolphins are," he says. "They're as smart as humans, and I believe they're capable of <u>empathy</u>. When I was being attacked that day, maybe they were trying to protect their young or acting on instinct. But they drove the shark away. If they hadn't, there's no doubt in my mind it would have come back."

To what does Endris attribute his rescue?

19   Six weeks after the attack, Endris stood at a mirror and checked out his scars. One snaked its way across his back and the other up and down his right leg. Even before he got a close look, he knew that he would return to the water. "I had to get on with it," he says. "I love the ocean too much."

1,435 words divided by _____ minutes = _____ words per minute

Reading 1 Thinking About What You Read

It is a good habit to summarize everything you read to strengthen your comprehension.

Directions: On the following lines, write a two- or three-sentence summary of the article "Shark!" In your own words, describe what the article was about and why the author wrote it.

....

....

....

....

....

Comprehension Questions

The following questions will help you to recall the main idea and the details of "Shark!" Review any parts of the article that you need to in order to find the correct answers.

LITERAL COMPREHENSION

1. What is the topic of this article?

   a. Todd Endris   **c.** a shark attack

   b. sharks   **d.** dangerous surfing

MAIN IDEA AND CENTRAL POINT

2. What is the central point (main idea) of the entire article?

   a. Sharks will swim away if a pod of dolphins come upon them.

   b. You should never swim or surf in shark-infested waters.

   c. Surfer Todd Endris was rescued from a shark attack.

   d. Todd Endris is a surfer who works for the preservation of dolphins.

SUPPORTING DETAILS

3. What did Todd Endris see just before the shark released him?

   a. the beach patrol coming to his aid

   b. a lifeguard splashing into the water toward him

   c. his whole life flashing before his eyes

   d. a pod of dolphins jumping over him

Reading 1
DRAWING CONCLUSIONS

4. Based on the story, which of the following is a logical conclusion?

   a. Todd Endris will never surf again.

   b. The dolphins swam around Todd Endris and drove away the shark.

   c. Marina State Beach will be closed to surfing because of the shark attack.

   d. Dolphins will usually attack sharks.

5. Why was the Great White shark swimming in Monterey Bay?

   a. It had come to feed on the seals and sea lions in the bay.

   b. It wanted to attack the dolphins in Monterey Bay.

   c. It wanted to attack surfers in the bay.

   d. It was driven there by warmer ocean temperatures.

PATTERNS OF ORGANIZATION

6. Identify the relationship within the following sentence: Working quickly, he wound a six-foot surfboard leash tightly around Endris's leg to help slow the bleeding.

   a. cause and effect   c. time order

   b. spatial order   d. compare and/or contrast

7. What is the overall pattern of organization?

   a. cause and effect   d. compare and/or contrast

   b. listing   d. time order

CRITICAL READING

8. Identify the following sentence as fact, opinion, or both: One of the most diverse protected ecosystems in the world, it includes the Red Triangle, an area that earned its ghoulish nickname for its history of shark attacks, particularly in the period from late August through November, when Great Whites come to feed on young seals and sea lions.

   a. fact

   b. opinion

   c. fact and opinion

9. Identify the following sentence as fact, opinion, or both: Six bottlenose dolphins were leaping in and out of the water, stirring up whitecaps.

   a. fact

   b. opinion

   c. fact and opinion

VOCABULARY IN CONTEXT

10. Identify the meaning of the underlined word in the following sentence: It was then that he saw the bright red ring of Endris's blood diffusing through the water.

    a. sinking   c. spreading

    b. floating   d. aspirating

Reading 1 Vocabulary Practice

Use the vocabulary words from the Word Bank to complete the following sentences. Write the words into the blanks provided.

WORD BANK

strenuously	traversing	chaos	catapulted	empathy
encompass	ghoulish	flukes	encounter	pods

1. My favorite novel is about a(n) .... vampire who preys upon the citizens of a small town at night.

2. In the sea mammal show, the orca whales wave goodbye with their ....

3. If you .... any bats in this cave, just wave your arms and they will leave.

4. Martin .... over the bar and broke the school's record for the high jump.

5. The rock climber pulled .... on his rope and reached the top of the cliff.

6. The surfers caught the biggest waves and began .... them.

7. All the mountains that .... this area are habitats for many wild animals, including the elk and deer.

8. Whales travel in groups, or .... , often with family members, and share the same dialect of vocal sounds.

9. When they announced on the news that a tornado was approaching, there was total .... as people rushed to shelters.

10. As Julia grieved over the death of her friend, her poodle dog stayed close to her and seemed to show .... for her feelings.

493

Reading 1 Questions for Writing and Discussion

Review any parts of the article you need to answer the following questions.

1. What evidence supports Todd Endris's theory that the dolphins came to his rescue?

2. Why did Joe Jansen change his mind and turn back?

3. Endris's survival was due to a number of factors that were in his favor. What were they?

4. In some areas of the world, when a wild animal attacks a human, the animal is hunted and killed. Do you think this is the best way to deal with animals that attack humans? Why or why not?

5. How would you explain the behavior of the dolphins that came to Todd Endris while the shark was attacking him?

Reading 1 Vocabulary Practice–Fast Match

strenuously	straining hard	traversing	going across
chaos	confusion	catapult	to send through the air
encompass	surrounding	ghoulish	monster-like
empathy	understanding another's feelings	tails	flukes
encounter	experience; meeting	pod	group of sea animals

1.

On a blank sheet, draw the 20 cards above and cut out as individual cards. Pair up with another person to play one against one.

2.

Shuffle the vocabulary and matching definition cards and lay them face down in four rows of five cards.

3.

Have another person keep time. Both players will have 60 seconds to make as many matching pairs of words and their definitions as they can. Both players play at the same time, turning over one card and then a second card. When a card is turned over and it doesn't match the second one turned over, both cards must be turned face down in the same places before turning over any other cards. If two players go for the same card at the same time, the player whose hand is most on the card gets to use it for his or her turn.

4.

As soon as a match is found, players take the matching cards and put them into a pile in front of them.

5.

When time is called, play stops, and the player with the most correct matches wins.

understanding another's feelings

empathy

Reading 2 Vocabulary Preview

The following words are from the article "Super Storm." With a partner or in a team, choose the correct meanings of the underlined words in the following sentences. Use context clues (LEADS), word part clues, and parts of speech to help you figure out the meanings.

1. That weird vampire movie was the eeriest (EAR-ee-ist) one I've ever seen.

   a. slowest

   b. inward

   c. strangest

   d. severe

2. In the morning, there were only remnants (REM-nants) of last night's party at the fraternity house: empty beer bottles, cold pizza, and trash piled up in the kitchen.

   a. leftover food

   b. remainders

   c. symptoms

   d. memories

3. After the earthquake, there was so much rubble (RUB-bul) in the streets that emergency vehicles could not get to where they were needed.

   a. broken pieces of rock, concrete, and so on

   b. dirt and mud

   c. water

   d. chaos

4. The power lines that had blown down during the storm were in a huge morass (more-AS).

   a. swamp

   b. tangled mess

   c. dilemma

   d. pallet

5. In the *Wizard of Oz*, Dorothy's house was sucked up into the vortex (VOR-tex) of a tornado.

   a. clouds

   b. lightning

   c. thunderstorm

   d. rotating column of air

6. An <u>apocalyptic</u> (ah-pah-kuh-LIP-tik) earthquake destroyed northwestern Turkey in 1999, killing more than 17,000 people.

   a. disastrous

   b. shattered

   c. tentative

   d. disarming

7. The strongest tornadoes usually form with <u>supercells</u> (SOO-per-sells) and can cause tremendous damage to life and property.

   a. cell phone towers

   b. huge thunderstorms

   c. lithographs

   d. portfolios

8. The strong, <u>turbulent</u> (TER-byu-lent) winds caused the airplane to dip and bump through the atmosphere.

   a. severed

   b. earmarked

   c. violently disturbed

   d. ragged

9. We tried various <u>configurations</u> (kon-fig-yur-AY-shuns) when deciding upon the final layout for our new home's plan.

   a. changes

   b. amputations

   c. impulses

   d. arrangements

10. My brother's bedroom looks like a disaster zone with his clothes and belongings all <u>strewn</u> (STROON) around his room.

    a. a dish of meat and vegetables

    b. scattered

    c. severed

    d. encompassed

Reading 2 ## What Do You Already Know?

1. Describe the worst storm you have ever personally seen or have heard about from someone.

2. What kind of natural disasters are common in your area? What preparations have you or your family taken to deal with them?

> **Directions:** As you read this article, practice the four-step reading process. Preview the article, and then write on the following lines one or two questions that you would hope to have answered.
>
> ....
>
> ....
>
> ....

As you read, answer the questions in the margins to check your comprehension.

"Super Storm"

BY CHRISTOPHER W. DAVIS

In *Reader's Digest*, September 2006. Copyright © 2006 by The Reader's Digest Association, Inc. Reprinted by permission of *Reader's Digest*.

A tornado half a mile wide was headed straight for town, but no one knew how disastrous it would be.

Sunday, April 2, 2006, 5:30 p.m.
Dyer County, Tennessee

1   The picture windows in Rick and Laura Gregory's home looked west over cotton fields toward the Mississippi River and the boot heel of Missouri beyond. As the sun went down, it played tricks with the sky, painting it yellow and orange. The news crawl at the bottom of the TV screen in the Gregory's family room said "Tornado watch." Laura was in the kitchen preparing an early dinner. Her husband, Rick, a patrol deputy for Dyer County, had just come off duty.

2   Then the newscasters came on to report that a tornado had hit Marmaduke, Arkansas, 60 miles to the west. When they started talking about Caruthersville, directly across the Mississippi, Rick was sure they

were in for it. He quickly finished his supper. Without a storm cellar, people said, the bathroom was the safest place. He turned to Laura and told her to get theirs ready. "If you hunker down in the tub with a cell phone, a candle and a battery-powered radio, you'll be okay." What Rick was about to see over the next 48 hours would change that belief forever.

3   Climbing into his patrol car, Rick began to study the sky. He had never seen anything like it, and never had such a ringside seat right on the edge of a supercell thunderstorm. It was as if the road was acting as a boundary. The entire sky to the left, southward, was a pleasant, warm blue with golden sunlight. But everything to the north was a turbulent, pitch-black mass of the meanest-looking cloud cover he'd ever seen. Rick got on the radio and told the team, "I'm heading down to the Great River Road to watch."

Why was Deputy Rick Gregory going to Great River Road?

4   Across town, Vanice and Larry Parker had moved into their new ranch house with cypress wood siding on Meacham Road just a week ago. They'd taken their time building, adding custom touches to the house and a large cabinetry workshop in the side yard.

5   Vanice and Larry had spent most of Sunday rearranging furniture, trying different configurations for the dining and living room areas. They unpacked boxes and planted a few trees. The day was unusually warm for April, so Vanice opened the windows in the living room. There was a nice breeze blowing in the afternoon. At 7 p.m. they settled down on the sofa in pajamas just as the movie *Crash* began.

6   Just 15 minutes into *Crash*, Vanice and Larry Parker, sitting with the windows still open, heard click-click-clicking noises outside. "It's hailing," Vanice said. Then they heard a roaring, grinding sound like a huge cement truck backing toward the house.

7   "Is that a tornado?" Larry asked. "It sounds like it."

8   "I don't know," Vanice said.

9   As they ran down the hall toward the west-facing bedroom, they saw it. It was huge, dark, sucking up the earth, and coming right for them. This wasn't any familiar funnel dancing across the landscape. It was an apocalyptic black curtain cutting off the sky, whipping round and round, snapping trees in half, tearing everything up. They had nowhere to go, no basement, nowhere to hide. Larry tried pulling the mattress off the bed to cover them in the tub, but it was too heavy and he couldn't budge it.

Describe the situation that Vanice and Larry are facing.

10   He and Vanice lay down side by side in the bathtub. She wrapped her arms around her husband. The roar got louder. It was louder than they thought noise could get. Their ears started popping as air being sucked into the vortex created a low-pressure zone. They could feel the whole house vibrating in their bones, shaking as violently as in an earthquake. Larry reached up and took hold of the faucet. He grasped it as if it were his last hold upon the earth. A split second later the lights went out.

Reading 2

11   When the tornado finally passed, Vanice and Larry Parker emerged from the bathtub and went to the living room. The furniture they'd been arranging and rearranging all day was piled in a heap in the dining room. Leaves and debris were scattered everywhere. Some of the screens on the open windows were blown in; others were blown out. Insulation had been sucked out of the wall, and ventilation ducts popped out of the floor. Somehow, though, their dream house had held together against the nightmare. They were two of the lucky ones.

12   Vanice opened the front door. A flash of lightning illuminated a ravaged battlefield: two houses on the McAndrews' property directly across the street, the stone main house and a smaller frame structure, were gone, just gone. Vanice felt herself go limp as she dialed 911 on her cell phone. "My neighbor's house has just been blown away by a tornado," she told the operator.

13   "Help is on the way," the dispatcher replied. Then Vanice's phone went dead. She stepped back outside. That's when she saw the two McAndrews kids and three of their friends, screaming and crying, running from the rubble across the way.

14   "Oh, thank God they're alive," Vanice thought. But as the youngsters got closer, she saw terror in their eyes. "Where's your mom and dad?" she asked. They said their parents were out to dinner in town. The kids had been in the smaller house watching television when one of their parents called and warned them about the approaching tornado. The kids went outside, saw the storm towering across the sky, and had only seconds to run for cover in the basement of the stone house. No sooner had they huddled together in one corner than the house was ripped apart. Shattered remnants collapsed into the basement, filling it with rubble. Only the spot where they hid was spared.

15   A neighbor named Steve Harness, in the home nearby, was okay, but in the next house down the road, Bill and Wanda Fay Taylor were not. That was the eeriest thing. The Taylors were found lying side by side, as if they had just gone to bed, right where the house had been, family photographs strewn around them.

16   On Biffle Road there was another heartbreak. A young couple told people that their 11-month-old son had been in the house with their mother and stepfather who were baby-sitting while the couple was away in town. Volunteers searched. The bodies of all three were found in a field across the road.

17   After watching the monster tornado drop out of the clouds and head toward his home, Deputy Rick Gregory pushed the gas pedal of his patrol car to the floor. "I've got to get home before it does," he said into the radio. Racing alongside the cotton fields, he watched the quarter-mile-wide storm twist steel power-line towers like pretzels. Then the full force

What did Vanice see when she opened the front door?

What happened to some other people in the town?

500

of the storm slammed into the bluff, bounced off, stalled, tried again, and a third time.

18 Finally, the massive cloud headed off to the left, away to the north and east. Sure that it had bypassed his house, Rick turned toward the bluff, chasing the vortex of wind. Already reports were coming in about homes damaged and people trapped. He headed up the road to the bluff, where he was stopped by a morass of huge, old trees. Uprooted, snapped and twisted apart, they blocked the narrow, winding road completely. Rick got out of his car and started to run through the devastation. He had been up and down this road a thousand times—now he didn't recognize the area at all.

What did Deputy Rick Gregory see when he returned home?

19 It was about 2 a.m. before Patrolman Rick Gregory got home and collapsed into bed. His house had been untouched. The next day he was up early to take a look at the devastation from a helicopter. He had seen some wild stuff in his day, but this storm was in a class all its own.

20 The tornado was a category F3 storm with winds up to 200 miles per hour. It had been a half-mile wide and carved an 18-mile-long path through Dyer County. In all, 24 lives were lost in Tennessee that evening, 16 of them in Dyer County and 8 in neighboring Gibson. According to the Red Cross, 141 single-family homes were completely destroyed, and 80 homes sustained major damage.

21 For the next week, it seemed like all Gregory and his fellow deputies did was patrol Harness Road to keep looters and gawkers away and to try to maintain some kind of order. After a couple of days, deputies were saying they'd had enough. They wanted duty in another part of the county.

22 Tales of amazing coincidence, heroism, and heartbreaking tragedy gradually spread across the county. There was the couple who survived when the husband lay on top of his wife holding her down on the floor while the wind pulled the rings off their fingers and the earrings from her ears. The farmer whose 5,000-pound plow had been moved 300 yards. A herd of miniature horses were found across the street from where they were penned—all survived save one.

What effects did the tornado have on the town?

23 The people began rebuilding their lives, grateful they had survived, mourning for those friends and neighbors who did not. They cleared away the rubble and tried to do what they could to salvage their homes and belongings. And no one knows when the next big twister will strike again.

1,615 words divided by _____ minutes = _____ words per minute

Reading 2 Thinking About What You Read

It is a good habit to summarize everything you read to strengthen your comprehension.

Directions: On the following lines, write a two- or three-sentence summary of the article "Super Storm." In your own words, describe what the article was about and why the author wrote it.

....

....

....

....

....

Comprehension Questions

The following questions will help you to recall the main idea and the details of "Super Storm." Review any parts of the article that you need to in order to find the correct answers.

LITERAL COMPREHENSION

1. **What is the topic of this article?**
   a. the damage caused by a tornado
   b. a tornado in Dyer County, Tennessee
   c. natural disasters
   d. how one couple survived a tornado

CENTRAL POINT

2. **What is the central point of the entire article?**
   a. Tornadoes are dangerous.
   b. A tornado killed many people.
   c. A huge tornado in Dyer County injured and killed residents and destroyed much property.
   d. If you are ever caught in a tornado, the bathroom or the basement are the two safest places to be.

SUPPORTING DETAILS

3. **What happened to Laura Gregory, the deputy's wife?**
   a. She was found dead among the rubble.
   b. She ran to a neighbor's house and stayed in the cellar until the storm passed.
   c. She escaped harm from the tornado.
   d. Her husband came home and took her to a shelter.

Reading 2

4. **What did Vanice and Larry Parker see when they emerged from the bathtub?**

    a. Their house was gone.

    b. Their house was untouched by the tornado.

    c. The tornado had taken off their roof.

    d. Their house was still standing, but the two buildings across the street were gone.

DRAWING CONCLUSIONS

5. **What happened after the storm that made the situation even more difficult for Rick Gregory and his deputies?**

    a. There was no water or electricity in the county.

    b. They had to keep looters and gawkers away from the damaged homes and businesses.

    c. Many deputies quit their jobs.

    d. There were no emergency services.

PATTERNS OF ORGANIZATION

6. **What is the overall pattern of organization for this article?**

    a. compare and/or contrast

    c. definition

    b. cause and effect

    d. time order

VOCABULARY IN CONTEXT

7. **Identify the meaning of the underlined word in the following sentence: A flash of lightning illuminated a <u>ravaged</u> battlefield.**

    a. ruined

    c. war-like

    b. intense

    d. disaste

8. **Identify the meaning of the underlined word in the following sentence: They cleared away the rubble and tried to do what they could to <u>salvage</u> their homes and belongings.**

    a. save

    c. investigate

    b. take apart

    d. find

9. **What is the author's tone?**

    a. angry

    c. excited

    b. objective

    d. disapproving

10. **Which of the following statements is an opinion?**

    a. He had been up and down this road a thousand times—now he didn't recognize the area at all.

    b. Vanice felt herself go limp as she dialed 911 on her cell phone.

    c. The furniture they'd been arranging and rearranging all day was piled in a heap in the dining room.

    d. They were two of the lucky ones.

Reading 2 Vocabulary Practice

Use the vocabulary words from the Word Bank to complete the following sentences. Write the words into the blanks provided.

WORD BANK

eeriest	remnants	rubble	morass	vortex
supercells	apocalyptic	turbulent	configurations	strewn

1. The .... we were given by the designer for our furniture don't really fit our room sizes.

2. .... of the storm were everywhere—in town, where vehicles were overturned, and in the countryside, where entire homes were leveled to the ground.

3. After the storm, the streets of the town were filled with .... , and light posts were strewn everywhere.

4. The passengers and crew on the flight to Chicago went through some .... weather and suffered some minor injuries.

5. Tornadoes are likely to occur when there are .... with violent winds and hail.

6. After the thunderstorm, leaves and branches were .... all over our front lawn.

7. In an F5 tornado, winds inside the .... have been recorded at over 300 miles per hour.

8. When I walked into the old deserted house, I got the .... feeling that I was not alone.

9. The tornado had left the mobile home community in a(n) .... of crumpled and torn metal.

10. The tornado that ripped through Dyer County was so .... that it will take years to get things back to normal.

Questions for Writing and Discussion

Review any parts of the article you need to answer the following questions.

1. According to the article, and based on what you've learned, what are some things you should do when a tornado approaches?

....

....

....

Reading 2

2. Natural disasters bring out the best and the worst in people. What are some examples of the "best" and the "worst" as described in the article?

....

....

....

3. "Storm chasers" are people who follow tornadoes and other extreme weather so they can experience the thrill of a violent storm. Do you think storm chasing would be something you would want to do? Why or why not?

....

....

....

4. Why would studying weather patterns be important for any country?

....

....

....

5. What can people who are not affected by a disaster do to help those who have suffered a natural disaster like those in Dyer County, Tennessee?

....

....

Vocabulary Practice—Guess the Phrase

Preparation: Your instructor will draw blank lines on the board for each letter of a phrase. Divide the class into two to four teams. The objective of the game is to be the first team to guess the phrase.

1.

After deciding which team will go first by a coin toss, the instructor will read a question about the vocabulary words from either Reading Assignment 1 or 2 to the first team. If the team gives a correct response within 10 seconds, that team can guess one letter of the phrase on the board. If the letter the team guessed is in the phrase, the instructor will write all instances of that letter on the board where it appears in the phrase. If the team answers incorrectly or doesn't respond in 10 seconds, that team may not guess a letter or try to solve the puzzle.

2.

The play then goes to the next team, which will receive a question. Play will continue until all the questions have been answered or the puzzle has been solved. Teams may only try to solve the puzzle (guess the entire phrase) when it is their turn.

VIEWPOINT: Oil Drilling in Alaska

Read the following letters to the editor about whether we should allow oil companies to drill for oil in the Alaskan wilderness. Then, answer the questions that follow.

Dear Editor:

The debate in Congress over whether to allow more oil drilling in Alaska's north shore has me very worried. We've been getting oil from the National Petroleum Reserve (about 400,000 acres) and sending it through the 800-mile-long Alaskan Pipeline to the Alaskan west coast. And now people think we should drill even more around the Arctic National Wildlife Refuge. These lands are the home of more than 160 bird species, fish and marine mammals, polar bears and grizzly bears, foxes, caribou, wolves, and musk oxen. Why must we keep taking away their habitats to support our gas-guzzling vehicles? Why not use other forms of energy? Crude oil is poisonous to *all* life. If we are not concerned about the welfare of animals, we should at least be concerned about our own lives.

Signed,

Ms. Green

Dear Editor:

Once again the tree-huggers are trying to stop oil drilling in the Alaska wilderness. Have they forgotten about what it was like to spend a small fortune at the gas pump? Not only do people depend on oil, but businesses depend on it, too. Nearly everything we buy has to be shipped from somewhere, and that takes fuel. It takes fuel to run our factories and heat our homes and businesses. Our nation needs to reduce its dependence on oil from foreign countries, which can push up prices whenever they wish. Without enough oil, our manufacturing and shipping costs will be much higher. Jobs will go to other countries where costs are less. Prices of just about everything would be even higher than they are now. Although hydrogen and other new fuels are cleaner, we don't have enough of those resources ready yet. We need this oil for our current needs, or else we'll all suffer.

Signed,

Mr. Black

Critical Thinking

1. A *point of view* is the author's opinion about a topic. To find the author's point of view, ask yourself, "How does this author feel about this issue?" What is the author's point of view about oil drilling in Alaska in the first letter?

   ....

   ....

2. What is the author's point of view about oil drilling in Alaska in the second letter?

   ....

   ....

   ....

3. Which letter do you agree with, and why?

   ....

   ....

   ....

4. What could be the consequences of allowing oil drilling in the Alaskan wilderness?

   ....

   ....

   ....

5. What could be the consequences of not drilling for oil in the Alaskan wilderness?

   ....

   ....

   ....

   ....

WRITE YOUR THOUGHTS

Write a letter to the editor stating your own feelings about drilling for oil in the Alaskan wilderness. Use a separate sheet of paper.

507

Dr. Scott Gearhart,
Veterinarian at Sea World, Orlando, Florida

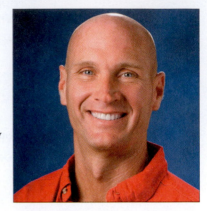

How did you become interested in veterinary medicine?
As far back as I can remember, I had always dreamed of becoming a veterinarian. I have *always* been interested in animals and was one of those kids who was always collecting whatever creatures I could get my hands on (much to my mother's chagrin!). Birds, rabbits, squirrels, snakes, toads, insects, you name it, and I likely had those individuals in my possession at some point in my youth. But, as corny as this may sound, what sealed my destiny in becoming a veterinarian was when I was 14, I rushed to the aid of a dog that had just been hit by a car, and it died in my arms. That was when I knew that this was a career that I had to pursue.

What is your training and educational background that prepared you for this job?
I acquired a B.A. degree in zoology before getting into veterinary school. While I was in college, I did some volunteer work at a local nature center, as well as spending some time with the companion animal veterinarian who provided the care for the wildlife that came into the center. Then, during my senior year of veterinary school, I was able to do an externship with a veterinarian in South Florida who worked with many exotic species as well as marine mammals. After I graduated, I worked for a small animal clinic in Las Vegas and then moved on to a mixed animal hospital. After a couple years there, I was hired into my first marine mammal veterinary position with a small park in Fort Lauderdale. After that park was closed, I went into a zoo, wildlife, and exotic animal internship at Kansas State University. From there, I took a job with the San Antonio Zoo, where I remained until I came here to Sea World. So, I have had a wide variety of experiences to get me to this point in my career.

While in school, did you have to overcome any obstacles? Did you ever feel like quitting?
I suppose the biggest obstacle that I had to overcome besides achieving good grades and meeting the veterinary prerequisites was gaining experience in the field, as there are not always a great number of ideal opportunities for students to participate and gain that hands-on experience. As far as feeling like quitting, I do not believe that that had ever crossed my mind, as I was truly driven to achieve my dream.

What do you like best about your job?
I have the greatest job in the world! The diverse collection of species that I get to work with is unmatched, and I also am incredibly fortunate to have ownership, which has the financial resources and desire to provide the very best of care to that collection.

What challenges do you face in your work?
Besides the very nature of my job, which is working with patients that cannot "tell me where it hurts," I face the additional challenge of working with animals who live their entire lives in water; thus, a lot of the more traditional diagnostic and therapeutic options available to other veterinarians working on terrestrial species are not practical for me to use. Because my patients are aquatic, they most often need to be removed from the water to be examined, which obviously presents its share of difficulties.

What advice do you have for college freshmen who are considering a career in veterinary medicine?
Obviously, achieving good grades is important, but it's also crucial to look for opportunities to gain experience in the field, even if it means cleaning kennels in a veterinary practice or doing volunteer work with a local wildlife rehabilitation center. It will help set you apart from other veterinary school candidates if you can demonstrate a long-standing interest in the profession.

What are your plans for the future?
I wish to continue working with marine animals, be it as a clinician or perhaps moving into a management position in my field. After that, hopefully a comfortable retirement!

BUILDING VOCABULARY

Throughout this course, you will be introduced to word parts that make up many words in the English language. Study the following word parts, and then answer the questions that follow.

Prefixes	Roots	Suffixes
bi- *two*	-angul-, -angle- *angle*	-ar *relating to*
tri- *three*	-ped-, -pod- *foot*	
quad-, quadr- *four*		
pent- *five*		
hexa- *six*		

What English words can you create from these word parts?

....

....

....

....

....

....

Using a dictionary, look up the meanings of any of the words you wrote that you can't define. Use one of the words you wrote in a sentence that reveals its meaning with a context clue:

....

....

....

Nutrition Labels

Reading nutrition labels is a good way to make sure you are buying food that is nutritious and good for your health. Foods with high amounts of calories, fat, cholesterol, sugar, and sodium are not good for you. Compare the following labels of two cereals, and then answer the questions that follow.

Here are the suggested amounts for healthy eating with a 2,000-calories-per-day diet:

Recommended Daily Total Amounts

Fat	less than 65 **g**	Cholesterol	less than 300 mg
Sodium	less than 2400 mg	Total carbohydrates	300 g

g = gram (A current U.S. penny weighs 2.5 grams.)

Kellogg's Special K Cereal

Nutrition Facts

Serving Size 1 Cup (31g/1.1 oz.)   Servings Per Container About 11

	Cereal	Cereal with 1/2 Cup Vitamins A&D Fat Free Milk
Amount Per Serving		
Calories	120	160
	% Daily Value**	
Total Fat 0.5g*	1%	1%
Saturated Fat 0g	0%	0%
Trans Fat 0g		
Cholesterol 0mg	0%	0%
Sodium 220mg	9%	12%
Potassium 50mg	1%	6%
Total Carbohydrate 23g	8%	10%
Dietary Fiber less than 1g	2%	2%
Sugars 4g		
Other Carbohydrate 19g		
Protein 6g		
Vitamin A	15%	20%
Vitamin C	35%	35%
Calcium	0%	15%
Iron	45%	45%
Vitamin E	35%	35%
Thiamin	35%	40%
Riboflavin	35%	45%
Niacin	35%	35%
Vitamin B6	100%	100%
Folic Acid	100%	100%
Vitamin B12	100%	110%
Phosphorus	4%	15%
Zinc	4%	6%
Selenium	10%	10%

* Amount in cereal. One half cup of fat free milk contributes an additional 40 calories, 65mg sodium, 6g total carbohydrates (6g sugars), and 4g protein.
** Percent Daily Values are based on a 2,000 calorie diet. Your daily values may be higher or lower depending on your calorie needs:

	2,000	2,500
Calories	2,000	2,500
Total Fat Less than	65g	80g
Saturated Fat Less than	20g	25g
Cholesterol Less than	300mg	300mg
Sodium Less than	2,400mg	2,400mg
Potassium	3,500mg	3,500mg
Total Carbohydrate	300g	375g
Dietary Fiber	25g	30g

Calories per gram: Fat 9 • Carbohydrate 4 • Protein 4

Store Brand Granola

Nutrition Facts

Serving Size 2/3 Cup (31g/1.1 oz.) Servings Per Container About 9

	Cereal	Cereal with 1/2 Cup Vitamins A&D Fat Free Milk
Amount Per Serving		
Calories	180	220
	% Daily Value**	
Total Fat 4.5g*	1%	1%
Saturated Fat 0g	0%	0%
Trans Fat 0g		
Cholesterol 0mg	0%	0%
Sodium 270mg	12%	15%
Potassium 50mg	1%	6%
Total Carbohydrate 26g	8%	10%
Dietary Fiber less than 4g	4%	4%
Sugars 10g		
Other Carbohydrate 26g		
Protein 8g		
Vitamin A	15%	20%
Vitamin C	35%	35%
Calcium	0%	15%
Iron	40%	40%
Vitamin E	30%	30%
Thiamin	25%	30%
Riboflavin	25%	35%
Niacin	20%	20%
Vitamin B6	35%	35%
Vitamin B12	30%	30%
Phosphorus	1%	12%

* Amount in cereal. One half cup of fat free milk contributes an additional 40 calories, 65mg sodium, 6g total carbohydrates (6g sugars), and 4g protein.
** Percent Daily Values are based on a 2,000 calorie diet. Your daily values may be higher or lower depending on your calorie needs:

	2,000	2,500
Calories	2,000	2,500
Total Fat Less than	90g	100g
Saturated Fat Less than	25g	30g
Cholesterol Less than	300mg	300mg
Sodium Less than	2,400mg	2,400mg
Potassium	3,500mg	3,500 mg
Total Carbohydrate	300g	375g
Dietary Fiber	25g	30g

Calories per gram: Fat 15 • Carbohydrate 8 • Protein 6

Questions

1. How much is one serving of cereal for Special K?

   a. 1 1/2 cups

   b. 1 cup

   c. 2/3 cups

   d. 2 cups

2. How much is one serving of cereal for Store Brand Granola?

   a. 1 1/2 cups

   b. 1 cup

   c. 2/3 cup

   d. 2 cups

3. How many more calories are in one serving of Store Brand Granola (without the milk) than Special K?

   a. 100 calories

   b. 90 calories

   c. 60 calories

   d. 20 calories

4. Which of these nutrients are higher in the Special K cereal than in the Store Brand Granola (both without milk)?

   a. sodium, vitamin E, and zinc

   b. cholesterol, sodium, and fat

   c. sugars, vitamin A, and selenium

   d. vitamin E, niacin, and iron

5. Which of these nutrients are higher in Store Brand Granola than in Special K?

   a. cholesterol, vitamin A, and iron

   b. calcium, sugar, and fat

   c. sugar, cholesterol, and vitamin A

   d. sugar, fat, and sodium

TEXTBOOK GRAPHIC AIDS

Study the following diagram, and then answer the questions that follow.

Anatomy of a Tornado

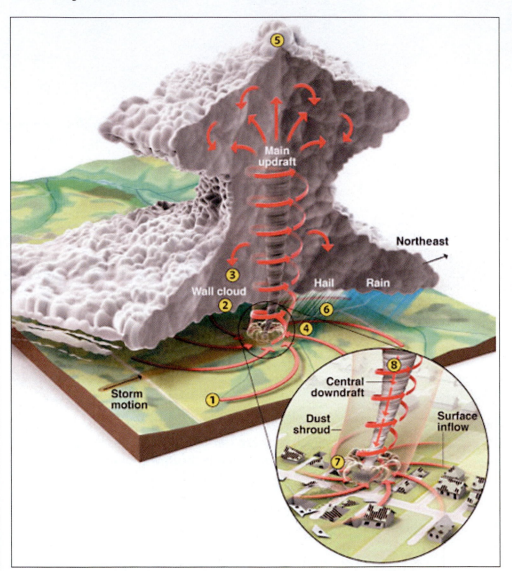

How Tornados Occur (from storm to major event):

1. Warm, moist air at the Earth's surface rises rapidly, creating an updraft.
2. Falling rain evaporates, cooling the air around it.
3. The wall cloud rotates as it is hit with winds from opposite directions.
4. As the rotation intensifies, a visible funnel drops out of the clouds.
5. A prominent cloud forms on top when the updraft is very strong.
6. Powerful updrafts give hail time to form.
7. A dust shroud is kicked up by the tornado's strong winds at ground level.
8. Central downdrafts appear in some tornadoes.
9. The rotating cloud gains strength and speed, some reaching speeds over 300 mph.

(By Joseph Lertola. Adapted from *Reader's Digest*, May 2009. Copyright © 2009 by Joseph Lertola. Reprinted with permission.)

1. Where does a tornado begin forming?

    a. up in the atmosphere

    b. at the ocean shores

    c. at the Earth's surface

    d. in the Northeast

2. What causes the spinning vortex to form?

    a. Warm, moist air at the Earth's surface rises rapidly, creating an updraft.

    b. The wall cloud rotates as it is hit with winds from opposite directions.

    c. A dust shroud is kicked up by the tornado's strong winds at ground level.

    d. Central downdrafts appear in some tornadoes.

3. According to the information above, which of the following are created by a tornado? (Choose all that apply.)

    a. strong updrafts

    b. lightning

    c. hail

    d. dust shrouds

4. When does the funnel or vortex appear?

    a. when the warm, moist air rises

    b. when the falling rain cools the air

    c. as wind hits a rotating cloud from opposite directions

    d. as the rotating cloud intensifies

5. How are objects removed from the surface of the Earth in a tornado?

    a. They are pushed out by the strong downdrafts.

    b. They are sucked upward by the surface inflow of the rotating vortex.

    c. They are scattered by the high winds.

    d. They are dragged along by a strong wind force.

CHAPTER REVIEW PRACTICE #1

Read the paragraph, and underline the main idea (if stated) and major details. Then, answer the questions that follow.

On May 18, 1980, one of the most tragic natural disasters occurred in Washington State. Mount St. Helens, a volcanic mountain, erupted with incredible force, flattening trees within a 160-mile radius. The eruption killed 59 people, including those who died from the intense heat and the clouds of ash and gases in the air. The gases and ash from the eruption shot more than 11 miles into the atmosphere. This caused crop damage in states as far away as the Midwest. The ash clouds over the city of Yakima, Washington, were so thick that it became as dark as night at noon. Mount St. Helens is one of 15 large volcanoes in the Cascade Mountain Range near the west coast of North America. Several others in this range could erupt in the future.

1. **What is the topic?**
   a. volcanoes
   b. volcanic eruptions
   c. a volcanic eruption at Mount St. Helens
   d. volcanoes in the Cascade Mountain Range

2. **What is the main idea?**
   a. Mount St. Helens is the worst natural disaster in recent history.
   b. Several volcanoes in the Cascade Mountain Range could erupt in the future.
   c. Volcanoes can cause great damage.
   d. On May 18, 1980, Mount St. Helens erupted in Washington State, destroying lives and property.

3. **Which of the following statements is an opinion?**
   a. On May 18, 1980, one of the most tragic natural disasters occurred in Washington State.
   b. The eruption killed 59 people, including those who died from the intense heat and the clouds of ash and gases in the air.
   c. The gases and ash from the eruption shot more than 11 miles into the atmosphere.
   d. The ash clouds over the city of Yakima, Washington, were so thick that it became as dark as night at noon.

4. **What is the author's purpose?**
   a. to entertain readers with a story about a volcano
   b. to persuade readers that volcanoes are dangerous
   c. to inform readers about the volcanic eruption at Mount St. Helens
   d. to explain how volcanoes form

5. **What is the author's tone?**
   a. discouraging
   b. serious
   c. critical
   d. amused

CHAPTER REVIEW PRACTICE #2

Read the following paragraph, and underline the main idea (if stated) and major details. Then, answer the questions that follow. Look for opinions and bias.

Seal hunters kill hundreds of thousands of baby seals each year in Canada, all for the sake of fashion. Baby seal fur is white and very soft, which makes it one of the most beautiful furs for coats and wraps. Trappers may use clubs or hooks to kill seals in horrible ways that cause pain and suffering to these animals just to avoid damaging the fur. Imagine the terrible suffering of the mother seal as she watches her babies being killed and dragged away. Canada has slowed the slaughter of seals, but it has not been completely stopped. We need to stop purchasing products with animal fur. We should demand that the Canadian government enforce laws to permanently stop the hunting of baby seals. Everyone can help by joining protest groups and contacting government officials to demand action to protect these innocent and beautiful animals.

1. What is the topic?

   a. seal hunting   **c.** baby seal hunting

   b. seals   **d.** how baby seals are killed

2. What is the implied main idea?

   a. The seal hunting industry depends on people who buy furs.

   b. Baby seal fur is white and very soft, which makes it one of the most desirable furs for coats and wraps.

   c. Seal hunters use painful methods to kill baby seals.

   d. We should permanently stop the hunting of baby seals in Canada.

3. Which of the following statements is a fact?

   a. Baby seal fur is white and very soft, which makes it one of the most beautiful furs for coats and wraps.

   b. Canada has slowed the slaughter of seals, but it has not been completely stopped.

   c. Imagine the terrible suffering of the mother seal as she watches her babies being killed and dragged away.

   d. We should demand that the Canadian government enforce laws to permanently stop the hunting of baby seals.

4. What is the author's tone?

   a. disapproving   **c.** straightforward

   b. objective   **d.** positive

5. Which of the following best describes this selection?

   a. the author is biased in favor of baby seal hunting

   b. the author is biased against baby seal hunting

   c. the author is unbiased

   d. none of the above

CHAPTER REVIEW PRACTICE #3

Read the following paragraph, and underline the main idea (if stated) and major details. Then, answer the questions that follow. Look for opinions and bias.

A rainbow is a natural event that is a symbol of hope and has been associated with many legends, such as the one that says there is a pot of gold at the end of every rainbow. Unfortunately, this is not true. Rainbows are created when there are rain clouds in the sky, usually just after a shower, and the sun is shining. When sunlight shines through the raindrops, the light is refracted, or bent. Light is made up of many different-colored light waves. Light is reflected off the inner surface of each raindrop and then bounces back through the side where it entered. As it passes through the raindrop, the light is divided into colorful bands: red, blue, and violet. The result is a colorful rainbow. We can only see part of the rainbow from the Earth's surface, but as you go higher, you can see more of it. From an airplane, the rainbow appears as a complete circle.

1. What is the topic?
   a. the colors of a rainbow
   b. rainbows
   c. how rainbows are formed
   d. the colors of light

2. What is the implied main idea?
   a. A rainbow is a beautiful natural event that is a symbol of hope and has been associated with many interesting legends, such as the one that says there is a pot of gold at the end of every rainbow.
   b. Rainbows occur after a shower when the there are rain clouds and the sun is still shining.
   c. Light is made up of many different-colored light waves.
   d. A rainbow is the result of light passing through raindrops and refracting into different colors.

3. Which of the following statements is an opinion?
   a. A rainbow is a natural event that is a symbol of hope and has been associated with many legends, such as the one that says there is a pot of gold at the end of every rainbow.
   b. Unfortunately, this is not true.
   c. Rainbows are created when there are rain clouds in the sky, usually just after a shower, and the sun is shining.
   d. Light is reflected off the inner surface of each raindrop and then bounces back through the side where it entered.

4. What is the author's purpose?

  a. to inform readers about how rainbows are created

  b. to entertain readers with a story about rainbows

  c. to persuade readers to look for rainbows in the sky

  d. to tell legends about rainbows

5. Which of the following best describes this selection?

  a. the author is biased in favor of rainbows   **c.** the author is unbiased

  b. the author is biased against rainbows   **d.** none of the above

TEXTBOOK PRACTICE

Read the following textbook selection, and underline the main idea (if stated) and major details. Then, answer the questions that follow. Look for opinions and bias.

How Can You Reduce Your Risk of Heart Disease?

Although cardiovascular disease remains the number-one killer in the United States, incidence of the disease has declined over the past 30 years. This drop has occurred primarily because people have reduced their risk factors for coronary heart disease (CHD). Table 9.2 lists the major CHD risk factors. Note that six of the nine major risk factors, and both of the contributing factors, can be modified by behavior. Therefore, you can modify 70 percent of CHD risk factors to reduce your risk of developing cardiovascular disease.

TABLE 9.2
Major and Contributory Risk Factors for Developing Coronary Heart Disease

Risk Factor	Classification	Is Behavior Modification Possible?	Behavior Modification to Reduce Risk
Smoking	Major	Yes	Smoking cessation
Hypertension	Major	Yes	Exercise, proper diet, and stress reduction
High blood cholesterol	Major	Yes	Exercise, proper diet, and medication
Diabetes mellitus	Major	Yes	Proper nutrition exercise
Obesity and overweight	Major	Yes	Weight loss, proper nutrition, exercise
Physical inactivity	Major	Yes	Exercise
Heredity	Major	No	
Gender	Major	No	
Increasing age	Major	No	
Stress	Contributes	Yes	Stress management, exercise
Alcohol	Contributes	Yes	Moderate consumption

(From *Total Fitness and Wellness*, Brief Edition, 3rd, by Scott K. Powers and Stephen L. Dodd. Copyright © 2009. Printed and Electronically reproduced by permission of Pearson Education, Inc., Upper Saddle River, NJ.)

1. What is the topic?

   a. coronary heart disease (CHD)

   b. bad health habits

   c. Americans at risk

   d. risk factors for CHD

2. What is the implied main idea?

   a. Many Americans are at risk for CHD.

   b. People's risk for CHD depends on their behavior, such as smoking.

   c. Although cardiovascular disease remains the number-one killer in the United States, we can often reduce the risk of CHD by modifying our behavior.

   d. Many people are in danger because of CHD.

3. What is the author's purpose?

   a. to persuade people to eat healthier

   b. to inform readers about risk factors for CHD

   c. to explain why people shouldn't smoke

   d. to entertain readers

4. According to the information in the table, which of these behavior modifications are the most helpful for reducing the risk of CHD? (Choose all that apply.)

   a. stress management

   b. exercise

   c. proper diet

   d medication

5. Which of the following best describes this selection?

   a. The author is biased against risk factors for CHD.

   b. The author is biased in favor of modifying behavior to lower the risk factors for CHD.

   c. The author is biased against diabetes.

   d. The author is unbiased.

STUDY SKILL CHAPTER REVIEW

A study guide is a list of topics with questions and answers. Study guides help you learn the most important information in a unit of study. Begin creating a study guide by listing the topics in the column on the far left. Next, in the middle column, write the most important skills or concepts about each topic in the form of a question. In the far-right column, write the answers to the questions. Complete the following study guide about the concepts you learned in this chapter, and then use it to quiz yourself or your study partners.

TOPIC	QUESTIONS	ANSWERS
Fact and Opinion	What is a fact?	....
	What is an opinion?	....
Author's Purpose	....	The reason why an author wrote something.
Intended Audience	What is the intended audience?	....
Author's Tone	What is author's tone?	....
Bias	....	....

519

READING LAB ASSIGNMENTS

SKILL PRACTICES

1. Go online to MyReadingLab, and click on "Study Skills Website" under "Other Resources." Next, click on "Critical Thinking," and print the self-assessment. Answer each question "yes" or "no."

COMPREHENSION IMPROVEMENT

2. Go online to MyReadingLab, and click on the Reading Level tab. Choose two stories to read, and answer the questions that follow.

CAREER EXPLORATION

3. Go online to www.bls.gov/oco and explore careers in science. Find a career that interests you, and print out the information. Print the article, and then preview, read, highlight, and annotate it. Underline five facts in the article.

SKILL APPLICATION

4. Find an article in the newspaper. The editorial section or the sports section is especially good for this practice. In the article, underline three facts and three opinions, labeling each statement as "F" or "O." Write the main idea of the article, and describe the author's tone, purpose, and intended audience.

LEARNING REFLECTION

Think about the skills and concepts in this chapter. What have you learned in this chapter that will help your reading comprehension and enable you to do well in college?

SELF-EVALUATION CHECKLIST

Rate yourself on the following items, using the following scale:

1 = strongly disagree

2 = disagree

3 = neither agree nor disagree

4 = agree

5 = strongly agree

1. I completed all of the assigned work on time. ....

2. I understand all of the concepts in this chapter ....

3. I contributed to teamwork and class discussions. ....

4. I completed all of the assigned lab work on time. ....

5. I came to class on time. ....

6. I attended class every day. ....

7. I studied for any quizzes or tests we had for this chapter. ....

8. I asked questions when I didn't understand something. ....

9. I checked my comprehension during reading. ....

10. I know what is expected of me in the coming week. ....

11. Are you still on track with the goals you set in Chapter 1? ....

12. What changes can you make to improve your performance in this course? ....

For support in meeting this chapter's objectives, go to the Study Plan in MyReadingLab and select Critical Thinking. Read and view the resources in the Review Materials section, and then complete the Recall, Apply, and Write exercises in the Activities section. Check your results by clicking on Gradebook.

STUDY SKILL: USING GRAPHIC AIDS TO IMPROVE COMPREHENSION

Graphic aids are visual features that help you to understand information and data. They may be charts, diagrams, graphs, maps, or even pictures. They are especially common in textbook reading, although they also appear in many research studies and articles.

As you are reading a selection, you might see a reference to a graphic aid. This sometimes appears as "See Figure 1.2" or in parentheses as "(Fig. 1.2)." This means that you should take a moment to study the figure because it will help your understanding of the concepts the author is discussing.

Graphs are charts that show values or amounts with bars, lines, circles, or icons. There are various types of graphs that you should be familiar with: bar graphs, line graphs, and pie (circle) graphs. When reading graphs, you should use the data to draw conclusions about the information. Each type of graph has a specific purpose. In general, when reading a graph, it is important to:

- Read the title. (What is the graph showing?)
- Read the data under the graph.
- Read the data along the left side of the graph.
- Read the units of measurement.
- Read the bars, lines, or segments of the circle (pie) graph.
- Read the date and source of the information.
- Read the key or legend that explains the colors, lines, or other format.

GRAPHS

Line graphs are used to show increases or decreases in data. *Pie charts* and *bar graphs* compare amounts. In a pie chart, a circle represents 100 percent and is divided up so each portion of the pie chart represents a part of the whole. Bar graphs compare the amounts of similar categories of data.

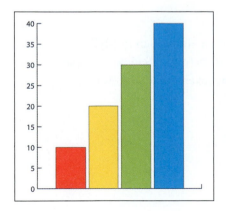

Bar graph

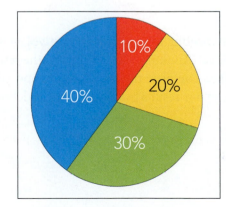

Pie chart

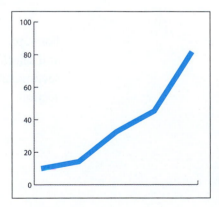

Line graph

FLOW CHARTS

Flow charts are images that represent a process. There are key items to look for when reading a diagram or flow chart:

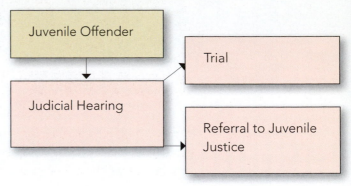

- Read the title and caption of the diagram or flow chart.
- Note where the process begins.
- Follow arrows carefully.
- Read the data inside the shapes and on the lines.
- Look for a legend or key that tells what certain types of lines or colors may mean.

DIAGRAMS

Diagrams are pictures that represent structure. They show where things are located, such as in the following diagram.

(From Belk, Colleen; Borden Maier, Virginia, From *Biology: Science for Life with Physiology,* 2nd by Colleen Belk and Virginia Borden. Copyright © 2007 by Pearson Education. Printed and Electronically reproduced by permission of Pearson Education, Inc., Upper Saddle River, NJ.)

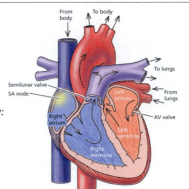

TABLES

Year	Number of cases
2010	15
2005	12
2000	8

Tables show information for comparison. They show data in rows and columns. When reading a table, there are several things to note:

- Read the title and headings on the top row and left column.
- Read the source and date of the information.
- Read the data under the columns and across the rows.

Match the information on the right with the graphic aid (on the left) that will best show that information.

1. _____ line graph   **a.** the skeletal structure of the human body

2. _____ pie chart   **b.** the healthiest weights for men and women by their ages and heights

3. _____ diagram   **c.** how much of the total budget is spent for each type of expense

4. _____ flow chart   **d.** the amount of increase in tuition over five years

5. _____ table   **e.** the process that is used to make paper

COMBINED SKILLS TESTS

Test 1

Read the next textbook selection, and then answer the questions that follow.

How Can I Prepare for a Classical Music Concert?

1 As often as possible, listen to recordings of the music that will be featured at the concert so you will become familiar with the music. We tend to enjoy the music we know best. Besides preparing for a concert, purchasing the recordings is an excellent way to build your personal music collection.

2 Municipal and university libraries also can be excellent resources. You can listen to recordings at the library or check them out for a few days. Also, pre-set your radio to your local classical music stations (usually FM stations), and you will become familiar with many styles of music. The Web also has satellite radio stations and streaming audio sites dedicated to classical music.

3 Each musical style has its own characteristics. Knowing how to listen to the various styles makes it easier to follow and enjoy the music.

4 Also, become familiar with the composer, the artists, and the background of the music. Sometimes this information is available on an insert accompanying a recording. Many of the greatest geniuses have been as imperfect and vulnerable as any other human being. Their stories are very moving and can give you greater insight into their works.

1. What is the topic?

   a. music

   b. concerts

   c. preparing for a classical music concert

   d. musical styles

2. What is the implied main idea?

   a. You should listen to recordings of music before you attend a concert.

   b. You should become familiar with the music, the composers, and background of the music before you go to a concert.

   c. Each musical style has its own characteristics.

   d. There are several things you should do to prepare before going to a classical music concert.

3. Identify the meaning of the underlined word in the following sentence: Their stories are very moving and can give you greater <u>insight</u> into their works.

   a. seeing into

   b. understanding

   c. enjoyment

   d. research

4. According to the selection, why should you become familiar with the music before going to the concert?

   a. so that you will not fall asleep during the concert

   b. so that you will buy the recording and support the artist

   c. so that you will understand and enjoy the music more

   d. to learn more about the composers and how they achieved success

5. According to the selection, what are some resources that you should use to prepare for the concert? (Choose all that apply.)

   a. your own music collection

   b. libraries

   c. the Internet

   d. classical radio stations

6. What is the overall pattern of organization in this selection?

   a. time order

   c. definition and example

   b. compare and/or contrast

   d. listing

7. Which of the following conclusions can be made from this selection?

   a. Understanding the background stories of the artists and composers can provide insight into their works.

   b. Understanding classical music can be difficult.

   c. Attending concerts can be expensive, but well worth the experience.

   d. You will learn more about composing if you attend more concerts.

8. Which of the following is an opinion?

   a. You can listen to recordings at the library or check them out for a few days.

   b. Municipal and university libraries can be excellent resources.

   c. The Web also has satellite radio stations and streaming audio sites dedicated to classical music.

   d. Each musical style has its own characteristics.

9. What is the author's purpose?

   a. to inform readers about concerts

   b. to explain how to understand music better

   c. to inform readers how to prepare before they attend a concert

   d. to entertain readers by telling them about how to enjoy a concert

10. Who is the intended audience for this selection?

    a. classical musicians

    c. ticket sellers

    b. classical music fans

    d. students in music classes

Test 2

Read the following textbook selection, and then answer the questions that follow.

Larceny-Theft Offenses

1 There are many types of larceny-theft offenses and their rate of occurrence is considerable. A lack of witnesses or other "concrete" evidence makes larceny a difficult crime to solve. In larceny-theft investigations, the state must show that there was a "taking" at least for a brief time and that the defendant had control over the property "of another." The taking must be deliberate and with the intent to steal.

2 The Uniform Crime Report defines larceny-theft as the unlawful taking, carrying, leading, or riding away of property from the possession or constructive possession of another. It includes crimes such as shoplifting, pocket picking, purse snatching, thefts from motor vehicles, thefts of motor vehicle parts and accessories, and bicycle thefts, in which no use of force, violence, or fraud occurs. In the Uniform Reporting Program, this crime category does not include embezzlement, confidence games, forgery, or worthless checks. Motor vehicle theft is also excluded from this category because it is a separate Crime Index offense.

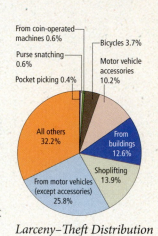

Larceny–Theft Distribution

1. **What is the topic of this textbook selection?**

   a. theft

   b. national crime

   c. investigating crime

   d. larceny-theft offenses

2. **What is the main idea?**

   a. There are many types of criminal offenses.

   b. There are many types of larceny-theft offenses, and their rate of occurrence is considerable.

   c. Larceny is defined as the taking of another's property with intent to steal.

   d. Larceny- theft crimes are difficult to prove.

3. **Identify the meaning of the underlined word in the following sentence: Although there are many different types of larceny-theft offenses, in this book we attempt to discuss only a few of the most problematic.**

   a. horrifying

   b. interesting

   c. easy to solve

   d. difficult

4. **According to the selection, why is larceny such a difficult crime to solve?**

   a. They are rarely reported.

   b. The methods to solve such offenses are ineffective.

    c. It is difficult to obtain witnesses or other "concrete" evidence.

    d. Police are unwilling to solve these crimes.

5. **According to the graph, which of the following conclusions is true?**

    a. There is a higher occurrence of theft from buildings than shoplifting.

    b. There is a lower occurrence of pocket picking than purse snatching.

    c. Bicycle theft is included in "All others."

    d. There is a higher occurrence of motor vehicle theft than shoplifting.

6. **According to the graph, what is the third largest type of theft committed?**

    a. all others

    b. motor vehicle accessories

    c. shoplifting

    d. from motor vehicles

7. **Which patterns of organization are used in paragraph 2?**

    a. definition and example   **c.** cause and effect

    b. compare and contrast   **d.** time order and listing

8. **Identify the relationship within the following sentence: Motor vehicle theft is also excluded from this category because it is a separate Crime Index offense.**

    a. cause and effect   **c.** definition

    b. time order   **d.** listing

9. **Which of the following statements is an opinion?**

    a. There are many types of larceny-theft offenses, and their rate of occurrence is considerable.

    b. The taking must be deliberate and with the intent to steal.

    c. The Uniform Crime Report defines larceny-theft as the unlawful taking, carrying, leading, or riding away of property from the possession or constructive possession of another.

    d. Motor vehicle theft is also excluded from this category inasmuch as it is a separate Crime Index offense.

10. **Which of the following best describes the author's purpose and tone?**

    a. purpose: to warn readers about the dangers of larceny-theft; tone: concerned

    b. purpose: to persuade readers to study the types of larceny-theft; tone: serious

    c. purpose: to inform readers about the types of larceny-theft; tone: objective

    d. purpose: to entertain readers with stories about theft; tone: amusing

Test 3

Read the following textbook selection, and then answer the questions that follow.

terra cotta: a reddish clay used in pottery and sculpture

1 In 1974, two Chinese farmers in Shaanxi Province found broken pieces of **terra cotta** on their land. Shortly thereafter, the tomb of the Chinese emperor Shihuangdi (who ruled 221–210 B.C.) was opened, and excavations began. Shihuangdi unified China and established a code of laws, a writing system, and standardized measurements. He had monumental works of art and architecture made, built roads throughout the country, and defended its borders by extending and completing most of the Great Wall of China.

2 When he died, Shihuangdi decided he would take life with him. So he assembled over 7,000 life-size terra-cotta soldiers and horses to guard him after death. Most were arranged in rows, like military battalions, standing at attention in trenches. Others are shown kneeling and holding the reins of horses. The figures were constructed in sections— torso, limbs, and head— on a base; their remarkably lifelike appearance was achieved by the use of different paint and slight variations in the features. It was not for public viewing, for the emperor had no idea that his soldiers would be excavated, photographed, copied in various sizes for sale, and exhibited throughout the world.

3 Since its discovery, the terra-cotta army has become an international attraction, and visitors to China regularly include this in their travels.

1. **What is the topic?**

   a. Emperor Shihuangdi's terra-cotta army

   b. Chinese art

   c. Shaanxi Province in China

   d. Chinese emperor Shihuangdi

2. **What is the main idea?**

   a. Shihuangdi unified China and established a code of laws, a writing system, and standardized measurements.

   b. When he died, Shihuangdi decided he would take life with him.

   c. In 1974, two Chinese farmers in Shaanxi Province found broken pieces of terra cotta on their land.

   d. Chinese Emperor Shihuangdi assembled 7,000 life-size terra-cotta soldiers and horses to guard him after death.

3. **Identify the meaning of the underlined word in the following sentence: Shortly thereafter, the tomb of the Chinese emperor Shihuangdi (who ruled 221–210 B.C.) was opened, and <u>excavations</u> began.**

   a. construction

   b. digging out

   c. exaggerations

   d. expectations

4. According to the selection, how was the terra-cotta army discovered?

   a. Emperor Shihuangdi left it as a monument to his army.

   b. An archaeologist believed there was a burial tomb in the area and began digging.

   c. It was discovered when the Chinese government started construction on the Great Wall of China.

   d. The tomb was discovered in 1974, when two Chinese farmers in Shaanxi Province found broken pieces of terra cotta on their land.

5. According to the selection, how were the artists able to achieve such a lifelike appearance for the army?

   a. All the figures were exactly alike.

   b. They used different paint and slight variations in the features.

   c. Actual models posed for the statues.

   d. The figures were of real people that the emperor knew.

6. Which of the following conclusions can be made from this selection?

   a. Emperor Shihuangdi believed that he would live on after he died.

   b. Emperor Shihuangdi loved his army and wanted to build a memorial to it.

   c. The Chinese are superstitious people.

   d. Emperor Shihuangdi wanted the people of the world to see his magnificent burial tomb.

7. Identify the relationship between the following sentences: When he died, Shihuangdi decided he would take life with him. So he assembled more than 7,000 life-size terra-cotta soldiers and horses to guard him after death.

   a. listing

   b. time order

   c. compare and/or contrast

   d. cause and effect

8. Which of the following correctly describes this sentence: "The figures were constructed in sections— torso, limbs, and head—on a base; their remarkably lifelike appearance was achieved by the use of different paint and slight variations in the features"?

   a. fact

   b. opinion

   c. fact and opinion

   d. expert opinion

9. What is the author's purpose?

   a. to entertain readers with a story about a Chinese emperor

   b. to persuade readers to visit the site of the terra-cotta army

   c. to inform readers about Emperor Shihuangdi's terra-cotta army

   d. to explain why the Emperor had the terra-cotta army created

10. What is the author's tone?

   a. concerned

   b. informative

   c. upset

   d. uninterested

Test 4

Read the following textbook selection, and then answer the questions that follow.

Modern Hydropower

1 Most of our hydroelectric power today comes from holding water in reservoirs behind concrete dams that block the flow of river water, and then letting that water pass through the dam. Because immense amounts of water are stored behind dams, this is called the storage technique. As reservoir water passes through a dam, it turns the blades of turbines, which cause a generator to generate electricity (Figure 16.9). Electricity generated in the powerhouse of a dam is transmitted to the electric grid by transmission lines, while the water flows into the riverbed below the dam to continue downriver. By storing water in reservoirs, dam operators can ensure a steady and predictable supply of electricity, even during times of naturally low river flow.

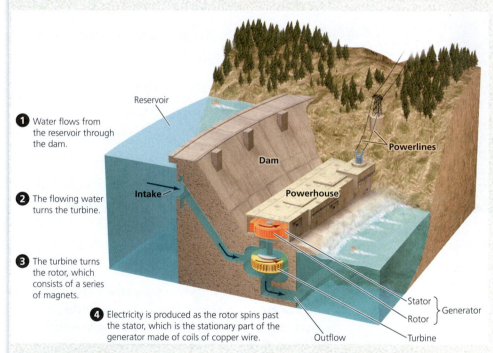

1 Water flows from the reservoir through the dam.

2 The flowing water turns the turbine.

3 The turbine turns the rotor, which consists of a series of magnets.

4 Electricity is produced as the rotor spins past the stator, which is the stationary part of the generator made of coils of copper wire.

Reservoir

Dam

Intake

Powerlines

Powerhouse

Stator ⎫
       ⎬ Generator
Rotor ⎭

Outflow

Turbine

Figure 16.9 Hydroelectric Power

2 Large dams generate substantial amounts of hydroelectric power. Inside these dams, flowing water is used to turn turbines and generate electricity. Water is funneled from the reservoir through a portion of the dam to rotate turbines, which turn rotors containing magnets. The spinning rotors generate electricity as their magnets pass coils of copper wire. Electrical current is transmitted away through power lines, and the river's water flows out through the base of the dam.

(From *Essential Environment: The Science Behind the Stories*, 3e by Jay H. Withgott and Scott R. Brennan. Copyright © 2009 by Jay H. Withgott and Scott R. Brennan. Reprinted by permission of Pearson Education, Inc., Upper Saddle River, NJ.)

1. **What is the topic?**
   a. dams
   b. electricity
   c. hydroelectric power
   d. how electricity is made

2. **What is the implied main idea?**
   a. Because immense amounts of water are stored behind dams, this is called the storage technique.
   b. The storage technique is used to generate electricity.
   c. Hydroelectric power is produced by letting water pass through a dam to operate a generator, which makes the electricity.
   d. Electricity generated in the powerhouse of a dam is transmitted to the electric grid by transmission lines.

3. **Identify the meaning of the underlined word in the following sentence: As reservoir water passes through a dam, it turns the blades of** turbines, **which cause a generator to generate electricity.**
   a. large motors, with blades that turn as air or water pass them
   b. a helicopter rotor
   c. blades of a fan for cooling air
   d. super charged

4. **According to the diagram, what happens after water flows from the reservoir through the dam?**
   a. Electricity is produced as the rotor spins past the stator, which is the stationary part of the generator made of coils of copper wire.
   b. The turbine turns the rotor, which has a series of magnets.
   c. The flowing water turns the turbine.
   d. Electrical current is transmitted away through power lines.

5. **According to the diagram, how is electricity produced?**
   a. Water is funneled from the reservoir through a portion of the dam to rotate turbines, which turn rotors containing magnets.
   b. The spinning rotors generate electrical current as their magnets pass coils of copper wire.
   c. Electrical current is transmitted away through power lines
   d. The river's water flows out through the base of the dam.

6. What conclusion can you draw from this selection?

    a. Electricity is inexpensive to produce.

    b. We should build more hydroelectric plants.

    c. Large bodies of water are possible sources for producing electricity.

    d. Hydroelectric power should be used instead of fossil fuels.

7. What is the pattern of organization in paragraph 2?

    a. time order

    b. space order

    c. listing

    d. process

8. What is the author's purpose?

    a. to persuade readers to use hydroelectric power

    b. to inform readers about how hydroelectric power is produced

    c. to entertain readers with a description of hydroelectric power

    d. to explain why hydroelectric power is a cleaner energy source

9. Identify the relationship within the following sentence: As reservoir water passes through a dam, it turns the blades of turbines, which cause a generator to generate electricity.

    a. cause and effect

    b. process

    c. time order

    d. listing

10. Which of the following correctly describes this sentence: "Because immense amounts of water are stored behind dams, this is called the storage technique"?

    a. opinion

    b. fact

    c. fact and opinion

    d. expert opinion

Test 5

Read the following textbook selection, and then answer the questions that follow.

Contract Manufacturing and Outsourcing

1 Because of high domestic labor costs, many U.S. companies manufacture their products in countries where labor costs are lower. This arrangement is called **international contract manufacturing** or **outsourcing**. A U.S. company might contract with a local company in a foreign country to manufacture one of its products. It will, however, retain control of product design and development and put its own label on the finished product. Thanks to 21st-century information technology, non-manufacturing functions can also be outsourced to nations with lower labor costs. U.S. companies increasingly draw upon a vast supply of relatively inexpensive skilled labor to perform various business services, such as software development, accounting, and claims processing.

2 For years, American insurance companies have processed much of their claims-related paperwork in Ireland. With a large well-educated population, India has become a center for software development and customer call centers for American companies. In the case of India, as you can see in Table 8.1, the attraction is not only a large pool of knowledgeable workers, but significantly lower wages as well.

Table 8.1 Selected Hourly Wages, United States and India

Occupation	U.S. Wage	Indian Wage
Telephone operator	$12.57	Under $1.00
Health-record technical worker/medical transcriber	$13.17	$1.50–$2.00
Payroll clerk	$15.17	$1.50–$2.00
Legal assistant/paralegal	$17.86	$6.00–$8.00
Accountant	$23.35	$6.00–$15.00
Financial researcher/analyst	$33.00–$35.00	$6.00–$15.00

(From *Exploring Business* by Karen Collins. Copyright © 2008 by Karen Collins. Reprinted by permission of the author.)

1. What is the topic?

   a. business

   b. wages in the United States and India

   c. contract manufacturing and outsourcing

   d. U.S. business in India and Ireland

2. What is the main idea?

   a. To reduce labor costs, many U.S. companies manufacture their products in other countries through international contract manufacturing or outsourcing.

   b. U.S. companies increasingly draw upon a vast supply of relatively inexpensive skilled labor to perform various business services, such as software development, accounting, and claims processing.

   c. A U.S. company might contract with a local company in a foreign country to manufacture one of its products but still keep control of it.

   d. For years, American insurance companies have processed much of their claims-related paperwork in Ireland.

3. Identify the meaning of the underlined word in the following sentence: It will, however, <u>retain</u> control of product design and development and put its own label on the finished product.

   a. give up

   b. recall

   c. bring back

   d. keep

4. According to the selection, what kinds of business services are outsourced? (Choose all that apply.)

   a. machine repairs

   b. claims processing

   c. software development

   d. telephone operator

5. According to the table, which jobs offer higher pay in the United States than in India? (Choose all that apply.)

   a. financial researcher/analyst

   b. machine operator

   c. legal assistant/paralegal

   d. automobile designer

6. According to the table, what is the difference in wages for a payroll clerk in the United States and India?

   a. about $17 more in India

   b. about $20 more in the United States

   c. about $17 less in the United States

   d. about $13 more in the United States

7. What is the overall pattern of organization used in paragraph 2?

    a. definition

    b. example

    c. cause and effect

    d. time order

8. According to this selection, why do U.S. companies outsource software development and customer call centers to India?

    a. India has cheaper prices than Ireland.

    b. The U.S. software business doesn't make enough money.

    c. India has a large pool of knowledgeable workers and lower labor costs.

    d. Companies in India do not have their own software developers or customer call centers.

9. Identify the relationship between the following sentences: A U.S. company might contract with a local company in a foreign country to manufacture one of its products. It will, however, retain control of product design and development and put its own label on the finished product.

    a. contrast

    b. comparison

    c. cause and effect

    d. process

10. Who is the intended audience for this selection?

    a. manufacturers in the United States

    b. business owners

    c. students

    d. librarians

APPENDIX
USING A GLOSSARY OR DICTIONARY
Using a Glossary

If context clues or word parts fail to provide enough information to figure out a word's meaning, check the back of your textbook for a glossary. A glossary is a list of terms used in the textbook that are essential for understanding the subject matter. The words and terms are listed in alphabetical order. Often they are followed by a page number, where you find the term to read more about it and see the context in which it is used. Below is an example of a glossary from a business textbook. The definition for "accounting equation" also includes another term in bold print, "owner's equity." This means that the definition for this term is also included in the glossary, and it would be found under the Os.

> ## A
> **accounting** System for measuring and summarizing business activities, interpreting financial information, and communicating the results to management and other decision makers. [225]
>
> **accounting equation** Accounting tool showing the resources of a business (assets) and the claims on those resources (liabilities and **owner's equity**). [231]
>
> **account payable** Record of cash owed to sellers from whom a business has purchased products on credit. [233]
>
> (From *Exploring Business* by Karen Collins. Copyright © 2008 by Karen Collins. Reprinted by permission of the author.)

Using a Dictionary

If the glossary doesn't define the word or term you need, or if there is no glossary, a dictionary is another option. Many students access online dictionaries through their cell phones or home computers. Online dictionaries provide most of the information you need, such as the definition, how to break the word into syllables, the parts of speech, how to pronounce the word, and its various meanings. Besides convenience, another advantage of using online dictionaries is that they will provide a list of suggestions if you misspell the word you are looking for. For example, if you were looking for *irresponsible* and spelled it *earesponsable*, the following list appears:

> Do you mean:
>
> irresponsible
>
> responsible
>
> responsibly
>
> Click on the correct spelling of the word to see its definitions.

Here is a sample page from an online dictionary:

If you type the word "rhythm" into the search box, the definitions will appear as follows:

rhythm [uncountable and countable]

1 ▶))) a regular repeated pattern of sounds or movements [metre]

Drums are used to keep the rhythm.

rhythm of
We were dancing to the rhythm of the music.
the steady rhythm of the rain on the roof

2 a pattern of changes or cycles
the natural rhythm of the body

rhythm of
The rhythm of a farmer's life moves with the seasons.

The entry word, "rhythm," is divided into syllables.

Next, the terms "uncountable" and "countable" tell us the type of nouns this word is considered to be. Countable nouns are things that can be counted, such as people or objects. Uncountable ("noncount") nouns are not countable and don't form plurals, such as *strength, confusion, truth*, etc.

The symbol to the left of the definition, ▶)), is a link to hear the word pronounced.

The word in brackets, [metre] is a synonym for *rhythm*.

The first definition is followed by an example of how the word is used in the first meaning. The phrase "rhythm of" follows the definition, and two examples of this phrase are provided. The second definition is also followed by an example and another example of how the phrase "rhythm of" can be used according to the second definition.

Using a Published Dictionary

The best dictionaries for students in college are college dictionaries. These contain most of the words you will need, and they are printed in paperbacks as well as hardcover editions. Although paperbacks may not have as many words as the larger hardcover editions, they are usually suitable for use in most college courses.

The words listed in bold print in dictionaries are called entries. To find a specific entry such as *jinni,* use the words at the top of the page to locate your word. These are called guide words. The word on the left is the first entry on the page, and the word on the right is the last entry. Like a glossary, all the words are listed in alphabetical order. On the page in this example, you will find all the words that come alphabetically between *jinn* and *jogger.* (The sample shows only the top half of the page.)

jinn   **jogger**

jinn (jin) n. *pi.* O/JINNI: popularly
regarded as a singular, with the pl. **jinns**
jin-ni (ji ne', jin'e) n. [Ar. *jinni*, pl. *jinn*]
Moslem Legend a supernatural being
that can take human or animal form
and influence human affairs
jin-rik-i-sha (jin rik'sAS, -sha) n.
[Jap, < *jin*, a man +*riki*, power + *sha*,
carriage] a small, two-wheeled carriage
with a hood, pulled by one or two men,
esp. formerly in the Orient; also sp. jin-
rick'sha, jin-rlk'sha
ji-pt-ja-pa (he'pe ha'pa) n. [Sp. < *Jipijapa*,
place in Ecuador] 1. a Central and South

job-ber-y (-ar e, -re) n. [see JOB1 (*vi.*
3)] [Chiefly Brit.] the carrying on of
public or official business dishonestly
for private gain
Job Corps a U.S. government program
for training underprivileged youth for
employment
job-hold-er (-hol'der) n. a person who
has a steady job; specif., a government
employee
job-less (-lis) adj. 1. without a job;
unemployed 2. having to do with the
unemployed—the **job less** those who
are unemployed—**job'less-ness** n.

The first entry on the page is *jinn*. The word *jinni* appears after it.

The two ways to pronounce the word are in parentheses, (ji-nē´, jin' ē). Notice the accent mark (') shows that the accent is on the second syllable in the first pronunciation and on the first syllable in the second pronunciation. Either one is correct. A key to all the symbols and abbreviations can be found in the first few pages of a dictionary.

At the bottom of the page or in the first few pages, you will find a guide for using the pronunciation symbols. Here is the pronunciation guide from the bottom of the sample page:

fat, āpe, cär, ten, ēven (…etc.)

This means that *a* = the *a* sound in fat
ā = the *a* sound in *ape*
ä = the *a* sound in *car*
e = the *e* sound in *ten*
ē = the *e* sound in *even*

The second item in the entry is the part of speech. In this case, *jinni* is a noun, shown by the *n*. Here are some common abbreviations for the parts of speech:

n. = noun
v. = verb
adj. = adjective
adv. = adverb
The symbol *pl* = plural (more than one)

In brackets, we find the origin of the word. The origin of *jinni* is [Ar. *jinni*, pl. *jinn*]. "Ar" means Arabic.

Next is the definition, with a note as to where the word was first used—in a Moslem legend: "*Moslem Legend* a supernatural being that can take human or animal form and influence human affairs"

541

FIGURATIVE SPEECH

Authors use many tools to clearly express their ideas. Sometimes they will rely on figurative language to help readers understand their messages. Following are some types of figurative language.

- Comparisons help readers to understand concepts by relating the new idea to something they already know. There are two types of comparisons: literal or figurative. Literal comparisons compare things from the same category. Figurative comparisons use different categories.

Literal comparison example: Like his father, Russ loves taking things apart and putting them back together.

Figurative comparison example: When she walks, she sways as gently as a willow in the wind.

- Any comparison that uses the words *like* or *as* is called a **simile** (SIM-uhl-lee). Notice how the comparisons above use the words *like* and *as*.
- Another type of comparison that does not use *like* or *as* is called a **metaphor** (MET-a-for). It usually states that something *is* or *was* something else. For example:

Metaphor: Life <u>is</u> just a big bag of mixed nuts.
Simile: Life is <u>like</u> a big bag of mixed nuts.

Metaphor: She <u>was</u> a bright star in her father's life.

Simile: She was <u>as</u> bright <u>as</u> a star in her father's life.

- Personification is another way authors try to convey meaning. Personification gives human actions or qualities to a thing or idea. For example:

The angry barren trees clawed at the sky in the bitter wind.

Time was unkind to Grandmother.

- Hyperbole (hi-PER-bo-lee) is deliberate exaggeration. For example:

This purse must weigh a ton!

I've been waiting for my dinner forever.

Denotation and Connotation

Words can have two kinds of meanings. One is the literal meaning—the definition that is found in the dictionary—and this is known as the word's **denotation**. But words also may have an emotional meaning, called **connotation**. For example: the denotative meaning of *skinny* is "thin," but the connotative meaning is more negative than the word *slender* or *thin*. Consider the following words and their connotations.

Words with positive connotations	Words with negative connotations
slender	skinny
crowd	mob
request	demand

IMPROVING READING RATE AND ENDURANCE

Students are often concerned about their reading rate. They want to read faster so they can get through their assignments more quickly. But the real goal of any reading course, first and foremost, is comprehension. When we discuss reading rate, we mean the number of words per minute that you can read with complete comprehension of the material. Here are some tips for improving your reading rate:

Before reading:

- Preview the material before you begin reading to get a general sense of what the passage is about.
- Try to predict what the author will say about the topic. Think of a couple questions that you would like to find the answers to by reading the selection.

During reading:

- Stay focused. Lead your eyes across the page with a pen, pencil, or your finger. Have it pointing one or two words ahead of where you are reading, so that your eyes are trying to "catch up" to the speed of your pencil or finger.
- Stop at the end of a section to recall and summarize what you just read: State the topic and the author's main point about the topic.
- If the material is easy, try to make your pencil or finger go a little faster. When you notice that you cannot summarize what you just read, then slow it down and try again.
- Easy materials that you read for fun, such as a magazine, or a short, easy passage can be read faster than more difficult materials. The level of difficulty for you depends on your vocabulary, your prior knowledge of the subject, and your fluency with language.

After reading:

- Check your comprehension again by summarizing the entire passage or chapter that you just read. Make notes and draw diagrams, charts, or illustrations to help you remember what you read.
- If there are comprehension questions in the book, do them by going back to reread parts of the passage that will help you get the correct answers.

Timed Readings

If you want to improve your reading speed, you can start with the articles in this book. Before you read, follow the steps above under "Before reading." Then, write down the time that you begin reading. When you finish a section without stopping, look at the time, and write it down. Subtract your starting time from your finishing time. Then, count the number of words in the passage. The reading assignment articles in this book have a word count at the end. When you are doing a timed reading, do not stop to answer the comprehension-check questions in the margins until after you have finished the entire article. If you can't answer the questions correctly, it means that you need to read more slowly. Build up your speed gradually. Just racing across a page of print is not reading. Being good at reading is like being good at anything else. It takes time, effort, and practice.

To determine your reading rate, divide the number of words in the passage by the number of minutes that it took you to read them. This will be your "words per minute" score, or your WPM.

$$\text{WPM} = \frac{\text{number of words in passage}}{\text{number of minutes}}$$

Example: If it takes someone 10 minutes to read 1500 words, this person would divide 1500 by 10, as follows:

$$\frac{1500 \text{ words in the passage}}{10 \text{ minutes}} = 150 \text{ WPM}$$

By following the techniques listed previously under "Before reading," "During reading," and "After reading," you may see an improvement in your WPM by the end of the semester. But keep in mind that it's better to read a little slower and have good comprehension than it is to read fast and have poor comprehension.

What Influences Your Rate?

You will find that reading about subjects that are familiar to you allows you to read much faster than when reading new material that is complex or contains many new terms. Other factors that slow your rate are habits like going back and rereading the same sentence or phrase. Getting stuck on unfamiliar words—trying to sound them out and figure out what they mean before moving on—can also slow you down. Subvocalizing means that you actually say the words out loud to yourself, although usually not loud enough for other people to hear. Reading aloud, moving your lips, or subvocalizing slows your reading rate. Becoming distracted while reading by things such as television, loud music, or other thoughts will pull you off track and interfere with your rate and your comprehension. For these reasons, it is recommended that you do the following:

- Read in a quiet, comfortable environment, away from noise. Playing soft music may help you relax but not if you're distracted by it.
- Avoid subvocalizing or reading aloud while timing yourself. However, reading aloud is a good strategy when you encounter something difficult.
- Keep your eyes moving forward at a steady pace, resisting the temptation to go back and reread sentences or phrases. You can go back after you have completed the timing to reread the details.
- If you feel tense or nervous, take slow, deep breaths or do some exercises before you start. Being relaxed helps your concentration and your comprehension.
- Try to read in phrases of three to four words instead of individual words. You can increase the number of words in the phrases you read very gradually over time.
- Avoid fixating, or stopping, between words. Try to keep moving ahead at a comfortable rate.
- Keep a notepad handy to write down thoughts that distract you, and then deal with them after you're done reading.
- Gradually increase your reading time period. If you start reading for 45 minutes in one sitting, try to increase it to 50 minutes, and then 55 minutes, and so on.

Post-Test Survey: How Did You Learn?

1. Are you satisfied with your test grade?

   ....

   ....

   ....

2. Did the study methods you used help you to master the concept? Why or why not?

   ....

   ....

   ....

3. What reading or study skills did you use as you took this test?

   ....

   ....

   ....

4. What were the most effective study methods you used? (For example: note cards, charts, pictures; group or study partner; self-testing; repeating things aloud; repeating things in writing; other methods.)

   ....

   ....

   ....

5. What will you do differently for your next test?

   ....

   ....

   ....

   ....

PHOTO CREDITS

FRONT MATTER

Page iii: © Vera Berger/Corbis; Page iv: Craig Fennessy; Page v: © Wally McNamee/Corbis; Page vi: Bill Bachmann/Alamy; Page vii: © MARKA/Alamy; Page viii: © Radius Images/Corbis; Page ix: Craig Fennessy; Page x: © Ocean/Corbis; Page xi: © Tomas Rodriguez/Corbis; Page xii: © HBSS/Corbis; Page xiii: © Hill Street Studios/Blend Images/Corbis

CHAPTER 1

Page 2: © Daniel Koebe/Corbis; Page 5: © Praymantis Images/Alamy; Page 7: Bruce Laurance/Getty Images; Page 17: © Chris Pearsall/Alamy

CHAPTER 2

Page 18: LWA/Getty Images; Page 19: © Oote Boe Photography/Alamy; Page 23: © Winston Link/Alamy; Page 25: © Ray A. Akey/Alamy; Page 27: © Michael Routh/Alamy; Page 35: © JHP Public Safety/Alamy; Page 41: © Oleksiy Maksymenko/Alamy; Page 46: Chris Hartlove; Page 49: Thierry Dosogne/Getty Images; Page 55: Craig Fennessy; Page 63: © amana images inc./Alamy

CHAPTER 3

Page 72: Neleman Initiative, LLC/Getty Images; Page 75: © JR Carvey/Streetfly Studio/Blend Images/Corbis; Page 80: © PhotoStock-Israel/Alamy; Page 83: © Richard T. Nowitz/Corbis; Page 89: ASSOCIATED PRESS; Page 91: © John Henshall/Alamy; Page 99: © Blue Shadows/Alamy; Page 107: © HG Delaney/Alamy; Page 111: © Custom Medical Stock Photo/Alamy; Page 112: Lieutenant David Scott; Page 119: © Wally McNamee/Corbis; Page 121: © Kate Kunz/Corbis

CHAPTER 4

Page 126: Michael Krasowitz/Getty Images; Page 138: FilmMagic/Getty Images; Page 144: © Allstar Picture Library; Page 150: © Blend Images/Alamy; Page 155: Getty Images; Page 160: © Garry Gay/Alamy; Page 163: Adrienne Metzinger; Page 166: © Jim Wileman/Alamy; Page 170: © D. Hurst/Alamy

CHAPTER 5

Page 180: © Gael Conrad/Corbis; Page 184: © Chris Pearsall/Alamy; Page 186: © Nik Wheeler/Corbis; Page 191: © Steven Vidler/Eurasia Press/Corbis; Page 193: © Danita Delimont/Alamy; Page 195: © David Zanzinger/Alamy; Page 197: © Martin Shields/Alamy; Page 199: © Gregory Wrona/Alamy; Page 202: © Walter McBride/Retna Ltd./Corbis; Page 208: © RF Food Shots/Alamy; Page 214: Give Kids the World; Page 217: Give Kids the World; Page 223: Craig Fennessy; Page 226: © Michael Willis/Alamy; Page 231: © Per Winbladh/Corbis

CHAPTER 6

Page 240: © JGI/Jamie Grill/Blend Images/Corbis; Page 243: © Colin Underhill/Alamy; Page 244: © blueduck/Asia Images/Corbis; Page 247: © JASON LEE/Reuters/Corbis; Page 249: Anthony Neste Page 259: © Dan Leeth/Alamy; Page 260: © Stebe Boyle/NewSport/Corbis; Page 263: © Chris Trotman/Duomo/Corbis; Page 266: © Radius Images/Alamy; Page 271: Washington Post/Getty Images; Page 276: © Mark Burnett/Alamy; Page 278: Peter Dazeley; Page 279: Rick Muhr; Page 284: © Andres Rodriguez/Alamy; Page 286: Getty Images; Page 287: © Joe Fox/Alamy; Page 291: © David Cook/blueshiftstudios/Alamy; Page 293: © Radius Images/Corbis; Page 296: © ALESSANDRO DELLA BELLA/Keystone/Corbis

CHAPTER 7

Page 298: © Image Source/Alamy; Page 302: © Pat Canova/Alamy; Page 308: © imagebroker/Alamy; Page 316: © imagestopshop/Alamy; Page 317: © Chris Willson/Alamy; Page 324: © BSIP SA/Alamy; Page 327: © Travis Rowan/Alamy; Page 328: Jupiterimages/Getty Images; Page 330: © Mark Thiessen/National Geographic Society/Corbis; Page 333: © Huntstock, Inc./Alamy; Page 338: Craig Fennessy; Page 340: © WoodyStock/Alamy; Page 341: Craig Fennessy; Page 344: © Martin Bennett/Alamy

CHAPTER 8

Page 354: JLP/Jose L. Palaez/Corbis; Page 355: Yuri Cortez/Agence France Presse/Getty Images; Page 361: © David R. Frazier/Photolibrary, Inc./Alamy; Page 365: © Paul A. Souders/Corbis; Page 368: © Mark Peterson/Corbis; Page 375: © Ted Soqui/Corbis; Page 376: Lori Stoll; Page 385: David Walter; Page 391: © Image Source/Corbis; Page 392: (top) © Nick Downes/The New Yorker Collection/www.cartoonbank.com, (bottom) © Kim Warp/www.cartoonbank.com; Page 393: www.CartoonStock.com; Page 395: Paul Ekman, Ph.D. Professor of Psychology, University of California, San Francisco; Page 397: © Laura Doss/Corbis

CHAPTER 9

Page 402: © Julia Grossi/Corbis; Page 404: © Chad McDermott/Alamy; Page 405: © EVERETT KENNEDY BROWN/epa/Corbis; Page 406: © Bob Krist/Corbis; Page 407: © Bruno Ehrs/Corbis; Page 408: © JOHN KELLERMAN/Alamy; Page 410: © philipus/Alamy; Page 415: © Mark Burnett/Alamy; Page 416: © Pictorial Press Ltd/Alamy; Page 420: © Ancient Art & Architecture Collection Ltd/Alamy; Page 425: Getty Images; Page 429: © Peter Noyce/Alamy; Page 437: Ed Kashi/Corbis; Page 448: Meaghan Girouard; Page 449: © Ingo Jezierski/Alamy; Page 453: © Photo Researchers/Alamy; Page 456: WireImage/Getty Images; Page 458: © Tomas Abad/Alamy

CHAPTER 10

Page 464: © Noel Hendrickson/Blend Images/Corbis; Page 467: © Jim Reed/Science Faction/Corbis; Page 468: © Jim Sugar/Corbis; Page 471: © SERDAR/Alamy; Page 474: © NASA/Alamy; Page 478: © Daniel J. Cox/Corbis; Page 481: © Eddie Gerald/Alamy; Page 487: © Arco Images GmbH/Alamy; Page 493: © Malcolm Schuyl/Alamy; Page 498: © Chuck Doswell/Visuals Unlimited/Corbis; Page 508: Scott Gearhart; Page 515: © Hans Reinhard/Corbis

END MATTER

Page 525: © image100/Alamy

INDEX